The Right to Privacy

Rights and Liberties under the Law

Richard A. Glenn

ABC-CLIO

Santa Barbara, California • Denver, Colorado • Oxford, England

Library of Congress Cataloging-in-Publication Data
Glenn, Richard A.
The right to privacy : rights and liberties under the law / Richard A. Glenn.
p. cm. —(America's freedoms)
Includes bibliographical references and index.
ISBN 1-57607-716-0 (hardcover : alk. paper); ISBN 1-57607-717-9 (e-book)
1. Privacy, Right of—United States—Juvenile literature. I. Title. II. Series.
KF1262.Z9G59 2003
342.73'0858--dc21 2003010050

08 07 06 05 04 03 10 9 8 7 6 5 4 3 2 1

This book is also available on the World Wide Web as an e-book. Visit abc-clio.com for details.

ABC-CLIO, Inc.
130 Cremona Drive, P.O. Box 1911
Santa Barbara, California 93116–1911

This book is printed on acid-free paper.
Manufactured in the United States of America

To Ryan, my son

Contents

Series Foreword

America's Freedoms promises a series of books that address the origin, development, meaning, and future of the nation's fundamental liberties, as well as the individuals, circumstances, and events that have shaped them. These freedoms are chiefly enshrined explicitly or implicitly in the Bill of Rights and other amendments to the Constitution of the United States and have much to do with the quality of life Americans enjoy. Without them, America would be a far different place in which to live. Oddly enough, however, the Constitution was drafted and signed in Philadelphia in 1787 without a bill of rights. That was an afterthought, emerging only after a debate among the foremost political minds of the day.

At the time, Thomas Jefferson was in France on a diplomatic mission. Upon receiving a copy of the proposed Constitution from his friend James Madison, who had helped write the document, Jefferson let him know as fast as the slow sailing-ship mails of the day allowed that the new plan of government suffered one major defect—it lacked a bill of rights. This, Jefferson argued, "is what the people are entitled to against every government on earth." Madison should not have been surprised at Jefferson's reaction. The Declaration of Independence of 1776 had largely been Jefferson's handiwork, including its core statement of principle:

> We hold these truths to be self-evident, that all men are created equal, that they are endowed by their Creator with certain unalienable Rights, that among these are Life, Liberty, and the pursuit of Happiness. That to secure these rights, Governments are instituted among Men, deriving their just powers from the consent of the governed.

Jefferson rejected the conclusion of many of the framers that the Constitution's design—a system of both separation of powers among the legislative, executive, and judicial branches, and a federal division of powers between national and state governments—would safeguard liberty. Even when combined with elections, he believed strongly that such structural checks would fall short.

Jefferson and other critics of the proposed Constitution ultimately had their way. In one of the first items of business in the First Congress in 1789, Madison, as a member of the House of Representatives from Virginia, introduced amendments to protect liberty. Ten were ratified by 1791 and have become known as the Bill of Rights.

America's Bill of Rights reflects the founding generation's understanding of the necessary link between personal freedom and representative government, as well as their experience with threats to liberty. The First Amendment protects expression—in speech, press, assembly, petition, and religion—and guards against a union of church and state. The Second Amendment secures liberty against national tyranny by affirming the self-defense of the states. Members of state-authorized local militia—citizens primarily, soldiers occasionally—retained a right to bear arms. The ban in the Third Amendment on forcibly quartering troops in houses reflects the emphasis the framers placed on the integrity and sanctity of the home.

Other provisions in the Fourth, Fifth, Sixth, Seventh, and Eighth Amendments safeguard freedom by setting forth standards that government must follow in administering the law, especially regarding persons accused of crimes. The framers knew firsthand the dangers that government-as-prosecutor could pose to liberty. Even today, authoritarian regimes in other lands routinely use the tools of law enforcement—arrests, searches, detentions, as well as trials—to squelch peaceful political opposition. Limits in the Bill of Rights on crime-fighting powers thus help maintain democracy by demanding a high level of legal scrutiny of the government's practices.

In addition, one clause in the Fifth Amendment forbids the taking of private property for public use without paying the owner just compensation and thereby limits the power of eminent domain, the authority to seize a person's property. Along with taxation and conscription, eminent domain is one of the most awesome powers any government can possess.

The Ninth Amendment makes sure that the listing of some rights does not imply that others necessarily have been abandoned. If the Ninth Amendment offered reassurances to the people, the Tenth Amendment was designed to reassure the states that they or the people retained those powers not delegated to the national government. Today, the Tenth Amendment is a reminder of the integral role states play in the federal plan of union that the Constitution ordained.

Despite this legacy of freedom, however, we Americans today sometimes wonder about the origin, development, meaning, and future of our liberties. This concern is entirely understandable, because liberty is central to the idea of what it means *to be American.* In this way, the United States stands apart from virtually every other nation on earth. Other countries typically define their national identities through a common ethnicity, origin, ancestral bond, religion, or history. But none of these accounts for the American identity. In terms of ethnicity, ancestry, and religion, the United States is the most diverse place on earth. From the beginning, America has been a land of immigrants. Neither is there a single historical experience to which all current citizens can directly relate: someone who arrived a decade ago from, say, Southeast Asia and was naturalized as a citizen only last year is just as much an American as someone whose forebears served in General George Washington's army at Valley Forge during the American War of Independence (1776–1783). In religious as in political affairs, the United States has been a beacon to those suffering oppression abroad: "the last, best hope of earth," Abraham Lincoln said. So, the American identity is ideological. It consists of faith in the value and importance of liberty for each individual.

Nonetheless, a longstanding consensus among Americans on the *principle* that individual liberty is essential, highly prized, and widely shared hardly assures agreement about liberty *in practice.* This is because the concept of liberty, as it has developed in the United States, has several dimensions.

First, there is an unavoidable tension between liberty and restraint. Liberty means freedom: we say that a person has a "right" to do this or that. But that *right* is meaningless unless there is a corresponding *duty* on the part of others (such as police officers and elected officials) not to interfere. Thus, protection of the liberty of one person necessarily involves restraints imposed on someone else. This is why we speak of a *civil* right or a *civil* liberty: it is a claim on the behavior of another that is enforceable through the legal process. Moreover, some degree of order (restrictions on the behavior of all) is necessary if everyone's liberties are to be protected. Just as too much order crushes freedom, too little invites social chaos that also threatens freedom. Determining the proper balance between freedom and order, however, is more easily sought than found. "To make a government requires no great prudence," declared English statesman and political philosopher Edmund Burke in 1790. "Settle the seat of power; teach obedience; and the work is done. To give freedom is still more easy. It is not necessary to guide; it only requires to let go the rein. But to form a *free government;*

that is, to temper together these opposite elements of liberty and restraint in one consistent work, requires much thought; deep reflection; a sagacious, powerful, and combining mind."

Second, the Constitution does not define the freedoms that it protects. Chief Justice John Marshall once acknowledged that the Constitution was a document "of enumeration, and not of definition." There are, for example, lists of the powers of Congress in Article I, or the rights of individuals in the Bill of Rights, but those powers and limitations are not explained. What is the "freedom of speech" that the First Amendment guarantees? What are "unreasonable searches and seizures" that are proscribed by the Fourth Amendment? What is the "due process of law" secured by both the Fifth and Fourteenth Amendments? Reasonable people, all of whom favor individual liberty, can arrive at very different answers to these questions.

A third dimension—breadth—is closely related to the second. How widely shared is a particular freedom? Consider voting, for example. One could write a political history of the United States by cataloging the efforts to extend the vote or franchise to groups such as women and nonwhites that had been previously excluded. Or consider the First Amendment's freedom of speech. Does it include the expression of *all* points of view or merely *some*? Does the same amendment's protection of the "free exercise of religion" include all faiths, even obscure ones that may seem weird or even irritating? At different times questions like these have yielded different answers.

Similarly, the historical record contains notorious lapses. Despite all the safeguards that are supposed to shore up freedom's foundations, constitutional protections have sometimes been worth the least when they have been desperately needed. In our history the most frequent and often the most serious threats to freedom have come not from people intent on throwing the Bill of Rights away outright but from well-meaning people who find the Bill of Rights a temporary bother, standing in the way of some objective they want to reach.

There is also a question that dates to the very beginning of American government under the Constitution. Does the Constitution protect rights not spelled out in, or fairly implied by, the words of the document? The answer to that question largely depends on what a person concludes about the source of rights. One tradition, reflected in the Declaration of Independence, asserts that rights predate government and that government's chief duty is to protect the rights that everyone naturally possesses. Thus, if the Constitution is read as a document designed, among other things, to protect liberty, then protected liberties are not limited to those in the text of the Constitution but may also be derived from experience, for example, or from one's assessment of the requirements of a free society. This tradition places a lot of discretion in the hands of judges, because in the American political system, it is largely the judiciary that decides what the Constitution means. Partly due to this dynamic, a competing tradition looks to the text of the Constitution, as well as to statutes passed consistent with the Constitution, as a *complete* code of law containing *all* the liberties that Americans possess. Judges, therefore, are not free to go outside the text to "discover" rights that the people, through the process of lawmaking and constitutional amendment, have not declared. Doing so is undemocratic because it bypasses "rule by the people." The tension between these two ways of thinking explains the ongoing debate about a right to privacy, itself nowhere mentioned in the words of the Constitution. "I like my privacy as well as the next one," once admitted Justice Hugo Black, "but I am nevertheless compelled to admit that government has a right to invade it unless prohibited by some specific constitutional provision." Otherwise, he said, judges are forced "to determine what is or is not constitutional on the basis of their own appraisal of what laws are unwise or unnecessary." Black thought that was the job of elected legislators who would answer to the people.

Fifth, it is often forgotten that at the outset, and for many years afterward, the Bill of Rights applied only to the national government, not to the states. Except for a very few restrictions, such as those in section 10 of Article I in the main body of the Constitution, which expressly limited state power, states were restrained only by their individual constitutions and state laws, not by the U.S. Bill of Rights. So, Pennsylvania or any other state, for example, could shut down a newspaper or barricade the doors of a church without violating the First Amendment. For many in the founding generation, the new central government loomed as a colossus that might threaten liberty. Few at that time thought that individual freedom needed *national* protection against *state* invasions of the rights of the people.

The first step in removing this double standard came with ratification of the Fourteenth Amendment after the Civil War in 1868. Section 1 contained majestic, but undefined, checks on states: "*No State* shall make or enforce any law which shall abridge the privileges or immunities of citizens of the United States; nor shall any *State* deprive any person of life, liberty, or property, without due process of law; nor deny to any person with in its jurisdiction the equal protections of the laws" (emphasis added). Such vague language begged for interpretation. In a series of cases mainly between 1920 and 1968, the Supreme Court construed the Fourteenth Amendment to include within its meaning almost every provision of the Bill of Rights. This process of "incorporation" (applying the Bill of Rights to the states by way of the Fourteenth Amendment) was the second step in eliminating the double standard of 1791. State and local governments became bound by the same restrictions that had applied all along to the national government. The consequences of this development scarcely can be exaggerated because most governmental action in the United States is the work of state and local governments. For instance, ordinary citizens are far more likely to encounter a local police officer than an agent of the Federal Bureau of Investigation or the Secret Service.

A sixth dimension reflects an irony. A society premised on individual freedom assumes not only the worth of each person but citizens capable of rational thought, considered judgment, and measured actions. Otherwise democratic government would be futile. Yet, we lodge the most important freedoms in the Constitution precisely because we want to give those freedoms extra protection. "The very purpose of a Bill of Rights was to . . . place [certain subjects] beyond the reach of majorities and officials and to establish them as legal principles to be applied by the courts," explained Justice Robert H. Jackson. "One's right to life, liberty, and property, to free speech, a free press, freedom of worship and assembly, and other fundamental rights may not be submitted to vote; they depend on the outcome of no elections." Jackson referred to a hard lesson learned from experience: basic rights require extra protection because they are fragile. On occasion, people have been willing to violate the freedoms of others. That reality demanded a written constitution.

This irony reflects the changing nature of a bill of rights in history. Americans did not invent the idea of a bill of rights in 1791. Instead it drew from and was inspired by colonial documents such as the Pennsylvania colony's Charter of Liberties (1701) and the English Bill of Rights (1689), Petition of Right (1628), and Magna Carta (1215). However, these early and often unsuccessful attempts to limit government power were devices to protect the many (the people) from the few (the English Crown). With the emergence of democratic political systems in the eighteenth century, however, political power shifted from the few to the many. The right to rule belonged to the person who received the most votes in an election, not necessarily to the firstborn, the wealthiest, or the most physically powerful. So the focus of a bill of rights had to shift too. No longer was it designed to shelter the majority from the minority, but to shelter the minority from the majority. "Wherever the real power in a Government lies, there is the danger of oppression," commented Madison in his exchange of letters with Jefferson in 1788. "In our Government, the real power lies in the majority of the Community, and the invasion of private rights is *chiefly* to be apprehended, not from acts of government contrary to the sense of its constituents, but from acts in which the Government is the mere instrument of the major number of the Constituents."

Americans, however, do deserve credit for having discovered a way to enforce a bill of rights. Without an enforcement mechanism, a bill of rights is no more than a list of aspirations: standards to aim for, but with no redress other than violent protest or revolution. Indeed this had been the experience in England with which the framers were thoroughly familiar. Thanks to judicial review—the authority courts in the United States possess to invalidate actions taken by the other branches of government that, in the judges' view, conflict with the Constitution—the provisions in the Bill of Rights and other constitutionally protected liberties became judicially enforceable.

Judicial review was a tradition that was beginning to emerge in the states on a small scale in the 1780s and 1790s and that would blossom in the U.S. Supreme Court in the nineteenth and twentieth centuries. "In the arguments in favor of a declaration of rights," Jefferson presciently told Madison in the late winter of 1789 after the Constitution had been ratified, "you omit one which has great weight with me, the legal check which it puts into the hands of the judiciary." This is the reason why each of the volumes in this series focuses extensively on judicial decisions. Liberties have largely been defined by judges in the context of deciding cases in situations where individuals thought the power of government extended too far.

Designed to help democracy protect itself, the Constitution ultimately needs the support of those—the majority—who endure its restraints. Without sufficient support among the people, its freedoms rest on a weak foundation. The earnest hope of *America's Freedoms* is that this series will offer Americans a renewed appreciation and understanding of their heritage of liberty.

Yet there would be no series on America's freedoms without the interest and support of Alicia Merritt at ABC-CLIO. The series was her idea. She approached me originally about the series and was very adept at overcoming my initial hesitations as series editor. She not only helped me shape the particular topics that the series would include but also guided me toward prospective authors. As a result, the topic of each book has been matched with the most appropriate person as author. The goal in each instance as been to pair topics with authors who are recognized teachers and scholars in their field. The results have been gratifying. A series editor could hardly wish for authors who have been more cooperative, helpful, and accommodating.

Donald Grier Stephenson, Jr.

Preface and Acknowledgments

The central philosophical premise of the Bill of Rights—the first ten amendments to the U.S. Constitution—is that citizens should be free from unwanted and unwarranted governmental interference. Thus, the Bill of Rights is an enumeration of specific freedoms from governmental interference, protected by judicial guardianship. Although it is true that the Bill of Rights lacks any textual reference to "privacy," several of its amendments protect individuals in their privacy. The First Amendment guarantees freedom of conscience in both religious and political matters and freedom of association. The Third and Fourth Amendments protect the privacy of the home. And the Fifth Amendment shields the privacy of one's thoughts.

But the freedoms mentioned in the Bill of Rights are not a complete catalogue of America's freedoms. The Ninth Amendment confirms as much when it notes that the listing of specific rights in the Bill of Rights "shall not be construed to deny or disparage others retained by the people." In 1965, the U.S. Supreme Court held that one of those additional rights, "retained by the people" and thus immune from governmental interference, was privacy. Since that time, the Ninth Amendment has become a highly visible and highly contentious source of limitations on the powers of government. No doubt this is so because the judiciary has invoked the Ninth Amendment in privacy cases dealing with such political hot-button issues as contraception, abortion, and sexual relations.

This book examines the most abstract, most broad, most ill-defined, and what many consider to be the most difficult to grasp of America's freedoms—the right to privacy. Its intent is neither to advocate nor criticize but rather to explain. Accordingly, its function is descriptive, not prescriptive. Because the primary audience consists of upper-level high school and college students, this book assumes that readers are being introduced to the topic for the first time. This book evidences thorough and well-balanced research and avoids technical terms wherever possible while defining clearly those terms that are necessary; it also simplifies complicated constitutional issues without obscuring the central and important problems presented by them. The primary purpose of this book is thus to provide readers of all levels with a rich and comprehensive source of information about the right to privacy.

To accomplish that purpose, this book (1) discusses the significance of the right to privacy as well as its implications for the American political system; (2) reveals the origins and early development of the right to privacy by looking at its philosophical, constitutional, and common law heritage; (3) explores the evolution and arguable devolution of the right to privacy in the twentieth century by analyzing significant judicial decisions; and (4) speculates on general trends in privacy jurisprudence by examining closely those issues and controversies that have been most visible in recent debates.

Chapter 1 introduces the subject matter. It begins with a short case study that illuminates the controversial nature of the constitutional right to privacy. It then proceeds to define privacy and makes clear the significance of privacy, the role of privacy in the American political system, and the current breadth of the right to privacy.

Chapter 2 explores the origins of the right to privacy, examining its philosophical, constitutional, and common law foundations. It begins with an overview of the philosophical foundations of privacy, looking selectively at the contributions of Thomas Hobbes, John Locke, and John Stuart Mill. Each of these philosophers grappled with the question, "What are the legitimate limits of governmental authority?" The right to privacy, after all, flows from the general concept that there are certain freedoms beyond the power of government to restrict. Next, Chapter 2 examines the constitutional foundations of privacy in the United States. The Constitution does more than grant power to the government; just as important, the document articulates certain prohibitions on the exercise of governmental authority. Because constitutional privacy is about the legitimate limits on governmental authority, it is important to explore the history, politics, and interpretations of the Constitution. Here we give particular attention to the first eight amendments (a list of specific freedoms *from* governmental interference); the Ninth Amendment (which indicates that the list of specific freedoms enumerated in the first eight amendments is not an exhaustive list); judicial review (the privacy doctrine holds that it is the judiciary's responsibility to determine when the government has encroached upon those freedoms); and substantive due process of law (which holds that the Constitution prohibits government from adopting and enforcing certain policies, even though those policies may not contravene any specific constitutional provision). Each of these constitutional components plays an important role in the development of the constitutional right to privacy. Finally, in this chapter we will consider the common law foundations of privacy. Formal legal protection for privacy interests in the United States did not emerge until the nineteenth century, and only then almost exclusively as a component of tort law in state judicial decisions. This segment analyzes the important *Harvard Law Review* article on privacy (which called for the courts to recognize privacy as a distinct and independent right) written in 1890 by Samuel Warren and Louis Brandeis; examines state judicial decisions involving the right to privacy in the nineteenth century; and concludes with a discussion of *Pavesich v. New England Life Insurance Company* (1905), the first case in which any state court of last resort recognized privacy as a distinct and independent right.

Chapter 3 examines the major themes that emerged in connection with the constitutional right to privacy during the twentieth century. From its beginnings in the late nineteenth century, privacy law gradually evolved to mean "the right to be let alone—the most comprehensive of rights and the most valued by civilized man." This chapter explores the evolution and arguable devolution of the constitutional right to privacy by focusing on defining decisions of the U.S. Supreme Court. When deciding cases about contraception, abortion, marriage, divorce, child rearing and education, and sexual relations, judges regularly employ the concept of constitutional privacy. In the twentieth century, constitutional privacy can be divided into four major areas: reproductive autonomy; family autonomy; sexual autonomy; and personal autonomy.

Chapter 4 examines the privacy issues that have been most visible and contentious of late in order to speculate on the future of privacy jurisprudence. During the twentieth century, the Supreme Court grappled with a variety of issues invoking the constitutional right to privacy. Although many judicial decisions on privacy acknowledged a liberty interest in independence in making certain kinds of important decisions, they did not mark clearly the outer limits of the right to privacy. Thus, new claims of constitutional privacy continue to confront the justices, and constitutional privacy remains a developing concept. In the 1990s, the most prominent privacy claims related to the right to die. Constitutional privacy has also been invoked with respect to polygamy, reproductive rights for prison inmates, same-sex marriages, child adoption by gay and lesbian couples, and the use of sexually stimulating devices. In addition, informational privacy—the liberty interest in avoiding disclosure of personal matters—has become of much greater concern in the digital age.

Chapter 5 offers an alphabetically organized reference section on important cases, concepts, persons, laws, and terms that are central to understanding the constitutional right to privacy. The entries included in Chapter 5 are related to, and drawn from, the material presented in Chapters 1–4.

Chapter 6 is a source materials section, consisting of critical primary documents—an article and some cases—reprinted in excerpted form. Each item in this section is preceded by a brief headnote explaining the significance and background of the reproduced material.

The book also includes a chronology of pertinent events as well as an annotated bibliography of useful works on constitutional privacy.

Acknowledgments

This book was made possible only through the assistance of a number of individuals. It is a pleasure to acknowledge those persons and to thank them.

D. Grier Stephenson, professor of government at Franklin and Marshall College and ABC-CLIO's *America's Freedoms* series editor, offered sound advice, thoughtful guidance, and welcomed encouragement at every stage of the project. I thank him not only for the opportunity to write this book but also for the considerate interest he has shown in my career.

Alicia Merritt, ABC-CLIO's senior acquisitions editor, and Melanie Stafford, ABC-CLIO's senior production editor, provided insightful comments and prompt responses to my inquiries.

Beth Glenn enhanced my understanding of the various life-sustaining medical technologies that affect the right to die.

Anthony M. Bottenfield provided valuable research assistance, particularly in the area of informational privacy.

Howard C. Ellis read and reread each chapter, always improving it. His contribution stretched far beyond what anyone would have the right to expect. I am fortunate to have a colleague of such insight and a friend of such kindness.

To my family I owe the most of all. To my parents, Kenneth and Beth, for a life filled with opportunity. To my wife, Lorena, for her love, her patience, and her extraordinary grace. To my son Ryan, for welcoming me home each evening with such pomp and circumstance—and a bat and a ball; and to Andrew, my younger son, who, as of this writing, is three weeks old. No words can adequately express my gratitude.

Richard A. Glenn
Millersville University

Prologue

As this book went to print, the U.S. Supreme Court decided a landmark case regarding constitutional privacy. As much as I would have preferred to incorporate this matter into the text of the book, technical reasons prohibited that. Therefore, this important case and its ramifications are discussed here. It may be that much of this prologue will be difficult for the reader to comprehend until he or she has read the text, particularly the section of Chapter 3 that deals with sexual autonomy. The reader should be aware, however, that this particular decision has enormous significance for constitutional privacy. I recommend that the reader return to the prologue after reading Chapters 1–4. An excerpt of the case is included in this prologue.

The constitutional privacy landscape changed dramatically on June 26, 2003, when the U.S. Supreme Court, in *Lawrence v. Texas* (2003 U.S. LEXIS 5013), struck down a Texas statute that made it a crime for two persons of the same sex to engage in certain intimate sexual conduct. Homosexuals are "entitled to respect for their private lives," wrote Justice Anthony Kennedy for the Court. "The state cannot demean their existence or control their destiny by making their private sexual conduct a crime. Their right to liberty under the Due Process Clause gives them the full right to engage in their conduct without intervention of the government" (2003 U.S. LEXIS 5013, at 36). Thus, for the first time, the Court, by acknowledging that constitutional privacy includes the right of consenting adults to engage in private sexual relations, extended constitutional privacy to include activities outside of the traditional categories of procreation, marriage, and family life.

In reaching this sweeping conclusion, the justices overturned *Bowers v. Hardwick* (478 U.S. 186; 1986), a case decided only seventeen years earlier in which the majority dismissed a similar claim as "facetious." (*Hardwick* is discussed in brief at the outset of Chapter 1; and in detail in Chapter 3.)

The challenge to the Texas homosexual conduct law was brought by John Geddes Lawrence and Tyron Garner, who were convicted of engaging in "deviate sexual intercourse with a member of the same sex" in the privacy of Lawrence's apartment. Lawrence and Garner were discovered by officers of the Harris Country Police Department who had been dispatched to the residence in response to a reported weapons disturbance. (The neighbor who reported the disturbance had notified the police that there was a man with a gun "going crazy" in the apartment. The neighbor was later convicted of filing a false report with the police.) Upon arrival at the apartment, the officers entered the residence through an unlocked door, at which time they observed the two men engaging in a sexual act. Lawrence and Garner were arrested, jailed overnight, charged, and convicted before a justice of the peace. At trial, the two men unsuccessfully challenged the statute as a violation of the Equal Protection Clause of the Fourteenth Amendment to the U.S. Constitution and of a similar provision of the Texas Constitution. The equal protection argument was based on the fact that the law criminalized sexual activity between homosexuals but not heterosexuals. The two then pleaded *nolo contendere* (a Latin phrase meaning "I will not contest it"), and each was fined $200 and assessed a court cost of $141.25.

On appeal, the lawyers representing Lawrence and Garner argued, in addition to the equal protection claims, that the statute constituted an invasion of privacy, as protected by the Due Process Clause of the Fourteenth Amendment. In mid-

2000, a three-judge panel of the Court of Appeals for the Texas Fourteenth District ruled that the convictions "impermissibly discriminated on the basis of sex" and thus violated the Texas Constitution (*Lawrence v. State*, 2000 Tex. App. Houston 14th District, June 8, 2000). Shortly thereafter, however, an *en banc* (full) panel of the court of appeals reversed the three-judge panel, rejecting the federal constitutional arguments under both the Equal Protection and Due Process Clauses (*Lawrence v. State*, 41 S.W. 3d 349; 2001). With respect to equal protection, the seven-judge majority, relying in part upon U.S. Supreme Court precedent, held that homosexuality—unlike race, gender, and nationality—was not a protected classification. Therefore, the Texas legislature had the right to discriminate against gays and lesbians so long as it had a legitimate interest in doing so. The court then agreed with the state that the statute had a legitimate interest—the preservation of public morality: "There has never been any doubt that the legislature, in the exercise of its police power, has authority to criminalize the commission of acts which are considered immoral." Per due process, the court of appeals considered *Hardwick*, which held that the U.S. Constitution did not confer a fundamental right upon homosexuals to engage in consensual sodomy (oral or anal sex) performed in the privacy of the home, to be the controlling principle. Accordingly, the court rejected the due process claim.

The Texas Court of Criminal Appeals—the highest state court for criminal cases—declined to review the case. Lawrence and Garner then sought review from the U.S. Supreme Court, which agreed to consider three questions: (1) whether Lawrence and Garner's criminal convictions under the Texas homosexual conduct law, which criminalized sexual intimacy by same-sex couples but not identical behavior by different-sex couples, violated the Fourteenth Amendment guarantee of equal protection under the law; (2) whether the criminal convictions for adult sexual intimacy in the home violated a person's vital interests in liberty and privacy protected by the Due Process Clause of the Fourteenth Amendment; and (3) whether *Hardwick* should be overturned. Oral arguments took place on March 26, 2003; the decision was announced exactly three months later.

Five of the members of the High Court—Justices Kennedy, John Paul Stevens, David Souter, Ruth Bader Ginsburg, and Stephen Breyer—agreed that the case should be resolved by determining whether consenting adults were free to engage in private sexual conduct in the exercise of their liberty under the Due Process Clause. To do so, however, required a reconsideration of the holding in *Hardwick*. (Only three members of the *Lawrence* Court—Chief Justice William Rehnquist, Justice Stevens and Justice Sandra Day O'Connor—had been on the Court when *Hardwick* was decided.) The majority criticized the *Hardwick* opinion for its failure to appreciate the extent of the liberty at stake in laws that criminalized certain sexual conduct. In *Hardwick*, the justices had stated the claim too narrowly—whether there was a fundamental right to engage in consensual homosexual sodomy. Instead of asking whether homosexual sodomy had traditionally enjoyed constitutional protection, which clearly it had not, the justices *should* have asked whether private relationships between consenting adults had traditionally enjoyed constitutional protection, which clearly they had. "The laws involved in [*Hardwick*] and here are, to be sure, statutes that purport to do no more than prohibit a particular sexual act," wrote Justice Kennedy.

> Their penalties and purposes, though, have more far-reaching consequences, touching upon the most pri-

> vate human conduct, sexual behavior, and in the most private of places, the home. The statutes do seek to control a personal relationship that ... is within the liberty of persons to choose without being punished as criminals.... [A]dults may choose to enter upon this relationship in the confines of their homes and their own private lives and still retain their dignity as free persons. When sexuality finds overt expression in intimate conduct with another person, the conduct can be but one element in a personal bond that is more enduring. The liberty protected by the Constitution allows homosexual persons the right to make this choice. (2003 U.S. LEXIS 5013, at 16–17)

The *Hardwick* Court had relied upon the "ancient roots" of proscriptions against homosexual conduct, the numerous state laws criminalizing homosexual conduct, and the constitutional privacy precedent to conclude that such conduct was neither "deeply rooted in this Nation's history and tradition" nor "implicit in the concept of ordered liberty." That historical evidence, however, was "more complex" than the majority and concurring opinions in *Hardwick* indicated, said the majority in *Lawrence*: "Their historical premises are not without doubt and, at the very least, are overstated." History notwithstanding, the *Lawrence* Court concluded that "laws and traditions in the past half century ... show an emerging awareness that liberty gives substantial protection to adult persons in deciding how to conduct their private lives in matters pertaining to sex" (2003 U.S. LEXIS 5013, at 23–25). To support this conclusion, Justice Kennedy cited some pre- and post-*Hardwick* data. Before 1961, all fifty states had outlawed sodomy, and at the time of the Court's decision in *Hardwick*, twenty-four states and the District of Columbia prohibited sodomy. But, by 2003, only thirteen states prohibited the relevant conduct, of which four—Kansas, Missouri, and Oklahoma are the others—enforced such laws exclusively against homosexuals. And in those states where sodomy was prohibited, there was a pattern of nonenforcement with respect to consenting adults acting in private. Additionally, Justice Kennedy noted that the foundations of *Hardwick* had been eroded by two subsequent decisions: *Planned Parenthood of Southeastern Pennsylvania v. Casey* (505 U.S. 833; 1992), in which the justices spoke of the respect the Constitution demanded for the autonomy of the person in making intimate and personal choices; and *Romer v. Evans* (517 U.S. 620; 1996), in which the Court struck down a state constitutional amendment that was "born of animosity" toward homosexuals and had no rational relationship to a legitimate governmental purpose. In short, the rationale of *Hardwick* was no longer viable. "Its continuance as precedent demeans the lives of homosexual persons.... [It] was not correct when it was decided, and it is not correct today. It ought not to remain binding precedent. *Bowers v. Hardwick* should be and now is overruled" (2003 U.S. LEXIS 5013, at 35–36). The Court then announced a new controlling principle: "[I]ndividual decisions by married [and unmarried] persons ... concerning the intimacies of their physical relationship, even when not intended to produce offspring, are a form of liberty protected by the Due Process Clause of the Fourteenth Amendment" (quoting from Justice Stevens's dissenting opinion in *Hardwick*, 478 U.S. at 216).

The fact that this decision is protected by the Due Process Clause, of course, does not necessarily mean that a state may not proscribe it. When a state chooses to enter into such a realm of personal liberty, to withstand constitutional scrutiny, it must be in furtherance of a legitimate state interest. Here, the interest asserted by Texas was the preservation of public morality. Simply because a governing majority considered a particular sexual practice to be immoral, however, was not a sufficient reason alone for upholding a law prohibiting the practice. In short, neither history nor tradition nor "moral disapproval" could justify this intrusion into the personal and private life of the individual.

Although recognizing that the equal protection claim was a "tenable" argument, the majority declined to address its merits. Justice Kennedy feared that if the Court refused to address the privacy question, and were to hold the statute invalid only under the Equal Protection Clause, a state could nonetheless criminalize intimate conduct so long as same-sex and opposite-sex participants were treated equally. There was, however, no need to examine the equal protection question, for the Court had already acknowledged that private sexual relations between all consenting adults were protected by the Due Process Clause.

Justice O'Connor refused to join the Court in overruling *Hardwick*. (She had concurred in *Hardwick*.) Nevertheless, she agreed that the Texas law was unconstitutional, basing her conclusion on the Equal Protection Clause. Because the statute treated the same conduct differently based solely on the sexual orientation of the participants, it made homosexuals "unequal in the eyes of the law" (2003 U.S. LEXIS 5013, at 41). Thus, according to Justice O'Connor, the proper inquiry in *Lawrence* was whether, under the Equal Protection Clause, moral disapproval was a legitimate state interest to justify a statute that banned homosexual sodomy, but not heterosexual sodomy. She concluded that it was not: "A law branding one class of persons as criminals solely based on the state's moral disapproval of that class and the conduct associated with that class runs contrary to the values of the Constitution and the Equal Protection Clause" (2003 U.S. LEXIS 5013, at 49).

Chief Justice Rehnquist and Justices Antonin Scalia and Clarence Thomas dissented. In a blistering dissent that he read from the bench (it is rare for a justice to read his or her dissent from the bench), Justice Scalia criticized the majority for taking sides in the culture war by signing on to "the so-called homosexual agenda." After a lengthy yet digressive discussion on why *Roe v. Wade* (410 U.S. 113; 1973) should be overturned, he turned to the crux of the matter. As with laws prohibiting prostitution and drug use, the Texas law "undoubtedly impose[d] constraints on liberty." But liberty interests that were not "deeply rooted in this Nation's history and tradition," such as homosexual sodomy, could be abridged or abrogated pursuant to a validly enacted state law so long as the law was rationally related to a legitimate state interest. "Countless judicial decisions," he wrote, had held that a governing majority's belief that certain sexual behavior was "immoral and unacceptable" constituted such a rational basis for this type of regulation (2003 U.S. LEXIS 5013, at 56). After all, this was the same interest furthered by criminal laws against fornication, bigamy, adultery, adult incest, bestiality, and obscenity. And if the promotion of majoritarian sexual morality were not a legitimate state interest, the dissenters warned that none of the abovementioned moral legislation could survive a constitutional challenge. Justice Scalia, ever consistent with his position on constitutional privacy, then concluded his dissent with a forceful argument for judicial restraint:

> Let me be clear that I have nothing against homosexuals ... promoting their agenda through normal

> democratic means.... But persuading one's fellow citizens is one thing, and imposing one's views in absence of democratic majority will is something else.... What Texas has chosen to do is well within the range of traditional democratic action, and its hand should not be stayed through the invention of a brand-new "constitutional right" by a Court that is impatient with democratic change. It is indeed true that "later generations can see laws that once thought necessary and proper in fact serve only to oppress," and when that happens, later generations can repeal those laws. But it is the premise of our system that those judgments are to be made by the people, and not imposed by a governing caste that knows best.... (2003 U.S. LEXIS 5013, at 79)

Justice Thomas also authored a dissenting opinion. He noted that he found the law "uncommonly silly" and would vote to repeal it if he were a member of the Texas legislature, but added that he could not overturn the law because he did not believe that the Constitution conferred upon the people "a general right of privacy."

There is considerable debate among interested persons about the impact of *Lawrence* on other matters involving homosexuals—including same-sex marriages, child adoption by gay and lesbian parents, and the military's prohibition on service by openly homosexual soldiers—and on other types of moral legislation. A quick glance at various national newspapers on the days following the decision indicates a high degree of misunderstanding about the decision. For example, numerous gay rights advocates have speculated that this decision paves the way for formal recognition of same-sex marriages.

Even Justice Scalia's dissenting opinion claimed that the ruling "dismantles the structure of constitutional law that ... permitted a distinction to be made between heterosexual and homosexual unions, insofar as formal recognition is concerned" (2003 U.S. LEXIS 5013, at 81). The majority—perhaps anticipating such comments from Justice Scalia, perhaps in response to them—denounced any such sweeping effect, stating clearly that its holding did not involve "whether the government must give formal recognition to any relationship that homosexual persons [sought] to enter" (2003 U.S. LEXIS 5013, at 49). (Marital rights, of course, belong to the virtually exclusive province of the states. Accordingly, states are free to recognize or not to recognize same-sex marriages.) Additionally, *Lawrence* did not speak in any direct way to child adoption by gay and lesbian parents and the military's proscription against homosexual soldiers. It does not logically follow from this decision that the justices in the majority would be willing to strike down prohibitions against child adoption by gays and lesbians or the military's ban on openly homosexual soldiers. Similarly, those displeased with the decision warned that the Court's rationale would lead to the end of all moral legislation. But Justice Kennedy went out of his way to assert that the right recognized here was limited to private sexual conduct between consenting adults. It does not logically follow from this decision that all moral legislation is in constitutional jeopardy.

This case is about sexual privacy, much more so than it is about homosexual privacy or discrimination against homosexuals or morality as a basis for certain legislation. It is about the liberty of adult persons—irrespective of sexual orientation—to engage in private sexual conduct free from the unwanted and unwarranted gaze of government.

Lawrence has real social, political, and legal implications for at least three reasons. First, the Supreme Court has now identified the homosexual rights movement as a basic civil rights issue. Second, nowhere does the Court's opinion declare that sexual privacy is a "fundamental right" under the Due Process Clause. If it did, all laws encroaching upon sexual privacy would be subjected to strict scrutiny. The absence of such a declaration arguably leaves the door open for states to proscribe certain sexual conduct if they can demonstrate a legitimate purpose—something more than moral disapproval—for doing so. The justices have indicated an unwillingness to uphold laws that prohibit a particular practice based *solely* on moral disapproval of that practice. This calls into question all such laws unless some additional justification can be produced. For example, states presumably have a legitimate interest, in addition to moral disapproval, in prohibiting statutory rape, prostitution, rape, polygamy, and incest. Statutory rape causes harm to minors. Prostitution involves public conduct. Rape is coercive and injurious. Polygamy jeopardizes family stability. And incest often leads to genetic abnormalities. But if the Court is not willing to recognize justifications other than moral disapproval, as was true in *Lawrence*, the law will not withstand constitutional scrutiny. This may well be a marked departure from the Court's previous jurisprudence. As it said in *Hardwick*, "[I]f all laws representing essentially moral choices are to be invalidated under the Due Process Clause, the courts will be very busy indeed" (478 U.S. at 196).

Third, and most important for this book, for the first time in more than a quarter of a century, the Supreme Court has expanded the scope of constitutional privacy. As recently as *Washington v. Glucksberg* (521 U.S. 702; 1997), the last constitutional privacy/constitutional liberty decision prior to *Lawrence*, the justices noted that, in addition to the specific freedoms protected by the Bill of Rights, the "liberty" specially protected by the Due Process Clause included the rights to marry, to have children, to direct the education and upbringing of one's children, to enjoy marital privacy, to use contraception, to preserve bodily integrity, and to have an abortion. (The *Glucksberg* Court also assumed, and strongly suggested, that the Due Process Clause protected the traditional right to refuse unwanted lifesaving medical treatment.) The right to marry had been affirmed in *Loving v. Virginia* (388 U.S. 1; 1967), the right to procreation in *Skinner v. Oklahoma* (316 U.S. 535; 1942); the right to direct the upbringing and education of one's children in *Meyer v. Nebraska* (262 U.S. 390; 1923) and *Pierce v. Society of Sisters* (268 U.S. 510; 1925); the right to marital privacy in *Griswold v. Connecticut* (381 U.S. 471; 1965); the right to use contraception in *Griswold* and *Eisenstadt v. Baird* (405 U.S. 438; 1972); the right to bodily integrity in *Rochin v. California* (342 U.S. 165; 1952); and the right to abortion in *Roe v. Wade* (410 U.S. 113; 1973). An examination of the dates of these decisions indicates that, despite numerous opportunities to do so, the justices have not "added" a new category to constitutional privacy since 1973. In 1997, when the justices rejected a due process right to physician-assisted suicide, constitutional privacy provided heightened protection only to those personal, intimate, and important choices relating to marriage, procreation, and family life. Yet, now, only six years later, the Court has added a new category to constitutional privacy—sexual autonomy—and this, a category that the justices had, at least in limited form, rejected only seventeen years earlier in *Hardwick*.

It is difficult to overstate the importance of *Lawrence v. Texas*. It does nothing less than add a chapter to our constitutional privacy law. It stands for the proposition that the constitutional right to privacy includes a general right for consenting adults to have sexual relations in the privacy of their homes. This is truly a landmark decision.

Lawrence v. Texas, 2003 U.S. LEXIS 5013 (2003)

Argued March 26, 2003; decided June 26, 2003

JUSTICE KENNEDY delivered the opinion of the Court.

Liberty protects the person from unwarranted government intrusions into a dwelling or other private places.... Liberty presumes an autonomy of self that includes freedom of thought, belief, expression, and certain intimate conduct. The instant case involves liberty of the person both in its spatial and more transcendent dimensions.... The question before the Court is the validity of a Texas statute making it a crime for two persons of the same sex to engage in certain intimate sexual conduct.... We conclude the case should be resolved by determining whether the petitioners were free as adults to engage in the private conduct in the exercise of their liberty under the Due Process Clause of the Fourteenth Amendment to the Constitution. For this inquiry we deem it necessary to reconsider the Court's holding in *Bowers* [*v. Hardwick*].There are broad statements of the substantive reach of liberty under the Due Process Clause in earlier cases, ... but the most pertinent beginning point is our decision in *Griswold v. Connecticut*....

In *Griswold*, ... the Court invalidated a state law prohibiting the use of drugs or devices of contraception and counseling or aiding and abetting the use of contraceptives. The Court described the protected interest as a right to privacy and placed emphasis on the marriage relation and the protected space of the marital bedroom. After *Griswold* it was established that the right to make certain decisions regarding sexual conduct extends beyond the marital relationship. In *Eisenstadt v. Baird*, ... the Court invalidated a law prohibiting the distribution of contraceptives to unmarried persons....

The opinions in *Griswold* and *Eisenstadt* were part of the background for the decision in *Roe v. Wade*.... *Roe* recognized the right of a woman to make certain fundamental decisions affecting her destiny and confirmed once more that the protection of liberty under the Due Process Clause has a substantive dimension of fundamental significance in defining the rights of the person....

The facts in *Bowers* had some similarities to the instant case.... One difference between the two cases is that the Georgia statute [at issue in *Bowers*] prohibited the conduct whether or not the participants were of the same sex, while the Texas statute, as we have seen, applies only to participants of the same sex....

The Court began its substantive discussion in *Bowers* as follows: "The issue presented is whether the Federal Constitution confers a fundamental right upon homosexuals to engage in sodomy and hence invalidates the laws of the many States that still make such conduct illegal and have done so for a very long time." That statement, we now conclude, discloses the Court's own failure to appreciate the extent of the liberty at stake.... The laws involved in *Bowers* and here are, to be sure, statutes that purport to do no more than prohibit a particular sexual act. Their penalties and purposes, though, have more far-reaching consequences, touching upon the most private human conduct, sexual behavior, and in the most private of places, the home. The statutes do seek to control a personal relationship that ... is within the liberty of persons to choose without being punished as criminals.... [A]dults may choose to enter upon this relationship in the confines of their homes and their own private lives and still retain their dignity as free persons. When sexuality finds overt expression in intimate conduct with another person, the conduct can be but one element in a personal bond that is more enduring. The liberty protected by the Constitution allows homosexual persons the right to make this choice.

... [T]he *Bowers* Court said: "Proscriptions against [homosexual sodomy] have ancient roots." ... [T]here are fundamental criticisms of the historical premises relied upon by the majority and concurring opinions in *Bowers*.... [T]here is no longstanding history in this country of laws directed at homosexual conduct as a distinct matter....

... [W]e think that our laws and traditions in the past half century are of most relevance here. These references show an emerging awareness that liberty gives substantial protection to adult persons in deciding how to conduct their private lives in matters pertaining to sex....

In *Bowers* the Court referred to the fact that before 1961 all 50 States had outlawed sodomy, and that at the time of the Court's decision 24 States and the District of Columbia had sodomy laws. Justice Powell pointed out that these prohibitions often were being ignored, however....

... The 25 States with laws prohibiting the relevant conduct referenced in the *Bowers* decision are reduced now to 13, of which 4 enforce their laws only against homosexual conduct. In those States where sodomy is still proscribed, whether for same-sex or heterosexual conduct, there is a pattern of nonenforcement with respect to consenting adults acting in private....

Two principal cases decided after *Bowers* cast its holding into even more doubt. In *Planned Parenthood of Southeastern P[ennsylvania] v. Casey,* ... the Court reaffirmed the substantive force of the liberty protected by the Due Process Clause. The *Casey* decision again confirmed that our laws and tradition afford constitutional protection to personal decisions relating to marriage, procreation, contraception, family relationships, child rearing, and education. In explaining the respect the Constitution demands for the autonomy of the person in making these choices, we stated as follows:

These matters, involving the most intimate and personal choices a person may make in a lifetime, choices central to personal dignity and autonomy, are central to the liberty protected by the Fourteenth Amendment. At the heart of liberty is the right to define one's own concept of existence, of meaning, of the universe, and of the mystery of human life. Beliefs about these matters could not define the attributes of personhood were they formed under compulsion of the State. *Persons in a homosexual relationship may seek autonomy for these purposes, just as heterosexual persons do. The decision in* Bowers *would deny them this right.*

The second post-*Bowers* case of principal relevance is *Romer v. Evans*.... There the Court struck down class-based legislation directed at homosexuals as a violation of the Equal Protection Clause. *Romer* invalidated an amendment to Colorado's constitution which named as a solitary class persons who were homosexuals, lesbians, or bisexual ... , and deprived them of protection under state antidiscrimination laws. We concluded that the provision was "born of animosity toward the class of persons affected" and further that it had no rational relation to a legitimate governmental purpose.

As an alternative argument in this case, counsel for the petitioners and some *amici* contend that *Romer* provides the basis for declaring the Texas statute invalid under the Equal Protection Clause. That is a tenable argument, but we conclude the instant case requires us to address whether *Bowers* itself has continuing validity. Were we to hold the statute invalid under the Equal Protection Clause some might question whether a prohibition would be valid if drawn differently, say, to prohibit the conduct both between same-sex and different-sex participants.... When homosexual conduct is made criminal by the law of the State, that declaration in and of itself is an invitation to subject homosexual persons to discrimination both in the public and in the private spheres. The central holding of *Bowers* has been brought in question by this case, and it should be addressed. Its continuance as precedent demeans the lives of homosexual persons. The stigma this criminal statute imposes, moreover, is not trivial. The offense, to be sure, is ... a minor offense in the Texas legal system. Still, it remains a criminal offense with all that imports for the dignity of the persons charged. The petitioners will bear on their record the history of their criminal convictions.... This underscores the consequential nature of the punishment and the state-sponsored condemnation attendant to the criminal prohibition. Furthermore, the Texas criminal conviction carries with it the other collateral consequences always following a conviction, such as notations on job application forms, to mention but one example....

The rationale of *Bowers* does not withstand careful analysis. In his dissenting opinion in *Bowers* Justice Stevens came to these conclusions: Our prior cases make two propositions abundantly clear. First, the fact that the governing majority in a State has traditionally viewed a particular practice as immoral is not a sufficient reason for upholding a law prohibiting the practice; neither history nor tradition could save a law prohibiting miscegenation from constitutional attack. Second, individual decisions by married persons, concerning the intimacies of their physical relationship, even when not intended to produce offspring, are a form of "liberty" protected by the Due Process Clause of the Fourteenth Amendment. Moreover, this protection extends to intimate choices by unmarried as well as married persons.

Justice Stevens' analysis, in our view, should have been controlling in *Bowers* and should control here. *Bowers* was not correct when it was decided, and it is not correct today. It ought not to remain binding precedent. *Bowers* v. *Hardwick* should be and now is overruled.

The present case does not involve minors. It does not involve persons who might be injured or coerced or who are situated in relationships where consent might not easily be refused. It does not involve public conduct or prostitution. It does not involve whether the government must give formal recognition to any relationship that homosexual persons seek to enter. The case does involve two adults who, with full and mutual consent from each other, engaged in sexual practices common to a homosexual lifestyle. The petitioners are entitled to respect for their private lives. The State cannot demean their existence or control their destiny by making their private sexual conduct a crime. Their right to liberty under the Due Process Clause gives them the full right to engage in their conduct without intervention of the government. "It is a promise of the Constitution that there is a realm of personal liberty which the government may not enter." The Texas statute furthers no legitimate state interest which can justify its intrusion into the personal and private life of the individual.

Had those who drew and ratified the Due Process Clauses of the Fifth Amendment or the Fourteenth Amendment known the components of liberty in its manifold possibilities, they might have been more specific. They did not presume to have this insight. They knew times can blind us to certain truths and later generations can see that laws once thought necessary and proper in fact serve only to oppress. As the Constitution endures, persons in every generation can invoke its principles in their own search for greater freedom.

The judgment of the Court of Appeals for the Texas Fourteenth District is reversed....

JUSTICE O'CONNOR, concurring in the judgment.

The Court today overrules *Bowers v. Hardwick*,.... I joined *Bowers*, and do not join the Court in overruling it. Nevertheless, I agree with the Court that Texas' statute banning same-sex sodomy is unconstitutional. Rather than relying on the substantive component of the Fourteenth Amendment's Due Process Clause, as the Court does, I base my conclusion on the Fourteenth Amendment's Equal Protection Clause....

The statute at issue here makes sodomy a crime only if a person "engages in deviate sexual intercourse with another individual of the same sex." Sodomy between opposite-sex partners, however, is not a crime in Texas. That is, Texas treats the same conduct differently based solely on the participants....

The Texas statute makes homosexuals unequal in the eyes of the law by making particular conduct—and only that conduct—subject to criminal sanction....

Texas attempts to justify its law, and the effects of the law, by arguing that the statute satisfies rational basis review because it furthers the legitimate governmental interest of the promotion of morality. In *Bowers*, we held that a state law criminalizing sodomy as applied to homosexual couples did not violate substantive due process. We rejected the argument that no rational basis existed to justify the law, pointing to the government's interest in promoting morality. The only question in front of the Court in *Bowers* was whether the substantive component of the Due Process Clause protected a right to engage in homosexual sodomy. *Bowers* did not hold that moral disapproval of a group is a rational basis under the Equal Protection Clause to criminalize homosexual sodomy when heterosexual sodomy is not punished.

This case raises a different issue than *Bowers:* whether, under the Equal Protection Clause, moral disapproval is a legitimate state interest to justify by itself a statute that bans homosexual sodomy, but not heterosexual sodomy. It is not. Moral disapproval of this group, like a bare desire to harm the group, is an interest that is insufficient to satisfy rational basis review under the Equal Protection Clause. Indeed, we have never held that moral disapproval, without any other asserted state interest, is a sufficient rationale under the Equal Protection Clause to justify a law that discriminates among groups of persons....

That this law as applied to private, consensual conduct is unconstitutional under the Equal Protection Clause does not mean that other laws distinguishing between heterosexuals and homosexuals would similarly fail under rational basis review. Texas cannot assert any legitimate state interest here, such as national security or preserving the traditional institution of marriage. Unlike the moral disapproval of same-sex relations—the asserted state interest in this case—other reasons exist to promote the institution of marriage beyond mere moral disapproval of an excluded group. A law branding one class of persons as criminal solely based on the State's moral disapproval of that class and the conduct associated with that class runs contrary to the values of the Constitution and the Equal Protection Clause, under any standard of review.

I therefore concur in the Court's judgment that Texas' sodomy law banning "deviate sexual intercourse" between consenting adults of the same sex, but not between consenting adults of different sexes, is unconstitutional.

JUSTICE SCALIA, with whom the CHIEF JUSTICE and JUSTICE THOMAS join, dissenting.

... I begin with the Court's surprising readiness to reconsider a decision rendered a mere 17 years ago in *Bowers* v. *Hardwick*....

... Countless judicial decisions and legislative enactments have relied on the ancient proposition that a governing majority's belief that certain sexual behavior is "immoral and unacceptable" constitutes a rational basis for regulation.... State laws against bigamy, same-sex marriage, adult incest, prostitution, masturbation, adultery, fornication, bestiality, and obscenity are likewise sustainable only in light of *Bowers'* validation of laws based on moral choices. Every single one of these laws is called into question by today's decision; the Court makes no effort to cabin the scope of its decision to exclude them from its holding. The impossibility of distinguishing homosexuality from other traditional "morals" offenses is precisely why *Bowers* rejected the rational-basis challenge. "The law," it said, "is constantly based on notions of morality, and if all laws representing essentially moral choices are to be invalidated under the Due Process Clause, the courts will be very busy indeed."

What a massive disruption of the current social order, therefore, the overruling of *Bowers* entails....

[The Texas law] undoubtedly imposes constraints on liberty. So do laws prohibiting prostitution, recreational use of heroin, and, for that matter, working more than 60 hours per week in a bakery. But there is no right to "liberty" under the Due Process Clause, though today's opinion repeatedly makes that claim. The Fourteenth Amendment *expressly allows* States to deprive their citizens of "liberty," *so long as "due process of law" is provided....*

Our opinions applying the doctrine known as "substantive due process" hold that the Due Process Clause prohibits States from infringing *fundamental* liberty interests, unless the infringement is narrowly tailored to serve a compelling state interest. We have held repeatedly ... that *only* fundamental rights qualify for this so-called "heightened scrutiny" protection—that is, rights which are "'deeply rooted in this Nation's history and tradition.'" All other liberty interests may be abridged or abrogated pursuant to a validly enacted state law if that law is rationally related to a legitimate state interest.

Bowers held, first, that criminal prohibitions of homosexual sodomy are not subject to heightened scrutiny because they do not implicate a "fundamental right" under the Due Process Clause. Noting that "proscriptions against that conduct have ancient roots," that "sodomy was a criminal offense at common law and was forbidden by the laws of the original 13 States when they ratified the Bill of Rights," and that many States had retained their bans on sodomy, *Bowers* concluded that a right to engage in homosexual sodomy was not "'deeply rooted in this Nation's history and tradition.'"

The Court today does not overrule this holding. Not once does it describe homosexual sodomy as a "fundamental right" or a "fundamental liberty interest," nor does it subject the Texas statute to strict scrutiny. Instead, having failed to establish that the right to homosexual sodomy is "'deeply rooted in this Nation's history and tradition,'" the Court concludes that the application of Texas's statute to petitioners' conduct fails the rational-basis test, and overrules *Bowers*' holding to the contrary....

Bowers' conclusion that homosexual sodomy is not a fundamental right "deeply rooted in this Nation's history and tradition" is utterly unassailable.

Realizing that fact, the Court instead says: "We think that our laws and traditions in the past half century are of most relevance here. These references show *an emerging awareness* that liberty gives substantial protection to adult persons in deciding how to conduct their private lives *in matters pertaining to sex*" (emphasis added). Apart from the fact that such an "emerging awareness" does not establish a "fundamental right," the statement is factually false. States continue to prosecute all sorts of crimes by adults "in matters pertaining to sex": prostitution, adult incest, adultery, obscenity, and child pornography. Sodomy laws, too, have been enforced "in the past half century," in which there have been 134 reported cases involving prosecutions for consensual, adult, homosexual sodomy....

I turn now to the ground on which the Court squarely rests its holding: the contention that there is no rational basis for the law here under attack. This proposition is so out of accord with our jurisprudence—indeed, with the jurisprudence of *any* society we know—that it requires little discussion. The Texas statute undeniably seeks to further the belief of its citizens that certain forms of sexual behavior are "immoral and unacceptable,"—the same interest furthered by criminal laws against fornication, bigamy, adultery, adult incest, bestiality, and obscenity. *Bowers* held that this *was* a legitimate state interest. The Court today reaches the opposite conclusion. The Texas statute, it says, "furthers *no legitimate state interest* which can justify its intrusion into the personal and private life of the individual" (emphasis added). The Court embraces instead Justice Stevens' declaration in his *Bowers* dissent, that "the fact that the governing majority in a State has traditionally viewed a particular practice as immoral is not a sufficient reason for upholding a law prohibiting the practice." This effectively decrees the end of all morals legislation. If, as the Court asserts, the promotion of majoritarian sexual morality is not even a *legitimate* state interest, none of the above-mentioned laws can survive rational-basis review....

Today's opinion is the product of a Court, which is the product of a law-profession culture, that has largely signed on to the so-called homosexual agenda, by which I mean the agenda promoted by some homosexual activists directed at eliminating the moral opprobrium that has traditionally attached to homosexual conduct....

Let me be clear that I have nothing against homosexuals, or any other group, promoting their agenda through normal democratic means. Social perceptions of sexual and other morality change over time, and every group has the right to persuade its fellow citizens that its view of such matters is the best. That homosexuals have achieved some success in that enterprise is attested to by the fact that Texas is one of the few remaining States that criminalize private, consensual homosexual acts. But persuading one's fellow citizens is one thing, and imposing one's views in absence of democratic majority will is something else. I would no more *require* a State to criminalize homosexual acts—or, for that matter, display *any* moral disapprobation of them—than I would *forbid* it to do so. What Texas has chosen to do is well within the range of traditional democratic action, and its hand should not be stayed through the invention of a brand-new "constitutional right" by a Court that is impatient of democratic change. It is indeed true that "later generations can see that laws once thought necessary and proper in fact serve only to oppress," and when that happens, later generations can repeal those laws. But it is the premise of our system that those judgments are to be made by the people, and not imposed by a governing caste that knows best....

... Texas's prohibition of sodomy neither infringes a "fundamental right" ... , nor is unsupported by a rational relation to what the Constitution considers a legitimate state interests, nor denies the equal protection of the laws.

JUSTICE THOMAS, dissenting.

... [T]he law before the Court today "is ... uncommonly silly." If I were a member of the Texas Legislature, I would vote to repeal it. Punishing someone for expressing his sexual preference through noncommercial consensual conduct with another adult does not appear to be a worthy way to expend valuable law enforcement resources. Notwithstanding this, I recognize that as a member of this Court I am not empowered to help petitioners and others similarly situated. My duty, rather, is to "decide cases 'agreeably to the Constitution and laws of the United States.'" And, just like Justice Stewart, I "can find [neither in the Bill of Rights nor any other part of the Constitution a] general right of privacy," or as the Court terms it today, the "liberty of the person both in its spatial and more transcendent dimensions."

1

INTRODUCTION

Michael Hardwick was a gay bartender in Atlanta, Georgia. In August 1982, he was arrested for performing consensual oral sex with another adult male in the privacy of his bedroom, thus violating Georgia's antisodomy statute, which prohibited "any sexual act involving the sex organs of one person and the mouth or anus of another." Hardwick and his partner were discovered by a police officer who had come to Hardwick's home to arrest him for failing to pay a fine for drinking in public. One of Hardwick's housemates, not knowing Hardwick's whereabouts, invited the officer into the house and gave the officer permission to check Hardwick's bedroom, where Hardwick and his partner were discovered.

The local district attorney chose not to prosecute Hardwick. Nevertheless, Hardwick brought a civil suit challenging the constitutionality of Georgia's law punishing heterosexual and homosexual sodomy. Hardwick alleged that the U.S. Constitution's implied right to privacy conferred upon him and other homosexuals the right to engage in consensual sodomy performed in the privacy of the home. The federal district court judge dismissed the suit, but the U.S. Court of Appeals for the Eleventh Circuit reversed, holding that the Georgia statute violated Hardwick's fundamental rights. Georgia's attorney general, Michael Bowers, then petitioned the U.S. Supreme Court for review.

In *Bowers v. Hardwick* (478 U.S. 186; 1986), the Supreme Court, dividing five to four, held that the U.S. Constitution did not confer a fundamental right upon homosexuals to engage in consensual sodomy performed in the privacy of the home. Justice Byron White wrote the majority opinion. (A *majority opinion* is an opinion that is supported by a majority of the justices who participated in the decision; in addition, justices may file separate concurring or dissenting opinions.) The opinion differentiated this case from earlier cases in which the constitutional right to privacy had been applied. Previously, the Court had recognized a constitutional right to privacy in limited matters, including those involving procreation, marriage, or family life. Those issues, however, bore no relation whatsoever to homosexual activity. Justice White then rejected Hardwick's contention that private sexual activity between consenting adults was beyond the authority of the state to regulate. Although it was true that the state could not abridge fundamental liberties that were "implicit in the concept of ordered liberty" or "deeply rooted in this Nation's history and tradition," Justice White conceded, neither of those formulations encompassed a fundamental right of homosexuals to engage in acts of consensual sodomy. To support this conclusion, the majority noted that homosexual sodomy was a criminal offense forbidden by the laws of the original thirteen states; that until 1961 homosexual sodomy was prohibited in all fifty states; and that even in 1986 almost half of the states continued to criminalize such behavior.

Five of the nine justices indicated clearly that the constitutional right to privacy was limited to those matters involving procreation, marriage, or family. Four justices, however, took exception to this limitation, calling for a more broadly defined constitutional right to privacy, one that included the right alleged here. Speaking for himself and three others, Justice Harry Blackmun dissented.

(A *dissenting opinion* is one written by a justice who disagrees with a particular result reached by the Court. By contrast, a *concurring opinion* is written by a justice who agrees with a particular result reached by the Court but disagrees with some or all of the reasons for that result. A concurring opinion often outlines different or additional reasons for the same result.) He noted that the proscribed activity clearly implicated the right to privacy—in its decisional aspect, which protected the fundamental interest all individuals have in controlling the nature of their intimate associations with others; and in its spatial aspect, which gave special protection to the intimacy of the home.

Although the majority was convinced that the constitutional right to privacy did not include private homosexual sodomy between consenting adults, it was equally obvious to the four dissenters that the constitutional right to privacy, if it meant anything, meant that consenting adults could engage in homosexual sodomy in their own bedrooms.

Definitions of Privacy

There is little consensus in the academic literature on a definition of privacy. Privacy is, to be certain, an elusive concept. For some, privacy is simply a condition of physical separation—the right to be apart, to live one's life in seclusion. For others, privacy is about control—the right to control the intimacies of life. For still others, privacy is about secrecy—the right to determine for oneself if and to what extent personal information is disseminated. To seek a definition of privacy is to set forth upon a monumental quest.

Etymologically, the word *privacy* stems from the words *privation* and *deprivation.* Originally, to be private was to be deprived. Thus, the term *privacy* initially had unfavorable connotations: isolation meant loneliness; seclusion was an effective method of punishment. Eventually, individuals discovered the value of occasional isolation—to ponder without interruption and to conceal selected aspects of one's thoughts and activities, so as to enjoy the confidences of others. Late in the nineteenth century, E. L. Godkin (1890, 65) noted that it had been "the ambition of nearly all civilized men and women . . . [to determine] for themselves how much or how little publicity should surround their daily lives."

Today, however, privacy means much more than physical isolation or protecting one's reputation. In 1880, Thomas Cooley (1880, 29) defined privacy as "a right of complete immunity: to be let alone." Two generations later, Justice Louis Brandeis, dissenting in *Olmstead v. United States* (277 U.S. 438; 1928), declared that this right to be let alone was "the most comprehensive of rights and the right most valued by civilized men" (277 U.S. at 478). Yet Cooley's definition, like most definitions of privacy, reveals a number of important limitations.

First, Cooley's definition fails to mention what specific rights, if any, are essential to maintaining privacy. Thus, some duly constituted authority, presumably a legislative or judicial entity, must state precisely those rights that fall under the rubric of privacy and then delineate clearly legitimate limits on intrusions into those areas. On these points, disagreement is a near certainty.

Second, this definition is too narrow. It fails to take into account the many ways in which we may be "left alone" while, at the same time, deprived of our privacy. Consider, for example, the hypothetical scenario proposed by Judith Thomsen (1975, 295). The police, acting without a warrant, employ a special X-ray monitoring device that permits them to watch a suspected criminal through the walls of his residence. In addition, the police train an amplifying device on the residence, so as to be able to hear everything said by the suspect in his home. Those who believe in a right to privacy are certain that the suspect's right to privacy has been violated. Yet those same individuals would be hard-pressed to articulate convincingly how the police had deprived the suspect of his right to privacy, assuming, of course, that the right to privacy is the "right to be let alone." Strictly speaking, the police let him alone. They never trespassed on his property. They never entered his residence. They never made physical contact with him. Their devices operated at a distance. The right to privacy has to be something more than just the right to be let alone.

Third, Cooley's definition is too broad. It makes almost any violation of a right a violation of the right to privacy. For example, if one individual clobbers another on the head with a brick, the first individual has clearly denied to the second individual her right to be let alone. But it is equally evident that the second individual has not been denied her right to privacy. Not all encroachments of the right to be let alone are encroachments of the right to privacy. The right to privacy has to be something less than that, for a right that seeks to embrace everything quickly endangers itself by embracing nothing.

Cooley's definition of privacy, of course, is an expression of his faith in the doctrine that holds that individual freedom is more cherished than all other values. Yet to promulgate a definition for privacy from a theoretical proposition is a difficult task. Justice Hugo Black noted as much when, dissenting in *Griswold v. Connecticut* (381 U.S. 479, 509; 1965), he remarked that constitutional privacy was a "broad, abstract, and ambiguous concept." It evades simple definition.

Categorically, two types of privacy exist. Certain privacy encroachments stem from the actions of private individuals, and other privacy encroachments result from intrusive governmental action. The first type of privacy encroachment I will call *tort privacy.* A *tort* is a private or civil injury to a person, property, or reputation. The individual who has been injured may bring a lawsuit against the wrongdoer, requesting that a court provide a remedy in the form of an action for damages. For example, if a journalist were to overstep bounds of propriety in covering what was intended to be a private wedding ceremony—say, by publishing lurid photographs or revealing highly intimate and embarrassing details—the aggrieved party may seek damages against the journalist in a court of law. Or if a candidate for local public office were to have her shady credit report broadcast against her will, she may file a tort claim against the individual responsible for the dissemination of the credit report. Tort law thus permits individuals who believe they have been wronged to seek redress in a court of law, instead of taking matters into their own hands. Tort privacy permits those who are of the opinion that their privacy has been invaded or denied to request from a court of law an action for damages against the person or persons who have committed the wrong. For well over a century, privacy law was considered to be one of the components within the larger category of tort law.

The second type of privacy encroachment I will call *constitutional privacy.* Although tort privacy preceded constitutional privacy, it is the latter that is the primary concern of this text. Constitutional privacy has come to mean the right of the individual to be free from unwanted and unwarranted governmental intrusion in matters affecting fundamental rights. These "autonomy interests"—some clearly, others marginally, still others allegedly subsumed under the rubric of privacy—include reproductive freedom; family relationships; sexuality; personal autonomy; decisions about dying and death; and informational privacy. The interests protected under the constitutional right to privacy may be quantified, for we have judicial decisions that tell us so. A state law proscribing first-trimester abortions, for example, runs afoul of the privacy protected by the U.S. Constitution. The general right to privacy, though, cannot be quantified so easily. Such is the nature of the concept. There is no universal agreement on what separates warranted from unwarranted governmental intrusion or what differentiates a fundamental right from a secondary right. Moreover, there is widespread disagreement on what autonomy interests should be included within the general right to privacy. Perhaps Judge Cooley understood full well this dilemma when he defined the right to privacy simply as the "right to be let alone."

Constitutional privacy also embraces the right of the individual not to have certain private information gathered, preserved, or disseminated by government. Thus, constitutional privacy involves at least two separate kinds of interests—one in independence in making certain kinds of important decisions, the other in avoiding disclosure by government of personal matters.

One thing is more certain: constitutional privacy does not mean the right of the individual to do as he or she pleases. Absolute individual autonomy would make a civilized society impossible. Laws, by necessity, infringe upon individual freedoms in numerous ways. The challenge is to strike the appropriate balance between the desire for liberty and the need for order. And no bright line separates desirable governmental action from oppressive governmental action.

The Significance of Privacy

Privacy is a valued condition of human life. Numerous legal and moral philosophers have suggested that privacy is valued because it satisfies a number of primary human needs. Alan F. Westin (1967, 32–39) has argued that privacy, in a democratic society, performs four basic functions for the individual: personal autonomy; emotional release; self-evaluation; and limited and protected communication.

Personal Autonomy

Most democratic societies accept the premise that the each individual is uniquely created, and thus worthy of respect, as self-evident. Psychologists and sociologist are in agreement that this sense of individuality can be maintained only where the individual is autonomous—free from the manipulation and dominance of others. The most serious threat to this autonomy is the penetration of the "core self," the inner circle within each individual that houses his "ultimate secrets." Any encroachment of this "protective shell, [this] psychological armor, would leave him naked to ridicule and shame and would put him under control of those who knew his secrets." Thus, most democratic societies accept the argument that one of government's primary responsibilities is to maintain social processes that safeguard the individual's sacred dignity. Clinton Rossiter and Milton Konvitz (1958, 15–17) stressed the significance of privacy in securing personal autonomy:

> Privacy is a special kind of independence, which can be understood as an attempt to secure autonomy in at least a few personal and spiritual concerns, if necessary in defiance of all the pressures of modern society. . . . [I]t seeks to erect an unbreachable wall of dignity and reserve against the entire world. The free man is the private man, the man who still keeps some of his thoughts and judgments entirely to himself, who feels no over-riding compulsion to share everything of value with others, not even those he loves and trusts.

Emotional Release

Privacy has value because it provides for emotional release. Life generates tension; periods of rest and relaxation are thus necessary to secure and maintain physical and psychological health. Each of us is constrained by the pressures that come with playing social roles. But like actors in a drama, we are unable to sustain those roles beyond a reasonable period of time. As such, each of us needs time among quiet waters, time to unwind and be ourselves, outside of the public glare. Privacy in this aspect, Westin maintains, gives us "a chance to lay [our] masks aside" to secure the rest so vital to the preservation of the human organism. Other forms of emotional release are made possible by privacy. Privacy ensures protection for permissible deviations from social norms.

Should all noncompliance with social norms be revealed, most individuals would be subject to formal discipline, perhaps even incarcerated, or curtailed in their actions by the threat of such punishment. Privacy thus serves a safety-valve function, allowing individuals the opportunity to vent their anger at those with whom they disagree. This aspect of privacy encourages persons to utter behind closed doors commentary that may be unfair, frivolous, nasty, and libelous. This commentary is not subject to social constraints, though, because it is spoken in private. Privacy is also required for management of bodily and sexual functions, as well as for resolve and recovery in times of loss, shock, sorrow, anxiety, and uncertainty.

Self-Evaluation

True self-evaluation is made possible only through privacy. Each of us needs time to reflect on past experiences, to anticipate future ones, to evaluate old ideas, and to originate new ones. This function of privacy includes a major moral dimension—the exercise of conscience by which the individual "repossesses himself." Jeffery H. Reiman (1976, 26) has written that privacy is "an essential part of the complex social practice by means of which the social group recognizes—and communicates to the individual—that his existence is his own." This function also gives the individual the appropriate amount of time to consider if and when one's private reflections become public matters.

Limited and Protected Communication

Privacy also provides for limited and protected communication among individuals, especially in the crowded environment of urban life. Individuals are free to share their intimacies with those deemed trustworthy—perhaps one's spouse, family, personal friends, and close associates—knowing that the confidences disclosed in private will not be disseminated in public. The sacred communication between a husband and wife, a lawyer and client, priest and penitent, and physician and patient are all aspects of this function of privacy. Limited communication also sets necessary boundaries of mental distance in interpersonal situations, even in marriage. Husbands and wives need spaces in their togetherness, standing together, just not too near together.

Richard C. Turkington and Anita L. Allen (1999, 27–28) have suggested that privacy promotes two ideals: human personhood, the recognition of individuals as rational, self-determining, and morally autonomous; and human relationships, the recognition that intimate associations make life more complete. Privacy encourages rest, reflection, experimentation, and independent action. This, in turn, prepares individuals for meeting their responsibilities as citizens and caretakers. Privacy thus helps to create and preserve social civility.

Charles Fried (1968, 477–478) has noted that without privacy relations of the most fundamental sort—respect, love, friendship, and trust—are simply inconceivable. Privacy is an absolute necessity to achieving these relations. "To respect, love, trust, feel affection for others and to regard ourselves as the objects of love, trust, and affection," he states, "is at the heart of our notion of ourselves as persons among persons, and privacy is the necessary atmosphere for these attitudes and actions, as oxygen is for combustion."

Privacy thus clearly has intrinsic value. It is a basic human good, central to our existence as individuals and as members of a community.

Privacy in the U.S. Political System

The United States is a liberal democracy. Liberal democracies generally fear excessive governmental authority; thus, they tend to be organized in such a way as to promote two values. Central to liberal democracies is the principle of *limited government.* This principle recognizes that there are formal restraints on the exercise of governmental authority. In certain areas, government is powerless to act. Equally important to liberal democracies is the idea of *self-determination.* Individuals must be free to express opinions and make choices, even unpopular ones, absent governmental interference. The U.S. Constitution, after all, was designed to "secure the Blessings of Liberty to ourselves and our Posterity." The right to privacy in the United States flows from these two values.

The right to privacy, though, is not mentioned specifically in the U.S. Constitution or in the Bill of Rights. The absence of such explicit recognition, however, should not be interpreted as the absence of concern for privacy interests. Long before the American Revolution, laws throughout this land provided protection for privacy interests. David H. Flaherty (1972) documents the extent to which American society recognized the right to privacy in the decades prior to independence from England. Westin (1967) demonstrates how the concept of privacy was dealt with in the early years of the republic, concluding that American law, heavily concerned about privacy interests, set up a "brilliant framework" for addressing such interests.

The legal system in the United States is based upon the common law. The *common law* is the body of principles that originate from judicial decrees that reflect prevailing usages and customs. Common law is thus judge-made law, as distinguished from statutory law, which is law created by the enactment of legislatures. As these judicial decrees are reapplied to similar situations, the body of principles gradually becomes "common" to the whole nation. Throughout the nineteenth century, common law courts in the United States began to acknowledge a legal right to privacy, most often as a tort protection. In other words, invasions of privacy were considered civil injuries, remedied through actions for damages. In 1905, however, the Georgia Supreme Court formally recognized privacy as an independent and distinct right (unrelated to tort law) under the Georgia Constitution. That case, *Pavesich v. New England Life Insurance Company* (50 S.E. 68; [Ga. 1905]), constituted the first time any court of last resort in the United States recognized an independent constitutional right to privacy. Over the next fifty years, a majority of the states adopted a common law principle of an independent right to privacy. Today, the right to privacy exists, in some form or another, in all fifty states.

It was not until sixty years after *Pavesich* that the U.S. Supreme Court formally announced that an independent right to privacy existed under the U.S. Constitution. (The Court, to be clear, acknowledged privacy interests under the Fourth and Fifth Amendments in the late nineteenth century but did not declare privacy to be an independent constitutional right prior to 1965.) In *Griswold v. Connecticut* (381 U.S. 479, 484; 1965), the U.S. Supreme Court held that the right to privacy could be found by looking in the shadows, by reading carefully between the lines, of the First, Third, Fourth, Fifth, and Ninth Amendments: "[S]pecific guarantees in the Bill of Rights have penumbras, formed by emanations from those guarantees that help give them life and substance." (A *penumbra* is a partial shadow surrounding a fuller and darker shadow, as in an eclipse.) In short, the *Griswold* Court held that certain specifically enumerated rights protected in the Bill of Rights, when considered along with their "emanations" and "penumbras," implied other rights, including an independent, general right to privacy. The Court's recognition of privacy as a distinct and independent right has generated much debate, and *Griswold* remains one of the most discussed and controversial Supreme Court decisions of all time.

CURRENT BREADTH OF THE RIGHT TO PRIVACY

Though the independent right to privacy arrived late to the common law, the last four decades have witnessed an undeniable expansion of privacy rights. This extension led Paul Freund (1971,

192) to call constitutional privacy a "greedy little concept," one not easily limited once recognized. The Supreme Court has been unable to resist the opportunity to enlarge the autonomy interests protected under the right to privacy. What has emerged from its decisions defies simple categorization. At a minimum, however, the right to privacy includes the right to be free from governmental surveillance and intrusion in most matters deemed personal, as well as the right not to have private affairs made public by the government. As such, since 1965, the Supreme Court has held that the right to privacy includes the freedom of the individual to make most decisions regarding such fundamental rights as procreation, marriage, family life, sexuality, and the unnecessary public dissemination of personal information by government. Choices about contraception, pregnancy, childbearing, abortion, marriage, divorce, rearing and educating children, maintaining family ties, family living arrangements, and sexual activities are highly private ones; thus, most decisions pertaining to these matters have earned constitutional protection. Informational privacy—the right of the individual to control the dissemination by government of information concerning his or her person—is an important component of the constitutional right to privacy as well.

In addition, the right to privacy has been asserted successfully in a number of state courts to include the right of a competent adult to refuse medical treatment, to terminate artificial life-support, to obtain assistance from a physician for the purposes of ending life, and to engage in homosexual sexual relations. The U.S. Supreme Court, however, has, up to the present, been unwilling to extend the right to privacy under the U.S. Constitution to include these activities. Without question, these and other privacy issues will continue to confront the justices.

Judicial decisions in this area have not laid to rest the debate over the constitutional right to privacy. Privacy is, to be sure, a developing concept. The *Griswold* Court held that privacy was a penumbral right. Yet the justices did not say how broad that penumbra was. Bitter disagreement separates those who define the constitutional right to privacy broadly from those who prefer a more narrow definition of the right. Homosexual sodomy is but one example of that division.

REFERENCES AND FURTHER READING

Bates, Alan. 1964. "Privacy—A Useful Concept." *Social Forces* 42: 429–434.

Cooley, Thomas McIntyre. 1880. *A Treatise on the Law of Torts.* Chicago: Callaghan.

Flaherty, David H. 1972. *Privacy in Colonial New England.* Charlottesville: University Press of Virginia.

Freund, Paul A. 1971. "Privacy: One Concept or Many." In *Privacy,* edited by J. Roland Pennock and John W. Chapman. New York: Atherton Press.

Fried, Charles. 1968. "Privacy." *Yale Law Journal* 77: 475–493.

Godkin, E. L. 1890. "The Rights of the Citizen—IV: To His Reputation." *Scribner's* 8: 58–68.

Konvitz, Milton R. 1966. "Privacy and the Law: A Philosophical Prelude." *Law and Contemporary Problems* 31: 272–280.

Kurland, Philip B. 1976. *Some Reflections on Privacy and the Constitution.* Chicago: University of Chicago Center for Policy Study.

Parker, Richard B. 1974. "A Definition of Privacy." *Rutgers Law Review* 1974: 275–296.

Posner, Richard A. 1979. "The Uncertain Protection of Privacy by the Supreme Court." *Supreme Court Review* 1979: 173–216.

Prosser, William L. 1960. "Privacy." *California Law Review* 48: 383–423.

Reiman, Jeffery. 1976. "Privacy, Intimacy, and Personhood." *Philosophy and Public Affairs* 6: 26–44.

Rossiter, Clinton, and Milton R. Konvitz. 1958. *Aspects of Liberty.* Ithaca, NY: Cornell University Press.

Thomsen, Judith Jarvis. 1975. "The Right to Privacy." *Philosophy and Public Affairs* 4: 295–314.

Turkington, Richard C., and Anita L. Allen. 1999. *Privacy Law.* St. Paul, MN: West Group.

Westin, Alan F. 1967. *Privacy and Freedom.* New York: Atheneum.

2

Origins

Privacy is not a new right; it has been an important condition of almost all civilizations, however primitive. As Milton R. Konvitz (1966, 272) noted, privacy has been "marked off, hinted at, or groped for in some of our oldest legal codes and in the most influential philosophical writings and traditions." Long before the United States existed, the philosophical and constitutional foundations for privacy interests were laid. And long before the U.S. Supreme Court formally recognized privacy as a constitutionally protected right, the common law foundations were laid.

The Philosophical Foundations

Natural Law and Natural Rights

In the fourth century B.C., the Greek philosopher Aristotle was among the first to articulate the doctrine of natural law, the notion that human affairs should be governed by certain immutable, ethically binding principles. Three centuries later, Cicero (1928, 211) defined this "higher law" as a "sacred obligation" to which no person may be released, "but one eternal and unchangeable law valid for all nations and all time." In the thirteenth century A.D., St. Thomas Aquinas incorporated natural law with Christianity, positing that the two went hand in hand because God was the creator of the natural law that established individual natural rights.

This doctrine was further developed by the political philosophers of the seventeenth and eighteenth centuries. In the seventeenth century, Thomas Hobbes and John Locke, among others, advanced what would become the animating principle of the American Revolution and its subsequent government—the *social contract theory.* This theory posits that all men are born free and equal by God-given right and, therefore, must give their consent to be governed. Two centuries later, John Stuart Mill joined the debate, exploring the limits of governmental authority.

Thomas Hobbes

Thomas Hobbes, in *The Leviathan* (1651), argued that man's natural condition was evil. This "state of nature" was one of "force and fraud," in which "every man [was] to every man a wolf." Consequently, life was "solitary, poor, nasty, brutish, and short" (98–102). This dismal condition continued until people discovered through reason that they could enter into a mutually beneficial arrangement to protect their lives. This social contract, however, was impossible without an entity that possessed enforcement powers. Thus, government was a necessity. As such, citizens agreed to transfer to a sovereign certain liberties in exchange for physical protection. But what if the sovereign did not act in a manner acceptable to the people? According to Hobbes, no remedy existed. Even a bad government, he maintained, was preferable to a constant state of anarchy. In short, a civilized society required strict adherence to a set of rules promulgated by a single ruler.

John Locke

John Locke, in "An Essay Concerning Civil Government," published in *Two Treatises of Government* (1690), agreed with Hobbes that government was the proper remedy for the inconvenience brought about by the natural "state of war." Yet Locke maintained that creating a sovereign powerful enough to take away basic liberties, even if taken in the interest of preserving order, defeated the very purpose of government. Rather, individuals entered into a contract to preserve their *natural rights*—"lives, liberties, and estates," which Locke called by their general name: "property" (395). These rights preceded government; thus, government was not their source. Instead, government was simply the protector of preexisting rights. In short, individual rights came first; government came second solely as a means of securing individual rights.

To secure these rights, Locke advocated a fiduciary arrangement between the ruled and ruler. Within this arrangement, Locke called for a limited amount of power that the government (trustee) may exercise as long as it adhered to the will of the people (trustors). Locke believed the authority of the government lay in people willing to relinquish *limited* power to government. But what if the government did not act in a manner pleasing to the people? In such a case, the people possessed the authority to ask the government to cease and desist. If the government refused to comply, the people could remove the government by revolution and then establish a new government.

John Locke's *Two Treatises of Government* embodied the principles of natural rights, limited government, and the right of revolution, each widely referenced by the colonists in the years preceding the American Revolution. Witness, for example, the invocation of natural rights in the Declaration of Independence: "We hold these Truths to be self-evident, that all Men are created equal, that they are endowed by their Creator with certain inalienable Rights, that among these are Life, Liberty, and the Pursuit of Happiness." This appeal to "inalienable rights" was not novel; the Declaration of Independence was simply a concise restatement of the natural law–natural rights doctrines that had been developed centuries before the American Revolution. Notice as well that these "inalienable rights" came not from government but rather from a "Creator." In addition, the document asserted the sole justification for governmental power—to secure life, liberty, and the pursuit of happiness. Observe the document's incantation of limited government: "That to secure these Rights, Governments are instituted among Men, deriving their just Powers from the Consent of the Governed." Moreover, it affirmed the illegitimacy of any government that failed to live up to this standard. Consider its justification for revolution: "[T]hat whenever any Form of Government becomes destructive of these Ends, it is the Right of the People to alter or to abolish it, and to institute new Government, laying its Foundation on such Principles, and organizing its powers in such Form, as to them shall seem most likely to effect their Safety and Happiness."

The Declaration of Independence was a summation of fundamental principles: (1) individuals possessed rights outside of those granted or recognized by government; (2) government may exercise power only with the consent of the governed; and (3) if the government acted improperly, its contract with the people was broken and the people could abolish the existing government and institute a new one.

John Stuart Mill

John Stuart Mill was the most widely recognized British political writer of the nineteenth century. His most famous political tract, *On Liberty* (1859), explored the struggle between individual autonomy and governmental authority. The essay began with a question: What are the legitimate limits of the collective society over the individual? He then answered the question by articulating "a very simple principle": the only reason for interfering with anyone's liberty, against that individual's will, was self-preservation—to prevent harm to others. Power could not be exercised over the individual because it would make him happier, or, in the opinions of others, to do so would be wise or even right. The appropriate place to draw the line between state and individual power was where someone else might be hurt by another's actions.

> The only part of the conduct of anyone for which he is amenable to society is that which concerns others. In that part which merely concerns himself, his independence is, of right, absolute. Over himself, over his own body and mind, the individual is sovereign. . . . [T]here is a sphere of action in which society, as distinguished from the individual, has, if any, only an indirect interest: comprehending all that portion of a person's life and conduct which affects only himself or, if it also affects others, only with their free, voluntary, and undeceived consent and participation. (13, 15–16)

Notice, though, that the individual was not sovereign. As soon as any part of a person's conduct affected prejudicially the interests of others, society had jurisdiction over it, and the question whether the general welfare would or would not be promoted by interfering with it became open to discussion. Of course, Mill recognized that it was difficult to determine the precise point at which the conduct of the individual became the concern of society. As a general rule, however, *On Liberty* posited that government should make every effort to leave most matters to the individual.

To be certain, the right to privacy has many philosophical roots. It stems from Aristotle's doctrine of natural law, grows with Locke's defense of natural rights and a limited government to preserve those rights, and finds anchor in Mill's understanding of the primacy of the individual and the limitations of governmental authority.

THE CONSTITUTIONAL FOUNDATIONS

State Constitutions and Bills of Rights

Patriot leaders recognized the formation of legally constituted state governments as a strategic move in the revolutionary process. The prevailing political philosophy held that a revolution destroyed all existing political compacts and left the people free to enter into a new political compact setting up government once more. New Hampshire adopted a brief, temporary constitution in January 1776, and South Carolina did the same in March 1776. Between 1776 and 1780, all of the states save two—Rhode Island and Connecticut—adopted new written constitutions. Compared with the constitutions of later days, those of 1776 are notable for their brevity, most of them being five to seven pages in length. Even so, most of these documents acknowledged the presence of natural rights and all enumerated formal limitations on government. Seven of these state constitutions contained separate bills of rights, and the remainder incorporated similar provisions. (In genral, a *bill of rights* is a list of restrictions of the powers of the government.)

For example, drafted largely by George Mason and adopted in June 1776, the Virginia Bill of Rights, the most famous of the declarations of rights of the original state constitutions, declared that all men are "by nature equally free and independent, and have certain inherent rights, of which, when they enter into a state of society, they cannot, by any compact, deprive or divest their posterity; namely, the enjoyment of life and liberty, with the means of acquiring property, and pursuing and obtaining happiness and safety" (Poore 1877, I, 1908). In similar fashion, the Massachusetts

Bill of Rights, adopted in 1780, stated that all men "have certain natural, essential, and unalienable rights; among which may be reckoned the right of enjoying and defending their lives and liberties; that of acquiring, possessing, and protecting their property; in fine, that of seeking and obtaining their safety and happiness" (Poore 1877, I, 957). These two documents also prohibited writs of assistance, taxation without representation, and standing armies without consent; and guaranteed the right to trial by jury, moderate bail, fair procedure in criminal cases, freedom of the press, a free militia, and religious liberty. These documents, among others, attempted to articulate the fundamental rights of all persons, rights deemed by the Americans to be natural and inalienable.

The U.S. Constitution

The Constitutional Convention convened on May 25, 1787, in Philadelphia, Pennsylvania. American political thought at that time rested primarily upon four assumptions: individualism, popular consent, limited government, and private property. *Individualism* is the notion that the individual is more important than the state and its component ideas of individual worth, private religious judgment, private economic motive, and direct legal rights for individuals. Closely akin to the social contract theory, *popular consent* holds that a just government derives its powers from the consent of the people it governs. The principle of *limited government* recognizes legal, written restraints on governmental authority and "the moral primacy of the private over the public sphere of society" (Westin 1970, 330). Finally, *private property* was antecedent to government; as such, private property was morally beyond the reach of popular majorities. Each of these assumptions stemmed from a common purpose—to free citizens from government control (as had been the case when the colonists were "subjects" of the British Crown). Thus, the U.S. Constitution became the "tangible embodiment" of these principles, "brought down from the rarified stratosphere of natural law-natural rights theorizing and made concrete" (Dixon 1976, 46).

On September 17, 1787, the Constitution was signed, and the convention adjourned. Ten days later, an unenthusiastic Congress submitted the Constitution to the states for ratification. Ensuring ratification of the document, however, was no easy task. Nevertheless, the delegates took some critical steps to enhance chances for ratification. First, the delegates rejected a call for another convention. The states would have to ratify the document as it was, imperfections and all, or suffer the consequences. Second, the Constitution was to be ratified by popularly elected state conventions and not state legislatures. Under the Articles of Confederation, the then-existing compact, the states were sovereign; under the federal Constitution, the newly proposed charter, the states shared power with the national government. Thus, the Framers required that the people, and not the states, accept or reject the proposed charter. Third, unanimity was not required: the Constitution would take effect if and when nine of the thirteen states ratified it.

In the course of the fight for adoption, supporters of the instrument of government became known as Federalists, led by James Madison of Virginia and Alexander Hamilton of New York. Those opposed to ratification were known as the Antifederalists, led by Patrick Henry of Virginia. The Antifederalists feared that the new government would destroy the sovereignty and autonomy of the states. In addition, the Antifederalists clamored for a federal bill of rights, a list of restrictions on the powers of the national government.

The ten-month struggle for ratification produced several noteworthy pieces of political literature. The most important of these was *The Federalist,* inspired by Alexander Hamilton, who was concerned about the number of Antifederalist pamphlets appearing in New York. Hamilton, Madison, and John Jay published a series of scholarly articles, eighty-five in all, that examined the

Constitution clause by clause. Many of these articles were devoted to explanations of the various provisions of the Constitution and to reassurances that the new government would not destroy the states or become an instrument of tyranny. To this day, *The Federalist* remains one of the great treatises on the American constitutional system. Hamilton, Madison, and Jay were able to predict, with amazing precision and accuracy, the operations of a government that existed only on paper.

The Federalist was persuasive in a number of states, most notably Virginia and New York. Yet it was another agreement that solidified ratification. A promise was made to the Antifederalists: should the document be ratified, the First Congress would move for adoption of a bill of rights. Delaware was the first to ratify, in December 1787. The ninth state, New Hampshire, ratified on June 21, 1788. Virginia and New York ratified soon thereafter. Rhode Island, which never sent delegates to the convention, was the last of the original thirteen states to ratify, in 1790.

The four defining principles of the new Constitution were federalism, separation of powers, checks and balances, and individual rights. The incorporation of the first three principles minimized the threat of tyranny from any one government or any single branch of the national government. The incorporation of the fourth principle indicated the Framers' highest ideals—protection of the liberty and property of the individual. Although it is true the original Constitution contained few explicit guarantees with respect to individual rights, it is worth noting that many of the delegates assumed that the soon-to-be created *limited* national government would not be a threat to individual rights. Nevertheless, to be more certain, the delegates promised a written bill of rights should ratification occur.

Federalism is a system of government in which a constitution divides power between a national government and subnational governments. Neither the national government nor the state governments receives its powers from the other. Instead, both governments derive their powers from the U.S. Constitution. The Framers viewed the division of governmental authority as a means of checking power with power and providing "double security" to the people. The national government would keep the state governments in check, and the state governments would prevent excesses by the national government. In a federal system, both types of governments may act directly upon the people.

Separation of powers is a way of parceling out power among the three branches of the national government. Well aware of Montesquieu's concerns regarding the concentration of power, Madison wrote in *Federalist No. 47* that "the accumulation of all powers, legislative, executive, and judiciary, in the same hands . . . may justly be pronounced the very definition of tyranny." As such, the Constitution assigns the legislative, executive, and judicial powers of the national government to three separate, independent branches of government. This separation, Madison maintained, provided an "essential precaution in favor of liberty" (Hamilton, Madison, and Jay 1961, 301).

In addition, power is *checked* and *balanced.* The legislative, executive, and judicial branches of the national government share certain powers so that no branch has exclusive domain over any activity. "The great security against the gradual concentration of several powers in the same department," Madison noted in *Federalist No. 51,* "consists in giving to those who administer each department the necessary constitutional means and personal motives to resist encroachment by the others. . . . Ambition must be made to counteract ambition. . . . [E]xperience has taught mankind the necessity of auxiliary precautions" (Hamilton, Madison, and Jay 1961, 321–322). The Constitution thus contains a number of "auxiliary precautions" so that each branch may "resist encroachment" by the others. For example, the legislature may check the executive by overriding a presidential veto, impeaching and removing the president, and rejecting presidential nominees, including federal judges. The legislature may check the judiciary by determining the jurisdiction of federal courts and by rejecting, impeaching, and removing federal judges. The executive may check the legislature by rejecting bills passed by Congress, and it may check the judiciary by appointing all federal judges and by pardoning those accused or convicted of federal crimes. Much less was said about the powers of the judiciary. In fact, the Constitution is silent with respect to the means by which the judiciary may "resist encroachment" of the legislative and executive branches.

Judicial Review

Judicial review has come to mean the power of the federal judiciary to review and, if warranted, declare unconstitutional the acts and proceedings of other branches and levels of government. In effect, judicial review is the power of the federal courts to determine the constitutionality of governmental action; and if that action should be deemed inconsistent with the Constitution, then the judiciary has the power to nullify the will of the elected representatives of the people.

The notion that the courts should exercise such power stems from the rejection of the supremacy and inviolability of enacted law. Cicero (1928, 343) recognized in the first century B.C. that it was a "most foolish notion" to conclude that "everything is just which is found in the customs or laws of nations." The English jurist Sir Edward Coke went one step further in *Dr. Bonham's Case* (8 Coke Reports 114; 1610), in which he stated that courts could nullify legislative acts. In his now famous dictum, Coke noted, "[W]hen an act of Parliament is against common right and reason, or repugnant, or impossible to perform, the common law will controul it and adjudge such act to be void" (8 Coke Reports at 118). Whatever promise judicial review held in England, however, waned following the Glorious Revolution of 1688, which established clearly the supremacy of Parliament.

Sir William Blackstone (1765, I, 160–161), perhaps the most influential jurist of the eighteenth century, specifically rejected judicial review: if the legislature "think fit *positively* to enact a law there is no power which can countrol them . . . the judges are not at liberty, although it appear to them to be *unreasonable,* to reject it; for this were to set the *judicial* above the legislative, which would be subversive to all government." Thus, for the century leading up to the promulgation of the U.S. Constitution, the Blackstonian concept of legislative supremacy prevailed in England. That principle, however, did not apply with equal fervor in the colonies. Robert K. Carr (1942, 43) noted that the British Privy Council exercised judicial review 469 times over acts passed by the colonial legislatures in the seventeenth and eighteenth centuries.

The doctrine of judicial review found a more accepting audience in the colonies. According to Charles Grove Haines (1959):

> The gradual emergence of the principles that constitutions are fundamental laws with a peculiar sanctity, that legislatures are limited and receive the commission for their authority from the constitution, and that courts are to be considered the special guardians of the superior written laws may be observed in the evolution of political ideas which accompanied the separation from the British Empire and the establishment of an independent government in America. (66)

In 1761, for example, colonial lawyer James Otis spoke in opposition to "writs of assistance," general warrants permitting agents of the British Crown to search for smuggled materials without any limitations. Elaborating on the principle of judicial review announced by Sir William Coke in *Dr. Bonham's Case* (1610), Otis remarked, "An Act against the Constitution is void; an act against natural equity is void; and if an act of Parliament should be made, in the very words of this petition it would be void. The executive courts must pass such acts into disuse" (Commager 1958, 45). As tension between the Parliament and the "subjects" mounted, the colonists increasingly turned to judicial bodies for resolution, so much so that by 1776 judicial review had taken a firm hold.

In spite of the fact that judicial review may have been considered an important component of constitutional government by the time of America's founding, judicial review is nowhere specifically mentioned in the Constitution. In fact, Article III of the Constitution—dealing with the judicial branch—is the shortest and least detailed of the articles. Section 1 provides that "the judicial Power of the United States, shall be vested in one supreme Court, and in such inferior Courts as the Congress may from time to time ordain and establish." Yet it does not clarify what constitutes "judicial power." Section 2 specifies the types of cases and controversies that fall within the jurisdiction of the federal courts. And section 3 does not even deal with judicial matters.

Nonetheless, in *Federalist No. 78,* Alexander Hamilton (1961, 466–467) asserted a justification for judicial review. Because the Constitution granted only limited powers to government, it necessarily followed that other powers were outside the pale of governmental authority.

> This implied prohibition against certain powers could be preserved in practice no other way than the medium of courts of justice, whose duty it must be to declare all acts contrary to the manifest tenor of the Constitution void. . . . It is not otherwise to be supposed that the constitution could intend to enable the representatives of the people to substitute their *will* to that of their constituencies. It is far more rational to suppose that the courts were designed to be an intermediate body between the people and the legislature, in order, among other things, to keep the latter within the limits assigned to their authority. The interpretation of the laws is the proper and peculiar province of the courts. A constitution is in fact, and must be, regarded by the judges as a fundamental law. It therefore belongs to them as to ascer-

> tain its meaning as well as the meaning of any particular act proceeding from the legislative body. If there should happen to be an irreconcilable variance between the two, that which has the superior obligation and validity ought of course to be preferred; or in other words, the constitution ought to be preferred to the statute, the intention of the people to the intention of their agents.

Hamilton was not the only influential delegate to the convention who expressed support for judicial review. James Madison noted that the judiciary was necessary to prevent "nullification, anarchy, and confusion" (Warren 1937, 740). James Wilson observed that because the Constitution was supreme, those laws inconsistent with the Constitution must be declared so by those responsible for declaring and applying the law. Simply because one branch of government infringed the Constitution, it did not follow that the judiciary should aid in such infringement (Warren 1937, 460).

In addition, seven states—Rhode Island, New York, Connecticut, Massachusetts, New Jersey, North Carolina, and South Carolina—debated and accepted the doctrine of judicial review in their ratifying conventions. Still, the Constitution did not specifically provide for judicial review. And it would be well over a decade before the U.S. Supreme Court would assume the power for itself and the rest of the federal judiciary.

In the landmark ruling of *Marbury v. Madison* (5 U.S. 137; 1803), the U.S. Supreme Court, for the first time, declared an act of Congress unconstitutional. The opinion, written by Chief Justice John Marshall, justified judicial review in terms of the fundamental principles of constitutional government and employed language and logic similar to that used by Sir Edward Coke two centuries earlier and Alexander Hamilton fifteen years earlier. Recognizing the Constitution as the "fundamental and paramount law of the nation," the Court held that an act of the legislature repugnant to the Constitution was void. Moreover, it was the duty of the judiciary to make such a declaration.

> It is emphatically the province and duty of the judicial department to say what the law is. Those who apply the rule to particular cases, must of necessity expound and interpret that rule. If two laws conflict with each other, the courts must decided the operation of each.
>
> So if a law be in opposition to the constitution; if both the law and the constitution apply to a particular case, so that the court must either decide that case conformably to the law, disregarding the constitution, or conformably to the constitution, disregarding the law, the court must determine which of these conflicting rules governs the case. This is the very essence of judicial duty. (5 U.S. at 177–178)

The opinion then concluded by referencing Article VI, Clause 2 of the Constitution, which specified that all federal laws must be made "in pursuance" of the Constitution. It was the judiciary's responsibility, Marshall presumed, to determine which laws were pursuant to the Constitution and which ones were contradictory.

The Bill of Rights

The drive for the Bill of Rights was fed by a general distrust of a national government far removed from the governed. James Madison expressed his fear of "the abuse of the powers of the General Government" (U.S. Congress, *Annals* 1834, I, 432). Elbridge Gerry of Massachusetts noted that many states never would have ratified the Constitution had they not been ensured that their objections to the absence of a Bill of Rights restricting the national government "would have been duly attended to by Congress" (U.S. Congress, *Annals* 1834, I, 446–447). Thomas Jefferson, not a delegate to the Convention but an interested observer from his ambassadorial post in Paris, France, approved of a bill of rights: "You must specify your liberties, and put them down on paper," he wrote. In a letter to his protégé, Madison, Jefferson noted that even though a bill of rights might "cramp government," it was "what the people are entitled to against every government on earth, general or particular, and what no just government should refuse or rest on inferences" (Jefferson 1904, V, 371).

Alexander Hamilton, however, was opposed to the Bill of Rights on two counts. First, the national government was already limited to specific enumerated rights. Hamilton (Hamilton, Madison, and Jay 1961, 513–514) asked in *Federalist No. 84:* "Why declare that things shall not be done which there is no power to do? Why, for instance, should it be said that the liberty of the press shall not be restrained, when no power is given by which restrictions may be imposed?" Madison even acknowledged that the amendments "may be deemed unnecessary; but there can be no harm in making such a declaration" (U.S. Congress, *Annals* 1834, I, 441). Thus viewed, the Bill of Rights added nothing; it was unnecessary, a mere declaration that the national government could not do what it had no power to do. Second, Hamilton feared that to enumerate certain liberties might in the future lead to the conclusion that the *mentioned* liberties were the *only* liberties.

Nevertheless, on June 8, 1789, Madison introduced a proposed Bill of Rights, twelve amendments to the Constitution. During debate on the House floor, Madison reminded his colleagues that the proposed amendments were "most strenuously required" by the Antifederalists in the state ratifying conventions (U.S. Congress, *Annals* 1834, I, 746). And near the conclusion of the First Congress, Gerry reminded his colleagues of its purpose: "This declaration of rights . . . is intended to secure the people against the mal-administration of the [federal] government" (U.S. Congress, *Annals* 1834, I, 749). Quite obviously, the memory of King George III remained a seminal force behind the Bill of Rights. Congress adopted the twelve amendments in September 1789. Ten of the twelve amendments were ratified by the states in December 1791.

The Bill of Rights may be properly viewed as a general expression of the drafters' prevalent fear of fundamental rights being deprived by government. Several of the provisions in the Bill of Rights were adopted to protect individuals in their privacy. The First, Third, Fourth, and Fifth Amendments all contained some privacy component.

The First Amendment guaranteed freedom of conscience in both religious and political matters and freedom of association, thus protecting the autonomy of the individual. Joseph Story (1851, 591, 600), associate justice of the U.S. Supreme Court from 1812 to 1845, noted that these freedoms were intended to secure the rights of "private sentiment" and "private judgment." This amendment similarly protected those who wished to publish anonymously or under a pseudonym.

The Third Amendment specifically protected the privacy of the home in peacetime from soldiers seeking quarters without the owner's consent. The obvious purpose of this provision was "to secure the perfect enjoyment of that great right, of the [English] common law, that a man's house shall be his own castle, privileged against all civil and military intrusion" (Story 1851, 608).

In addition, official intrusions into dwellings were prohibited in the interests of privacy. The Fourth Amendment reads, "The right of the people to be secure in their persons, houses, papers, and effects, against unreasonable searches and seizures, shall not be violated." This amendment was "indispensable to the full enjoyment of the rights of personal security, personal liberty, and private property" (Story 1851, 608–609). In short, privacy in the home was virtually guaranteed. Francis Lieber (1853, 44–47) maintained that the purpose of the Fourth Amendment was twofold: (1) to acknowledge a man's sovereignty in his home; and (2) to reject the notion of "police government," in which an officer of the law, acting without a warrant, could enter at any time any room or house, break any drawer, and seize any papers or other item deemed fit. Judge Thomas Cooley (1878, 367–368) noted that the justification for this amendment was the common law principle that "a man's house is his castle." And in that castle, the citizen was free from "the prying eyes of the government." Another bulwark of constitutional protection for privacy was the Fifth Amendment, which disallowed compulsory self-incrimination, thus protecting the privacy of one's thoughts.

Unenumerated Rights

Like Alexander Hamilton, James Madison was concerned that future generations might conclude that the *mentioned* liberties were the *only* liberties. He feared that the enumeration of some rights might imperil others if they were not enumerated. This fear led Madison to consider the Ninth Amendment. He noted:

> It has been objected also against a bill of rights, that, by enumerating particular exceptions to the grant of power, it would disparage rights which were not placed in that enumeration; and it might follow, by implication, that those rights which were singled out, were intended to be assigned into the hands of the General Government, and were consequently insecure. This is one of the most plausible arguments I have ever heard urged against the admission of a bill of rights unto this system; but, I conceive, that it may be guarded against. I have attempted it, as gentlemen may see by turning to the last clause of the fourth resolution. (U.S. Congress, *Annals* 1834, I, 456)

That "fourth resolution" referred to the now-existing Ninth Amendment, which made it clear that the listing of certain rights did not mean that others did not exist: "The enumeration in the Constitution of certain rights, shall not be construed to deny or disparage others retained by the people." Madison further held that the fourth resolution was "the most valuable amendment in the whole list" (U.S. Congress, *Annals* 1834, I, 784).

There is great debate over whether the Ninth Amendment confers additional rights to the people, or whether it simply recognizes that there remain reserved to the people an area of unsurrendered rights. Complicating the debate is the unclear language of the provision. As constitutional scholar John Hart Ely (1980, 34) has noted, the Ninth Amendment, "read for what it says, . . . seems open-textured enough to support almost anything one might wish to argue, and that thought can get pretty scary."

Some conclude that the Ninth Amendment was not meant to add anything to the meaning of the Constitution: "[It] was designed to obviate the possibility of applying the maxim *expressio unuis exclusion alterius* [what is expressed excludes what is not] in interpreting the Constitution. It was adopted in order to eliminate the grant of powers by implication" (Dumbauld 1957, 63). In other words, the Framers feared that an enumeration of some rights might deliver those not enumerated into the hands of the national government. To assuage their fears, the Framers included the Ninth Amendment, which simply "demarked an area in which the 'General Government' ha[d] no power whatsoever" (Berger 1980, 23).

Others disagree. In *The Forgotten Ninth Amendment,* for example, Bennett Patterson (1955, 13) devotes 132 pages to appendices and a reprint of the legislative history. He concludes that the Ninth Amendment was definitely intended as a general declaration of "individual inherent rights," unenumerated *and* independent of constitutional grant. Quite possibly, these "unenumerated" rights are the "inalienable" ones mentioned in the Declaration of Independence—life, liberty, and the pursuit of happiness. It is from this premise that many argue that privacy is an unenumerated, yet unalienable, right.

Judicial Review and Unenumerated Rights

Much of constitutional thought today posits that the only rights possessed by the people are those explicitly stated in the Constitution or granted via the legislature. This is known as legal positivism or, put differently, "first comes government, then come individual rights." Legal positivism further holds that judges are authorized to recognize only those rights found in constitutional provisions or legislative statutes. "A judge may never restrict the act of a duly elected legislature unless such a restriction is specifically authorized by the Constitution. A judge is authorized to enforce only those strictures that are actually written in the Constitution (and those that may fairly be implied)" (Barnett 1987, 101–102).

A second school of constitutional thought, however, holds that individuals possess certain fundamental rights, even though such rights are not mentioned in the Constitution or recognized by enacted law. This approach is more Lockean in nature: individual rights come first; government follows to secure those rights. As such, a judge may restrict the act of a duly elected legislature even if that act does not violate a specific constitutional provision. This approach does not recognize the finite Constitution as the sole authority on individual rights.

The earliest judicial statement on unenumerated rights came in 1798. In *Calder v. Bull* (3 U.S. 386; 1798), the U.S. Supreme Court declined to assert its power when ruling that conflicts between state laws and state constitutions were matters for state, not federal, courts to resolve. Justice Samuel Chase, however, contended that the Court had the power to overturn laws that violated fundamental principles, explaining,

> I cannot subscribe to the omnipotence of a State Legislature, or that it is absolute and without controul. . . . There are acts which the Federal, or State, Legislature cannot do, without exceeding their authority. . . . An act of the Legislature (for I cannot call it a law) contrary to the great first principles of the social compact, cannot be considered a rightful exercise of legislative authority. It is against all reason and justice to entrust a Legislature with SUCH [despotic] powers; and there-

> fore, it cannot be presumed that [the people] have done it. (3 U.S. at 387–388)

Yet this principle was not generally agreed upon by all of the justices. By contrast, Justice James Iredell, a Southerner and strong proponent of states' rights, maintained that a state law might run against principles of "natural justice" and the Court still lacked the power to strike it down: "If . . . the legislature of any member of the union, shall pass a law, within the general scope of their constitutional power, the court cannot pronounce it to be void, merely because it is, in their judgment, contrary to the principles of natural justice" (3 U.S. at 399). Justice Iredell went on to note, however, that the courts could overrule acts of elected representatives if some specific provision of a constitution or bill of rights had been clearly violated.

Later in the nineteenth century, Thomas Cooley (1878) published a treatise on constitutional limitations in which he supported judicial review of state legislation that infringed upon natural law rights such as those of contract and property. Writing much later, Edward S. Corwin (1955) noted that natural law rights could not have been preserved without judicial review—a safeguard against legislative sovereignty.

To be certain, the right to privacy is nowhere *specifically* mentioned in the U.S. Constitution or in the Bill of Rights. Nevertheless, because privacy flows from the general concept that there are certain freedoms beyond the power of government to restrict, many view the federal Bill of Rights as a firm judicial mandate empowering the courts to protect both enumerated *and* unenumerated rights.

Incorporation: Beginnings

There is little doubt that at the time of its ratification the Bill of Rights was perceived as imposing limitations on the actions of the national government only. The prevailing view of the Bill of Rights in the nineteenth century was well stated by Chief Justice John Marshall in *Barron v. Baltimore* (32 U.S. 243; 1833). After reviewing the history of the Bill of Rights, Marshall concluded that because there was no evidence indicating an intent to apply the provisions of the Bill of Rights to the states, the Supreme Court was powerless to do so: "We are of the opinion, that, the provision in the Fifth Amendment to the Constitution, declaring that private property shall not be taken for public use without just compensation, is intended solely as a limitation on the power of the United States, and is not applicable to the legislation of the states" (32 U.S. at 250–251).

Ratification of the Fourteenth Amendment in 1868, however, introduced the possibility of a formal linkage between the federal Bill of Rights and the states. Section 1 of the Fourteenth Amendment denied to each *state* the power to "make or enforce any law which shall abridge the privileges or immunities of citizens of the United States . . . [or] deprive any person of life, liberty, or property, without due process of law . . . [or] deny to any person within its jurisdiction the equal protection of the laws." Some members of Congress, including the two primary authors of the Fourteenth Amendment—Representative John A. Bingham of Ohio and Senator Jacob M. Howard of Michigan—maintained that one objective of the Fourteenth Amendment was to make the Bill of Rights applicable to the states. The record of the Thirty-ninth Congress on this question, however, is far from conclusive. Nevertheless, plaintiffs in federal cases began to make this argument shortly after ratification.

The amendment's Privileges or Immunities Clause ("No State shall make or enforce any law which shall abridge the privileges or immunities of citizens of the United State") appeared to be the most direct limitation on the activities of the state. Bingham, the primary author, expected that this clause would be interpreted to protect fundamental rights from state encroachment. Similarly,

Howard stated during floor debate in the Senate that the purpose of the clause was to deny states the power to deprive citizens of "the personal rights guaranteed and secured by the first eight amendments of the Constitution" (*Congressional Globe* 1866, 2764–2765).

Whatever potential for incorporation the Privileges or Immunities Clause had was soon dashed in *Butchers' Benevolent Association v. Crescent City Livestock Landing and Slaughterhouse Company* (83 U.S. 36; 1873). Upholding a Louisiana law that created a monopoly on the operation of slaughterhouses, the Supreme Court, per Justice Samuel Miller, concluded that state citizenship was distinct and separate from national citizenship and that the Privileges or Immunities Clause protected only those privileges and immunities that arose out of the nature and essential character of the national government and the provisions of its Constitution. Here, the plaintiffs had alleged a denial of a privilege—the right to engage in lawful trade. Yet that privilege was among the privileges of state and not national citizenship. As such, protection of that privilege was left to the state governments.

Justice Stephen Field dissented. Speaking for three others, he echoed the sentiments expressed by Bingham and Howard: Congress intended the Fourteenth Amendment to offer protection against state encroachments on the guarantees in the Bill of Rights, including the fundamental right to secure lawful employment in a lawful manner.

In the nineteenth century, the Supreme Court, with only one exception, similarly refused to employ the Due Process Clause of the Fourteenth Amendment ("No state shall . . . deprive any person of life, liberty, or property, without due process of law") to limit the activities of the state with respect to the guarantees of the Bill of Rights. That exception came in *Chicago, Burlington, and Quincy Railway Company v. Chicago* (166 U.S. 226; 1897), where the justices held that the Due Process Clause of the Fourteenth

Amendment required that the states honor the provision of the Fifth Amendment that prohibited the taking of private property for public use without just compensation. This case was the first manifestation of the doctrine that held that the Fourteenth Amendment's Due Process Clause made the Bill of Rights, or at least one provision of the Bill of Rights, applicable to the states. This case also revealed the justices' strong allegiance to laissez-faire capitalism and protection of substantive property rights.

Not until well into the twentieth century, however, would the Supreme Court accept the argument that the Fourteenth Amendment's Due Process Clause "incorporated" most of the provisions of the Bill of Rights, thereby making them binding upon state governments in addition to the federal government.

Substantive Due Process

Despite refusing to nationalize the Bill of Rights, the Supreme Court could not escape responsibility for giving meaning to the Due Process Clause. The Fourteenth Amendment is clear: states may not take life, liberty, or property without due process of law. Yet the concept of due process itself defies simple definition and explanation. As Robert G. Dixon Jr. (1976, 43) noted, the concept has a "vague, open-ended, developmental quality."

In its most generic sense, *due process* refers to the methods by which governmental authority is exercised. In this sense, commonly known as *procedural due process,* it obliges government, at a minimum, to provide an individual with fair notice and a fair hearing prior to depriving that individual of life, liberty, or property. To paraphrase Daniel Webster, due process requires a procedure that "hears before it condemns, proceeds upon inquiry, and renders judgment only after a trial." In short, this concept places limits on *how* government may exercise its power. For example, in the case of *In re Gault* (387 U.S. 1; 1967), the Supreme Court held that the state of Arizona's juvenile code failed to afford juveniles numerous constitutional guarantees. These *procedural* guarantees—written notification, representation by counsel, freedom from compulsory self-incrimination—were required by the Due Process Clause of the Fourteenth Amendment. In essence, the Court held that juvenile delinquency proceedings must measure up to the essentials of due process and fair treatment.

The Due Process Clause, however, provides more than procedural protections. Due process of law has also been interpreted as imposing certain *substantive* limitations on governmental policies. This concept, known as *substantive due process,* holds that the government is barred from adopting and enforcing policies that are irrational, unreasonable, unfair, or unjust, even though those policies may not infringe upon specific constitutional prohibitions. In short, this concept places limits on *what* government may do. Many scholars trace the genesis of substantive due process to a decision of the New York Court of Appeals, *Wynehamer v. People of the State of New York* (13 N.Y. 378; [N.Y. 1856]). (The New York Court of Appeals is the highest court in the state.) In this case, decided prior to the adoption of the Fourteenth Amendment, the court overturned a state law that prohibited the sale of liquor. For the first time, a court of last resort discovered that the concept of due process encompassed more than just procedures. It mattered not that the New York legislature followed proper procedures in enacting the criminal statute, for the statute deprived individuals of certain *substantive* rights protected under New York's constitution, most notably property and the liberty to practice a livelihood. In spite of this decision, few other courts, state or federal, were eager to acknowledge a substantive component to due process. Yet in 1877 the U.S. Supreme Court, under the leadership of Chief Justice Morrison Waite, hinted at such a component.

The dominant economic theory among businessmen and many lawyers of the time was that the best government policy was laissez-faire. That theory, however, had not been formally adopted by the Supreme Court. In *Munn v. Illinois* (94 U.S. 13; 1877), the Court upheld an Illinois law regulating grain elevators. Because the grain elevators were businesses "clothed in the public interest," the state could regulate them under its *police powers*—the state's authority to legislate to protect public health, safety, welfare, and morality. Even though the law was upheld, the justices appeared to acknowledge that certain economic regulations, perhaps those of businesses whose operations were *not* clothed in the public interest, might constitute the taking of private property in violation of the Due Process Clause of the Fourteenth Amendment. Thus, plaintiffs, most often businesses, began challenging state economic legislation as a deprivation of substantive due process of law.

Between 1877 and 1890, the Supreme Court—with a number of former corporate lawyers now seated on it—became more committed to a philosophy of laissez-faire capitalism. This guardianship of economic liberty manifested itself in various ways. For example, in *Santa Clara County v. Southern Pacific Railroad Company* (118 U.S. 398; 1886), the Court declared that corporations were "legal persons" entitled to full protection under the Fourteenth Amendment. Eleven years later, in *Allgeyer v. Louisiana* (165 U.S. 578; 1897), the Court, for the first time, recognized substantive protections under the Due Process Clause. In this case, the majority invalidated a Louisiana statute that prohibited any act in the state to affect a contract for marine insurance on Louisiana property with a company not licensed to do business in Louisiana because it interfered with the "liberty of contract" protected by the Due Process Clause of the Fourteenth Amendment. The "liberty" mentioned in the Fourteenth Amendment, Justice Rufus Peckham noted for the Court,

> means more than just the right of the citizen to be free from the mere physical restraint of his person, as by incarceration; the term also embraces the right of the citizen to be free in the enjoyment of all his fac-

> ulties; to be free to use them in all lawful ways; to live and work where he will; to earn his livelihood by any lawful calling; to pursue any livelihood or avocation; and, for that purpose, to enter into all contracts that may be proper, necessary, and essential to carrying out to a successful conclusion the purposes mentioned above. (165 U.S. at 589)

In short, even though the state legislature had followed proper procedures in enacting the statute, and even though Allgeyer had been afforded a fair trial, the *substance* of the statute was deemed to be unreasonable. According to constitutional scholar Laurence H. Tribe (1988, 567), with this decision, the "floodgates of substantive due process . . . opened." With increasing frequency, the Court employed this doctrine to strike down legislation that interfered with economic liberty.

The heyday of economic substantive due process came in *Lochner v. New York* (198 U.S. 45; 1905), in which a narrowly divided Supreme Court struck down a New York labor law limiting the number of hours that bakers could work. Justice Rufus Peckham noted for the majority that the right to purchase and sell labor was part of the liberty protected from state encroachment under the Due Process Clause. "There is a limit to the valid exercise of the police power by the state . . . ," Peckham wrote, "[o]therwise the Fourteenth Amendment would have no efficacy and the legislatures of the state would have unbounded power" (198 U.S. at 56).

Justice Oliver Wendell Holmes Jr., in one of his most famous dissents, chastised his colleagues for reinterpreting the Constitution to support their own conservative economic ideology:

> This case is decided upon an economic theory which a large part of this country does not entertain. If it were a question whether I agreed with that theory, I should desire to study it further and long before making up my mind. But I do not conceive that to be my duty, because I strongly believe that my agreement or disagreement has nothing to do with the right of a majority to embody their opinions in law.

Holmes concluded,

> I think the word "liberty," in the Fourteenth Amendment, is perverted when it is held to prevent the natural outcome of a dominant opinion, unless . . . the statute proposed would infringe fundamental principles as they have been understood by the traditions of our people and our law. (198 U.S. at 75, 76)

For more than four decades, the Supreme Court embarked upon a full-scale substantive due process review, invalidating numerous state and federal economic (including labor) regulations. In fact, it has been estimated that the justices struck down close to 200 state and federal statutes pursuant to the Due Process Clause between 1897 and 1937. Time and time again, the Court demonstrated its allegiance to property and the liberty of contract under the Due Process Clauses of the Fifth Amendment (which limited the activities of the national government) and Fourteenth Amendment. The only exceptions to this general defense of economic liberty were those acknowledged in *Munn v. Illinois* (1877): laws that protected the public health, safety, welfare, and morals; or laws that regulated businesses clothed in the public interest. To be certain, though, the Court defined such exceptions narrowly.

Justice Holmes had lost the argument, and the philosophy of laissez-faire capitalism prevailed among the justices of the Supreme Court well into the 1930s. Holmes, however, was not alone. Louis Brandeis, himself an important figure in the development of the privacy doctrine, joined the Court in 1916, as did Harlan F. Stone in 1925. In 1930, Charles Evans Hughes was appointed chief justice, leaving the dissenters one vote shy of a majority. Benjamin N. Cardozo, who replaced Holmes in 1932, agreed with his predecessor that the Constitution embodied no particular economic theory.

Economic substantive due process met its demise in the 1930s. The Great Depression, with its spiraling unemployment, declining production, and waning prosperity, necessitated a government that was proactive in economic affairs. Yet during President Franklin Delano Roosevelt's first term (1933–1937), the Supreme Court, on substantive due process grounds, invalidated much of his New Deal economic legislation, thereby dismantling his plans for recovery. Following reelection in 1936, in which he secured 523 out of a possible 531 electoral votes, President Roosevelt boldly proposed an increase in the size of the Court. This Court-packing plan, had it been adopted, would have allowed the president to appoint an additional justice for every sitting justice over the age of seventy, up to a total of fifteen justices.

The plan was rendered unnecessary in the spring of 1937, however, when the Supreme Court surprisingly sustained both state and federal economic regulations. Prior to this "switch in time that saved nine," the justices, divided 5-4, typically found constitutional problems with economic legislation. Justices Willis Van Devanter, James C. McReynolds, George Sutherland, and Pierce Butler—the so-called Four Horsemen—consistently opposed economic legislation pursuant to due process and were joined most often by Justice Owen Roberts. Chief Justice Hughes and Justices Brandeis, Stone, and Cardozo supported progressive economic legislation. Yet for reasons that have never been explained fully, Chief Justice Hughes was able to convince Justice Roberts to switch his vote in *West Coast Hotel v. Parrish* (300 U.S. 379; 1937), in which the Court upheld a minimum-wage law in the state of Washington. Two weeks later, in *National Labor Relations Board v. Jones and Laughlin Steel Corporation* (301 U.S. 1; 1937), the Court sustained a major piece of New Deal legislation, the National Labor Relations Act. Justice Roberts, once again, proved to be the swing vote.

Shortly thereafter, Justice Van Devanter announced his resignation. The following year, Justice Sutherland resigned, as did Justices Butler and McReynolds in 1940 and 1941, respectively. President Roosevelt was thus able to appoint individuals to the Supreme Court who shared his political philosophy, thereby bringing an end to the era of economic substantive due process.

Since this constitutional revolution of 1937, the Court has consistently refused to invoke the Due Process Clause to limit the power of government to regulate the economy. Instead, the Court has proceeded upon the assumption that economic regulations must rest upon some rational basis.

Substantive Due Process of the Law and Privacy

Two additional points merit consideration. First, it was during the era of economic substantive due process (1897–1937) that the Supreme Court initially acknowledged protection under the Due Process Clause of the Fourteenth Amendment for personal privacy in the areas of education and child rearing. In *Meyer v. Nebraska* (262 U.S. 390; 1923), the Court struck down a state law forbidding the teaching of German and modern languages other than English in private and public schools. Two years later, *Pierce v. Society of Sisters* (268 U.S. 510; 1925) overturned an Oregon law requiring primary and secondary school children to attend public rather than private schools on the grounds that it interfered with the liberty of parents and guardians to direct the upbringing and education of their children. These cases—the progenitors of the privacy doctrine—will be discussed in detail in Chapter 3.

Second, the doctrine of substantive due process is not moribund. Although it is true that the Supreme Court has rejected the liberty-of-contract version of the doctrine, substantive due process continues under a different rubric: the right to privacy. Beginning in 1965, the justices held that privacy was a fundamental right enforceable against the states through the Due Process Clause of the Fourteenth Amendment. In *Griswold v. Connecticut* (381 U.S. 479; 1965), the right to privacy was invoked to invalidate a state law that prohibited the use of birth-control devices. (This case, too, will be discussed in detail in Chapter 3.) Thus, to the extent that the right to privacy relies upon the Due Process Clauses of the Fifth and Fourteenth Amendments, that right may be properly viewed as a modern example of substantive due process.

The Common Law Foundations

The Warren and Brandeis Article (1890)

In December 1890, the *Harvard Law Review* published an article written by Samuel Warren and Louis Brandeis, two young Boston lawyers. Warren, a prominent member of Boston society, was frustrated as a result of numerous intrusions into his family's personal and social affairs by the Boston press. When the press went overboard on the occasion of his daughter's wedding, the annoyed Warren secured the assistance of his law partner, Brandeis, to coauthor an article proposing a remedy for invasions of personal privacy resulting from so-called yellow journalism. Their article (entitled "The Right to Privacy") ranks high on any list of the most important law review articles ever published.

The article traced the genealogy of privacy back to the common law of England. Examining judicial decisions in which relief had been afforded on the basis of defamation, or the invasion of some property right, or a breach of confidence or an implied contract, Warren and Brandeis (1890, 193) concluded that such decisions were based primarily on a much broader principle, one worthy of recognition in and of itself: the right to privacy, or, as the authors defined it, the more general right "to enjoy life, . . . to be let alone."

The primary threat to this right to privacy, the authors maintained, was the invasion of privacy through the publication of personal information and gossip. The growing abuses of the press, which subjected individuals to unnecessary "mental pain and distress," made such a declaration essential: "Of the desirability—indeed of the necessity—of some such protection, there can, it is believed, be no doubt. The press is overstepping in every direction the obvious bounds of propriety and of decency" (Warren and Brandeis 1890, 196).

Thus, Warren and Brandeis called upon the courts, not the legislatures, to recognize a general right to privacy based on the right to an "inviolate personality." The authors called upon the courts, and not the legislatures, to recognize such a right because they knew well the capacity of the common law to meet the demands of society. The common law, via judicial decision, was ever-evolving—from protection of the physical person and tangible property to protection of man's sensations, emotions, spiritual nature, and intangible property; from protection against trespass and battery to protection against nuisance, slander, and libel. These protections, however, were not based on property rights; rather they were merely examples of the enforcement of a more general right of the individual to be let alone.

The common law had already secured "to each individual the right of determining ordinarily, to what extent his thoughts, sentiments, and emotions shall be communicated to others." It was thus "inevitable" that the next step required recognition of the right to be let alone: "The principle which protects personal writings and any other productions of the intellect or of the emotions, is the right to privacy," the authors noted, "and the law has no new principle to formulate when it extends this protection to the personal appearance, sayings, acts, and to personal relation, domestic or otherwise" (Warren and Brandeis 1890, 213).

The Warren and Brandeis article has assumed a hallowed place in legal circles; it has been dubbed by more than a few scholars as the most influential law review article of all time. Roscoe Pound went so far as to claim that the article did "nothing less than add a chapter to our law" (Mason 1946, 70). Many scholars thus praise the authors as having originated a new legal right. Warren and Brandeis might object to such praise and adoration, however, for they knew full well that they were not the originators of a new legal right. Instead, they simply drew upon established legal doctrines that already protected personal privacy to propose remedies against an invasive press.

Alan F. Westin (1970, 337–338) has noted that the notion put forward by some commentators that privacy was a "modern" legal right that began to take form only in the late nineteenth century is "simply bad history and bad law." For well more than a half-century preceding the publication of the Warren-Brandeis article, governments in the United States had a "thorough and effective set of rules with which to protect individual and group privacy from the means of compulsory disclosure and physical surveillance known in that era." In short, the law provided numerous and specific protections against invasions of privacy, as well as remedies when that privacy was encroached. This is not to minimize the contribution of Warren and Brandeis. Their article was significant as the first to call upon courts to recognize a specific legal right to privacy, a right independent of property and liberty, a right unrelated to tort law.

Privacy in the Nineteenth Century

Privacy has been a significant value in American society since colonial days (Flaherty 1972; Westin 1970, 330–338). By the early 1800s, privacy interests were being protected by the common law largely under traditional tort or contract doctrines. Long before Warren and Brandeis championed privacy as an independent right, numerous courts had recognized privacy as a significant value. These judicial decisions can be divided into four categories: (1) the inviolability of the home; (2) the inviolability of the person; (3) the sanctity of confidential communications; and (4) the sacredness of personal information.

The Inviolability of the Home. The sanctity of the home has a long history in the common law. In his famous oration against the writs of assistance in 1761, James Otis spoke of the sanctity of the home as being one of the fundamental principles of the law: "A man who is quiet, is as secure in his house, as a prince in a castle" (Commager 1958, 45). Shortly thereafter, Sir William Blackstone (1765, I, 223) noted that the law has "so particular and tender a regard to the immunity of a man's house that it stiles it his castle, and will never suffer it to be violated with impunity." William Pitt, in a speech before the English House of Commons in 1763, articulated his understanding of the inviolability of the dwelling place: "The poorest man may in his cottage bid defiance to all the forces of the Crown. It may be frail; its roof may shake; the wind may blow through it; the storm may enter; the rain may enter; but the King of England cannot enter—all his forces dare not cross the threshold of the ruined tenement" (Lieber 1853, 45). Even those living in poverty were protected from the power of the state in the privacies of their homes.

The Fourth Amendment to the U.S. Constitution similarly sought to guarantee a man's sovereignty in his home: "The right of the people to be secure in their persons, houses, papers, and effects, against unreasonable searches and seizures, shall not be violated." Warren and Brandeis (1890, 220) correctly noted in their article that nineteenth-century common law consistently "recognized a man's house as his castle, impregnable, often, even to its own officers engaged in the execution of its commands." The Fourth Amendment, it must be reminded, was not applicable to the state governments in the nineteenth century. Nevertheless, most states adopted provisions similar to the Fourth Amendment in their state constitutions. New York, for example, adopted such a provision in its 1787 constitution, employing the exact language of the U.S. Constitution.

And in other states, common law courts recognized the sanctity of the home. For example, the law of nuisance prevented unreasonable noises and smells that interfered with the "quiet enjoyment" of property by its owners. In 1816, a Massachusetts court recognized a legal right against "intrusion upon the repose and tranquility of families within the dwellinghouse." In 1822, a North Carolina court recognized a householder's "right of shutting his own door." In 1851, a New York court found that individuals could be compensated for "invasion of the privacy, and interference with the comfort of the plaintiff and his family." Two decades later, in *Weimer v. Bunbury* (30 Mich. 201; [Mich. 1874]), the Michigan Supreme Court interpreted its constitution "to make sacred the privacy of the citizen's dwelling and person against everything but process issued upon a showing of legal cause for invading it" (30 Mich. at 208). In 1880, a Vermont court spoke of a right to privacy involving intrusion by the owner of a house into a guest's room for the purposes of sexual assault. In 1892, a court in Alabama acknowledged "the sanctity and inviolability of one's house." And in 1889, a Kentucky court held that a home was "the place of family repose." Courts in Pennsylvania, Vermont, and Michigan held similarly. In effect, the laws against trespass protected domestic privacy.

Under the law of trespass, an individual was prohibited from entry onto private property absent consent. Yet invasions that fell short of physical trespass were handled under the criminal law of many states also. A court in Tennessee sustained a conviction for eavesdropping as early as 1808. So did a Pennsylvania court in *Commonwealth v. Lovett* (6 Pa. L.J.R. 226; [Pa. 1831]), noting: "I consider this a serious kind of offense. Every man's house is his castle, where no man has a right to intrude for any purpose whatever. No man has a right to pry into your secrecy in your own house. . . . [I]t is important to all persons that our families should be sacred from the intrusion of every person" (6 Pa. L.J.R. at 227). By the late nineteenth century, privacy interests had spurred the common law "to erect high walls around the family home by extending criminal penalties for and civil remedies against intrusion by strangers" ("The Right to Privacy" 1981, 1896).

In *Boyd v. United States* (116 U.S. 616; 1886), the U.S. Supreme Court initially recognized protection for privacy interests under the Fourth and Fifth Amendments. Here the justices declared unconstitutional a part of the Federal Customs Act (which required a person to produce his business papers in court when his goods had been seized as contraband or else have the charges of fraudulent importing taken as "confessed" and thus forfeiting the goods). Noting that a close and literal construction of the constitutional provisions for the security of person and property would deprive them of "half their efficacy, and lead . . . to gradual depreciation," the Court held that the amendments applied "to all invasions on the part of government and its employees of the sanctity of a man's home and the privacies of his life." "It is not the breaking of his doors, and the rummaging of his drawers, that constitutes the essence of the offence," Justice Joseph Bradley wrote, "but it is the invasion of his indefeasible right of personal security, personal liberty and private property" (116 U.S. at 630). In short, the Court linked the Fourth Amendment's protection against unreasonable search and seizure to the Fifth Amendment's guarantee against self-incrimination to provide protection to "the sanctity of a man's home and the privacies of his life."

The Inviolability of the Person. Thomas Cooley (1880, 29) made one of the first references to privacy in the academic literature in 1880, defining privacy as "a right of complete immunity: to be let alone." The following year, the Michigan Supreme Court, in *De May v. Roberts* (9 N.W. 146; [Mich. 1881]), recognized such a right when deciding a case concerning the presence of a young unmarried man (presumed to be a medical assistant) in a private room during the birth of a child. Instead of relying on the theory of trespass, the court held that the doctor had invaded the plaintiff's privacy: "The plaintiff had a legal right to the privacy of her apartment at such a time and the law secures to her this right by requiring others to observe it" (9 N.W. at 149).

In 1890, E. L. Godkin (1890, 65–66), in an article on the importance of state protection of the interest in a good reputation, spoke of

> the ambition of nearly all civilized men and women . . . [to determine] for themselves how much or how little publicity should surround

> their daily lives. . . . The right to decide how much knowledge of this personal thought and feeling, and how much knowledge, therefore, of his tastes, and habits, of his own private doings and affairs, and those of his family living under his roof, the public at large shall have is as much one of his natural rights as his right to decide how he shall eat and drink, what he shall wear, and in what manner he shall pass his leisure hours.

Elbridge Adams (1905, 37) suggested that Godkin's piece was the motivation for the Warren-Brandeis piece.

Manola v. Stevens (1890), an unreported decision of a New York trial court, was the first case to permit recovery on the independent basis of the right to privacy. Without permission, a photographer took a picture of an actress appearing on stage in tights. The trial judge enjoined the stage manager from publishing the picture for promotional purposes. Soon thereafter, other courts in New York (1891, 1893, and 1895) and Massachusetts (1894) permitted recovery on the independent basis of the right to privacy (Prosser 1960, 385).

The principle met with rejection, however, twelve years later, when the highest court in New York heard a case with similar facts. Without consent, a defendant used a picture of an attractive young lady to promote a particular brand of flour. In this proceeding, however, the plaintiff sought damages and an injunction. As no prior decision had granted or denied relief in similar circumstance, this was a case of first impression. In *Roberson v. Rochester Folding Box Company* (64 N.E. 442; [N.Y. 1902]), the Court of Appeals of New York, in a 4-3 decision, rejected the logic of Warren and Brandeis and denied recovery to Roberson, holding that she had no property right in her photographic likeness. More important, though, the court flatly refused to recognize an independent right to privacy, stating that the establishment of such a right was best left to a legislative body. The primary justification for this decision was a lack of precedent. Per Chief Justice Parker (64 N.E. at 443), the court stated:

> Mention of [a right to privacy] is not to be found in Blackstone, Kent, or any other of the great commentators upon the law; nor, so far as the learning of counsel or the courts in this case have been able to discover, does its existence seem to have been asserted prior to about the year 1890, when it was presented with attractiveness, and no inconsiderable ability in the *Harvard Law Review.*
>
> The so-called "right of privacy" is, as the phrase suggests, founded upon the claim that a man has the right to pass through this world, if he wills, without having his picture published, his business enterprises discussed, his successful experiments written up for the benefit of others, or his eccentricities commented upon either in hand bills or newspapers; and, necessarily, that the things which may not be written and published of him, must not be spoken of him by his neighbors, whether the comment be favorable or otherwise.

In effect, Roberson was asking the court to increase the ambit of legal protection by creating a new tort. On the grounds of judicial restraint, the justices refused to do so. This decision was so controversial and upsetting to many within the state that one of the concurring justices—Denis O'Brien (1902)—published a law review article in defense of his decision. In spite of the court's decision, the New York legislature soon thereafter enacted a statute prohibiting such action.

The U.S. Supreme Court specifically mentioned the "right to be let alone" in *Union Pacific Railroad v. Botsford* (141 U.S. 250; 1891). In holding that an individual seeking remedies against a railroad company for personal injuries could not be forced to submit to a medical examination, Justice Horace Gray noted that "no right is held more sacred, or is more carefully guarded, by the common law, than the right of every individual to the possession and control of his own person, free from all restraint or interference of others, unless by clear and unquestionable authority of law" (141 U.S. at 251). Justice Gray then quoted Thomas Cooley: "The right to one's person may be said to be a right of complete immunity: to be let alone."

The Sanctity of Confidential Communications. From the outset, American law recognized the importance of confidential communications. Even the constitutional convention met in secrecy; no reports were published, so as to preserve full and free discussion. The law in this country also established the right of government entities to claim privacy for internal proceedings. Juries, judicial conferences, and legislative committees, for example, rarely were public matters. "The law's protection of confidential communications . . . served to preserve the privacy without which free interchange was considered impossible" ("The Right to Privacy in Nineteenth Century America" 1981, 1904).

As such, the U.S. Congress recognized the "sanctity of the mails." A federal act in 1792 made it illegal for any postal worker to open a letter. In 1825, Congress prohibited anyone from opening a letter "to pry into another's business or secrets" while en route. Many states (e.g., California in 1872) made it a crime for any person to open, read, or publish any sealed letter not addressed to himself without authorization. Affirming this principle, the U.S. Supreme Court, in *Ex parte Jackson* (96 U.S. 727; 1878), noted that mailed letters and packages are "as fully guarded from examination and inspection, except as to their outward form and weight, as if they were retained by the parties forwarding them in their own domiciles. The constitutional guaranty of the right of the people to be secure in their papers against unreasonable searches and seizures extends to their papers, thus closed against inspection, wherever they may be" (96 U.S. at 733).

The common law also protected against the unauthorized publication of the contents of letters. In 1811, in *Dennis v. Leclerc* (1 Mart. (o.s.) 297; [La. 1811]), a Louisiana court held that the recipient of a letter had no right to publish its contents absent consent of the sender. Justice Joseph Story (1839, 946) noted that the publication of communications meant to be confidential "strikes at the root of all that free and mutual interchange of advice, opinions, and sentiments, between relatives and friends, and correspondents, which is so essential to the well-being of society, and to the spirit of a liberal courtesy and refinement." In addition, wiretapping was prohibited in many states.

Letters produced in court received special consideration: after being read privately by a judge, information not relevant or material, or what might be injurious to third parties, was not revealed (Greenleaf 1842, 253). When a plaintiff requested of a defendant secure information in which the plaintiff had no interest other than "to gratify his malice, or his curiosity," the request would be "denominated a mere fishing bill" (Story 1839, 711).

As mentioned earlier, the U.S. Supreme Court held in *Boyd v. United States* (1886) that the Fifth Amendment prohibited the compulsory production of personal papers. Many states similarly recognized a privacy component in their own state prohibitions against compulsory testimony by defendants. To preserve "the sacred confidences which subsist between husband and wife," spousal communications were protected from disclosure in courtroom testimony. This had been firmly established since colonial days, as had the attorney-client privilege. In 1813, a New York court held that privacy and confidentiality necessitated the priest-penitent privilege, to shield a priest from testifying as to the substance of a confession given in closed chambers. And in 1828, the New York legislature provided for a doctor-patient privilege. Most of the states followed New York's lead, protecting confidential communication.

The Sacredness of Personal Information. In the nineteenth century, as government demanded more personal and financial information, courts and legislatures demanded greater confidentiality by limiting the access of others to such information (Note 1981, 1907). For example, beginning in 1840, census returns were treated as confidential. When the census asked about secret diseases or home mortgages—information deemed "too personal"—

a storm of public protest followed. In 1889, a $500 penalty for disclosure of census information was enacted. Records of financial affairs were initially kept confidential. Land titles were on a need-to-know basis. Idle curiosity was insufficient justification for making private affairs public.

Nineteenth-century Americans resented exposure by the press, written and photographic. The development of the penny press in the 1830s encouraged publishers to abandon the narrow focus on commercial news and politics and to provide a variety of stories—often mere gossip or scandal—that would be interesting to the increasing number of literate individuals. Yet the widespread dissatisfaction with available remedies against an invasive press led to the common law recognition of privacy rights for personal information. Just as the government protected against railroad monopolies, it was time for new defenses to be erected against the omnipresent press: "Nothing is better worthy of legal protection than private life, or, in other words, the right of every man to keep his affairs to himself, and to decide for himself to what extent they shall be the subject of public observation and discussion," Godkin (1880, 80, 82) wrote. "The press has no longer anything to fear from legal restriction of any kind, as regards its influence or material prosperity; while the community has a good deal to fear from what may be called excessive publicity, or rather from the loss by individuals of the right of privacy."

In addition, American law promoted religious freedom. Most every state constitution included a component that guaranteed the free exercise and enjoyment of religious profession and worship, without discrimination or preference. The single reference to religion in the U.S. Constitution prohibited religious tests as a qualification for any office or public trust. The prominence of religious freedom was evidenced by its inclusion as the first guarantee found in the First Amendment: "Congress shall make no law respecting an establishment of religion, or prohibiting the free exercise thereof."

CONCLUSION

Without question, privacy had become a significant value in American society by the end of the nineteenth century. Yet at no time in the nineteenth century did any court of last resort specifically recognize an independent right to privacy. The natural law–natural rights bend of the Declaration of Independence clearly hinted at it. The Constitution and the Bill of Rights each has components that embodied it. State and federal courts often spoke to its importance. Warren and Brandeis called for judicial recognition of it. But no court of last resort specifically recognized it as an independent right in the nineteenth century.

Not until 1905 would privacy be deemed by a state court to be an independent right under a state constitution; and not until 1965 would the U.S. Supreme Court make such a declaration with respect to the U.S. Constitution. The Georgia constitution was the first state constitution to be interpreted to convey a general right to privacy to its citizens. In that case, the New England Life Insurance Company, without consent, made use of a plaintiff's name and picture, along with a testimonial. In *Pavesich v. New England Life Insurance Company* (50 S.E. 68; [Ga. 1905]), the Georgia Supreme Court, accepting the views of Warren and Brandeis, expressly recognized the existence of a general and independent right to privacy: Georgia citizens have a "liberty of privacy" guaranteed by the Georgia constitutional provision, which declares that "no person shall be deprived of liberty except by due process of law." Per Judge Andrew J. Cobb (50 S.E. at 69), the court grounded the right to privacy in the doctrine of natural law:

> The right of privacy has its foundations in the instincts of nature. It is recognized intuitively, consciousness being witness that can be called to establish its existence. Any person whose intellect is in a normal condition recognizes at once that as to each individual member of society there are matters private and there are matters public so far as the

> individual is concerned. Each individual as instinctively resents any encroachment by the public upon his rights which are of a private nature as he does the withdrawal of those rights which are of a public nature. A right of privacy in matters purely private is therefore derived from natural law.

Here, the court found the right to privacy to be "ancient law," with "its foundation in the instincts of nature[,]" derived from "the Roman's conception of justice" and natural law, making it immutable and absolute (50 S.E. at 69). The opinion described the liberty interest derived from natural law as "embrac[ing] the right of man to be free in the enjoyment of the faculties with which he has been endowed by his Creator, subject only to such restraints as are necessary for the common good." "Liberty" included "the right to live as one will, so long as that will [did] not interfere with the rights of another or of the public" and entitled the individual "to a liberty of choice as to his manner of life," free from arbitrary deprivation by another individual or the public. The *Pavesich* court further recognized that this "right of personal liberty" encompassed "the right to withdraw from the public gaze at such times as a person may see fit, when his presence in public is not demanded by any rule of law" (50 S.E. at 70). Stated succinctly, the state high court ringingly endorsed the "right 'to be let alone' so long as [one] was not interfering with the rights of other individuals or of the public" (50 S.E. at 71).

This decision constituted the first time any court of last resort in the United States recognized an independent constitutional right to privacy. Predictably, *Pavesich* "became the leading case" (Prosser 1960, 386). Over the next fifty years, a majority of the states, including four via legislation, adopted a common law principle of an individual right to privacy. In that same time period, more than 300 right-to-privacy cases were decided. By the turn of the twentieth century, the right to privacy was well on its way to full recognition under the common law.

REFERENCES AND FURTHER READING

Adams, Elbridge. 1905. "The Right to Privacy, and Its Relation to the Law of Libel." *American Law Review* 39: 37–58.

Barnett, Randy E. 1987. "Are Enumerated Rights the Only Rights We Have? The Case of Associational Freedom." *Harvard Journal of Law and Public Policy* 10: 101–115.

———. 1989. *The Rights Retained by the People: The History and Meaning of the Ninth Amendment.* 2 vols. Fairfax, VA: George Mason University Press.

Barron, James H. 1979. "Warren and Brandeis: The Right to Privacy, 4 *Harv. L. Rev.* 193 (1890): Demystifying a Landmark Citation." *Suffolk University Law Review* 13: 875–922.

Berger, Raoul. 1980. "The Ninth Amendment." *Cornell Law Review* 66: 1–26.

Blackstone, Sir William. 1765–1769. *Commentaries on the Laws of England.* 4 vols. Oxford, UK: Clarendon Press.

Breckenridge, Adam Carlyle. 1970. *The Right to Privacy.* Lincoln: University of Nebraska Press.

Carr, Robert K. 1942. *The Supreme Court and Judicial Review.* New York: Farrer and Rinehart.

Cicero, Marcus Tullius. [44 B.C.] 1928. *De Re Publica, De Legibus.* Translated by Clinton Walker Keyes. Cambridge, MA: Harvard University Press.

Commager, Henry Steele. 1958. *Documents of American History.* 6th ed. New York: Appleton-Century-Crofts.

Congressional Globe, Thirty-ninth Congress, First Session. 1866.

Cooley, Thomas McIntyre. 1878. *A Treatise on Constitutional Limitations which Rests upon the Legislative Power of the States.* 4th ed. Boston: Little, Brown.

———. 1880. *A Treatise on the Law of Torts.* Chicago: Callaghan and Company.

Corwin, Edward S. [1929] 1955. *The Higher Law Background of American Constitutional Law.* Reprint. Ithaca, NY: Cornell University Press.

Dixon, Robert G., Jr. 1976. "The 'New' Substantive Due Process and the Democratic Ethic: A Prolegomenon." *Brigham Young University Law Review* 1976: 43–88.

Dumbauld, Edward. 1957. *The Bill of Rights and What It Means Today.* Norman: University of Oklahoma Press.

Dunbar, Leslie. 1956. "James Madison and the Ninth Amendment." *Virginia Law Review* 42: 627–643.

Elliot, Jonathan. [1836] 1974. *The Debates in the Several State Conventions on the Adoption of the Federal Constitution.* 4 vols. Reprint. New York: Burt Franklin.

Ely, John Hart. 1980. *Democracy and Distrust.* Cambridge, MA: Harvard University Press.

Flaherty, David H. 1972. *Privacy in Colonial New England.* Charlottesville: University Press of Virginia.

Godkin, E. L. 1880. "Libel and Its Legal Remedy." *Journal of Social Science* 12: 69–83.

———. 1890. "The Rights of the Citizen—IV: To His Reputation." *Scribner's* 8: 58–68.

Greenleaf, Simon. 1842. *A Treatise on the Law of Evidence.* Boston: C. C. Little and J. Brown.

Haines, Charles Grove. 1959. *The American Doctrine of Judicial Supremacy.* New York: Russell and Russell.

Hamilton, Alexander, James Madison, and John Jay. [1787–1788] 1961. *The Federalist Papers.* New York: Mentor.

Hobbes, Thomas. [1651] 1962. *The Leviathan.* New York: Collier Macmillan.

Hofstadter, Samuel H. 1954. *The Development of the Right of Privacy in New York.* New York: Grosby Press.

Jefferson, Thomas. 1904. *The Works of Thomas Jefferson.* Edited by Phil Leicester Ford. 16 vols. New York: G. P. Putnam's Sons.

Konvitz, Milton R. 1966. "Privacy and the Law: A Philosophical Prelude." *Law and Contemporary Problems* 31: 272–280.

Lieber, Francis. 1853. *On Civil Liberty and Self Government.* London: Trubner.

Locke, John. [1690] 1960. "An Essay Concerning Civil Government." In *Two Treatises of Government.* Reprint. New York: Mentor.

Maier, Pauline. 1997. *American Scripture: Making the Declaration of Independence.* New York: Knopf.

Mason, Alpheas Thomas. 1946. *Brandeis: A Free Man's Life.* New York: Viking Press.

McWhirter, Darien A., and Jon D. Bible. 1992. *Privacy as a Constitutional Right.* New York: Quorum.

Mill, John Stuart. [1859] 1956. *On Liberty.* Reprint. Indianapolis, IN: Bobbs-Merrill.

O'Brien, Denis. 1902. "The Right of Privacy." *Columbia Law Review* 2: 437–448.

Patterson, Bennett. 1955. *The Forgotten Ninth Amendment.* Indianapolis, IN: Bobbs-Merrill.

Poore, Ben. 1877. *The Federal and State Constitutions, Colonial Charters, and Other Organic Laws of the United States.* 2 vols. Washington, DC: U.S. Government Printing Office.

Prosser, William L. 1960. "Privacy." *California Law Review* 48: 383–423.

Redlich, Norman. 1962. "Are There 'Certain Rights . . . Retained by the People'?" *New York University Law Review* 37: 787–812.

"The Right to Privacy in Nineteenth Century America." 1981. *Harvard Law Review* 94: 1892–1910.

Story, Joseph. 1839. *Commentaries on Equity Jurisprudence.* 2d ed. Boston: C. C. Little and J. Brown.

———. 1851. *Commentaries on the Constitution of the United States.* 2d ed. Boston: C. C. Little and J. Brown.

Tribe, Laurence H. 1988. *American Constitutional Law.* 2d ed. New York: Foundation Press.

U.S. Congress. 1834. *Annals of Congress.* 42 vols. Washington, DC: Gales and Seaton.

Warren, Charles. 1937. *The Supreme Court in United States History.* Boston: Little, Brown.

Warren, Samuel D., and Louis D. Brandeis. 1890. "The Right to Privacy." *Harvard Law Review* 9: 193–220.

Westin, Alan F. 1970. *Privacy and Freedom.* New York: Atheneum.

3

Twentieth-Century Issues

In 1916, President Woodrow Wilson appointed Louis Brandeis, author of the famous 1890 *Harvard Law Review* article on privacy, to the U.S. Supreme Court. Twelve years later, at the age of seventy-one, Justice Brandeis had a second, and more formal, opportunity to make the case for constitutional privacy. He did so in dissent in a Fourth Amendment case, *Olmstead v. United States* (277 U.S. 438; 1928). Roy Olmstead was convicted in federal district court of transporting and selling liquor in violation of the National Prohibition Act. The evidence used to convict Olmstead was secured by a warrantless wiretap placed by federal agents on telephone lines between Olmstead's home and office. Olmstead challenged the admission of this evidence on the grounds that it was obtained in violation of the Fourth Amendment's guarantee against unreasonable searches and seizures. The Supreme Court held 5-4 that because the interception of telephone conversations occurred without "trespass" on private property there was no "search" of a constitutionally protected area—"persons, houses, papers, and effects." According to Chief Justice William H. Taft, who authored the Court's opinion, the Fourth Amendment was not meant to include within its protection telephone wires that reached to the whole world; those wires "are not part of his house or office, any more than are the highways along which they are stretched" (277 U.S. at 465). Moreover, conversations were not tangible items that could be "seized."

In dissent, Justice Louis Brandeis argued that the Fourth Amendment should not be interpreted so strictly. He contended that the amendment conferred upon each individual a general right to privacy, one not confined to traditional categories of searches involving actual trespass on private property or seizures of tangible items. In other words, it was possible for government to violate Olmstead's right to privacy without trespassing upon his property or seizing his belongings. The danger in concluding otherwise was far too great. Without privacy, government could, "by means far more effective than stretching upon the rack," disclose in court what was "whispered in the closet" (277 U.S. at 473). "Ways may some day be developed," Justice Brandeis warned, "by which the government, without removing papers from secret drawers, can reproduce them in court, and by which it will be enabled to expose to a jury the most intimate occurrences of the home. . . . Can it be that the Constitution affords no protection against such invasions of individual security?" (277 U.S. at 474). Then, in words similar to those he used thirty-eight years earlier in his pioneering article in the *Harvard Law Review,* Justice Brandeis noted:

> The makers of our Constitution undertook to secure conditions favorable to the pursuit of happiness. They recognized the significance of man's spiritual nature, of his feelings and of his intellect. They knew that only a part of the pain, pleasure and satisfactions of life are to be found in material things. They sought to protect Americans in their beliefs, their thoughts, their emotions and their sensations. They conferred, as against the government, the right to be let alone—the most comprehensive of rights and the right most valued by civilized men. To protect that right, every unjustifiable intrusion by the government

> upon the privacy of the individual, whatever the means employed, must be deemed a violation of the Fourth Amendment. (277 U.S. at 478)

Although Justice Brandeis's argument failed to prevail in this case, thirty-seven years later, in *Griswold v. Connecticut* (381 U.S. 489; 1965), the Supreme Court adopted the idea of a constitutional right to privacy. Thus, the emergence of a constitutional right to privacy is of relatively recent origin. This does not mean, however, that *Griswold* marked the first time the Supreme Court reached beyond the specific language of the Constitution to declare as inconsistent with it state or federal legislation. As far back as the late nineteenth century, the Court categorized certain unlisted rights as fundamental and immunized them from most governmental encroachment. The Supreme Court had recognized at least the following unlisted rights as fundamental prior to *Griswold:* to have a presumption of innocence and to demand proof beyond a reasonable doubt before being convicted of a crime (*Coffin v. United States,* 156 U.S. 432; 1895); to work for a living in the common occupations of the community (*Truax v. Raich,* 239 U.S. 33; 1915); to teach a foreign language (*Meyer v. Nebraska,* 262 U.S. 390; 1923); to direct the upbringing and education of one's children (*Pierce v. Society of Sisters,* 268 U.S. 510; 1925); to retain procreative capabilities (*Skinner v. Oklahoma,* 316 U.S. 535; 1942); to receive equal protection of the laws from the federal government (*Bolling v. Sharpe,* 347 U.S. 497; 1954); to access the federal courts and other governmental institutions (*Griffin v. Illinois,* 351 U.S. 12; 1956); to travel abroad (*Kent v. Dulles,* 357 U.S. 116; 1958); to associate with others (*NAACP v. Alabama,* 357 U.S. 449; 1958); and to cast a ballot of equal weight to that of other citizens (*Reynolds v. Sims,* 377 U.S. 533; 1964).

Although Justice Brandeis's influential dissent in *Olmstead* derived from a Fourth Amendment case, constitutional privacy must not be confused with expectations of privacy secured by the

Fourth Amendment. In a Fourth Amendment context, the right to privacy is invoked to govern the conduct of government when it intrudes in various ways upon a citizen's life. By contrast, constitutional privacy attaches to the rightholder's own decisions, and it immunizes certain conduct stemming from those decisions—such as using contraceptives, aborting a pregnancy, marrying someone of a different race, or rearing children—from state proscription or penalty. Laws struck down under the rubric of constitutional privacy have gravitated around three principal areas: procreation, marriage, and family life.

According to Jed Rubenfeld (1989), the prevailing method of privacy analysis holds that democratic government may not proscribe those decisions that substantially shape a person's life. Certain decisions are fundamental and are thus immune from the control and direction of the state. To permit government to make those decisions for all people would be tantamount to allowing government to direct the day-to-day activities of peoples' individual lives. That, in turn, would make the individual the mere instrument of the state, a notion incompatible in a liberal democracy based upon the principle of limited government. Each of us has the right to be let alone, if by that term we mean the right not to have the course of our life dictated by the state.

The right to be let alone, however, does not translate into the right to make whatever decision we desire. The judiciary has not accepted every claim of constitutional privacy. For example, it has been argued that constitutional privacy includes private sexual activity between consenting adult homosexuals and the right to die. Up to this point, the Supreme Court has specifically refused to include these particular interests under the rubric of privacy. Only fundamental rights merit constitutional protection. But what is "fundamental"? In determining what rights are fundamental, judges are not to rely solely or even primarily upon their personal and private notions. Instead, judges are to look "to the traditions and [collective] conscience of our people" to determine whether a principle is "so rooted [there] . . . as to be ranked as fundamental" (*Snyder v. Massachusetts,* 291 U.S. 97, 105; 1934). Judges are not to rely solely upon the express language of the Bill of Rights to make that determination, either. The Court has concluded that the language and history of the Ninth Amendment reveal that there are additional fundamental rights, protected against governmental infringement, that exist in addition to those rights specifically articulated in the first eight amendments. Since *Griswold,* the right to privacy has been one of those additional, fundamental rights.

In a series of decisions beginning in 1897, the Supreme Court held that the Fourteenth Amendment's Due Process Clause absorbed and applied to the states most but not all of the specific liberties mentioned in the first eight amendments. In *Palko v. Connecticut* (302 U.S. 319; 1937), the Court, per Justice Benjamin Cardozo, rationalized the selective application of the guarantees of the Bill of Rights. According to this theory, often known as *selective incorporation,* only fundamental rights are applied to the states. For a right to be fundamental, it either had to be "implicit in the concept of ordered liberty" or "deeply rooted in this Nation's history and tradition" (302 U.S. at 325). The Court's position in 1937 was thus threefold. First, certain liberties mentioned in the Bill of Rights were fundamental and thus binding upon the states through the process of incorporation. Second, other liberties mentioned in the Bill of Rights were not fundamental and thus not binding upon the states. (Even now, several provisions of the Bill of Rights—the Second Amendment, the Third Amendment, the Grand Jury Clause of the Fifth Amendment, the Seventh Amendment, and the Excessive Bail and Fines Clauses of the Eighth Amendment—are not applicable to the states.) And still other liberties, though not mentioned in the Bill of Rights, were fundamental and thus immune from federal *and* state governmental proscription. This incorporation of the Bill of Rights has generated much criticism. Charles Fairman (1949), Leslie Dunbar (1956), and Raoul Berger (1980) are adamant that the Fourteenth

Amendment's Due Process Clause was misused by courts to incorporate the Bill of Rights.

This chapter will analyze the major themes that have emerged in connection with the right to privacy during the twentieth century. When deciding cases about contraception, abortion, marriage, divorce, child rearing and education, sexual relations, the right to refuse medical treatment, and euthanasia (the act of inducing a gentle and easy death), judges regularly employ the concept of constitutional privacy. Constitutional privacy in the twentieth century can be divided into five major areas: reproductive autonomy; family autonomy; sexual autonomy; personal autonomy; and the right to die. *Reproductive autonomy* includes sterilization, contraception, pregnancy and childbirth, and abortion. Marriage, divorce, rearing and educating children, maintaining family ties, and family living arrangements will be covered in *family autonomy. Sexual autonomy* consists of sexual relations and sexual orientation. Liberty claims involving matters of *personal autonomy* such as viewing obscenity, physical appearance, and private recreational and medicinal drug use invoke values of privacy. And the *right to die* encompasses the termination of life-sustaining medical treatment, as well as suicide and physician-assisted suicide. This chapter will trace the development of the first four of these branches of constitutional privacy in some detail. Because the claim to a constitutional right to die is of relatively recent origin and remains mostly undeveloped, it will be discussed in Chapter 4, which will look at recent privacy issues that have been most visible and contentious.

REPRODUCTIVE AUTONOMY

Sterilization

As discussed in Chapter 2, by the turn of the twentieth century the right to privacy was well on its way to full recognition under the common law. This emerging right to privacy suffered a temporary setback, however, in *Buck v. Bell* (274 U.S. 200; 1927), where the justices considered a Virginia law, passed in 1924 in response to the eugenics movement, that required the sterilization of persons indefinitely confined to state mental health institutions. Carrie Buck, a feebleminded eighteen-year-old, became pregnant as a result of a rape. After psychological examinations determined that her mental age was nine, she was committed to the State Colony for Epileptics and Feeble-Minded, where her mother was also confined. Following the birth of Buck's mentally retarded daughter, the director of the institution recommended that she be sterilized pursuant to the state statute. Buck's attorneys then challenged the constitutionality of the statute. After the plaintiff unsuccessfully challenged the statute in the lower courts, an appeal was made to the U.S. Supreme Court.

Buck's attorneys argued that the compulsory surgical sterilization deprived Buck of her constitutional right to "bodily integrity" and was therefore repugnant to the Due Process Clause of the Fourteenth Amendment. "A reign of doctors will be inaugurated and in the name of science new classes will be added, even races may be brought within the scope of such regulation, and the worst forms of tyranny practiced," Buck's lawyers predicted. Despite these warnings, the Supreme Court, in an 8-1 opinion written by Justice Oliver Wendell Holmes, upheld the sterilization law. Justice Holmes defended the statute: if the country were constitutionally permitted to "call upon their best citizens for their lives" in times of war, "it would be strange if it could not call upon those who already sap the strength of the State for these lesser sacrifices. . . . It is better for all the world, if instead of waiting to execute degenerate offspring for crime, or to let them starve for their imbecility, society can prevent those who are manifestly unfit from continuing their kind." In the now infamous phrase, Justice Holmes went on to write that "three generations of imbeciles are enough" (274 U.S. at 207).

Only fifteen years later, in *Skinner v. Oklahoma* (316 U.S. 535; 1942), the Supreme Court struck down the Oklahoma Habitual

Criminal Sterilization Act. The act defined *habitual criminal* as one who had been convicted three or more times for felonies involving "moral turpitude." If a court or jury found that the defendant was a habitual criminal and could be surgically rendered sexually sterile without detriment to his or her general health, then the court could so order. Interestingly, though, the act exempted persons convicted of prohibitory laws, revenue acts, embezzlement, and political offenses. Jack Skinner was a thrice-convicted felon—once for stealing chickens and twice for robbery with firearms. Two years after his third conviction, the state attorney general instituted proceedings against him under the act. Skinner challenged the constitutionality of the law, alleging that it violated both the Equal Protection Clause ("No state shall . . . deny to any person within its jurisdiction the equal protection of the laws") and the Due Process Clause of the Fourteenth Amendment. His challenge was unsuccessful in the lower courts.

In striking down the act, the Supreme Court relied upon the inequalities inherent in the statute. A person convicted of stealing chickens committed a felony and, if convicted three times of such crime, could be sterilized. Yet if the same person were entrusted with the chicken coop and fraudulently appropriated it, he or she was an embezzler and not subject to sterilization no matter how habitual his or her proclivities for embezzlement happened to be. Though the nature of the two crimes—larceny and embezzlement—was inherently the same, they were not punishable in the same manner. Because the law treated unequally those who committed intrinsically the same quality of offense by sterilizing one and not the other, the Equal Protection Clause was offended.

More important for purposes of constitutional privacy, though, the majority opinion went on to suggest that a more deep-seated principle was at stake. "We are dealing here with legislation which involves one of the basic civil rights of man. Marriage and procreation are fundamental to the very existence and survival of the race," wrote Justice William Douglas. "The power to sterilize, if exercised, may have subtle, far-reaching and devastating effects. In evil or reckless hands it can cause races or types which are inimical to the dominant group to wither and disappear. There is no redemption for the individual whom the law touches. Any experiment which the State conducts is to his irreparable injury. He is forever deprived of a basic liberty" (316 U.S. at 541).

Because the Court in *Skinner* chose to rely upon the Equal Protection Clause, however, *Buck* has never been formally overturned. Nevertheless, it appears to be at odds with modern privacy jurisprudence. It is highly unlikely that such a position would command a majority of the justices today.

Skinner was the first major ruling extending constitutional protection to procreation. Although the Supreme Court did not declare *all* compulsory sterilization laws unconstitutional, the justices concluded that laws that deprived individuals of fundamental liberties, such as the right to have offspring, should be evaluated under the higher standard of strict scrutiny. "Strict scrutiny" is the standard of review under the Equal Protection and Due Process Clauses used by courts to evaluate laws that discriminate against suspect classifications or curtail fundamental rights. A *suspect classification* is a class of people deliberately subjected to such unequal treatment in the past, or relegated by society to a position of such political powerlessness, as to require extraordinary judicial protection. More than a half-century ago, for example, the U.S. Supreme Court declared that race was a suspect classification. A fundamental right, to recall, is a right either "implicit in the concept of ordered liberty" or "deeply rooted in this Nation's history and tradition." A law that discriminates against a suspect classification or curtails a fundamental right is inherently suspect. Operationally, this means that the law is presumptively unconstitutional. To justify such a restriction, the government has the heavy burden of persuading a court that there is a compelling state interest in the law and that there is no other, less restrictive way to accomplish that interest. By contrast, a law that discriminates against a nonsuspect classification—homosexuality, for example—or curtails a nonfundamental right is generally subjected to the "rational basis" test. When the rational basis test is applied, the burden is on those attacking the law, and courts are likely to sustain the law as long as it is reasonably related to a legitimate state interest.

Forced Sterilization

A half-century after *Skinner* was decided, the issue of compulsory sterilization reappeared in a highly emotional case involving Darlene Johnson, a young unmarried mother of four children (pregnant with her fifth child) who pleaded guilty to child abuse. California state judge Howard Broadman ordered that Johnson spend one year in jail, followed by three years of probation, during which time she would have six matchstick-sized birth control rods implanted into her upper arm. By releasing very small amounts of a hormone that keeps the ovaries from releasing eggs, these rods prevented conception. If Johnson rejected the temporary sterilization, the judge would sentence her to more time in jail. In short, Johnson had to choose between contraception and jail. Supporters of this form of creative sentencing pointed to the fact that the state had broad latitude to punish child abusers, including lengthy prison terms that precluded the opportunity for procreation. Moreover, felons often bargained away certain rights. For example, as a condition of probation, a felon may agree to wear a bracelet that monitored his or her whereabouts, to abide by a judge-imposed house curfew, or not to associate with certain undesirables. Opponents echoed *Skinner,* arguing that procreation was "one of the basic civil rights of man . . . fundamental to the very existence and survival of the race." They considered the option of contraception or incarceration to be overly coercive and perhaps genocidal, alleging that poor black women would be the prime targets of this type of sentencing (MacKenzie 1991, A22).

Johnson initially agreed to the conditions but soon decided against it and requested that the judge reconsider the sentencing order in light of her constitutional right to reproduce. With assistance from the American Civil Liberties Union and Planned Parenthood, Johnson was able to obtain a stay of the order while she appealed the unusual sentence. During that stay, however, Johnson tested positive for cocaine (the test being required as a separate condition of her probation) and was sentenced to prison. The appellate court accordingly found that the temporary sterilization sentence was no longer relevant and dismissed the appeal. Thus, no appellate court has ruled on the question of whether court-ordered temporary sterilization as a condition of liberty constitutes an infringement upon the fundamental right to procreation recognized in *Skinner.*

Recently, a prison inmate asserted that his fundamental right to procreate with his spouse survived incarceration. This matter will be discussed in Chapter 4.

Contraception

Few decisions, if any, are more profound and intimate than "whether, when, and how one's body is to become the vehicle for another human being's creation" (Tribe 1988, 1338). Even so, laws regulating contraception date back to the middle of the nineteenth century. (*Contraception* is the intentional prevention of impregnation through the use of various devices, agents, or drugs.) In 1832, Charles Knowlton, a Massachusetts physician, published the first American medical treatise on contraception. Although there were no statutes or common law precedents declaring such information illegal, Knowlton was indicted, fined, and sentenced to three months of hard labor. Nevertheless, for most of the nineteenth century contraception remained a private issue, largely ignored by the law. Federal intervention came in 1873. At the encouragement of vice crusaders and purity societies, Congress passed the Comstock Act, which made it a crime to sell, lend, distribute, publish, or possess devices or literature pertaining to birth control or abortion. Many states soon followed suit, promulgating legislation addressing this subject, with twenty-four states criminalizing birth control and abortion. These statutes remained largely in effect until the late 1960s, by which time various cultural forces—the military's distribution of condoms to prevent venereal disease in World War I, which increased the supply and demand for such products; liberalization of sexual mores after World War I; opportunities for nonmarital sexual contacts in automobiles and dancehalls in the 1920s; greater financial pressure to curtail fertility during the Depression in the 1930s; expanding economic opportunities for women in the 1940s and 1950s; and concerns for global overpopulation—weakened legal restraints on birth control (Rhode 1989, 202–207).

By the middle of the twentieth century, the Supreme Court had rejected numerous opportunities to review the constitutionality of bans on birth control. In *Poe v. Ullman* (367 U.S. 497; 1961), for example, the justices refused to rule on the constitutionality of an 1879 Connecticut statute that criminalized the use of any drug, medicinal article, or instrument for the purpose of preventing conception. The law also provided that any person who assisted another to use contraception could be prosecuted and punished. Because neither the fictitiously named plaintiff, Pauline Poe, nor her physician, Dr. C. Lee Buxton, had been prosecuted, the Court held that the matter was not ripe for constitutional adjudication.

Justice John Marshall Harlan, however, dissented, holding that the statute violated the right to privacy as guaranteed by the Bill of Rights and the Fourteenth Amendment. (This dissent had a significant influence on the development of privacy jurisprudence, as evidenced by the Supreme Court's opinion four years later in *Griswold.*) To punish married couples for the use of contraceptives, he maintained, was "an intolerable and unjustifiable invasion of privacy in the conduct of the most intimate concerns of an individual's personal life" (367 U.S. at 539). To do so implicated "a most fundamental aspect of 'liberty,' the privacy of the home in its most basic sense" (367 U.S. at 548). Two constitutional provisions supported Justice Harlan's argument concerning the privacy of the home—the Third Amendment, which related to the quartering of soldiers, and the Fourth Amendment, which prohibited unreasonable searches and seizures. Neither of those amendments, however, was directly implicated, for the Connecticut statute did not invade the home "in the usual sense." Justice Harlan, much like Justice Brandeis thirty-four years earlier in *Olmstead,* argued that the Bill of Rights should not be interpreted so literally: "It would surely be an extreme instance of sacrificing substance to form were it to be held that the constitutional principle of privacy against arbitrary official intrusion comprehends only physical invasions by the police." Although the intrusion here was not *into the home,* it was *on the life* that had its place in the home. "And the integrity of that life is something so fundamental that it has been found to draw to its protection the principles of more than one explicitly granted Constitutional right" (367 U.S. at 551).

Justice Harlan was careful to distinguish this type of privacy—marital privacy in the home, which deserved constitutional protection—from privacy claims involving adultery, homosexuality, fornication, and incest, even if privately practiced, which did not deserve constitutional protection. "The intrusion of the whole machinery of the criminal law into the very heart of marital privacy, requiring husband and wife to render an account before a criminal tribunal of their uses of that intimacy," he reasoned, "is surely a very different thing indeed from punishing those who establish intimacies which the law has always forbidden and which can have no claim to social protection" (367 U.S. at 553).

Only four years after Justice Harlan's dissent in *Poe,* the Supreme Court, in *Griswold v. Connecticut* (1965), announced a new privacy doctrine. In *Griswold,* the Court invalidated a state statute that criminalized counseling about contraception and the use of contraceptive devices by married persons. Estelle Griswold, the executive director of the Planned Parenthood League of Connecticut, and Dr. C. Lee Buxton (the same physician whose challenge was dismissed on technical grounds in *Poe*) were convicted as accessories for giving married persons information, instruction, and medical advice concerning the means of preventing conception. Each was fined $100. The Supreme Court, dividing 7-2, reversed the lower court decision and declared the law violative of the constitutional right to privacy. This constitutional right to privacy was located in the "penumbras" of various guarantees of the Bill of Rights, and it was broad enough to include the freedom of married couples to use contraceptives in the privacy of their bedrooms.

At the outset of the majority opinion, Justice Douglas attempted to distinguish privacy jurisprudence from the discredited jurisprudence of *Lochner v. New York* (198 U.S. 45; 1905). (In *Lochner*, the justices read into the Fourteenth Amendment's Due Process Clause a liberty of contract to strike down economic legislation. The case thus symbolized substantive judicial analysis of economic regulation based on the constitutional principles of due process, property rights, and liberty. Although this position was later reversed, *Lochner* was emblematic of the Court's creation and enforcement of an unenumerated right; see Chapter 2) "We do not sit as a super-legislature to determine the wisdom, need, and propriety of laws that touch economic problems, business affairs, of social conditions," Justice Douglas wrote, in obvious reference to the pre–New Deal Court. This law was different, however; it operated "directly on an intimate relation of husband and wife and their physician's role in one aspect of that relation" (381 U.S. at 482).

Justice Douglas asserted that specific guarantees in the Bill of Rights "have penumbras, formed by emanations from those guarantees that help give them life and substance" (381 U.S. at 484). In other words, the right to privacy derived from rights explicitly protected in the Bill of Rights. More specifically, the First, Third, Fourth, Fifth, and Ninth Amendments created "zones of privacy." For example, freedom of association was not mentioned in the Constitution or in the Bill of Rights. Nevertheless, in *NAACP v. Alabama* (357 U.S. 449; 1958), the Supreme Court protected the freedom of association as a peripheral First Amendment right. The Constitution was silent on the right to educate a child in a school of the parent's choice, whether public, private, or parochial. Yet in *Pierce v. Society of Sisters* (268 U.S. 510; 1925), the Court protected the right of parents to educate their children as they chose. Neither was the right to study any particular subject or any foreign language granted by the Constitution. The Court, however, in *Meyer v. Nebraska* (262 U.S. 390; 1923), held that students had the right to study the German language in a private school. All these cases suggested that the First Amendment had numerous penumbras wherein privacy was protected from governmental intrusion.

The Third Amendment, which guarded against the quartering of soldiers "in any house" in a time of peace without the consent of the owner, was another facet of privacy. The Fourth Amendment explicitly affirmed the "right of the people to be secure in their persons, houses, papers, and effects, against unreasonable searches and seizures." Only four years earlier, in *Mapp v. Ohio* (367 U.S. 643; 1961), the Court had held that this amendment created a right to privacy no less important than other rights reserved to the people. The Fifth Amendment in its Self-Incrimination Clause enabled a citizen to create a zone of privacy that government could not force him to surrender to his detriment. This penumbral right was hardly novel. In the late nineteenth century, the justices had remarked in *Boyd v. United States* (116 U.S. 616, 630; 1886) that the Fourth and Fifth Amendments protected against all governmental invasions "of the sanctity of a man's home and the privacies of his life." In addition, the Ninth Amendment pointed to the conclusion that certain rights, though not specifically listed in the Bill of Rights, were still protected against governmental encroachment.

Justice Douglas then appeared to downplay the significance of this decision. The Constitution and these and other cases "bear witness that the right of privacy which presses for recognition here is a legitimate one. . . . We deal with a right of privacy older than the Bill of Rights—older than our political parties, older than our school system" (381 U.S. at 485–486). In short, this declaration was not a departure from precedent.

Having made the case for constitutional privacy, Justice Douglas cursorily concluded that a law that criminalized a married couple's decision to prevent conception would have a "maximum destructive impact" upon the marital relationship. In language clearly expressing his outrage at the thought of the means necessary to enforce the law, he wrote, "Would we allow the police to search the sacred precincts of marital bedrooms for telltale signs of the use of contraceptives? The very idea is repulsive to the notions of privacy surrounding the marriage relationship" (381 U.S. at 485–486).

Justice Arthur Goldberg, who was joined by Chief Justice Earl Warren and Justice William Brennan, concurred. Instead of relying primarily upon the penumbras of specific guarantees of the Bill of Rights, Justice Goldberg rested his argument upon the Ninth Amendment as the source of unenumerated rights. His argument was threefold. First, the Framers did not believe that the fundamental rights listed in the first eight amendments were exclusive of other fundamental rights protected from governmental infringement. To hold otherwise was to ignore the Ninth Amendment. Second, judges, in determining what additional fundamental rights existed alongside those specifically mentioned, were to look to the "traditions and [collective] conscience of our people." And third, though the Constitution did not speak in so many words of the right to marital privacy, the right was "so basic and fundamental and so deep-rooted in our society" that it was retained by the people within the meaning of the Ninth Amendment (381 U.S. at 491, 499).

Justice Harlan also concurred, stating that the proper constitutional inquiry was whether the Due Process Clause of the Fourteenth Amendment violated basic values "implicit in the concept of ordered liberty" (quoting *Palko v. Connecticut,* 302 U.S. at 325; 1937). The Court did not need to invoke either the penumbras of various provisions of the Bill of Rights or the Ninth Amendment. The Fourteenth Amendment stood "on its own bottom" (381 U.S. at 500). Justice Byron White concurred as well, for much the same reason.

Justices Hugo Black and Potter Stewart dissented. Although he found the law offensive, Justice Black criticized the majority for its eagerness to amend the Constitution by judicial fiat. Although he had no difficulty striking down acts that violated specific provisions of the Constitution, Justice Black refused to do so for acts that ran afoul of no specific constitutional provision. Put simply, there was no constitutional right to privacy. And for the Court to make such a determination placed the justices in the indefensible position of substituting their own subjective considerations of due process for those of a state legislature, a formula that Justice Black thought marked an eerie return to discredited reasoning of *Lochner.* "That formula . . . is no less dangerous when used to enforce this Court's views about personal rights than those about economic rights. I thought that we had laid that formula, as a means of striking down state legislation, to rest once and for all . . . ," he wrote (381 U.S. at 522). Justice Stewart, who found the law "uncommonly silly," nevertheless agreed with Justice Black that no such general right to privacy could be found in the Constitution, the Bill of Rights, or any case ever decided by the Supreme Court.

Griswold was the first case in which the Supreme Court specifically recognized an independent and fundamental right to privacy. Justice Brandeis's dissenting opinion in *Olmstead* had finally prevailed. Yet there was considerable disagreement among the justices with respect to the source of the right to privacy. Five members of the Court were willing to recognize a specific constitutional right to privacy: Justices Douglas and Tom Clark in the "penumbras"; and Justice Goldberg, Chief Justice Warren, and Justice Brennan in the Ninth Amendment. In making the argument for striking down the law, Justices Harlan and White relied upon the standard substantive due process analysis under the Due Process Clause of the Fourteenth Amendment, not the right to privacy. And Justices Black and Stewart, fearing the specter of *Lochner* and the olden days of substantive due process, did not believe the Court had the power to declare the law unconstitutional because privacy was not a specific constitutional right.

Critics of *Griswold* find fault with the decision in three areas: the constitutional basis for the decision; the definition of *privacy;* and the misrepresentation of *Griswold* vis-à-vis *Lochner.* First, critics fault the majority opinion for its excessive reliance upon the imagery of penumbras and emanations. The essential argument in defense of penumbral rights is simply stated: "Each specific constitutional provision fully protects matters within its domain. Yet, to assure that those matters actually received the full protection to which they are entitled, it is necessary to protect matters outside the domain of the specific amendments" (Tushnet 1991, 76). Stated otherwise, a judge should not err by sticking too closely to the relatively precise and therefore limited nature of specific amendments when those amendments imported a broader principal. Nevertheless, the decision has been labeled "unprincipled" for the way in which the justices derived a new constitutional right (Bork 1971, 7–10). The complaint is as follows: although specific individual amendments have specific penumbral rights—the First Amendment's freedom of association, for example—those penumbras have no life on their own as rights independent of a value specified in the Bill of Rights. Justice Douglas never disclosed how a series of specific, enumerated rights combined to create a new, nonspecific, and unlisted right. Critics of *Griswold* bemoan that the decision appears to have licensed the judiciary to engage in a variety of substantive innovations. Courts that do so cannot be squared with the presuppositions of democracy. To be so squared, judges must assiduously avoid making value choices; they must be controlled by principles exterior to their own will.

Second, the decision is faulted for its failure to define adequately the newly created right to privacy. Because the opinion focused primarily on making the case for privacy as a constitutional right, Justice Douglas failed to articulate what specific rights, other than the right of married couples to use contraceptive devices, were to be included under the umbrella of privacy. He "skipped through the Bill of Rights like a cheerleader—'Give me a P . . . give me an R . . . and I . . . ,' and so on, and found P-R-I-V-A-C-Y as a derivative or penumbral right" (Dixon 1976, 84). But that is it; he went no further. He never said, "The constitutional right to privacy includes the following liberties." Neither did he say, even as Justice Harlan had said in dissent in *Poe,* that the constitutional right to privacy did not include adultery, homosexuality, fornication, incest, and so forth. Critics complain that this lack of definition permitted the "wonder-working Warren Court to transform the fourteenth amendment into a cornucopia of 'rights' *excluded* by the framers" (Berger 1980, 12).

Third, *Griswold* is denounced for failing to distinguish itself sufficiently from the discredited jurisprudence of *Lochner.* Justice Douglas attempted to do so rather perfunctorily: *Lochner* involved laws that touched economic problems; *Griswold* operated directly on marital intimacy. But he never stated why laws operating on marital intimacy deserved more judicial scrutiny than laws regulating contracts and property. Clearly the answer cannot be that privacy is a penumbral right of the First, Third, Fourth, Fifth, and Ninth Amendments and contracts and property are not penumbral rights of Article I, Section 10, and the Due Process Clause of the Fourteenth Amendment.

Although *Griswold* generated a tremendous amount of debate within legal circles, it did not receive the public attention that accompanied the school desegregation cases of the 1950s, the school prayer decisions of the early 1960s, and the subsequent abortion decisions. Most persons are much more interested in the substantive policy outputs of the Supreme Court than in the rather mundane legal aspects of specific cases. Court-watchers, however, speculated on just how far the right to privacy would go. The answer, of course, was not too far. Clearly, the justices have broadened constitutional privacy, yet they have also limited it to matters affecting procreation, marriage, and family life, although many have argued for a broader application of the principle.

In 1972, the Supreme Court extended the holding in *Griswold* to unmarried persons. Massachusetts law forbade the distribution to and use of contraceptives to unmarried persons. William Baird displayed contraceptive devices while delivering a lecture on the topic to students at Boston University and gave a young unmarried woman a package of vaginal cream at the close of his address. In *Eisenstadt v. Baird* (405 U.S. 438; 1972), the justices struck down the law, holding that whatever the rights of the individual to access to contraceptives were, they had to be the same for the unmarried and the married alike. For the Court, Justice William Brennan noted:

> It is true that in *Griswold* the right of privacy in question inhered in the marital relationship. Yet the marital couple is not an independent entity with a mind and heart of its own, but an association of two individuals each with a separate intellectual and emotional makeup. If the right to privacy means anything, it is the right of the individual, married or single, to be free from unwarranted governmental intrusion into matters so fundamental affecting a person as whether to bear or begat a child (405 U.S. at 453).

The Court specified here that constitutional privacy inhered in the individual, not in the marital couple or in the marital bedroom. Thus, this case had the effect of identifying the dispositive factor in *Griswold:* reproductive autonomy. In spite of *Griswold*'s numerous references to marital intimacy, *Eisenstadt* made clear that reproductive autonomy was the chief value to be protected. This holding, therefore, was entirely consistent with *Skinner,* in which the Court characterized the right to reproduce as "one of the basic civil rights of man." Laurence Tribe (1988, 1340) has noted that the meaning of *Skinner* was that "*whether one person's body shall be the source of another life must be left to that person and that person alone to decide.*" If that is accurate, then *Eisenstadt* should be interpreted as a simple reaffirmation of *Skinner* and a logical extension of *Griswold.*

Five years after *Eisenstadt,* the Supreme Court declared unconstitutional a New York statute that criminalized the distribution of contraceptive devices to anyone under the age of sixteen, the distribution of contraceptive devices by anyone other than a licensed pharmacist, and advertisement or display of contraceptives. Justice Brennan made clear in *Carey v. Population Services International* (431 U.S. 678, 684; 1977) that the decision whether or not to beget or bear a child was "at the very heart of this cluster of constitutionally protected choices."

Once the Supreme Court struck down legal barriers to the advertising, distribution, and use of contraceptive devices, the pharmaceutical industry presented consumers with a wide array of birth-control products: condoms, topical spermicides, diaphragms, and oral contraceptives. The intrauterine device, or IUD, emerged as a popular form of birth control in the 1960s and 1970s. In the 1980s mifepristone, or RU-486, a pill that expelled fertilized eggs from the womb, was developed in France. By 1990, the sale of oral contraceptives alone reached $900 million. Late in 1990, the Food and Drug Administration approved a product called Norplant, the first subdermal implant, for commercial use. (Norplant was the specific contraceptive device required by Judge Howard Broadman when he sentenced Darlene Johnson.)

Though there were numerous birth-control methods widely available by the end of the twentieth century, pharmaceutical companies continued to develop new, highly effective, and easy-to-use contraceptives. In the fall of 2001, the Food and Drug Administration approved two such methods: Ortho Evra, the first birth control patch, which could be applied to one of four places on the body; and NuvaRing, a slender, flexible, transparent vaginal ring that provided month-long protection and could be inserted and removed by the woman in the privacy of her home. Neither of these forms of contraception required a physician's prescription.

Pregnancy and Childbirth

Privacy rights are often implicated when a state seeks to regulate the conduct of pregnant women. In support of such regulations, states contend that women who decide against terminating their pregnancies should be held to certain standards of responsibility for the health of their unborn child. Three situations have raised concerns in this respect (Turkington and Allen 1999, 661–664): (1) a pregnant woman engages in conduct that, even though lawful, nevertheless poses a health risk to the unborn child—for example, smoking cigarettes, consuming alcohol, or failing to heed her physician's medical advice about prenatal care; (2) a pregnant woman knowingly ingests controlled substances; and (3) a pregnant women refuses medical care recommend by her physician. Lower courts have authorized certain medical procedures, such as blood transfusions and Caesarian surgical delivery, to be performed on pregnant women without their consent and have jailed pregnant women for prenatal negligence. Barbara Shelly (1988), among others, has proposed criminal punishment for women who make unwise decisions regarding the health of their unborn child. The Supreme Court, though, has yet to rule on whether procreative choice and bodily integrity protect the right of the mother to engage in conduct that may or will be harmful to her unborn child. In *Cleveland Board of Education v. LaFleur* (414 U.S. 632; 1974), a challenge to a school board policy mandating unpaid maternity leave five months prior to the expected date of childbirth, however, the justices noted that concern for the unborn child did not necessarily trump women's autonomy. Overly restrictive maternity leave regulations, though perhaps well-intentioned, might have the effect of penalizing a pregnant woman for deciding to bear a child. The Due Process Clause of the Fourteenth Amendment required that such regulations not "needlessly, arbitrarily, or capriciously" impinge upon the exercise of a basic civil right (414 U.S. at 639).

Abortion

Griswold invalidated state laws erecting barriers to access to contraceptives. The case left open the question of whether states could prohibit abortion. The decision about whether to become pregnant—the principle behind *Griswold*—is fundamentally different than the decision to terminate pregnancy, for abortion implicates certain state interests—protecting potential life and safeguarding a woman's physical and psychological well-being, for example—in ways that contraception does not. Accordingly, the law treats access to contraception and access to abortion as separate matters.

The first abortion statutes in the United States, enacted between 1820 and 1840, prohibited only those abortions that occurred postquickening. (*Quickening* is the stage of pregnancy at which the unborn child shows signs of life.)

Cultural trends in the mid–nineteenth century contributed to more stringent legislation. As Debra Rhode (1989, 202) has noted, "Increased advertising of birth control and abortion made these practices more visible; expanded opportunities for women outside the domestic sphere made such techniques more desirable." By the end of the nineteenth century, almost three-quarters of all women practiced some method of birth control, and the ratio of abortion to live births was between 1:3 and 1:5. As such, the birth rate in 1900 was about half of what it had been a century earlier.

Opposition to birth control and abortion reflected various concerns. Vice crusaders and purity societies, interested in promoting civic morality, were concerned that separating sexual relations from procreation would increase venereal disease, psychological derangement, and social instability. Members of the upper classes, aware of their declining fertility and the exploding population growth among immigrants, were fearful of so-called race suicide. Doctors, seeking to assert technical, ethical, and social superiority over their less-educated competitors, mobilized against abortion. The crusade against birth control and abortion was effective. The aforementioned Comstock Act, passed by Congress in 1873, made it a crime to sell, lend, distribute, publish, or possess devices or literature pertaining to birth control or abortion. Over the next several decades, all but one state—Kentucky—made abortion a felony. Many of these laws, enacted in response to the first women's rights movement, were designed to keep women in their place and were premised in part upon the serious danger to health and life caused by abortions at that time.

It was not until 1973 that the U.S. Supreme Court addressed the constitutionality of statutes proscribing abortion. First, the justices had to determine what precisely was at stake for the pregnant woman. Second, they had to determine how the interests of the pregnant woman were to be balanced against the interests of the state seeking to restrict abortion. That opportunity came in *Roe v. Wade* (410 U.S. 113; 1973). In 1969, Norma McCorvey, a poor, unmarried Dallas woman who had become pregnant allegedly because she had been raped, unsuccessfully sought an abortion in Texas. Texas, like most other states at the time, prohibited abortions unless necessary to save a woman's life, providing for a prison term of up to ten years. McCorvey carried her pregnancy to term and gave up the child she bore for adoption. She then decided to challenge the constitutionality of the antiabortion law, and McCorvey became "Jane Roe" in a test case against Henry Wade, the criminal district attorney for Dallas County, Texas. (Using pseudonyms in legal cases is quite common, particularly in abortion cases, to protect the privacy of young women who did not want others to know that they had sought or obtained an abortion.) Roe claimed that she had a right to choose to terminate her pregnancy, a right found in the concept of personal liberty found in the Due Process Clause of the Fourteenth Amendment; in personal, marital, familial, and sexual privacy protected by the Bill of Rights and its penumbras; and among those rights reserved to the people by the Ninth Amendment. On January 23, 1973, the justices, dividing 7-2, declared the Texas law violative of the constitutional right to privacy.

Speaking for the Court, Justice Harry Blackmun began by reviewing the history of antiabortion statutes. He concluded that such statutes were of relatively recent vintage. Abortions were legal in ancient Greece and Rome and under ancient English law, as long as they were performed prior to quickening. Even when the Constitution was drafted, a woman enjoyed a substantially broader right to terminate a pregnancy than she did in 1973. Simply because abortion statutes were of relatively recent vintage, however, was insufficient justification for declaring one of them unconstitutional. So Justice Blackmun drew the connection between abortion rights and constitutional privacy.

It was true, he conceded, that the Constitution did not explicitly mention any right to privacy. In a series of decisions going back as far as the late nineteenth century, however, the Court had recognized that a right of personal privacy, or a guarantee of certain areas or zones of privacy, existed under the Constitution and that the right had application to activities relating to procreation, marriage, and child rearing. It was a logical extension, therefore, to conclude that constitutional privacy was "broad enough to encompass a woman's decision whether or not to terminate her pregnancy" (410 U.S. at 153).

The majority's argument was fourfold. First, certain liberties, though not mentioned in the Bill of Rights, were fundamental and therefore immune from state governmental proscription. Second, privacy was one of those unenumerated yet fundamental liberties. Third, privacy included rights of individual choice pertaining to marriage, procreation, and child rearing. And fourth, the right to terminate a pregnancy fell squarely within this long-established area of private decisionmaking in matters affecting fundamental rights such as procreation.

The detriment that the state would impose upon the pregnant woman by denying this choice altogether was far too great. Justice Blackmun noted:

> Specific and direct harm medically diagnosable even in early pregnancy may be involved. Maternity, or additional off-spring, may force upon the woman a distressful life and future. Psychological harm may be imminent. Mental and physical health may be taxed by child care. There is also the distress, for all concerned, associated with the unwanted child, and there is the problem of bringing the child into a family already unable, psychologically or otherwise, to care for it. In other cases, as in this one, the additional difficulties and continuing stigma of unwed motherhood may be involved. (410 U.S. at 153)

Wade argued for the state of Texas that the unborn child was a *person* within the language and meaning of the Fourteenth Amendment and therefore entitled to constitutional protection. The justices *specifically* rejected this claim. No instance in the Constitution indicated that the word *person* had "any possible pre-natal application" (410 U.S. at 157). In addition, because physicians, philosophers, and theologians had been unable to arrive at any consensus on when life begins, the majority opted not to speculate as to the answer, though Justice Blackmun pointed out that throughout most of Western history the medical profession considered birth to be the critical point.

Roe argued that her right to terminate her pregnancy at whatever time, in whatever way, and for whatever reason she alone chose was absolute. The justices *specifically* rejected this claim also. The privacy right involved here, like other constitutional rights, "cannot be said to be absolute." Because a woman's right to terminate her pregnancy was fundamental, though, only a compelling interest could justify a state regulation that infringed upon that right. (To recall, laws that curtail fundamental rights are generally subjected to the strict scrutiny test; see Table 3.1.) In abortion matters, a state might properly assert three important interests: safeguarding maternal health, maintaining medical standards, and protecting potential life. At some point during the pregnancy, those interests became sufficiently compelling to sustain abortion regulations. The Court was clear: a pregnant woman was not isolated in her privacy. Any right to privacy had to be measured accordingly.

To balance the interests of a woman seeking an abortion with those of the states seeking to regulate or proscribe abortion, Justice Blackmun contrived a trimester framework, breaking the nine-month pregnancy into three successive three-month periods. Prior to the end of the first trimester of pregnancy, the state may not interfere with a woman's decision, reached in consultation with her physician, to terminate her pregnancy. After the first trimester, and until the point in time when the unborn child becomes viable (capable of maintaining a separate existence outside of the mother's womb), the state may regulate the abortion procedure only in ways that are reasonably related to the preservation and protection of maternal health. From the point of viability, the state may regulate, and even prohibit altogether, abortions, except those necessary to preserve the life or health of the mother. Thus, *Roe* stands for the proposition that constitutional privacy prote *to some extent* the right of a woman to terminate her preg

...ts
...ancy.

...andards of Review under the Equal Protection and Due Process Clauses for Privacy Issues

	Classifications	*Rights*	*Standards of Review*
...ect ...s and fundamental rights)	**Suspect:** Race	**Fundamental:** Procreation, Contraception, Abortion, Marriage, Divorce, Family Living Arrangements	**Strict Scrutiny:** The government has the heavy burden of persuading a court that there is a compelling state interest in the law and that there is no other, less restrictive way to accomplish that interest
Lower Tier (applies to nonsuspect classifications and nonfundamental rights)	**Nonsuspect:** Homosexuality	**Nonfundamental:** Homosexual Sodomy, Physician-Assisted Suicide	**Rational Basis:** The burden is on those attacking the law, and the courts are likely to sustain the law so long as it is a rationally (reasonably) related to a legitimate state interest

Abortions in the last three months of pregnancy could be subjected to a legislative veto if the state wanted (except, of course, those abortions necessary to save the life or health of the pregnant woman).

Calling the decision an "improvident and extravagant exercise" of judicial power, Justice Byron White dissented. He believed that the Constitution conferred a general right to privacy (witness his concurrence in *Griswold*), but he did not believe that such a right included abortion. The Constitution did not "value . . . the convenience, whim, or caprice of the putative mother more than the potential life of the fetus" (410 U.S. at 221). (A *fetus* is an unborn human more than eight weeks after conception.) Justice White chastised the majority for fashioning and announcing a new constitutional right to abortion. That issue, he thought, was better left to the people and the political processes.

Justice William Rehnquist, who had not been on the Supreme Court when *Griswold* was decided, dissented as well. He objected to the majority's application of the compelling state interest test. The fact that a majority of the states had restricted abortion for more than a century, Justice Rehnquist observed, indicated that abortion was not so rooted in the traditions and consciences of the people as to be ranked as fundamental. Therefore, the majority should have applied the far more deferential rational basis standard, asking only if the statute had a rational relation to a valid state objective (see Table 3.1. Justice Rehnquist conceded that a law that prohibited an abortion when the mother's life was threatened would lack a rational relation to a valid state objective.

Roe v. Wade was the most controversial Supreme Court opinion since the 1954 school desegregation case *Brown v. Board of Education* (347 U.S. 483) and has become the most debated privacy case ever. It elevated abortion to the national political agenda. It was praised by many for its recognition that the decision whether to abort or give birth was essential to the independence of women, that control over a woman's body and her reproductive destiny belonged to the woman; and it was criticized by an equal number for its lack of concern for potential life and perceived support of infanticide. (*Infanticide* is the killing of a child during the earliest period of life or when the child is still unborn.)

Those who support *Roe* tend to focus on the consequences of forcing a woman to bear a child against her will. Rubenfeld (1989, 788–791), for example, has written compellingly of the tremendous capacity of antiabortion laws to reshape and redirect forcefully a woman's life. "[I]t is difficult to imagine a state-enforced rule whose ramifications within the actual, everyday life of the actor are more far-reaching. For a period of months and quite possibly years, forced motherhood shapes women's occupations and preoccupations in the minutest detail; it creates a perceived identity for women and confines them to it." Another consequence brought by antiabortion laws is bodily intrusion—the requirement that a woman carry a unborn child to term, deliver the baby, and nurture the child for its first few years. These processes "involve the most intimate and strenuous exercises of the female body. The woman's body will be subjected to a continuous regimen of diet, exercise, medical examination, and possible surgical procedures. Her most elemental biological and psychological impulses will be enlisted in the process." In addition to the physical intervention, antiabortion laws also create physiological and psychological attachments between mother and child.

Those who oppose *Roe* offer numerous criticisms. First, judges should be extraordinarily cautious when second-guessing legislative action with respect to unlisted liberties. This risk of "government by judiciary" is far too great when unelected judges have the power to call an unlisted liberty "fundamental" and by fiat declare it beyond the reach of legislative majorities. Second, the trimester approach smacks of judicial legislating. By adopting a specific, statutory-like framework for state regulation of abortions—

breaking the pregnancy into three distinct terms and outlining the permissible restrictions the state may impose in each term—the justices legislated from the bench. Third, although antiabortion legislation "may cramp the lifestyle of an unwilling mother," it does so no more than antihomosexuality or antibigamy statutes cramp the lifestyle of homosexuals or bigamists (Ely 1973, 924). Virtually all laws impose some disability; such is the nature of law. Fourth, abortion takes the life of a human being other than the one making the choice. Protecting human life, the argument continues, is sufficient justification for limiting sharply, perhaps even eliminating, abortion rights. And fifth, *Roe* delegitimizes the rights of the father. Although perhaps it is plausible to conclude that the unborn child does not deserve constitutional protection, it is unfair to assert either that the father has no claim or interest in the unborn child or that the mother's claim or interest is always superior to the father's.

In the aftermath of *Roe*—and in large part because a reversal by the Supreme Court itself was highly unlikely—opponents of the ruling focused their efforts in four areas: (1) promoting a constitutional amendment to reverse the decision; (2) convincing Congress to curb federal support for abortion; (3) encouraging state legislatures to pass laws restricting the availability of abortions; and (4) electing a prolife president who would appoint only those opposed to abortion to the federal bench.

Shortly after *Roe,* proposed constitutional amendments to overturn the Supreme Court's ruling were introduced in both houses of Congress. (The standard method by which to amend the Constitution requires approval by two-thirds of *both* houses of Congress *and* ratification by three-fourths of the state legislatures. This process is quite slow and laborious, and most proposed amendments never even achieve congressional approval.) The most prominent of those proposed amendments, each of which declared that life began at conception, was the so-called Human Life Amendment. It read:

> Section 1: With respect to the right to life, the word 'person' as used in this article and in the Fifth and Fourteenth Amendments to the Constitution of the United States applies to all human beings irrespective of age, health, function, or condition of dependency, including the unborn offspring at every stage of their biological development.
>
> Section 2: No unborn person shall be deprived of life by any person; provided, however, that nothing in this article shall prohibit a law permitting only those medical procedures required to prevent the death of the mother.
>
> Section 3: The Congress and the several States shall have the power to enforce this article by appropriate legislation.

This proposal never secured the level of support required to be reported out of Congress to the states. (Those who supported it have noted that between 1973 and 1980 Democratic majorities controlled both houses of Congress.) In 1983 supporters attempted another constitutional amendment. This one simply stated, "A right to abortion is not secured by this Constitution." The results were similar: on June 26, 1983, the Senate defeated the proposal 50-49, far short of the sixty-seven votes required for passage. Presumably either of these amendments would have reversed *Roe* and meant that states were free to restrict or prohibit abortions.

Though disappointed in the results of their efforts to bring about a constitutional amendment, opponents of abortion were able to convince federal lawmakers to pass legislation to curb federal support for abortion. In the fifteen years following *Roe,* Congress enacted more than thirty laws restricting the availability of abortions. For example, shortly after *Roe* and without any congressional action, the federal government, primarily through the Medicaid program, began paying for abortions. By 1976, Medicaid alone was funding approximately 300,000 elective abortions per year for poor women. That year, Congress passed the so-called Hyde Amendment (not a constitutional amendment), which excluded abortion from the comprehensive health care services provided to indigent persons by the federal government through Medicaid, though an exception was granted if the abortion was necessary to save the life of the mother. In 1994, Congress broadened the Hyde Amendment to permit federal funding in cases of rape or incest and when the mother's life was endangered by physical disorder, illness, or injury.

In the years following *Roe,* more than a dozen states, anticipating that the decision would be overturned, refused to repeal their presumably unconstitutional antiabortion laws. Other states passed new antiabortion laws, most of which were consistent with the holding in *Roe* and simply prohibited abortions in the third trimester. And still other states attempted to restrict the availability of abortions by requiring informed consent, waiting periods, parental approval for a minor to obtain an abortion, and spousal notification; by prohibiting abortion clinics from advertising; and by refusing to provide state funds for abortions. The Supreme Court has ruled on the constitutionality of many of these post-*Roe* state legislative measures.

In *Doe v. Bolton* (410 U.S. 179; 1973), decided on the same day as *Roe,* the Supreme Court invalidated three parts of a Georgia statute that regulated abortions. Georgia permitted abortions in limited circumstances yet required that they be performed in licensed hospitals; that hospital staff committees approve abortions in advance; and that two physicians concur in the abortion decision. The justices struck down the requirements as not reasonably related to the safety or necessity of the abortion. Two years later, in *Bigelow v. Virginia* (421 U.S. 809; 1975), the Court struck down a Virginia statute that prohibited advertisements for abortions or abortion-related services. In both of these cases, the only dissenters were Justices White and Rehnquist, the same two who had dissented in *Roe.*

Seventeen months after *Roe,* Missouri's general assembly enacted a bill that imposed a structure for the control and regulation of abortions performed in the state during all stages of pregnancy. Specifically, it required that before submitting to an abortion during the first twelve weeks of pregnancy a woman (1) consent in writing to the procedure and certify that her consent was informed, freely given, and not the result of coercion; (2) obtain written consent of a spouse, unless a licensed physician certified that the procedure was necessary to save the woman's life; and (3) secure the written consent of a parent or person in loco parentis (in the place of a parent) if unmarried and under the age of eighteen. In *Planned Parenthood of Central Missouri v. Danforth* (428 U.S. 52; 1976), the Supreme Court sustained the first requirement, as long as the state's interest was related to maternal health and did not interfere unduly with the doctor-patient relationship, and declared unconstitutional the second and third requirements. Spousal and parental requirements were unconstitutional because they delegated to third parties an absolute veto power that the state did not itself possess. Because the state could not regulate or prescribe abortions in the first trimester, Justice Blackmun wrote, the state could not delegate that authority to any particular person during the same period. The majority opinion recognized that this holding permitted a woman to terminate her pregnancy without informing her spouse or parent. Nevertheless, because the woman carried the child and was more directly and immediately affected by the pregnancy, the balance "weigh[ed] in her favor" (428 U.S. at 71).

In the mid-1970s, the Massachusetts general assembly adopted a statute that required a minor seeking an abortion to obtain parental consent. If either or both of the parents refused consent, the law provided for a "judicial bypass" whereby a judge could authorize the abortion. The law also stipulated that the parents be notified when the minor filed the petition for the judicial waiver; and that the judge could deny the petition if the judge found that the abortion would be against the best interests of the minor. In *Bellotti v. Baird* (443 U.S. 622; 1979), the Supreme Court declared the statute unconstitutional, holding that all minors had to have the opportunity to approach a judge for an abortion order *without first consulting* their parents and that those proceedings had to be confidential. In addition, a pregnant minor must be afforded an opportunity to receive an independent judicial determination of whether she was mature enough to consent to an abortion; if so, the "mature" minor could obtain an abortion regardless of her parents' wishes or the judge's view as to her best interests.

These four cases—*Doe, Bigelow, Danforth,* and *Bellotti*—were logical and anticipated corollaries to *Roe. Roe* did not declare an unqualified right to abortion; rather, it protected a woman from unduly burdensome interference with her freedom to decide whether to terminate her pregnancy. These cases reaffirmed as much: states were prohibited from making abortions unreasonably difficult to obtain.

This principle, however, did not imply that states had an obligation to make abortions easy to obtain. The Supreme Court confirmed as much in *Maher v. Roe* (432 U.S. 634; 1977), an equal protection challenge to a Connecticut law that authorized reimbursement to Medicaid recipients for medical expenses incident to childbirth but not to abortion. The Court drew a distinction between direct state interference with the freedom to choose to terminate a pregnancy and whatever deterrence of the abortion choice resulted from the state's decision to pay for medical expenses related to childbirth but not to provide corresponding support for the same woman if she chose to terminate the pregnancy. The right to abortion, Justice Lewis Powell noted, implied "no limitation on the authority of a State to make a value judgment favoring childbirth over abortion, and to implement that judgment by the allocation of public funds" (432 U.S. at 474). In short, the state may subsidize some but not other medical expenses.

That same year, in *Poelker v. Doe* (432 U.S. 519; 1977), the justices found no constitutional violation by the city of St. Louis, Missouri, in electing, as a policy choice, to provide publicly financed hospital services for childbirth without providing analogous services for nontherapeutic abortions. Thus, even though abortion was a constitutionally protected right, *public* hospitals had no obligation to provide for them, even for indigent women. Three years later, in *Harris v. McRae* (448 U.S. 297; 1980), the Supreme Court upheld the aforementioned Hyde Amendment, which limited federal funding for nontherapeutic abortions, noting that a woman's right to an abortion did not require Congress to appropriate funds to enable an indigent woman to obtain the procedure.

In the final analysis, *Maher, Poelker,* and *Harris* have the same justification: an indigent woman had the same access to abortion as she would have had had the local, state, or federal government chosen not to subsidize any health care costs at all. As such, the city of St. Louis, the state of Connecticut, and the Congress of the United States interfered in no significant way with a woman's freedom to terminate her pregnancy. Justice Stewart summarized this position well in *Harris:* "It cannot be that because government may not prohibit the use of contraceptives . . . or prevent parents from sending their child to a private school . . . government, therefore, has an affirmative constitutional obligation to ensure that all persons have the financial resources to obtain contraceptives or send their children to private schools" (448 U.S. at 318). In other words, a constitutional prerogative to exercise certain liberties did not imply a governmental obligation to fund the exercise of those liberties.

Critics of *Maher, Poelker,* and *Harris* point out that policies such as these discriminate against poor women by making abortions more difficult to obtain and potentially more dangerous. Women who are denied such services often use alternatives, such as self-induced termination or so-called back-alley abortions, which are dangerous to their health. Also, there are increased health risks for women who postpone the procedure to raise the necessary funds to obtain it.

In 1980, opponents of abortion were buoyed by the results of the national elections. Voters elected a prolife president, Ronald

Reagan, and also made the Republican Party, with a staunch prolife position in its official platform, the majority party in the Senate. The elections of 1980 thus brought about renewed potential for limiting the impact of *Roe* and its progeny. (Under the Constitution, the president appoints all federal judges, subject to confirmation by simple majority vote of the Senate.) The combination of a prolife president and a Republican-controlled Senate provided the opportunity to appoint to the federal bench only individuals opposed to abortion. And with just *three* prolife appointments to the Supreme Court, *Roe* might be overturned. The justices were split 7-2 in *Roe.* The only change in the Court's composition since *Roe* was the retirement of Justice Douglas, the author of the *Griswold* decision, in 1975. President Gerald Ford had appointed John Paul Stevens to the vacancy. In his first six years, Justice Stevens tended to favor abortion rights. Therefore, when President Reagan took office in early 1981, the split among the justices on the issue of abortion as a constitutionally protected right appeared to remain seven in favor and two opposed.

In June 1981, Justice Potter Stewart, who had dissented in *Griswold* (expressing the view that neither the Constitution nor the Bill of Rights contained a general right to privacy) but concurred in *Roe* (asserting that the right to abortion was within the liberty protected by the Due Process Clause of the Fourteenth Amendment), resigned. President Reagan, who had promised in his campaign to appoint the first female justice to the Supreme Court, nominated Sandra Day O'Connor, a move that surprisingly sparked a noisy public debate. Many of President Reagan's more conservative supporters opposed O'Connor's nomination, largely because of the moderate views on abortion she had expressed as an Arizona state legislator. Most of the prominent women's interest groups, however, approved of the selection, no doubt in part due to its symbolic victory for women's rights. At her confirmation hearings before the Senate Judiciary Committee, O'Connor steadfastly declined to speculate how she would vote as a justice on the matter of abortion. Nevertheless, seventeen of the eighteen members of the Judiciary Committee recommended her nomination. One member voted "present" because of O'Connor's refusal to condemn *Roe* when specifically given the opportunity to do so. In September the Senate confirmed Justice O'Connor by a vote of 99-0.

Justice O'Connor's first abortion case came in her second term on the high court bench. *Akron v. Akron Center for Reproductive Health* (462 U.S. 416; 1983) was a challenge to an Akron, Ohio, ordinance that required (1) all abortions after the first trimester of pregnancy be performed in full-service hospitals (as opposed to clinics); (2) minors under fifteen to obtain parental or judicial consent for an abortion; (3) the attending physician to provide the woman with specific information relevant to informed consent, including details of fetal anatomy, a statement that human life begins at "the moment of conception," a list of risks and consequences associated with the abortion procedure, and the availability of agencies to provide the woman with assistance and information with respect to birth control, adoption, and childbirth; (4) a woman to wait twenty-four hours between consenting to and receiving an abortion; and (5) physicians performing abortions to dispose of fetal remains in a "humane and sanitary manner."

Per Justice Powell, the Court, split 6-3, invalidated all five sections of the city ordinance. First, the hospitalization requirement unduly interfered with a woman's access to abortion services without protecting her health, because the most common method of midtrimester abortion—dilation and evacuation (D&E)—could be performed as safely in outpatient facilities as in full-service hospitals. This requirement thus imposed a heavy and unnecessary burden on women's access to a relatively inexpensive, otherwise accessible, and safe abortion procedure and had the likely effect of inhibiting the vast majority of abortions after the first trimester. Second, the parental-consent and judicial-bypass provisions failed to provide for an individual determination of whether the minor was mature enough to make the decision on her own (as required by *Bellotti*). Such a blanket determination that all minors under the age of fifteen were too immature to make an abortion decision prohibited case-by-case evaluations of the maturity of pregnant minors. Third, the informed-consent "script" intruded upon the physician's judgment as to what was best for the individual woman and, instead of merely describing the general subject matter, contained information clearly designed to dissuade the woman from having an abortion. Fourth, the twenty-four-hour waiting period did not serve the state's interests in protecting the woman's health (the only compelling state interest prior to the last trimester, according to *Roe*) and in ensuring her informed consent. There was simply no evidence to indicate the procedure would be performed more safely after the waiting period. It simply increased costs by requiring an additional trip to the physician and was unnecessarily arbitrary and inflexible. Fifth, the "humane and sanitary" disposal of fetal remains requirement was too vague to give fair warning to physicians of what the law required.

To the surprise and delight of abortion opponents, Justice O'-Connor, joined by Justices White and Rehnquist (the two dissenters in *Roe*), dissented. She claimed that the analytical framework of *Roe,* which varied according to the "stage" of pregnancy, was "completely unworkable" because it was incapable of "continuity over significant periods of time." It was not unreasonable to conclude that advances in medical technology may make possible fetal viability in the first trimester. Those same advances may also increase the time for which a safe abortion could be obtained well into the third trimester. Advances in medical technology thus worked both ways—improving the ability of physicians to save a fetus removed from the womb during the first trimester (which would extend the length of the third trimester) and increasing the time for which a safe abortion could be obtained (which would increase the length of the first trimester). Because the trimester approach was "clearly on a collision course with itself," Justice O'-Connor advocated its abandonment (462 U.S. at 458). Relying on language in cases decided after *Roe,* she suggested instead that abortion regulations be declared unconstitutional only if they posed on "undue burden" on a woman seeking an abortion. This standard was to be applied throughout the entire pregnancy, irrespective of the particular stage of pregnancy involved.

Akron was perceived by most as a significant victory for pro-choice advocates, a solidifying of the right to abortion. In an unusual act, President Reagan released a printed statement expressing his "profound disappointment" at the Supreme Court's reaffirmation of the constitutional right to abortion. The president called upon Congress to "make its voice heard" by adopting legal protections for the unborn whether by statute or constitutional amendment. President Reagan also cited favorably the dissent written by his appointee, Justice O'Connor (Clines 1983, A16). The decision in *Akron* galvanized antiabortion groups, many of which redoubled their efforts to win passage of a constitutional amendment. Less than two weeks after *Akron* was decided, however, the Senate defeated an amendment that read in its entirety, "A right to abortion is not secured by this Constitution." David Garrow (1994, 644) captured the significance of the defeat when he noted, "That vote effectively signaled an end to meaningful congressional efforts to overturn *Roe* and its legacy; and the fall of 1983 was as quiet a period of abortion battles as anytime in over a decade."

Three years later, in *Thornburgh v. American College of Obstetricians and Gynecologists* (476 U.S. 747; 1986), the Supreme Court, despite direct invitations from the Reagan administration to overturn *Roe,* once again reaffirmed the general principles laid down in *Roe* and confirmed in *Akron* only three years prior. The Pennsylvania law required (1) a woman seeking an abortion to give her informed consent, after she had been given specified information, including the potential medical, physical, and psychological effects of the procedure; the availability of medical assistance benefits for prenatal care, childbirth, and neonatal care; a list of agencies offering alternatives to abortion; and a state-produced brochure describing the unborn child; (2) detailed reporting to the state by providers on each abortion, with reports open for public inspection; (3) a physician performing a postviability abortion to use the abortion method most likely to result in fetal survival unless it would cause "significantly" greater risk to a woman's life or health; and (4) the presence of a second physician during abortions when viability was a possibility. The Court struck down each of the provisions, the first because it was intended to dissuade women from having abortions, the second because it could easily lead to public disclosure of the woman's identity, the third because it required a woman to bear an increased risk to her health in order to maximize the chances of fetal survival, and the fourth because it made no exception for emergencies.

More generally, *Thornburgh* held that states could not, under the guise of protecting maternal health or potential life, intimidate women into continuing their pregnancies. "Few decisions are more personal and intimate, more properly private, or more basic to individual dignity and autonomy, than a woman's decision—with the guidance of her physician and within the limits specified by *Roe*—whether to end her pregnancy," wrote Justice Blackmun. "A woman's right to make that choice freely is fundamental. Any other result . . . would protect inadequately a central part of the sphere of liberty that our law guarantees equally to all" (476 U.S. at 772).

Advocates of a woman's right to choose applauded the decision, yet with some trepidation. *Roe* was decided by a vote of 7-2; *Thornburgh,* however, commanded the support of but five of the nine justices. Chief Justice Warren Burger, though he had been in the majority both in *Roe* thirteen years earlier and in *Akron* (which strongly reaffirmed *Roe*) only three years hence, dissented, as did Justices White, Rehnquist, and O'Connor.

The chief justice's new position was based upon his understanding that the Supreme Court, contrary to his original expectations, had ignored that portion of *Roe* specifying abortion was only a qualified right that had to be balanced against important state interests in regulation. Instead, the Court had extended *Roe* to sanction "abortion on demand" (476 U.S. at 782). Each of the dissenters found the challenged law entirely consistent with the Court's holding in *Roe,* which permitted states to regulate second-trimester abortions to protect a woman's health and third-trimester abortions to protect potential human life.

The shift in Chief Justice Burger's position, resulting in a perceived narrowing margin of support for *Roe,* suggested that the Supreme Court might consider reversing itself or even abandoning the constitutional right to abortion if any justice in the majority were replaced by a new one who shared the views of the dissenters. Abortion foes were encouraged that they were but one vote away from overturning *Roe.* That probably was not the case, however. Only two of the four dissenters, Justices White and Rehnquist, called for *Roe* to be overturned. That pair rejected the idea of a constitutionally protected right to abortion and would permit the states, at whatever stage during the pregnancy, to regulate or even prohibit abortion. Such had been their position in 1973 as well. The remaining two dissenters, Chief Justice Burger and Justice O'Connor, though unhappy with *Roe,* were unwilling to join their colleagues who called for its abandonment. Rather than declaring that no constitutional right to abortion existed, this pair simply advocated for a more limited right, one in which the states were permitted to play a far greater regulatory role. *Thornburgh* demonstrated how closely the justices were divided over the issue of state regulation of abortion, but not so much over the constitutional right to abortion. The significant split in *Thornburgh* was thus between those five justices who appeared willing to strike down most state regulations of abortion automatically and the two dissenters who supported the constitutional right to abortion but preferred a balancing approach more favorable to state regulations.

Although *Roe* was probably not one vote away from being overturned, it was only one vote away from being reexamined. Support for *Roe* among the justices had declined from seven (*Roe*) to six (*Akron*) to five (*Thornburgh*). In 1986, Chief Justice Burger announced his resignation from the Court. President Reagan promptly elevated Justice Rehnquist to the chief justiceship and named Antonin Scalia, an opponent of the constitutional right to abortion, to the newly vacated seat. Scalia's appointment, therefore, altered the split among the justices on the issue of abortion. When Justice Lewis Powell, who had been in the majority in *Roe, Akron,* and *Thornburgh,* announced his resignation the following year, both sides of the abortion debate recognized its importance: one of the "fragile five" who had supported *Roe* was leaving.

After two unsuccessful nominations, President Reagan appointed Anthony Kennedy. At his confirmation hearings, Kennedy declared that while he had no "fixed view" on abortion or limitations on privacy rights, he believed that constitutional liberty included "protection of the value we call privacy." On the day Kennedy made those remarks, the Supreme Court, dividing 4-4, let stand an appellate court decision striking down an Illinois law that required all teenagers to notify their parents prior to having an abortion. That decision underscored the critical role that Kennedy would play on this issue if confirmed. His refusal to commit to abortion rights annoyed prochoice groups; his acceptance of a general right to privacy raised concerns among prolife groups. Nevertheless, he was confirmed easily by the Senate. The opportunity to reexamine the general principles laid down in *Roe* came in Justice Kennedy's first full term.

Webster v. Reproductive Health Services (492 U.S. 490; 1989) was a challenge to a 1986 Missouri statute regulating the performance of abortions, the preamble of which declared that life began at conception and that the unborn child had "protectable interest in life, health, and well-being." More important, the act (1) forbade the use of public facilities for abortions not necessary to save a woman's life; (2) made it unlawful to use public funds for the purpose of counseling a woman to have an abortion not necessary to save her life; and (3) required physicians to perform various medical tests on all fetuses to determine viability where, in the doctor's judgment, the fetus was twenty or more weeks of gestational age. The federal district court, relying upon *Roe* and subsequent cases, declared the preamble and the three challenged provisions unconstitutional and enjoined their enforcement; the U.S. Court of Appeals for the Eighth Circuit affirmed.

A splintered Supreme Court, with the core majority made up of the two *Roe* dissenters—Justices White and Rehnquist—and the three Reagan appointees—Justices O'Connor, Scalia, and Kennedy, upheld the two most controversial provisions. (The Court refused to rule on the constitutionality of the preamble, because it did not regulate abortion or any other aspect of the medical practice of health care professionals offering abortion services or pregnancy counseling, and the counseling prohibition, because no litigant had been adversely affected by it.) The first provision—prohibiting the use of public facilities for abortions not necessary to save the mother's life—was permissible because it placed no *governmental* obstacle in the path of a woman who chose an abortion. A pregnant woman was left with the same choices as she would have had if the state had chosen not to operate any public hospitals at all. Nothing in the Constitution, Chief Justice Rehnquist wrote for the majority, required Missouri to enter or remain in the business of performing abortions; neither did private physicians or their patients have a constitutional right of access to public facilities for the performance of abortions. The third provision—viability testing—was constitutional because it furthered the state's interest in protecting potential human life. Under the framework established in *Roe*, twenty weeks fell within the second trimester, where regulation was permissible only to the extent that such regulation was related to the preservation and protection of maternal health. Clearly this regulation was not so related. Nevertheless, a plurality held that the state's interest in protecting human life was of equal weight throughout the pregnancy. (A *plurality opinion* is an opinion that states the holding of the Court but is supported by less than a majority of the justices participating in the decision.) Because viability testing promoted a legitimate state interest, it was constitutional, irrespective of the stage at which it was required.

Webster provided the justices with the opportunity to overturn *Roe.* Yet they specifically declined to do so. A plurality—the chief justice and Justices White and Kennedy (in his first abortion case)—wanted to abandon the trimester-and-viability framework of *Roe,* but not *Roe* itself, because this case afforded no occasion to do so. Justice O'Connor hinted that she might be willing to replace the framework of *Roe* with the undue burden analysis (see her dissent in *Akron*) but that this case was an inappropriate vehicle for doing so. She preferred to wait for the right case, one in which a state statute actually turned on the constitutional validity of *Roe.* Only Justice Scalia (in his first abortion case as well) voted in favor of an outright reversal of *Roe.* So while five justices expressed dislike for *Roe,* they could not agree on a new legal test that would be used to evaluate state regulations. There was no doubt, however, that after *Webster* states possessed far greater power to regulate when, where, and how a woman could terminate her pregnancy.

The dissenters, placed in that position on this issue for the first time, could not mask their disappointment. "The plurality repudiates every principle for which *Roe* stands," Justice Blackmun wrote. "Thus, not with a bang, but a whimper, the plurality discards a landmark case of the last generation and casts into darkness the hopes and visions of every woman in this country who had come to believe that the Constitution guaranteed her the right to exercise some control over her unique ability to bear children"

(492 U.S. at 557). The public facilities and employees provision brought to bear the full force of the state's economic power and control over essential facilities to discourage its citizens from exercising their constitutional rights. And the viability-testing provision imposed a burden on second-trimester abortions as a way of furthering the state's interest in potential life, as opposed to maternal health. "For today the women of this nation still retain the liberty to control their destinies. But the signs are evident and very ominous, and a chill wind blows," Justice Blackmun concluded.

The public reaction to *Webster* was as expected. John C. Willkie, president of the National Right to Life Committee, remarked, "Now we see a halt in this genocidal movement. . . . We are hopeful and confident. We have our thumbs up. We are smiling" (Kamen 1989, 1). President George H. W. Bush, who had taken office less than six months earlier, praised the decision and called for further action "to restore to the people the ability to protect the unborn." He suggested a right-to-life constitutional amendment as a means to resolve this emotional controversy. Antiabortion forces responded to the call. Senator Jesse Helms (R–NC) introduced a proposed constitutional amendment that would have protected human life from the moment of conception, by expanding the definition of "person" under the Fourteenth Amendment's Due Process and Equal Protection Clauses. The proposed amendment was defeated in the Senate. Many state legislatures were encouraged to adopt new, more restrictive laws. Other states began enforcing certain antiabortion statutes that had not been enforced for years and were presumed unconstitutional after *Roe* and subsequent cases but never repealed. One of those, a Minnesota statute requiring a forty-eight-hour waiting period for minors seeking an abortion, was upheld by the Supreme Court the following year in *Hodgson v. Minnesota* (497 U.S. 417; 1990).

Interpreting *Webster* as an assault on the independence of women and fearing the demise of the constitutional right to abortion, prochoice groups mobilized as well. The Freedom of Choice Act was introduced in Congress in 1989. Though never approved, this act would have prohibited states from enacting restrictions on abortion prior to viability. And a handful of state legislatures, including Connecticut's, enacted statutes that guaranteed abortion as a matter of state law.

Shortly after *Webster,* Justices William Brennan and Thurgood Marshall, two ardent supporters both of the constitutional right to abortion and *Roe,* retired. President George H. W. Bush nominated David Souter and Clarence Thomas, respectively, to replace the departing justices. At the confirmation hearings, neither nominee engaged inquiring senators in any substantive discussion of abortion rights or *Roe.* Souter said that he had not decided what he thought about the holding in *Roe* and that it therefore would be inappropriate to engage in any dialogue on the constitutional right to abortion. Thomas similarly deferred, claiming that he had no opinion as to whether the Constitution protected the right to abortion. With respect to privacy, Thomas said that he believed privacy for married couples was a fundamental constitutional right. He did not say whether that right extended beyond the marital setting, however. Following their confirmations, and in spite of these nondiscussions on abortion, many observers assumed, perhaps because the new justices were appointees of a prolife president, that the Rehnquist Court was once again on the verge of overruling *Roe.* That assumption was proved at least in partial error only three years later.

The Pennsylvania Abortion Control Act, as amended in 1989, required except in narrowly defined medical emergencies that (1) a woman wait twenty-four hours between consenting to and receiving an abortion; (2) a woman be given state-mandated information about abortion and offered state-authored materials on fetal development; (3) a married woman inform her husband of her intent to have an abortion; and (4) minors obtain consent of one parent or guardian, or a judicial waiver, prior to receiving an abortion. In addition, physicians and clinics performing abortions were required to provide to the state annual statistical reports on abortions performed during the year, including the names of referring physicians. In *Planned Parenthood of Southeastern Pennsylvania v. Casey* (505 U.S. 833; 1992), the Supreme Court, by the narrowest of margins, upheld all of the restrictions except for the husband-notification requirement.

The holding in *Casey* was not that simple, however. Though the ruling limited the constitutional right to an abortion by permitting some state restrictions never before sustained by the Court (in fact, by permitting some state restrictions struck down by the Court less than a decade earlier in *Akron* and *Thornburgh*), it also reaffirmed the essential holding of *Roe*—that viability marked the earliest point at which the state's interest in fetal life was constitutionally adequate to justify a legislative ban on nontherapeutic abortions. In an extraordinary opinion written jointly by Justices O'Connor, Kennedy, and Souter, and joined in part by Justices Blackmun and Stevens, the majority said that *Roe* established a "rule of law and a component of liberty we cannot renounce" (505 U.S. at 871). Nevertheless, the majority rejected the trimester framework, which it did not consider to be part of the essential holding in *Roe.* Instead of the traditional trimester framework, the Court applied for the first time in a majority opinion the undue burden analysis, which asked whether restrictive laws had the purpose or effect of placing a "substantial obstacle in the path of a woman seeking an abortion of a nonviable fetus" (505 U.S. at 877). Applying that standard to the Pennsylvania law, a separate majority concluded that three of the four provisions were not unduly burdensome merely because they attempted to persuade a woman to carry her pregnancy to term. The spousal-notification requirement, however, operated as a substantial obstacle to a woman's choice to undergo an abortion. Because women have very good reasons—physical or psychological abuse, child abuse, the destruction of possessions, physical confinement to the house, the disclosure of the abortion to family and friends, for example—for not wanting to inform their husbands, this requirement was likely to prevent a significant number of women from terminating their pregnancies.

Justice Stevens would have declared unconstitutional all of the provisions except the parental-consent requirement. Justice Blackmun would have struck down all of the provisions, and he alone asserted that the trimester approach of *Roe* should not be disturbed. In angry separate opinions, Chief Justice Rehnquist and Justices White, Scalia, and Thomas advocated overruling *Roe* and extracting the Supreme Court from this area of the law. Without a fifth vote, however, the four settled on expressing the view that the statute should be sustained in its entirety as rationally related to a legitimate state interest. According to these four, the legitimate state interest in spousal notification was attempting to improve truthful communications between spouses and encouraging collaborative decisionmaking.

Without question, *Casey* redefined and narrowed the constitutional right to abortion. Yet it also offered significantly more protection for abortion rights than most prochoice groups expected from a Supreme Court that was supposedly primed to overrule *Roe.* This case pointed to the emergence of a new bloc of justices committed to preserving the right of a woman to terminate her pregnancy prior to fetal viability. The solidity of their position was underscored by the joint authorship of the opinion, typically meant to give added weight to the decision. It would therefore be a mistake to cast *Casey* as a major victory for abortion opponents. It would be appropriate to cast it as a watershed decision, though, for the Court had adopted a new standard, one that permitted considerably more abortion regulation during the first and second trimesters.

The following eighteen months witnessed a wave of violence directed against abortion clinics and other reproductive health care providers. Six individuals—three doctors, two receptionists, and an escort—were shot to death, a police officer responding to a bomb threat was killed, and dozens of others were wounded in attacks associated with abortion clinics. Congress responded to this violence by passing the Freedom of Access to Clinic Entrances (FACE) Act of 1994, which made the use of force or the threat of force, or physical obstruction for the purpose of injuring, intimidating, or interfering with a person seeking to obtain or provide reproductive health services, a federal offense with penalties up to ten years' imprisonment. In April 2001, the Supreme Court, without comment, refused to hear a constitutional challenge to the act.

Casey was the last major broadside attack on the constitutional right to abortion. Eight years later, abortion returned to the Supreme Court's docket in *Stenberg v. Carhart* (530 U.S. 914; 2000). By this time, Justices Blackmun and White—one abortion rights proponent and one abortion rights opponent—had been replaced by Justices Ruth Bader Ginsburg and Stephen Breyer, appointees of President Bill Clinton. At the confirmation hearings, Ginsburg voiced general support for abortion rights, noting that governmental control over such a decision was tantamount to treating a woman as "less than a fully adult person." Although less certain than Ginsburg, Breyer also expressed support for legal precedents that protected abortion.

The issue in *Stenberg* was not abortion itself but rather a particular form of abortion. Nebraska, like thirty other states, prohibited so-called partial-birth abortions unless necessary to save the life of the mother. (In 1996, President Clinton vetoed the federal Partial Birth Abortion Ban Act, which would have criminalized most such abortions.) The statute defined *partial birth abortion* as a procedure "in which the person performing the abortion partially delivers vaginally a living unborn child before killing the unborn child and completing the delivery." The phrase "partially delivers vaginally a living unborn child" was defined as "intentionally delivering into the vagina a living unborn child, or a substantial portion thereof." In an opinion written by Justice Breyer, the Court in *Stenberg* declared the act unconstitutional because it prohibited a safe abortion procedure, lacked an exception for the preservation of the health of the mother, and imposed an undue burden upon a woman's right to choose an abortion.

Because the statute targeted only one method of abortion, the majority opinion devoted significant ink to describing different abortion procedures. During the second trimester, the most common abortion procedure was dilation and, whereby the fetal tissue was evacuated from the uterus after dilation of the cervix. The risks that accompanied D&E were significantly lower than induced delivery, the next safest second-trimester abortion. A variation of D&E, known as intact D&E, which involved removing the fetus from the uterus through the cervix intact, was commonly used after the sixteenth week. The feet-first method, commonly known as dilation and extraction (D&X), was ordinarily associated with partial birth abortion. After surveying medical opinion on the subject, the Court's opinion concluded that convincing evidence established that the method of abortion proscribed here might well be the safest and most medically appropriate abortion procedure.

A second shortcoming of the statute was its lack of an exception for the preservation of the health of the mother. Although a state was permitted to regulate methods of abortion, it could not do so in a manner that endangered a woman's health. The Supreme Court rejected Nebraska's contention that the procedure was used infrequently and other safe alternatives remained available; those facts were "not highly relevant." The state could not prohibit a procedure simply by pointing out that most people did not need it.

Finally, the majority held that the statute imposed an undue burden on a woman's right and ability to choose an abortion. The language of the statute was too broad: it banned both D&X and D&E. Even D&E, the most commonly used method of abortion, often involved a physician pulling an arm, leg, or other "substantial portion" of a still-living fetus into the vagina prior to the fetus's death. Because the statutory terms did not distinguish between D&X and D&E, the law could be used to pursue physicians performing previability second-trimester abortions. And if those who performed the most common type of abortions feared prosecution, conviction, and imprisonment, a woman's right to terminate her pregnancy would be unduly burdened.

Of particular significance in *Stenberg* was the dissent penned by Justice Kennedy, who had been in the majority eight years earlier in *Casey* when the Supreme Court reaffirmed most of the *Roe* holding. Indicating his displeasure with the majority's misapplication of *Casey,* which said nothing about cases in which a physician considered one prohibited method of abortion to be preferable to other permissible methods, Justice Kennedy emphasized the "consequential moral difference" between partial-birth and other methods of abortion, the former being considered by "many decent and civilized people . . . to be among the most serious of crimes against human life" (530 U.S. at 979). In sum, though a woman had a constitutional right to choose an abortion, she had no such right to choose a particular method of abortion. State laws that attempted to promote the life of the unborn and to ensure respect for all human life and its potential by proscribing certain methods of abortion placed no undue burden upon a woman seeking an abortion. The other dissenters—Chief Justice Rehnquist and Justices Scalia and Thomas—repeated a familiar refrain: nothing in the Constitution required a state to permit abortion. *Roe* was decided incorrectly. So was *Casey.* Both should be overruled.

Although *Stenberg* appeared to be a victory for abortion-rights supporters, it certainly energized antiabortion advocates, who were encouraged by the closeness of the vote and the public's perception of partial-birth abortion as a particularly gruesome procedure. Within hours of the announcement, antiabortion advocates were saying that their loss before the High Court could translate into a gain at the ballot box because many centrist voters, even those who supported abortion rights generally, were uncomfortable with this particular procedure. Electing Texas governor George W. Bush in the November 2000 presidential election, they informed voters, would most likely produce a Supreme Court that would sustain state restrictions on partial-birth abortions and return the abortion decision back to the states, which would be free to eliminate the right altogether. Recognizing that it would take just one vote to reverse the result, abortion-rights supporters turned their attention to the November election as well, asserting that only if Vice President Al Gore were elected would a woman's right to choose be protected. On the very day *Stenberg* was decided, President Clinton captured the importance of the pending presidential election when he stated that abortion rights hung "in the balance" of the next president's appointments to the high court (Rubin 2000, A12).

The *Skinner-Griswold-Roe* trilogy characterized reproductive rights as fundamental rights of privacy, inviolate against any but compelling state interests and narrowly tailored remedies, and requiring strict judicial scrutiny of restrictive legislation. In *Casey,* however, the justices held that strict scrutiny of abortion-related statutes was not required where challenged legislation did not unduly burden the right to abortion. So, what is the current state of constitutional law on abortion? Constitutional privacy guarantees women the right to choose an abortion prior to viability of the fetus (*Roe*), but states may enact restrictions on abortion as long as those restrictions do not pose an undue burden on women seeking to terminate their pregnancies (*Casey*). Accordingly, states may insist that a woman seeking an abortion wait twenty-four hours between consenting to and receiving an abortion; and that she be given state-mandated information about abortion and offered state-authored materials on fetal development (*Casey*). Blanket requirements of third-party consent are unconstitutional. The Supreme Court has been unwilling to give either the pregnant woman's spouse or parents (in case of a minor) an absolute veto over an abortion that the state itself is powerless to proscribe (*Danforth*). Requirements of parental consent must allow for a judicial bypass for a minor who is sufficiently mature to make the decision herself or who can demonstrate that an abortion is in her best interests (*Belloti*). Minors, however, may be required to notify a parent and wait forty-eight hours between consenting to and receiving an abortion (*Hodgson*). States may not mandate that all abortions after the first trimester be performed in full-service hospitals (*Akron*) or require that a married woman inform her husband of her intent to have an abortion (*Casey*). Neither the federal government (*Harris*) nor the states (*Maher*) has an obligation to pay for an abortion, even if it is medically necessary to preserve the mother's health or even save the mother's life. Those states that opt to pay for medical expenses related to childbirth may still refuse to pay for abortion procedures (*Maher*). States may forbid the use of public facilities for abortions not necessary to save a woman's life (*Webster*). And physicians and clinics performing abortions may be required to provide detailed information to the state, such as annual statistical reports on abortions performed during the year, including the names of referring physicians (*Casey*), as long as that information does not lead to public disclosure of the woman's identity (*Thornburgh*).

Support for the principles of *Roe* has gradually shrunk among the justices. In addition, many of the arguments advanced in dissent are now more concerned with opposition to the central premise of reproductive autonomy than with the application of *Roe*'s principles to specific abortion regulations. It appears that the Supreme Court has a number of options, none of which commands solid support from a majority of justices.

First, the justices could overturn *Roe,* returning the matter to the states. This option assumes that the democratic process within each state is the most legitimate procedure to solve the abortion issue; it also holds that recent history demonstrates the incapability of the federal judiciary to do so. In addition, letting states go their separate ways averts future culture wars brought about by the nationalization of abortion law. Opponents of this option assume that the democratic process is incapable of solving profound problems. Deferring to the states is, therefore, the least legitimate procedure, for it would do nothing more than "delegate the fate of mothers and unborn children alike to shifting majorities in fifty legislatures. The rights of women would be trampled in some states; the rights of unborn sacrificed in others" (Koukoutchos 1985, A23). Fundamental rights, the argument continues, cannot be reduced to political interests. As Justice Robert Jackson remarked more than sixty years ago in *West Virginia Board of Education v. Barnette* (319 U.S. 624, 638; 1943), "The very purpose of the Bill of Rights was to withdraw certain subjects from the vicissitudes of political controversy. . . . Fundamental rights may not be submitted to a vote; they depend on the outcome of no elections." If abortion were returned to the states, some state legislatures no doubt would proscribe all abortions, others would limit their availability, and still others would guarantee access to, perhaps even provide public funding for, abortion. Already, appellate courts in four states—California (1981), New Jersey (1982), Connecticut (1986), and New York (1993)—have held that the freedom to choose abortion is a fundamental right protected *under the state constitution.* As such, the right to abortion in these states is insulated from any retreat by the U.S. Supreme Court. Laurence Tribe (1988, 1351) suggests that Abraham Lincoln's warning, voiced at a time when the nation was deeply divided over another fundamental matter, is worth recalling: if the Union could not long endure "half-slave and half-free" back then, could it long endure "half-prochoice and half-prolife" now?

Second, the Supreme Court could say that life begins at conception, thereby providing constitutional protection to the unborn child. This approach might not permit states to proscribe all abortions, though. Presumably states would still be required to make exceptions for the preservation of the health and life of the mother.

Third, the justices could retain the undue burden analysis, keeping most previability abortions legal while permitting regulation of them. This is clearly the most likely option, as it has more support among the justices than the other two.

Much like the nation, the Supreme Court remains bitterly divided on this matter. The current Court (as of mid-2003) is made up of members nominated by presidents Richard Nixon (one), Gerald Ford (one), Ronald Reagan (three), George H. W. Bush (two), and Bill Clinton (two). Three justices tend to vote in a bloc to sustain abortion regulations. Chief Justice Rehnquist, one of the original dissenters in *Roe,* continues to maintain that *Roe* and its progeny were wrongly decided and should be overruled. Justice Scalia believes that *Roe* was "plainly wrong" because the Constitution says nothing whatsoever about abortion and the longstanding traditions of U.S. society have permitted abortion to be legally proscribed. He asserts that the entire federal judiciary should get out of this area of the law, where it has no right to be. "The Court should return this matter to the people—where the Constitution, by its silence on the subject, left it—and let *them* decide, State by State, whether [abortion] should be allowed," he wrote in *Stenberg* (530 U.S. at 956). Though he claimed at his confirmation hearing never to have considered *Roe,* Justice Thomas has consistently sided against its provisions.

Three justices clearly support the general principles enunciated in *Roe.* Justice John Paul Stevens, the oldest member of the Supreme Court, is a firm supporter of abortion rights. Although early in his tenure he voted in a number of cases to uphold limited restrictions on abortion, he has in the last fifteen years emerged as a solid vote in opposition to most barriers to abortion, including the distribution of antiabortion information and waiting periods. In *Casey,* he called *Roe* "an integral part of a correct understanding of . . . the concept of liberty" (505 U.S. at 912). Justices Ruth Bader Ginsburg and Stephen Breyer, though having participated in only a few abortion cases, support a woman's right to choose.

Prior to arriving at the Court, then Judge Ginsburg (1985) wrote that the reproductive rights have significant import for the autonomy and equality of women. In *Stenberg,* Justice Breyer asserted that *Roe* was settled law.

The remaining three members—Justices O'Connor, Kennedy, and Souter—are on record as supporting the "essential holding" of *Roe.* But they coauthored the plurality opinion in *Casey,* which held that strict scrutiny of abortion restrictions was not required as long as the restrictions did not "unduly burden" the right of a woman to terminate her pregnancy prior to viability of the fetus. That ruling upheld informed-consent requirements and mandatory waiting periods. It is fair to say that these jurists hold the balance on abortion rights. When given the opportunity to join an opinion overruling *Roe,* each declined to do so. Yet each has also voted on numerous occasions to curtail the right to abortion. Moreover, Justice Kennedy's dissent in *Stenberg* raises serious doubts about his continued support of abortion rights.

Clearly the Supreme Court has not spoken its final word on the abortion issue. Given the narrow margin of recent votes, the contrast in Justice Kennedy's position in *Casey* in 1992 and his position on the more focused question in *Stenberg* in 2000, the ever-increasing state legislative restrictions on abortion, the near-retirement ages of Chief Justice Rehnquist and Justices Stevens and O'Connor, and the promise of President George W. Bush to appoint individuals similar in ideology to Justices Scalia and Thomas, his two favorites, it is a certainty that the high court will continue to grapple with this emotionally charged, politically divisive, and seemingly intractable issue.

Family Autonomy

Long before the founding of the United States, the English legal system perceived of the family as an autonomous entity and intervened only in the most extreme circumstances. Thus, though the word *family* does not appear in the U.S. Constitution, the family has traditionally enjoyed special status under the Constitution. The family does not simply "co-exist with our constitutional system," write Philip Heymann and Douglas Barzelay (1973, 772–773). "Because our political system is superimposed on and presupposes a social system of family units, not just isolated individuals, . . . the family unit is an integral part of [the constitutional system]. . . . No assumption more deeply underlies our society." Limitations on autonomy in the private realm of family life became somewhat commonplace in the late nineteenth and early twentieth centuries, however, when numerous aspects of family life were brought under the supervision of the state. In a series of cases beginning in the 1920s, the Supreme Court looked to the history and tradition of the family to conclude that family privacy, though lacking clear constitutional roots, was among the unenumerated yet fundamental rights immune from the control and direction of the state. The Supreme Court has thus long recognized that freedom of personal choice in matters of marriage and family life is one of the liberties protected by the Due Process Clause of the Fourteenth Amendment. These matters include the right to marry, to divorce, to direct the upbringing and education of one's children, to maintain family ties, and to live with family members.

Marital Rights: Marriage and Divorce

Marriage. Traditionally, the law considered marriage to be a contract based upon a voluntary private agreement between a man and a woman to become husband and wife, a permanent and indissoluble union that the state should protect. As such, well past the middle of the nineteenth century, the states did not make their courts available "for resolving disputes between husband and wife or among other family members" (Minow 1990, 269–270). Although marriage is essentially a private matter, government regularly regulates the practice. Marital rights, both in marriage and its dissolution, belong to the virtually exclusive province of the states. The Supreme Court has long held that states may prescribe most of the conditions of marriage and divorce, including at what age a person may marry, how one may marry, the persons whom one may marry, the duties and obligations of the parties, the property rights of the parties, and how a marriage may be dissolved.

The Supreme Court did not characterize the personal interest in choosing whom to marry as a fundamental right to privacy until the 1960s. *Loving v. Virginia* (388 U.S. 1; 1967) was a challenge to a Virginia law that criminalized miscegenation in which a white person was a party. *Miscegenation,* from the Latin *miscere* (to mix) and *genus* (race), means marriage between persons of different races. Antimiscegenation laws in Virginia dated from early in the colonial period. Virginia was one of sixteen southern states that prohibited interracial marriage well into the twentieth century. In 1958, two residents of Virginia, Mildred Jeter, a black woman, and Richard Loving, a white man, were married in the District of Columbia. Shortly thereafter, the Lovings established residency and their marital abode in Virginia. The following year, the Lovings were charged with violating the antimiscegenation law, whereupon they pleaded guilty and were sentenced to one year in jail. The trial judge, however, suspended the sentence for twenty-five years, upon the condition that the Lovings leave the state and not return during that period. In his opinion, the trial judge wrote, "Almighty God created the races white, black, yellow, malay and red, and he placed them on separate continents. And but for the interference with his arrangement there would be no cause for such marriages. The fact that he separated the races shows that he did not intend for the races to mix" (quoted in *Loving,* 388 U.S. at 3).

A unanimous Supreme Court invalidated the law as an invidious racial classification patently lacking a compelling state interest and was therefore inconsistent with the Equal Protection Clause of the Fourteenth Amendment (see Table 3.1). The fact that Virginia prohibited only interracial marriages involving white persons demonstrated clearly that the racial classifications were designed to maintain white supremacy. But eight of the nine justices were willing to declare the statute violative of the Due Process Clause as well. "The freedom to marry has long been recognized as one of the vital personal rights essential to the orderly pursuit of happiness by free men," Chief Justice Warren wrote. "To deny this fundamental freedom on so unsupportable a basis as the racial classifications embodied in these statutes . . . is surely to deprive all the State's citizens of liberty without due process of law. Under our Constitution, the freedom to marry, or not marry, a person of another race resides with the individual and cannot be infringed by the State" (388 U.S. at 12).

The Supreme Court affirmed in *Loving* that marital choice was among those personal and private decisions that the individual had the freedom to make without unwanted and unwarranted governmental interference. But it did not imply then, or has it since, that all or even most restrictions on marriage were unacceptable. Although decided almost a century earlier, *Reynolds v. United States* (98 U.S. 145; 1879) demonstrates well that the right to marry—fundamental or not—must sometimes yield to societal interests. Here the Supreme Court recognized the "evil consequences" that flowed from plural marriages when it sustained a territorial statute prohibiting polygamy (the condition of having more than one spouse at a time). Because the territorial legislative powers determined that monogamy (the condition of having one spouse at a time) was preferable to polygamy, and because this determination was widely shared by comparable legal systems and had a profound impact on society, the justices ruled that it was a *sufficient* assertion of public morality. Accordingly, Utah's interest in prohibiting polygamy was compelling enough to outweigh the individual's freedom to marry.

Just more than a decade after *Loving,* the Supreme Court reaffirmed the fundamental character of the right to marry when striking down a Wisconsin statute that denied parents who failed to meet child-support obligations the right to remarry without a court's permission. The constitutional question in *Zablocki v. Redhail* (434 U.S. 374; 1978)—whether a state could impinge upon the individual's choice of *whether* to marry—was thus significantly different than the issue before the Court in *Loving*—whether a state could impinge upon the individual's choice of *whom* to marry. The Court deemed the law a "serious intrusion" on the right to marry, absolutely preventing some from getting married and effectively coercing others into forgoing their right to marry. The justices made clear in *Zablocki* that marital choice was a function of constitutional privacy. "[I]t would make little sense to recognize a right of privacy with respect to other matters of family life and not with respect to the decision to enter the relationship that is the foundation of the family in our society," wrote Justice Thurgood Marshall (434 U.S. at 386). The opinion then equated marital rights with reproductive rights. If a woman who desired to marry had a fundamental right to seek an abortion of her expected child, or to bring the child into life to suffer the myriad social and economic disabilities that the status of illegitimacy brought, surely the decision to marry and raise the child in a traditional family setting had to receive equivalent constitutional protection. And because Wisconsin prohibited sexual relations outside of marriage, the right to procreation had to imply some right to enter the only relationship where those relations legally could take place. The characterization of marriage as a constitutional right was reaffirmed more recently in *Turner v. Safley* (482 U.S. 78; 1987), in which a unanimous Supreme Court struck down a Missouri statute that prohibited most marriages involving prison inmates as impermissibly burdening a fundamental liberty.

The Supreme Court's declarations notwithstanding, the fundamental right to marry does not confer upon the individual the prerogative to marry whomever he or she wishes. At present, all states ban polygamy, require that a previously married person be legally released from a marital relationship either by death, divorce, or annulment prior to entering into a new marital relationship, and prohibit marriages involving children (typically younger than sixteen or eighteen years of age). Most states also require blood tests and good mental capacity as preconditions for marriage and that the participants are not close blood relatives. Forty-nine of the fifty states refuse to recognize same-sex marriages.

Two challenges remain in this area of constitutional privacy: polygamy and same-sex marriage. Immigrants to the United States, many arriving from nations where polygamy is commonplace and traditional, have expressed concerns about the legal nonrecognition of plural marriages. Those who desire multiple spouses fear that they will be unable to follow their traditions; those with multiple spouses, obviously, have much greater fears. And support for same-sex marriage appears to be gaining political and legal momentum. These two challenges to traditional marriage laws will be discussed in more detail in Chapter 4.

Divorce. A *divorce* is a legal dissolution of marriage, which results in both parties becoming single again. Like marriage, divorce is chiefly regulated by the states. Historically, states required proof by the requesting party that the spouse had committed some act—adultery or physical abuse, for example—sufficient to warrant the termination of the union. In 1969, California became the first state to adopt a no-fault divorce rule, which by the mid-1980s had become the national norm. (In a *no-fault divorce,* the parties are not required to prove fault or grounds for divorce beyond the showing of irretrievable breakdown of marriage or irreconcilable differences.)

If a state law could not unduly burden the fundamental right to marry (as *Loving, Zablocki,* and *Turner* held), it appears logical that such a rule should be similarly applied to restrictions on divorce. That was the issue before the Supreme Court in *Boddie v. Connecticut* (401 U.S. 371; 1971), a challenge to a Connecticut law that required payment of court costs prior to obtaining a divorce. The average cost for bringing an action for divorce was $60, which effectively prevented some indigent persons from obtaining a divorce. The Court found the denial of access a violation of due process rights. "Given the basic position of the marriage relationship in this society's hierarchy of values and the concomitant state monopolization of the means for legally dissolving this relationship," wrote Justice John Marshall Harlan, it was imperative that access to courts for individuals seeking a divorce be unimpeded (401 U.S. at 374). The opinion then equated, from a constitutional perspective, the right to a divorce with the right to marry. Because both were "precondition[s] to the adjustment of a fundamental human relationship," both deserved constitutional protection (401 U.S. at 383).

As with marriage, constitutional protection for divorce does not translate into the absence of state regulations on divorce. The Supreme Court has held that states may regulate divorce in reasonable ways. In *Sousna v. Iowa* (419 U.S. 393; 1975), for example, the justices sustained a one-year residency requirement as a precondition to obtaining a divorce. The majority distinguished this case from *Boddie* in two ways. First, Iowa had a reasonable interest in not becoming a "divorce mill for unhappy spouses" (whereas Connecticut had no reasonable interest for its statute). Second, the Iowa durational residency requirement did not irretrievably foreclose access to a divorce but only temporarily delayed such access (whereas Connecticut's filing fee might "exclude forever" a certain segment of the population from obtaining a divorce in the courts of Connecticut).

Rearing and Educating Children

One of the earliest cases to test the limits of public interference with private decisionmaking came in *Meyer v. Nebraska* (262 U.S. 390; 1923), a challenge to a Nebraska law that prohibited the teaching of any "modern" foreign language to schoolchildren who had not reached the ninth grade. The statute was sparked by anti-German sentiment during World War I, and its obvious purpose was to make English the mother tongue of all children educated in the state. Robert Meyer, a parochial school instructor, was convicted of teaching German to a child of ten. The Nebraska Supreme Court upheld the conviction, noting that to permit foreigners to read and educate their children in the language of their native land was "inimical to our own safety. . . . [It] was to educate them so that they must always think in that language, and, as a consequence, naturally inculcate in them the ideas and sentiments foreign to the best interests of this country" (quoted in *Meyer,* 262 U.S. at 398).

It was argued before the U.S. Supreme Court that the purpose of the statute was to promote "civic development." By "inhibiting . . . education of the immature in foreign tongues and ideals," students could learn English and acquire the preferable American ideals. In an opinion written by Justice James McReynolds, the Court rejected that argument and declared the statute outside of the competency of the state, noting that the individual had certain fundamental rights that had to be respected. The source of those fundamental rights was the Due Process Clause of the Fourteenth Amendment, which included rights of autonomous, private decisionmaking. The "liberty" protected by the Fourteenth Amendment

> denotes not merely freedom from bodily restraint but also the right of the individual to contract, to engage in any of the common occupations of life, to acquire useful knowledge, to marry, to establish a home and bring up children, to worship God according to the dictates of his own conscience, and generally to enjoy those privileges long recognized at common law as essential to the orderly pursuit of happiness of free men. (262 U.S. at 399)

Although the state had broad latitude "to improve the quality of its citizens, physically, mentally, and morally," certain policies—even "highly advantageous" ones—could not be coerced (262 U.S. at 401).

Pierce v. Society of Sisters (268 U.S. 510; 1925), though decided two years later, is perceived by many to be a companion case to *Meyer;* rarely is one mentioned without the other in the academic literature. In *Pierce,* the Supreme Court invalidated a state statute, motivated in part by anti-Catholic animus, that prohibited private elementary schooling, thus requiring all children between the ages of eight and sixteen to attend public schools. The state argued that the law was necessary to guarantee all students a basic education void of religious indoctrination and to prevent the teaching of disloyalty and subversive radicalism and bolshevism. The unanimous Court, once again per Justice McReynolds, disagreed, holding that the law interfered with the rights of parents and guardians to direct the upbringing and education of their children, subject only to *valid* regulations. For example, it was appropriate for the state to compel attendance at some school, to ensure that certain subjects "plainly essential to good citizenship" are taught, and to prohibit instruction "manifestly inimical to the public welfare." But the

> fundamental theory of liberty upon which all governments in this Union repose excludes any general power of the State to standardize its children by forcing them to accept instruction from public teachers only. The child is not the mere creature of the State; those who nurture him and direct his destiny have the right, coupled with the high duty, to recognize and prepare him for additional obligations. (268 U.S. at 535)

Meyer and *Pierce* imposed upon state legislative majorities "a duty not to preempt choices better left within the less centralized decision-making processes of children, their families, and occasionally their teachers" (Tribe 1988, 1318). In short, the Supreme Court interpreted the Constitution to protect the freedom of teachers to practice their profession and the rights of parents and guardians to direct the upbringing of the children under their control. Accordingly, a parent's decision concerning the manner in which his or her child was to be educated was a proper exercise of familial rights and responsibilities.

Meyer and *Pierce* are the first cases to hold that the Due Process Clause of the Fourteenth Amendment protected certain noneconomic aspects of individual autonomy. Prior to this time, substantive due process was primarily confined to the protection of economic liberties. These cases are thus appropriately viewed as denoting the emergence of a new branch of substantive due process, one that surfaced fully four decades later as an important precedent for constitutional privacy. Read together, *Meyer* and *Pierce* are the true progenitors of the privacy decisions. They demarcate limitations on governmental power to intrude upon matters affecting fundamental rights. The cardinal principle animating *Meyer* and *Pierce* was thus the "right to be let alone." Some decisions are simply better made *without* government. These two cases should not be interpreted as erecting impenetrable barriers to governmental regulation of public and private educational institutions, however. In *Runyon v. McCrary* (427 U.S. 160; 1976), for example, the Supreme Court upheld a federal law that prohibited private schools from denying admission to qualified children solely because of race. Although parents had a constitutional right to send their children to private schools, that constitutional right could be limited by overriding governmental concerns, in this case, racial equality.

Constitutional protection for family privacy was reinforced two decades after *Pierce* in *Prince v. Massachusetts* (321 U.S. 158; 1944). Though recognizing that the family was not beyond regulation, the majority opinion was unequivocal in its support of family privacy. "It is cardinal with us that the custody, care and nurture of the child reside first in the parents," wrote Justice Wiley Rutledge. "And it is in recognition of this that these decisions [*Meyer* and *Pierce*] have respected the private realm of family life which the state cannot enter" (321 U.S. at 166). As with other liberties, family life could be regulated, but only with substantial justification. For example, the state, seeking to protect the general welfare of the child, could compel school attendance, regulate child labor, and require certain vaccinations. Not even a parent had the liberty to expose the community or the child to communicable disease or the latter to ill health or death.

More recently, the Supreme Court reaffirmed the right of parents to direct the upbringing of their children in *Troxel v. Granville* (530 U.S. 57; 2000). Here, the Court struck down a Washington law that allowed a judge to order child visitation rights to grandparents against the wishes of the child's parents. Writing for a plurality, Justice O'Connor stated that the "liberty interest at issue in this case—the interests of parents in the care, custody, and control of their children—is perhaps the oldest of the fundamental liberty interests recognized by this Court" (530 U.S. at 65).

Maintaining Family Ties

As the previous cases indicate, the Supreme Court has long recognized the fundamental right of parents to make decisions concerning the care, custody, and control of their children. In *Stanley v. Illinois* (405 U.S. 645; 1972), the justices held that an unwed father had a privacy interest in the children he had sired and raised. *Stanley* was a challenge to an Illinois law, under which the children of unmarried fathers, upon the death of the mother, were declared wards of the state without any hearing on parental fitness and without proof of neglect. A hearing on parental fitness and proof of neglect were required before the state assumed custody of children of married or divorced parents and unmarried mothers. Joan and Peter Stanley lived together for eighteen years, during which time they had three children. When Joan Stanley died, the three children were placed in the custody of court-appointed guardians, though there was nothing in the record to indicate Peter Stanley had been an unfit parent. The justices invalidated the law, noting that the privacy interest "undeniably" deserved deference and, absent a more powerful countervailing interest, constitutional protection. The state could not, consistent with the Due Process Clause of the Fourteenth Amendment, automatically destroy the custodial relationship by assuming that unmarried fathers were unsuitable and neglectful parents. Because the issue at stake was "the dismemberment of his family," Peter Stanley was entitled to a hearing on his fitness as a parent before his children were taken from him (405 U.S. at 658).

Stanley was initially understood as establishing that biological fatherhood created a constitutionally protected privacy interest in a relationship with a child. Only eleven years later, however, the Supreme Court in *Lehr v. Robertson* (463 U.S. 248; 1983) upheld a New York provision that denied notice and opportunity to be heard to a father who had never had any significant custodial, personal, or financial relationship with his child. Read together, *Stanley* and *Lehr* appeared to establish that biological fatherhood *and* an established parental relationship created a constitutionally protected privacy interest in a relationship with a child.

But *Michael H. v. Gerald D.* (491 U.S. 110; 1989) clarified that such an assumption was not wholly accurate. Here, a father with a significant relationship to his child was denied *any* paternal rights, including visitation, because the child's mother was married to another man at the time of conception and birth. There was "no merit" to the father's claim that he had a constitutionally protected liberty interest in the parental relationship he had established with his child, wrote Justice Scalia, because paternal rights between the biological father and his child *in these circumstances* had not traditionally been accorded special protection. To the contrary, the plurality concluded, "our traditions have protected the marital family" (491 U.S. at 124).

Dissenters in *Michael H.* criticized the majority for several reasons. First, the Court relied far too heavily upon tradition. In drawing the conclusion that the Fourteenth Amendment offered shelter only to those interests specifically protected by historical practice, the plurality ignored the fact that we are "not an assimilative, homogenous society, but a facilitative, pluralistic one.... Even if we can agree ... that 'family' and 'parenthood' are part of the good life, it is absurd to assume that we can agree on the content of those terms and destructive to pretend that we do," wrote Justice William Brennan (491 U.S. at 141). Second, the opinion failed to concede that the search for tradition was a subjective one. For example, to support its conclusion (i.e., that this particular type of relationship had never been accorded constitutional protection), the plurality cited only English legal treatises and the *American Law Reports,* ignoring the equally important common law. Moreover, reasonable people often disagreed about the content of a particular tradition. And third, even if a consensus could be reached with respect to particular traditions, *Michael H.* erred by not identifying an objective standard by which to determine when a particular nontraditional interest earned constitutional protection. Traditions and history aside, dissenters alleged that a father's biological link to his child, when coupled with a substantial parent-child relationship, was sufficient to guarantee the father a liberty interest with the child.

Read collectively, *Stanley, Lehr,* and *Michael H.* stand for the proposition that biological fatherhood *and* an established parental relationship establish a constitutionally protected privacy interest in a relationship with a child, as long as the mother of the child is not in a traditional marital relationship with another man at the time of conception and birth.

The privacy interest between foster parent and child, however, is less protected. The issue in *Smith v. Organization for Foster Families for Equality and Reform* (431 U.S. 816; 1977) was whether a New York state regulation establishing the procedures for the removal of foster children violated the Fourteenth Amendment's "right to familial privacy." The Supreme Court sustained the regulation. Although affirming that biological relationships were not the sole determination of the existence of a family, the justices held that recognition of a privacy interest in relationships between foster parent and child did *not* require that foster families be treated as fully equivalent to biological families. Because the natural family had its origins entirely apart from the power of the state, its privacy was based upon intrinsic human rights. The foster family, by contrast, had its origins in state law and contractual arrangements: the state had been a partner in the foster family arrangement "from the outset" (431 U.S. at 845).

The holding in *Smith*—that family privacy inheres more in the natural family than in the foster family—has broad implications in the area of adoption. In 1977, Florida became the first state to ban adoption by gay or lesbian couples. Recently, that statute was challenged as violative of the constitutional rights to family privacy, intimate association, and family integrity. This topic will be discussed in more detail in Chapter 4.

Family Living Arrangements

A claim to constitutional privacy has also been invoked in challenges to regulations governing residential occupancy. In *Moore v. City of East Cleveland* (431 U.S. 494; 1977), the Supreme Court invalidated a city housing ordinance that essentially limited the occupancy of any dwelling to members of the same nuclear family. Inez Moore, a grandmother, was convicted of violating the ordinance and sentenced to five days in jail and fined $25. Her "crime" was having lived with her son and two grandsons, one of whom came to live with her following his mother's death. (The two grandsons were first cousins; had they been brothers the ordinance would not have been violated.)

Writing for a plurality, Justice Powell treated as fundamental the freedom of personal choice in matters of family living arrangements. Numerous decisions had taught that the Constitution protected the family precisely because the institution of the family was so deeply rooted in our history and tradition. That tradition was in no way limited to respect for the members of the nuclear family but included the sharing of a household with uncles, aunts, cousins, and especially grandparents. The city of East Cleveland could not "standardize its children—and its adults—by forcing all to live in certain narrowly defined family patterns." The history and tradition of the nation—what Justice Powell called the "accumulated wisdom of civilization"—compelled a larger conception of the family (431 U.S. at 505). Interestingly, however, the plurality opinion did not rely specifically upon the constitutional right to privacy but rather upon "the sanctity of the family" and "the basic values that underlie our society."

Justice Stewart said it well when he remarked in *Parham v. J.R.* (442 U.S. 584, 624–625; 1979) that "issues involving the family . . . are among the most difficult that courts have to face." The family is an integral part of our constitutional system and its sanctity long embedded in our legal traditions. One is hard-pressed to contrive a principle more important to our society. This principle suggests correctly that any governmental decision to control the basic functions of the family is constitutionally suspect. The Supreme Court has affirmed this position time and time again in the twentieth century. It did so when it struck down state laws prohibiting instruction in foreign languages and private education, recognizing that parents are the ones primarily responsible for the care, custody, and control of their children. It did so again when it held that marital rights were vital personal rights essential to the orderly pursuit of happiness, so fundamental that states could not ban interracial marriages or place financial obstacles in the paths of couples seeking to be married or divorced. The sanctity of the family was the central factor as well in decisions affirming the right of biological fathers to maintain relationships with their children and of extended families to live together. These and other decisions illustrate well that the family has traditionally enjoyed special status under the Constitution. The U.S. judiciary has long recognized that freedom of personal choice in matters of family life is one of the liberties protected by the constitutional right to privacy and the Due Process Clause of the Fourteenth Amendment.

SEXUAL AUTONOMY

By the end of the 1970s the Supreme Court had held that numerous liberty interests were included within the constitutional right to privacy. Although many of those related to sexual relations, the justices had never answered the question of whether that general right included the right to have sexual relations and, if so, what kind of sexual relations. Legal scholars were divided over whether *Griswold* and *Eisenstadt* conferred such a right upon the people. Some (Hafen 1983; Grey 1980) have pointed out that *Griswold* and *Eisenstadt* were not really about sexual relations per se but rather about preventing conception and controlling a family. The right to *prevent* conception, they argued, was not tantamount to the right to *cause* conception. Neither should the right to have and control a family be interpreted as the right to have sexual relations.

Others have interpreted *Griswold* and *Eisenstadt* together as protecting the right of all persons to receive *and* use contraceptives. After all, what good was a constitutional right to receive contraceptives if unable to use them? Surely, if married and unmarried individuals could purchase contraceptives, they could use them in the privacy of their home without governmental interference. This logic proved persuasive to the New Jersey Supreme Court when it struck down an antifornication statute, as applied to consensual, noncommercial, heterosexual activity between adults. In *State v. Saunders* (381 A.2d 333; [N.J. 1977]), the court opined that it would be ridiculous to conclude that the right to privacy protected the right to receive contraceptives but not the right to have sexual relations. The court also noted that procreation was a fundamental right. Without the right to have sexual relations, procreation was a virtual impossibility.

The absence of guidance from the U.S. Supreme Court on whether the right to privacy included the right to have sexual relations and, if so, what kind of sexual relations has prompted diverse and often contrasting holdings among lower state courts. This is especially true when dealing with statutes prohibiting sodomy (typically defined as oral or anal copulation). Some state courts have recognized sodomy rights, whereas others have upheld antisodomy statutes, and some holdings have been dependent upon the marital status of the participants. For example, the Iowa Supreme Court, in *State v. Pilcher* (242 N.W.2d 348, 359; [Iowa 1976]), invalidated an antisodomy statute as an invasion of fundamental rights, including the personal right to privacy. That court ruled that Iowa had no compelling state interest in "the manner of sexual relations performed in private between consenting adults of the opposite sex not married to each other." The court did not address the issue of private sex between homosexuals, however. Two state supreme courts declared all sodomy laws unconstitutional regardless of their application to heterosexuals or homosexuals. The Pennsylvania Supreme Court held that to regulate the private sexual conduct of consenting adults was beyond the power of the state in *Commonwealth v. Bonadio* (415 A.2d 47; [Pa. 1980]). In *People v. Onofre* (415 N.E.2d 936; [N.Y. 1980]), the Court of Appeals in New York, the highest court in that state, declared violative of the right to privacy a state law criminalizing sodomy. The state argued that *Griswold* protected "marital intimacy" and "procreative choice" but not sexual relations. The court disagreed, concluding that adults could seek sexual gratification from what "at least once was commonly regarded as 'deviant' conduct," as long as the decision to participate was voluntary and the activity occurred in a private setting (415 N.E.2d at 940).

By contrast, the Arizona Supreme Court concluded that the right to privacy did not give unmarried heterosexual adults the right to perform "unnatural copulation." *State v. Bateman* (547 P.2d 6; [Ariz. 1976]) clarified, though, that similar activity conducted by married persons could not be criminalized. Appellate courts in North Carolina and Rhode Island reached similar conclusions in *State v. Poe* (252 S.E.2d 843; [N.C. App. 1979]) and *State v. Santos* (413 A.2d 58; [R.I. 1980]).

When a Virginia statute making sodomy a crime was challenged in *federal* court as a denial of constitutional privacy, a lower federal court rejected the challenge, concluding that the statute did not offend either the U.S. Constitution or the Bill of Rights. In *Doe v. Commonwealth's Attorney* (425 U.S. 901; 1976), the Supreme Court summarily affirmed the lower court's decision. (A *summary decision* is rendered when the Supreme Court does not hear oral argument or give full consideration to a case yet wants either to affirm or to reverse a lower court ruling. Although such decisions allow the Court to reduce its workload, they also bring about confusion, for the Court has held that summarily decided cases do not have the same precedential weight as *plenary cases,* which are decided after full consideration.) Because *Doe* was a summary decision, it was not conclusive in settling the constitutionality of criminal laws proscribing sodomy. The Supreme Court avoided directly ruling on claims that constitutional privacy included private, consensual, adult sexual relations until a decade later.

Bowers v. Hardwick (476 U.S. 186; 1986), discussed in brief at the beginning of this book, was a challenge to a Georgia statute criminalizing sodomy. Michael Hardwick, a sexually active homosexual, was arrested in his bedroom for committing sodomy. Although the state chose not to prosecute, Hardwick challenged the constitutionality of the act, claiming that he was in imminent danger of arrest for his lifestyle. On the basis of *Doe,* the federal district court dismissed the challenge. The U.S. Court of Appeals for the Eleventh Circuit, however, reversed, asserting that private sexual activity between consenting adults was immune from state proscription under the Ninth Amendment and the Due Process Clause of the Fourteenth Amendment. The judges rejected the lower court's reliance on *Doe,* claiming that because it was summarily decided it was not binding precedent; it also noted that no Supreme Court precedent denied constitutional protection to consensual sexual behavior between consenting adults.

In a 5-4 decision, the Supreme Court reversed the decision of the Eleventh Circuit and upheld the Georgia statute. The crux of the majority opinion, announced by Justice White, can be stated in four conclusions. First, prior right-to-privacy cases could not be construed to confer a fundamental right to homosexual sodomy. None of the privacy rights announced in those cases—procreation, marriage, and family life—bore any resemblance to homosexual sodomy. Thus, *Griswold,* its antecedents, and its progeny could not be used to infer constitutional protection for all consensual sexual relations.

Second, homosexual sodomy was not a fundamental right. To be characterized as fundamental, and thus to qualify for heightened judicial scrutiny, a right had to be either "implicit in the concept of ordered liberty" or "deeply rooted in our Nation's history and tradition." Homosexual sodomy was neither; it had been a crime throughout our nation's history. At the time of ratification of the Bill of Rights, the laws of all thirteen states forbade sodomy. When the Fourteenth Amendment was ratified, thirty-two of the thirty-seven states criminalized sodomy. By 1961, all fifty states proscribed sodomy; and twenty-four states and the District of Columbia currently do so. It was therefore "facetious" even to suggest that consensual private homosexual behavior amounted to an intimate association entitled to constitutional protection. Accordingly, the justices were not inclined "to take a more expansive view of our authority" to discover a new fundamental right located in the Due Process Clause. "The Court is most vulnerable and comes nearest to illegitimacy," Justice White warned, "when it deals with judge-made constitutional law having little or no cognizable roots in the language or design of the Constitution" (478 U.S. at 194).

Third, Hardwick's contention that the conduct should be afforded greater protection because it took place in the privacy of his home was unpersuasive. Illegal conduct could not always escape the law simply because that conduct occurred in the home. If that were the case, Justice White maintained, it would be difficult to prosecute adultery, incest, and other sexual crimes committed in the home. The justices saw no way, "except by fiat," to excuse the claimed right to homosexual conduct while leaving other serious crimes committed in the home exposed to prosecution (478 U.S. at 195–196).

Finally, the legislature's determination that homosexual sodomy was "immoral and unacceptable" was an adequate basis for the law. The majority noted that law was often based on notions of morality. And if the Due Process Clause invalidated all laws representing moral choices, the courts would "be very busy indeed" (478 U.S. at 196).

Chief Justice Burger wrote separately to reinforce the majority's finding that homosexuality was not a fundamental right. After citing Roman law, the English common law, and Sir William Blackstone, Chief Justice Burger concluded that to hold that homosexual conduct was protected as a fundamental right would be "to cast aside millennia of moral teaching" (478 U.S. at 197). Justice Powell concurred to note that, while there was no substantive right to engage in consensual sodomy, imposing a long prison sentence for "a single, private, consensual act of sodomy" might implicate the Eighth Amendment's prohibition against cruel and unusual punishments. Interestingly, Justice Powell, though casting the controlling vote in this case, publicly regretted his vote after his retirement from the bench.

In a blistering dissent, Justice Blackmun lambasted the majority for its "almost obsessive focus on homosexual activity" (478 U.S. at 200). Under the statute the sex and sexual orientation of the persons who committed the act were irrelevant. The Court, therefore, should have examined the statute as it applied to heterosexual sodomy as well. He also accused the majority of dismissing too readily Hardwick's privacy interests. Instead of relying upon history and tradition to determine fundamental rights, the justices should have examined more closely the underlying values of constitutional privacy. Constitutional privacy, he asserted, protected more than procreation, marriage, and family life; it also protected—indeed, chiefly protected—decisions that were central to an individual's life. Because sexual conduct was one way through which individuals defined themselves "in a significant way," it deserved constitutional protection. The dissent also took exception to the justification for the statute offered by Georgia. First, nothing in the record suggested that homosexual sodomy had any "adverse consequences" for the general health and welfare or was physically dangerous to those who participated in it. (Given the AIDS epidemic among the homosexual community today, it would be interesting to know whether Justice Blackmun, if alive, would still hold to this view.) Second, the historical belief that homosexual sodomy was immoral was insufficient to justify its proscription. His frustration evident, Justice Blackmun concluded: "depriving individuals of the right to choose for themselves how to conduct their intimate relationships poses a far greater threat to the values most deeply rooted in our nation's history than tolerance of nonconformity could ever do" (478 U.S. at 214).

Justice John Paul Stevens also dissented. The statute was unconstitutional for two reasons, he explained. First, the fact that a governing majority considered a practice to be immoral was not sufficient reason for upholding a law prohibiting the practice. If that were true, the Supreme Court should not have struck down the antimiscegenation law in *Loving* (1967). Second, the statute, because it was enforceable against married and unmarried persons, categorically proscribed sodomy in violation of the Due Process Clause. Prior cases made it abundantly clear that "individual decisions by married [and unmarried] persons . . . concerning the intimacies of their physical relationship" were protected under the rubric of constitutional privacy (478 U.S. at 216).

Hardwick, without question, represented a considerable narrowing of the privacy doctrine; some (e.g., Rubenfeld 1989, 747) speculated on the "dark days" ahead for constitutional privacy. That fear was motivated in part by the majority's edict that constitutional privacy was *strictly* limited to the traditional categories of private life—procreation, marriage, and family life. Many asserted that this conclusion was a disingenuous distortion of precedent and a complete reconceptualization of the right to privacy. In numerous cases, the Supreme Court had affirmed the fundamental nature and the accompanying constitutional protection of the individual's freedom to enter into and carry on intimate associations, whether married or unmarried. Yet here, because the intimacy was homosexual, the justices refused to extend constitutional protection. Critics suggested that by adopting such a formalistic approach—listing previously protected privacy rights and then concluding that the list was exhaustive—the justices ignored the underlying and more important values (recognized in earlier cases) of individual autonomy and freedom of choice in conducting intimate relationships. Laurence Tribe (1988, 1423), who represented Hardwick before the Supreme Court, complained that the *Hardwick* majority treated *Griswold* and *Eisenstadt* as if they involved "the right to buy and use a particular pharmaceutical product, rather than the right to engage in sexual intimacy as such." The gist of this criticism is that the majority failed to define constitutional privacy at a high enough level of generality. Instead of asking whether oral sex among homosexuals had traditionally enjoyed constitutional protection, the justices should have asked whether private sexual conduct between consenting adults was included within the traditionally revered liberties of intimate association and individual autonomy. Tribe (1988, 1428) concluded that if the judicial inquiry were shifted from particular proscribed acts (and the homosexuals who engaged in them) to the more important value of sexual intimacy between consenting adults, it would be obvious that the proscriptions infringed upon fundamental liberties. The relevant question, therefore, was not "what Michael Hardwick was doing in the privacy of his own bedroom, but what the State of Georgia was doing there."

The criticisms notwithstanding, *Hardwick* may not be as detrimental to constitutional privacy as initially feared by some. Quite obviously, *Hardwick* appealed to the justices' pragmatism: if the Supreme Court granted this right, it would be hard-pressed to draw the line on other proscribed conduct—illegal drug use, for example—that occurred in the privacy of the home. In addition, because of the majority's "almost obsessive focus on homosexual activity," *Hardwick* should not be interpreted as rejecting all sexual privacy claims arising out of nonprocreative sex between consenting adults. During oral argument in *Hardwick,* the attorney general of Georgia, who argued in favor of the antisodomy statute, concluded it would be unconstitutional to enforce it against married couples. Yet because the majority framed the issue narrowly—the right of homosexuals to engage in sodomy—*Hardwick* left uncertain private, consensual sodomy between married and unmarried heterosexuals. After *Hardwick,* however, the Supreme Court denied a request for certiorari in *Post v. State* (715 P. 1105; [Okla. 1986]), a decision of the Oklahoma Supreme Court of Criminal Appeals striking down a statute that prohibited sodomy between consenting adult heterosexuals. (*Certiorari* is the primary method by which the Supreme Court accepts a case for its review.) Presumably, if the justices had wanted to settle the issue of consensual sodomy between heterosexuals, they could have done so in this case, although it is doubtful the justices could have done so by relying on *Hardwick* alone. Although homosexual sodomy (the issue in *Hardwick*) bore no resemblance to the traditional categories of privacy—procreation, marriage, and family life—heterosexual sodomy (the issue in *Post*), at least between spouses, clearly implicated marriage. In addition, the *Hardwick* opinion referenced repeatedly "ancient prohibitions" against homosexual sodomy, not ancient prohibitions against heterosexual sodomy.

Thus, in spite of *Hardwick,* it is still not clear what sexual activity between consenting adults is included under the rubric of constitutional privacy. Traditional sex within a marriage (*Griswold*) and traditional heterosexual sex outside of a marriage (*Eisenstadt*) are clearly protected. What good is a constitutional right to receive contraception if you cannot use it? (Prisoners have often alleged that because married and unmarried persons have a fundamental right to privacy in their sexual relations, they should be permitted physical intimacy with their spouses or lovers. Conjugal visitation and the right to privacy will be discussed in Chapter 4.) Heterosexual sodomy performed by married adults (*Hardwick*'s almost obsessive focus on homosexual sodomy) or unmarried adults (denial of certiorari in *Post v. State*) is apparently protected. And homosexual sodomy performed by adults (*Hardwick*) is not protected by the U.S. Constitution, although some state supreme courts have been willing to extend protection to this conduct as a matter of state constitutional law. For example, in *Commonwealth of Kentucky v. Wasson* (842 S.W.2d 487; [Ky. 1992]), the Kentucky Supreme Court held that the state constitution offered greater protection of the right to privacy than the U.S. Constitution in striking down a state law against homosexual sodomy. More recently, in *Powell v. State* (510 S.E.2d 18; [Ga. 1998]), the Georgia Supreme Court invalidated a criminal sodomy statute on state-law privacy grounds. The court concluded that the right to be let alone guaranteed by the Georgia constitution was far more extensive than the right to privacy protected by the U.S. Constitution: "Adults who withdraw from the public gaze to engage in private consensual sexual behavior are exercising a right . . . at the heart of the Georgia Constitution's protection of the right of privacy" (510 S.E.2d at 24).

Personal Autonomy

Although not relying per se on the doctrine of constitutional privacy, the Supreme Court has held that certain other personal liberty interests, each of which invokes values of privacy, are worthy of constitutional protection. For example, in *Stanley v. Georgia* (394 U.S. 557; 1969), a unanimous Supreme Court decided that a state could not punish the mere private possession of obscene material in the home. Robert Stanley was charged with violating a Georgia statute that made it a crime to possess obscene material. When legally searching his home for evidence of bookmaking activities, police discovered in a desk drawer in Stanley's bedroom numerous reels of film. A viewing revealed that the reels contained legally obscene material. Stanley was arrested and convicted. Relying heavily upon the language and logic of Justice Brandeis's dissenting opinion in *Olmstead,* Justice Thurgood Marshall's opinion for the majority held that the Constitution protected the right to receive information and ideas, regardless of their social worth, and to be generally free from "unwanted governmental intrusions into one's privacy" (394 U.S. at 564). Although the holding was certain, the basis for the holding was unclear. Different pluralities among the justices invoked different justifications. Read together, three constitutional rights—freedom of speech, freedom from unreasonable searches and seizures, *and* the right to privacy—prohibited the state from criminalizing the private possession of obscene materials.

Not all privacy-related interests have received constitutional protection. The efforts of states to regulate personal appearance are especially noteworthy. In hundreds of cases over the last forty years, individuals have challenged regulations pertaining to personal appearance. The plaintiffs have included high school and college students, teachers, national guardsmen, active military personnel, reservists, prisoners, probation officers, policemen, firemen, and attorneys. *Kelley v. Johnson* (425 U.S. 238; 1976) involved a challenge to a police department regulation directed at personal grooming, under which the style and length of hair, sideburns, and mustaches were limited and beards and goatees were prohibited except for medical reasons. A police officer challenged the regulations as violative of the guarantees of due process. Concluding that the liberty interest claimed here involved no substantial infringement on the individual's freedom of choice with respect to procreation, marriage, or family life, the Supreme Court upheld the regulations. None of the privacy cases—not *Meyer* or *Griswold* or *Eisenstadt* or *Roe*—even so much as hinted that the citizenry had some sort of liberty interest in personal appearance, Justice Rehnquist concluded. Justices Brennan and Marshall dissented: to say that the liberty guaranteed by the Fourteenth Amendment did not safeguard personal appearance was "fundamentally inconsistent" with the values of privacy, self-identity, and autonomy that the Constitution was designed to secure.

Even though efforts to legalize marijuana and other drugs for medical purposes have been successful in a number of states, courts have generally rejected the argument that the right to privacy includes the right to possess and use illegal drugs, even for medical purposes. In *Ravin v. State* (537 P.2d 494; [Alaska 1975]), however, the Alaska Supreme Court held that the right to privacy under both the federal and state constitutions protected the possession of small quantities of marijuana for personal, private use by adults in their homes. Even if the U.S. Supreme Court were to declare that constitutional privacy did not encompass the private use of certain drugs, a state supreme decision to the contrary would still be valid because a state supreme court is the definitive interpreter of the state constitution.

Conclusion

The twentieth century witnessed the formal emergence of the constitutional right to privacy in U.S. jurisprudence. From the earliest calls for its recognition in the late nineteenth century, the constitutional right to privacy gradually evolved to mean the right of the individual to be free from unwanted and unwarranted governmental intrusion in matters affecting fundamental rights. By the 1940s, the Supreme Court had acknowledged the privacy interests inherent in exercising such fundamental rights as rearing and educating children and procreation. Those decisions paved the way for the Court's eventual declaration of a new constitutional right in 1965. Though there was considerable discord within the Court as to the source and definition of that new constitutional right, *Griswold* nevertheless specifically recognized an independent and fundamental right to privacy under the U.S. Constitution. Because *Griswold* failed to articulate what specific rights (other than the right of married couples to use contraceptive devices) were to be included under the umbrella of privacy, the justices spent much of the remainder of the twentieth century debating that matter.

Notwithstanding serious disagreements among the justices, the Supreme Court went on to expand constitutional privacy to protect the right of individuals to marry outside of their own race; the right of single persons to receive contraceptives; the right of a pregnant mother to abort her unborn child prior to viability, subject to reasonable regulations; the right of indigents to marry and divorce, even if they cannot afford to pay required fees; the right of widowed fathers to retain custody of their children; and the right to live with relatives, among other rights. From those declarations, a consensus emerged: constitutional privacy protected the right of the individual to be let alone in matters affecting procreation, marriage, and family life. The future of privacy rights remained uncertain, however, when, in 1986, the Court declined to extend constitutional privacy to include the right of consenting adults to engage in homosexual sodomy. The following decade, in separate cases (to be discussed in Chapter 4), the justices similarly refused to make the decision to terminate life-sustaining medical treatment or the decision to obtain assistance from a physician for the purposes of ending life constitutional privacy rights, although in the latter case a majority indicated that it might be willing to do so under different circumstances. The status of the right-to-die claim, therefore, remains unsettled.

The privacy doctrine has been assailed both by opponents and proponents of constitutional privacy. On the one hand, the justices faced criticism for their intolerable assumption of complete governing power and its resulting extension of constitutional protection to certain allegedly immoral activities—most notably abortion, but also miscegenation and fornication. This inflation of enumerated rights and the creation of unenumerated rights deprived states of their proper authority to regulate the lives of their citizens in reasonable ways, opponents maintained. On the other hand, the justices engendered criticism for their steadfast allegiance to orthodoxy—procreation, marriage, and family life—as the determining factor in defining the limits of constitutional privacy. Proponents complained that this excessive reliance upon history and tradition resulted in a privacy doctrine that failed to protect adequately certain important autonomy interests.

REFERENCES AND FURTHER READING

Berger, Raoul. 1980. "The Ninth Amendment." *Cornell Law Review* 66: 1–26.

Bork, Robert H. 1971. "Neutral Principles and Some First Amendment Problems." *Indiana Law Journal* 47: 1–35.

Clines, Francis X. 1983. "Reagan Urges Congress to Nullify Supreme Court's Abortion Rulings." *New York Times,* June 16, at A16.

Craig, Barbara Hinkson, and David M. O'Brien. 1993. *Abortion and American Politics.* Chattam, NJ: Chattam House Publishers.

Dixon, Robert G., Jr. 1976. "The 'New' Substantive Due Process and the Democratic Ethic: A Prolegomenon." *Brigham Young University Law Review* 1976: 43–88.

Dunbar, Leslie. 1956. "James Madison and the Ninth Amendment." *Virginia Law Review* 42: 627–643.

Ely, John Hart. 1973. "The Wages of Crying Wolf: A Comment on *Roe v. Wade.*" *Yale Law Review* 82: 920–949.

Fairman, Charles. 1949. "Does the Fourteenth Amendment Incorporate the Bill of Rights?" *Stanford Law Review* 2: 5–139.

Garrow, David J. 1994. *Liberty and Sexuality: The Right to Privacy and the Making of* Roe v. Wade. New York: Macmillan Publishing.

Ginsburg, Ruth Bader. 1985. "Some Thoughts on Autonomy and Equality in Relation to *Roe v. Wade.*" *North Carolina Law Review* 63: 375–386.

Greenhouse, Linda. 1989. "Supreme Court, 5-4, Narrowing *Roe v. Wade,* Upholds Sharp State Limits on Abortions." *New York Times,* July 4, at A1.

Grey, Thomas. 1980. "Eros, Civilization, and the Burger Court." *Law and Contemporary Problems* 43: 83–100.

Grossberg, Michael. 1985. *Governing the Hearth: Law and Family in Nineteenth Century America.* Chapel Hill: University of North Carolina Press.

Hafen, Bruce. 1983. "The Constitutional Status of Marriage, Kinship, and Sexual Privacy—Balancing the Individual and Social Interests." *Michigan Law Review* 81: 463–574.

Heymann, Philip B., and Douglas E. Barzelay. 1973. "The Forest and the Trees: *Roe v. Wade* and Its Critics." *Boston University Law Review* 53: 765–784.

Kamen, Al. 1989. "Supreme Court Restricts Right to Abortion, Giving States Wide Latitude for Regulation: 5-4 Ruling Stops Short of Overturning *Roe.*" *Washington Post,* July 4, at A1.

Kauper, Paul C. 1965. "Penumbras, Peripheries, Emanations, Things Fundamental, and Things Forgotten." *Michigan Law Review* 64: 235–258.

Keynes, Edward. 1996. *Liberty, Property, and Privacy.* University Park: Pennsylvania State University Press.

Koukoutchos, Brian S. 1985. "A No-Win Proposal on Abortion Rights." *New York Times,* July 25, at A23.

Lombardo, Paul A. 1985. "Three Generations, No Imbeciles: New Light on *Buck v. Bell.*" *New York Law Review* 60: 30–62.

MacKenzie, John P. 1991. "Whose Choice Is It, Anyway?" *New York Times,* January 28, at A22.

Minow, Martha. 1990. *Making All the Difference: Inclusion, Exclusion, and American Law.* Ithaca, NY: Cornell University Press.

O'Brien, David M. 1979. *Privacy, Law, and Public Policy.* New York: Praeger.

Rhode, Debra. 1989. *Justice and Gender: Sex Discrimination and the Law.* Cambridge, MA: Harvard University Press.

Richard, David A. J. 1986. *Toleration and the Constitution.* New York: Oxford University Press.

Rubenfeld, Jed. 1989. "The Right of Privacy." *Harvard Law Review* 102: 737–807.

Rubin, Alissa J. 2000. "Supreme Court Decisions; Ruling May Energize Abortion Foes." *New York Times,* June 29, at A12.

Shelly, Barbara. 1988. "Maternal Substance Abuse: The Next Step in the Protection of Fetal Rights." *Dickinson Law Review* 92: 691–715.

Strickman, Leonard P. 1982. "Marriage, Divorce, and the Constitution." *Family Law Quarterly* 15: 259–348.

Tribe, Laurence H. 1988. *American Constitutional Law.* 2d ed. New York: Foundation Press.

Turkington, Richard C., and Anita L. Allen. 1999. *Privacy Law.* St. Paul, MN: West Group.

Tushnet, Mark. 1991. "Two Notes on the Jurisprudence of Privacy." *Constitutional Commentary* 8: 75–85.

Wadlington, Walter. 1966. "The *Loving* Case: Virginia's Anti-Miscegenation Statute in Historical Perspective." *Virginia Law Review* 52: 1189–1223.

Weddington, Sarah. 1992. *A Question of Choice.* New York: G. P. Putnam's Sons.

Woodhouse, Barbara Bennett. 1992. "Who Owns the Child? *Meyer* and *Pierce* and the Child as Property." *William and Mary Law Review* 33: 995–1122.

4

The Twenty-first Century

In the twentieth century, the Supreme Court recognized that one of the liberties protected by the Bill of Rights and the Due Process Clause of the Fourteenth Amendment was the right to personal privacy. From child rearing, family life, and procreation in the first half of the century, to contraception in the 1960s, abortion in the 1970s, and homosexual sodomy in the 1980s, the High Court justices grappled with a variety of issues invoking the constitutional right to privacy. Although many of these privacy decisions acknowledged a liberty interest in one's independence in making certain kinds of important decisions, they did not mark clearly the outer limits of the right to privacy. Thus, new claims of constitutional privacy continue to confront the justices, and constitutional privacy remains a developing concept.

In the 1990s, the most prominent privacy claims related to the right to die. More recently, constitutional privacy has been invoked with respect to polygamy, reproductive rights for prison inmates, same-sex marriages, child adoption by gay and lesbian couples, and the use of sexually stimulating devices. In addition, informational privacy—the liberty interest in avoiding disclosure of personal matters—has become of much greater concern in the digital age.

THE RIGHT TO DIE

Death, and the manner in which it occurs, is an inherently complicated matter. Advances in medical technology have obfuscated certain legal concepts, most notably the traditional definition of *death.* Historically and until relatively recently, the criterion for death was the cessation of the functions of the heart and lungs. As recently as 1968, *Black's Law Dictionary* (4th ed. 1968) defined death as "the cessation of life; the ceasing to exist; defined by physicians as the total stoppage of the circulation of the blood." With no respiration, the brain would be deprived of oxygen, resulting in the death of all cognitive and conscious functions. Accordingly, the failure of the heart marked the onset of death. Today, however, the medical profession can sustain human life long after the heart and lungs cease to function properly on their own. Cardiopulmonary resuscitation (known as CPR), mechanical ventilation (respirators), hydration and nutrition supplementation (feeding tubes), and cardiac regulation (artificial pacemakers), for example, all prolong the lives of patients who would otherwise most certainly expire. These modern resuscitative and supportive measures dramatically increase the ability to control the circumstances and timing of death. And this is true even where there is no possibility of a patient regaining consciousness following severe brain damage, where the patient is capable of existing only in a persistent vegetative state. The dilemma presented by this last possibility—an individual living but in an irreversible coma—prompted an ad hoc committee of the Harvard University Medical School in 1968 to recommend that a person who had suffered irreversible loss of function of the brain be considered legally dead. All states have since adopted brain-death statutes, with many enacting, sometimes with variations, the Uniform Determination of Death Act definition: "An individual who has sustained either (1) irreversible cessation of circulatory and respiratory function, or (2) irreversible cessation of all functions of the entire brain, including the brain stem, is dead." This changing definition is reflected in subsequent editions of *Black's Law Dictionary.* The 1979 edition defined death as "the cessation of life; permanent cessations of all vital functions and signs" (5th ed. 1979); and the most recent edition (6th ed. 1990) acknowledged that many states have enacted statutory definitions of death that include brain-related criteria.

Euthanasia (literally, "a good or happy death") is the means of bringing about a gentle and easy death of a person suffering from an incurable and extremely painful disease. Since the 1970s, euthanasia has come to mean the implementation of any one of four specific practices: passive voluntary euthanasia, passive involuntary euthanasia, active voluntary euthanasia, and active involuntary euthanasia.

Passive voluntary euthanasia is hastening the death of a person, with that person's consent, by discontinuing artificial means of support. It is passive because it is permitting, not causing, an individual to die a natural death. It is voluntary because it occurs with the person's consent. Passive voluntary euthanasia differs significantly from suicide in that the patient is not taking his or her life but rather attempting to control the timing and manner of an impending death. Perhaps the most common form of this type of euthanasia is an elderly person requesting to have a respirator or feeding tube removed so as to bring about death.

Passive involuntary euthanasia is hastening the death of a person by discontinuing artificial means of support, but it occurs without the person's consent. Thus, it is involuntary. Family members often elect to discontinue artificial means of support for patients in a persistent vegetative state.

Active voluntary euthanasia is the willing participation of a person in direct action that will cause his or her death. It is active because it is causing, not simply permitting, death. It is voluntary because the person taking direct action does so willingly. Active voluntary euthanasia is so closely akin to suicide as to be practically indistinguishable. When the person seeking death requires assistance, it is known as *assisted suicide;* when that assistance comes from a medical doctor, it is known as *physician-assisted suicide.* In an assisted suicide, the assistant either directly brings about death (e.g., by injecting a terminally ill patient, upon his or her request, with controlled substances) or supplies the means of death (providing a prescription for a lethal dose of morphine, a supply of carbon monoxide and a facemask, or a machine that will deliver death-inducing medications when prompted) so that the patient can bring about his or her own death.

Active involuntary euthanasia, quite similar to homicide, is causing the death of a person who has not requested assistance in dying. Sometimes known as *mercy killing,* this type of euthanasia occurs when, for example, an elderly man kills his wife of many years, without her consent, to end her tremendous suffering from Alzheimer's disease or osteoporosis.

The right to die is thus about controlling the timing and manner of one's own death. More specifically, it is the right to refuse unwanted medical treatment or to have ongoing medical care withdrawn even though the refusal or withdrawal will most likely result in death; it is also the right to terminate one's own life or obtain assistance for the purposes of doing so. In recent decades, the right to die has generated significant political attention and legal action. Patients and their families, challenging the use of ever more sophisticated life-sustaining technology, have asserted a constitutional right to die a natural death. Others have alleged that the Fourteenth Amendment's guarantee of liberty protects the decision of a mentally competent, terminally ill adult to bring about impending death in a humane and dignified manner. In more than two hundred cases since the mid-1970s, courts have been asked to resolve disputes involving these and other issues. In those cases, judges have attempted to answer three questions. First, does the Constitution protect a competent individual in his or her decision to terminate life-prolonging medical treatment? Second, to what extent does the Constitution allow guardians or family members to decide whether to remove life-prolonging medical treatment for incompetent patients (defined as one who has an irreversible lack of decisionmaking capacity)? And third, in what circumstances, and by what means—if any—does a person have a constitutional right to suicide or assisted suicide? At present, courts have yet to be asked to cloak active involuntary euthanasia with constitutional protection. In answering these questions, courts have recognized that assertions of patient autonomy and self-determination invoke important constitutional principles such as the right to control one's body, the right to privacy, and liberty interests under the Due Process Clause. And judges have consistently distinguished between passive and active euthanasia.

Passive Euthanasia: Refusing or Terminating Life-Sustaining Medical Treatment

An examination of twentieth-century state court decisions on the right to refuse or terminate medical treatment reveals "a surprising degree of homogeneity" (Hoefler 1994, 156). Three common premises emerge from these decisions. First, state courts have long recognized that a competent patient has the common law right to make decisions about his or her medical care. Early in the twentieth century, Justice Benjamin Cardozo of the Court of Appeals of New York, the state's highest court, declared in *Schloendorff v. Society of New York Hospital* (105 N.E. 92, 93; [N.Y. 1914]) that "[e]very human being of adult years and sound mind has a right to determine what shall be done with his own body." This statement is often cited as the genesis of the common law's recognition of the patient's right to control the decisionmaking of the physician; today, the doctrine is commonly known as *informed consent.* Informed consent requires that the patient be fully informed of the risks and benefits of any medical intervention *and* agree to a particular medical treatment. The logical corollary of the doctrine of informed consent is the right not to consent. State courts have thus generally agreed that a competent patient has the right to refuse or terminate medical treatment, even if doing so will result in certain death.

Second, most state courts have extended rights to incompetent patients comparable to those rights possessed by competent patients through the doctrine of *substituted judgment.* In a case of substituted judgment, the person previously authorized by the patient, when competent, to give consent on behalf of the incompetent patient attempts to determine what the patient would have wanted done had the patient understood the circumstances. The third party's best guess as to the wishes of the incompetent patient is then substituted for the expressed wishes of the incompetent patient, which cannot be obtained. The purpose of substituted judgment is to respect the autonomy of the incompetent patient by enforcing his or her likely wishes regarding medical care. Substituted judgment is, of course, an imperfect way to effectuate an incompetent patient's rights of self-determination. Nevertheless, most state courts have held that an incompetent patient's wishes are decisive as long as those wishes were articulated (not necessarily in writing) when the patient was competent. Where the wishes of the incompetent patient are not known or unclear, state courts have often permitted family members or close friends to surmise how the patient would have decided; alternatively, they have relied upon what was in the patient's best interests, as defined by the court, the patient's family, or a guardian ad litem (an advocate appointed by the court to represent the best interests of a child or incompetent individual).

Third, some state courts have found that the right to refuse or withdraw medical treatment is protected under the U.S. Constitution, either as a liberty interest under the Fourteenth Amendment or as a right to privacy. The liberty guaranteed by the Fourteenth Amendment, some state courts have held, prevents a physician from invading a patient's body in any manner without informed consent. Given that constitutional privacy is broad enough to protect decisions concerning procreation, marriage, and family life, other state courts have concluded that similar protection should be afforded to decisions about death. The right to refuse or withdraw medical treatment, those courts maintain, thus properly belongs in one of the zones of privacy that are immune from governmental encroachment.

The American Medical Association (AMA) estimates that each year 10,000 Americans fall into irreversible comas (Kamen 1989, 31). In most of those situations, the family members and attending physician agree that further medical attention is unwarranted; the respirators and feeding tubes are removed, and the patient dies a natural death. In some situations, however, the physician or hospital, for a variety of reasons, refuses the request of the patient's family to withhold or withdraw all means of life-prolonging medical treatment. That was precisely the scenario faced by the family of Karen Quinlan, whose irreversible coma gave rise to *In re Quinlan* (355 A.2d 647; [N.J. 1976]), the best-known state case involving both the doctrine of substituted judgment and the inclusion of the right to refuse medical treatment under the rubric of constitutional privacy.

After swallowing large quantities of alcohol and tranquilizers, Karen Quinlan, twenty-one years of age, became permanently comatose, unable to breathe without a ventilator. Yet because her brain maintained certain neurological functions—body temperature, breathing, and heart rate, for example—she was not legally dead under New Jersey law. When it became evident that she would not regain consciousness, her parents asked that she be removed from the respirator. The attending physician, mindful of medical traditions and no doubt fearing criminal prosecution and civil liability, refused to accede to the wishes of the family. Quinlan's father then unsuccessfully sought permission from the New Jersey Superior Court to be named guardian of the person and property of his daughter with express power to authorize the discontinuance of all extraordinary medical procedures sustaining her life.

On appeal, however, the New Jersey Supreme Court held that the constitutional right to privacy was broad enough to encompass a patient's decision to terminate medical treatment under certain circumstances. Although accepting the state's asserted interest in preserving human life, the court nevertheless held that the state's interest had to be balanced against the patient's interest in ending her life. And as the patient's prognosis dimmed, the state's interests weakened; eventually, the patient's interest trumped the state's interest. In this case, though, because the patient was unable to assert her own privacy interest, the court determined that her father could do so on her behalf. "The only practical way to prevent destruction of the right is to permit the guardian and family . . . to render their best judgment . . . as to whether she would exercise it in these circumstances" (355 A.2d at 664). To prevent abuse of this substituted judgment, the court spelled out a specific procedure to be followed: if the physician concluded that there was no reasonable possibility of the patient ever emerging from the comatose condition to a cognitive, sapient state, then the physician should consult with a hospital ethics committee. If that committee agreed with the prognosis, then, upon the wishes of the guardian and family, the life-support system could be removed. (Interestingly, after Karen Quinlan was removed from the respirator, she lived for nine more years in a vegetative state. Her parents never requested that the artificial hydration and nutrition be discontinued.)

In re Quinlan stands for two propositions. First, constitutional privacy protects a patient's decision to refuse or withdraw life-prolonging medical treatment *under certain circumstances.* (Although this was not the specific issue here, the opinion was unequivocal on this point.) Second, constitutional privacy protects a guardian's or family's decision to authorize termination of such treatment for comatose patients *under certain circumstances.* Much like the constitutional right to abortion (discussed in Chapter 3), these rights are not absolute but rather must be balanced against legitimate state interests. Because *In re Quinlan* was a decision of the New Jersey Supreme Court, however, it established no national precedent.

Following *In re Quinlan,* state legislatures fashioned a patchwork of laws concerning the right to refuse medical treatment (Hoefler 1994, 161). These laws differed greatly from state to state and were often inconsistent with state judicial pronouncements. Some states permitted life support to be withdrawn from a patient only if death were imminent, whereas others authorized withdrawal only if the life-support mechanism were responsible for keeping a terminally ill patient alive. Certain states included patients in a persistent vegetative state under the right-to-die blanket, others specifically excluded them, and still others made no reference to them. The removal of artificial hydration and nutrition was allowed in some states and proscribed in others. Some states made it possible for an individual to leave all medical decisionmaking to any duly appointed surrogate; a few states limited acceptable decisionmakers to family members and guardians (if no surrogate had been officially designated); and other states forbade proxy decisionmaking altogether. Missouri law, for example, permitted a surrogate to act for an incompetent patient in electing to have artificial hydration and nutrition withdrawn in such a way as to cause death but established a procedural safeguard to make certain that the decision of the surrogate conformed as best it may to the wishes expressed by the patient when competent. Specifically, the law required "clear and convincing, inherently reliable evidence" of the patient's wishes not to continue life-sustaining medical treatment. That law was the basis for the U.S. Supreme Court's first foray into the right-to-die issue.

In *Cruzan v. Missouri Department of Health* (497 U.S. 261; 1990), the justices considered whether the U.S. Constitution embraced a right to refuse lifesaving hydration and nutrition. As a result of an automobile accident and the subsequent deprivation of oxygen to the brain, twenty-five-year-old Nancy Cruzan suffered permanent brain damage. Despite rehabilitative efforts, she lived in a persistent vegetative state with no cognitive functions for nearly five years. When convinced that their daughter had no hope of regaining consciousness, Cruzan's parents, as her appointed guardians, requested that the artificial hydration and nutrition, with which their daughter could live indefinitely, be terminated. Because the termination of such hydration and nutrition would lead to certain death, the hospital refused to act without a court order. The parents then successfully petitioned a Missouri state court for authorization of their request. The trial court ruled that, under the Missouri and federal constitutions, a person had a fundamental privacy right to refuse or direct the withdrawal of life-prolonging procedures and that the patient had, prior to the accident, expressed her will to die if circumstances ever left her in a persistent vegetative state. The court, therefore, ordered the hospital to honor the family's request. The hospital refused to comply and appealed the decision to the Missouri Supreme Court.

Unable to find a fundamental unrestricted right to refuse medical treatment in the Missouri Constitution—and doubtful that such a right could be located in the U.S. Constitution—the Missouri Supreme Court reversed. It further held that any right to refuse medical treatment had to be balanced against Missouri's strong interest in the preservation of human life. Missouri's statute on living wills required "clear and convincing, inherently reliable evidence" of the patient's wishes not to continue life-sustaining medical treatment. (A *living will* is a formal document made by a patient while still competent, governing the withholding or withdrawal of life-sustaining medical treatment from a patient in the event he/she becomes permanently unconscious or terminally ill and is unable to make decisions regarding medical treatment.) In the absence of such evidence, as was the case here, the Missouri

Supreme Court refused to permit the parents to assume that choice for their incompetent daughter.

In a 5-4 decision, the U.S. Supreme Court affirmed. Writing for the majority, Chief Justice William Rehnquist quietly rejected the lower court's conclusion that the right to die was a fundamental privacy right. Instead, the majority opinion acknowledged both the common law right and constitutionally protected liberty interest in a *competent* person's decision to refuse medical treatment, including lifesaving hydration and nutrition. That liberty interest, however, was not absolute; it had to be balanced against relevant state interests, in this case Missouri's unqualified interest in the preservation of human life. Because Cruzan was incompetent, the state could legitimately seek to ensure that the choice to terminate treatment reflected the patient's actual preferences by imposing heightened evidentiary requirements. This clear and convincing evidence standard was permissible for two reasons. First, it guarded against potential abuses of the doctrine of substituted judgment. After all, there was no guarantee that the views of the family members would necessarily be the same as those of the patient. Second, the standard prevented irreversible error. Although an erroneous decision to terminate life-sustaining medical treatment was not susceptible to correction, an erroneous decision *not* to terminate simply maintained the status quo. In essence, if the state were going to err, it was preferable to do so in the interest of life.

Although joining the majority opinion, Justices Sandra Day O'Connor and Antonin Scalia wrote separately. Justice O'Connor's concurrence emphasized what the majority opinion did not say. Nothing in the Court's decision precluded a future determination by the Supreme Court that the Constitution required the states to implement the wishes of duly appointed substitute decisionmakers. She agreed with the majority, however, that the federal Constitution did not require a state to allow unauthorized parents to substitute their judgment for that of their incompetent adult child. Justice O'Connor encouraged the states to experiment with new methods that would safeguard the wishes of incompetents in similar situations, making clear, however, that the justices reserved the right to review those experiments at a later date. Justice Scalia reprimanded the majority for not explicitly stating that the federal courts "have no business in [the suicide] field" (497 U.S. at 293). In short, because the Constitution was silent on this matter, the justices should also be. Accordingly, even if it were demonstrated by clear and convincing evidence that the patient did not want life-sustaining medical treatment, Missouri could still elect not to honor that wish.

Justice William Brennan dissented. Although he agreed with the majority that the right to be free from unwanted medical treatment was among the liberty interests protected by the Due Process Clause, he argued that such a right was unquestionably so "deeply rooted in this Nation's history and tradition" as to be ranked as fundamental. Because it was fundamental, the right to be free from medical attention without consent could not be abridged simply because the patient was incompetent. Instead, the state had an obligation to provide the patient with an accurate as possible determination of how the patient would exercise her rights under such circumstances. Accordingly, the state could adopt any reasonable procedure it wanted *as long as* it earnestly sought to ascertain the wishes of the patient. The clear and convincing evidence standard failed to seek in a reliable manner the wishes of the patient for two reasons. First, it imposed upon the states "a markedly asymmetrical burden." Because no proof was required to support a finding that the incompetent patient would want to continue treatment, the proceedings to determine whether to terminate treatment almost always favored continuing treatment. Second, the standard discounted relevant—although perhaps not clear and convincing—evidence as to the patient's preferences, in this case, the patient's statements to her housemate and family members; testimony from the patient's family members that they were certain that the patient would want to discontinue artificial nutrition and hydration; and the conclusion of the guardian ad litem that there was clear and convincing evidence that the patient would want to discontinue medical treatment and that such discontinuance was in the patient's best interests. When the wishes of the patient were legitimately unknown, the Due Process Clause generally required that the state leave the decision with the duly appointed guardian, the person whom the patient would most likely have chosen as the guardian, or the patient's family (assuming, of course, that the party chosen had no improper motives).

Justice John Paul Stevens, also in dissent, argued that the Constitution required the state to ascertain and pursue the patient's best interests. Missouri, by refusing to consider quality of life in making decisions about extraordinary medical treatment, ignored Cruzan's best interests and unreasonably intruded upon traditionally private matters encompassed within the liberty interest protected by the Due Process Clause. In addition, by focusing solely upon prior expressions of intent, the majority limited the constitutional right to be free from unwanted medical treatment to those patients who had the foresight to declare formally and unambiguously their wishes while competent. Rather, the meaning and completion of Cruzan's life "should be controlled by persons who have her best interests at heart—not by a state legislature concerned only with the preservation of human life" (497 U.S. at 356).

Clearly, *Cruzan* did not bring the right to die under the rubric of constitutional privacy. Although many state courts had held that constitutional privacy included the right to refuse unwanted medical treatment (see *In re Quinlan*), the U.S. Supreme Court refused to do so here. That decision, however, was not entirely unexpected given the Court's long-standing opposition to extending constitutional privacy beyond the realm of procreation, marriage, and family life. The refusal to invoke constitutional privacy, however, should not overshadow the recognition of a constitutionally protected liberty interest in refusing unwanted medical treatment. (As a practical matter, there is little, if any, difference between a constitutionally protected privacy interest and a constitutionally protected liberty interest.) The majority construed the Fourteenth Amendment Due Process Clause to guarantee a liberty interest that protected the right of a *competent* patient to refuse unwanted medical treatment, that is, to participate in passive voluntary euthanasia. With the exception of Justice Scalia, every other justice (even those in dissent) endorsed this interpretation of the Fourteenth Amendment. Those same eight justices further agreed that an *incompetent* patient owned a liberty interest in refusing medical treatment. Accordingly, eight of the nine justices did not preclude incompetent patients from having their specific wishes respected. The majority, of course, limited the exercise of this liberty interest to those patients who had clearly expressed a desire to have medical treatment terminated in the event of permanent incapacitation. Finally, in noting that the Due Process Clause did not require a state to accept the substituted judgment of close family members *in the absence of* substantial proof that their views reflected the patient's, the majority indicated that, *with* such, the Due Process Clause required a state to accept the substituted judgment of close family members. Again, on this point, all but Justice Scalia agreed. Eight of the nine justices thus appeared to agree that the right to die deserved some constitutional protection; they simply disagreed on how the right should be balanced against relevant state interests.

Because this was the first case in which the Supreme Court was squarely confronted with the issue of whether the U.S. Constitution confers a right to die, the justices obviously trod lightly. The tentative tone of the majority opinion was evident from the outset, when the chief justice disavowed any effort "to cover every possible phase of [a] subject . . . of such magnitude and importance." Because each state approached this matter differently—

and because no approach had emerged as clearly superior to all others—the justices were content to defer to the states on this "perplexing question with unusually strong moral and ethical overtones" (497 U.S. at 277–278). In other words, let the states continue to experiment with various methods—subject to judicial review, of course—so as to discern the most effective means for handling these decisions. To hold otherwise was tantamount to a judicial decree that the Constitution required all states to adopt a particular national policy with respect to terminating medical treatment (as the Court had done with abortion). That decree was highly unlikely, for even among the justices (as among the states), there was little consensus on the preferable method of balancing the interests of the patient, the family, and the state. Some justices favored clear and convincing evidence of a prior choice; others were satisfied with reliable evidence of a prior choice. One suggested a best-interests test; another recommended no test whatsoever. Accordingly, the majority was content to let the matter play out in the fifty states, described many years ago by Justice Louis Brandeis as "the great laboratories of democracy." In this sense, *Cruzan* did not break new ground; it simply affirmed the legitimacy of what the states were already doing. (Following the Supreme Court decision, a state probate court decided that the Cruzan family had met the clear and convincing standard required by Missouri law. On December 14, 1990, upon the request of the parents, a judge authorized the cessation of artificial hydration and nutrition. Twelve days later, and nearly eight years after she had lapsed into an irreversible coma, Nancy Cruzan died.)

Shortly after *Cruzan,* and no doubt partly because of it, Congress codified the right to refuse medical treatment. The Patient Self-Determination Act of 1991 required all hospitals, skilled nursing facilities, home health agencies, hospice programs, and health maintenance organizations to guarantee that every adult receiving medical care be provided written information concerning advanced directives. More recently, state legislative action has become more consistent with judicial pronouncements. All fifty states now legitimize the use of advanced directives for end-of-life decisionmaking. (An *advanced directive* is a legal document expressing a patient's wishes about the kind of health care the patient desires should the patient become unable to make his or her own health care decisions. There are two types of advanced directives—the living will, discussed earlier, and the durable power of attorney for health care. A durable power of attorney for health care allows a patient to specify in advance who should make health care decisions for the patient if the patient is unable to make his or her own decisions. Unlike with a living will, the patient need not be in an irreversible coma or terminally ill for the durable power of attorney to take effect. To make the distinction clear: the living will is the patient's own choice of what should happen; the durable power of attorney is the patient's choice of another individual to decide what should happen.) Most states now permit, within certain limitations, the withdrawal of life-sustaining medical treatment and the termination of artificial hydration and nutrition for patients in a persistent vegetative state.

Active Euthanasia: Suicide and Assisted Suicide

Suicide is the deliberate termination of one's life. The moral permissibility of suicide has been debated among philosophers for millennia. Early Greek philosophers were divided: some found nothing blameworthy about choosing to end one's life; others found it contrary to the rule of life. Socrates, for example, pronounced that painful disease and suffering were legitimate reasons for ending one's life. Yet his student Plato thought suicide frustrated "the decree of destiny." The Stoic philosopher Seneca praised suicide as the final act of a free man. The later Christian philosophers condemned suicide on religious grounds. Saint Augustine labeled suicide as the most dangerous of all sins because it violated the sixth commandment—"Thou shalt not kill"—and denied the dead person time for true repentance. In *Summa Theologica* (1988, 70), St. Thomas Aquinas summarized the traditional Christian opposition to suicide: life was a gift from God; therefore, God alone had authority over life and death. Most Renaissance philosophers, however, rejected this argument of divine providence. In the sixteenth century, Michel Montaigne was among the first European philosophers to argue that suicide should be considered a fundamental human right. In "A Defense of Legal Suicide" (1580 II, 25), he wrote, "Life dependeth upon the will of others, death on ours." Two centuries later, Enlightenment philosophers Jean Jacques Rousseau and David Hume rejected the assertion that suicide violated God's prerogative to determine the duration of one's life by arguing that such an assertion, if true, would similarly deem any medical treatment as an interference with God's plan. Instead, because God gave to each of us the liberty to alter nature for our own happiness, and because suicide was an instance of that, suicide did not infringe upon God's plan.

Philosophical arguments notwithstanding, the English common law tradition has punished or otherwise disapproved of suicide since the thirteenth century. One of the first legal treatises, written by Henry de Bracton in 1268, observed that "just as a man may commit felony by slaying another so may he do so by slaying himself" (1968 II, 423). Other treatise writers—including the influential Sir Edward Coke and Sir William Blackstone, whose *Commentaries of the Laws of England* became the primary legal authority for eighteenth- and nineteenth-century lawyers in the United States—agreed with Bracton that suicide was criminally liable. The interest of the state in prohibiting suicide was first articulated in a sixteenth-century British case, *Hales v. Petit* (1 Plowd. Com. 253, 261; 1562). Here, the Court at Common Bench referred to suicide as an "Offence against Nature, against God, and against the King." Suicide was a crime against the king because it deprived the king of one of his subjects, thus interfering with one of his rights as a monarch. The standard punishment for suicide was forfeiture of property held and an ignominious burial, in reality a punishment of the family. Ironically, those who failed in their attempt to take their own lives were subject to being hanged by the state.

Most of the early American colonies—and later states—adopted the English common law tradition prohibiting suicide, but they did away with the harsh penalties imposed by the common law. These were abandoned not to legitimize the act but because of a growing consensus that punishing innocent family members for the suicide's wrongdoing was unfair. For a number of reasons, by the beginning of the twentieth century, suicide had been decriminalized. First, the punishment did not act as a deterrent. Second, prosecutors were reluctant to bring charges against, and juries were reluctant to convict, an individual recovering from a failed suicide attempt. And third, the general consensus was that mental illness was a primary reason for many suicides and attempts. One thing is certain: the decriminalization of suicide did not come about because suicide was deemed a "human right" or even because it was no longer considered reprehensible (Marzen 1985; Kamisar 1993). Though decriminalized in all fifty states, suicide is still largely perceived as a grave, albeit not felonious, public wrong.

The Anglo-American common law tradition has, even more so, disapproved of assisted suicide. At common law in England, assisted suicide was criminally liable. The earliest U.S. statute explicitly outlawing assisted suicide was enacted in New York in 1828. In 1850, California made it a felony to aid, advise, or encourage another to commit suicide. Most of the states soon adopted similar prohibitions. By the time of the adoption of the Fourteenth Amendment in 1868, twenty-one of the thirty-seven states specifically prohibited assisted suicide.

Prior to the 1990s, state courts were relatively silent on assisted suicide. The one exception to this silence came from a California appellate court in *Bouvia v. Superior Court of Los Angeles County*

(179 Cal. App. 3d. 1127; [Cal. 1986]). Though the case did not turn on the issue of assisted suicide, the majority flatly denied that a physician who facilitated death assisted suicide, because assisted suicide involved "affirmative, assertive, proximate, direct conduct such as furnishing a gun, poison, knife, or other instrumentality or usable means by which another could physically and immediately inflict some death-producing injury upon himself" (179 Cal. App. 3d. at 1145). Justice Lynn D. Compton wrote even more forcefully in a concurring opinion:

> The right to die is an integral part of our right to control our own destinies so long as the rights of others are not affected. That right should . . . include the ability to enlist assistance from others, including the medical profession, in making death as painless as possible. That ability should not be hampered by the state's threat to impose penal sanctions on those who might be disposed to lend assistance. . . . If there is ever a time when we ought to be able to get "government off our backs" it is when we face death—either by choice or otherwise. (127 Cal. App. 3d. at 1147–1148)

An important turning point in the assisted suicide debate came in the early 1990s when Dr. Jack Kevorkian, a Michigan physician, almost single-handedly elevated assisted suicide from a philosophical debate among philosophers, physicians, and priests to the national agenda. He did so by publicizing his assistance in the death of Janet Atkins in 1990 and dozens, perhaps hundreds, of others thereafter. Local judges dismissed charges against Kevorkian—dubbed "Dr. Death" by the media—in his first three assisted suicides because Michigan had no law explicitly prohibiting assisted suicide. In February 1993, however, Michigan adopted such a statute. But within the next twelve months, three judges in three separate proceedings struck down the assisted-suicide ban and dismissed charges against Kevorkian. In May 1993, Judge Cynthia Stevens of the Wayne County Circuit Court struck down the law on technical grounds but went on to make a substantive argument based on the U.S. Constitution: "The court cannot envisage a more fundamental right than the one of self-determination." On appeal, the law was reinstated, making it possible for Wayne County Circuit Court chief judge Richard C. Kaufman to strike it down on substantive grounds seven months later. Drawing motivation from *Cruzan,* Judge Kaufman opined that "when a person's quality of life is significantly impaired by a medical condition and the medical condition is extremely unlikely to improve" that person had a "constitutionally protected right to commit suicide" ("Suicide Law Struck Down," *New York Times,* December 14, 1993, at A18). Because the holding of the Wayne County Circuit Court held no sway in other counties, prosecutors in Oakland County pressed ahead with their prosecution of Kevorkian. In January 1994, Judge Jessica R. Cooper of the Oakland County Circuit Court invalidated the prohibition on technical grounds, although she held that "the right of self-determination, the right to control one's own body, has long been recognized in the common law of the United States" ("Aided Suicide Law Invalidated Again," *New York Times,* January 28, 1994, at A17). The disposition of these three cases reveals that the judges used the same strategy in formulating an opinion regarding physician-assisted suicide that earlier judges had used in withdrawal-of-treatment cases (Hoefler 1994, 168). Judge Stevens invoked notions of privacy and autonomy in speaking of fundamental rights inherent in the Bill of Rights. Judge Kaufman cited the liberty interest. And Judge Cooper, sounding much like Justice Cardozo in *Schloendorff,* relied upon the common law.

In December 1994, after numerous appeals, the Michigan Supreme Court upheld the constitutionality of the ban on assisted suicide (527 N.W. 2d 714; [Mich. 1994]). Mindful of the U.S. Supreme Court's consistent refusal to extend constitutional protection to rights that did not exist historically, the justices of the highest court in the state were unwilling to find a constitutionally protected liberty interest in an activity that historically had been, and remained, an ignominious criminal offense and a felony under the common law. That court, like others before it, acknowledged the real distinction between self-infliction of deadly harm (active euthanasia) and a self-determination against artificial life support (passive euthanasia). Relying upon *Cruzan,* the Michigan Supreme Court found that the distinction between letting a patient die and making a patient die was important, logical, rational, and well established.

Between 1995 and 1998, with the ban upheld, prosecutors attempted four times to convict Kevorkian for helping people use an apparatus known as a suicide machine to give themselves fatal injections. This suicide machine has three canisters attached to a metal frame. The first canister contains ordinary saline; the second barbiturates; and the third potassium chloride. Each canister has a syringe connected to an intravenous line in the person's arm. After the saline begins to flow, the person who wishes to die prompts the machine to deliver the sleep-inducing barbiturates. Once the person is asleep, a mechanical device triggered by the person's falling arm releases the lethal mixture of potassium chloride into the bloodstream. Death usually occurs within minutes. Three of Kevorkian's trials resulted in acquittals; the fourth ended in a mistrial. In September 1998, however, Kevorkian assisted in the death of Thomas Youk, a middle-aged man suffering from amyotrophic lateral sclerosis, commonly known as Lou Gehrig's disease. Michigan authorities initially declined to prosecute Kevorkian until he provided them with direct evidence: a videotape showing Kevorkian actually administering the lethal injection. Kevorkian gave the tape to the CBS news program *60 Minutes,* which aired it in November. That broadcast included an interview with Kevorkian in which he dared prosecutors to charge him. They did, and on March 26, 1999, a Michigan jury convicted him of second-degree murder. Shortly thereafter, he was sentenced to ten to twenty-five years in prison.

Since Dr. Kevorkian's public crusade began in the early 1990s, four states have considered citizen initiatives on physician-assisted suicide. Voters in Washington (in 1991), California (1992), and Michigan (1998) rejected ballot initiatives that would have legalized physician-assisted suicide. In 1994, Oregon voters, by a vote of 51 percent to 49 percent, statutorily decriminalized assisted suicide. The Oregon Death with Dignity Act permitted terminally ill Oregon residents to end their lives through the voluntary self-administration of lethal medications expressly prescribed by a physician for that purpose. Although the act legalized physician-assisted suicide, it specifically prohibited a physician or other person from directly administering a medication to end another's life.

Implementation of the act was delayed by a legal injunction. After three years of court challenges, including a petition that was denied by the U.S. Supreme Court, the law went into effect in 1997. When given the opportunity to repeal the act later that same year, Oregon voters chose to retain the act by a margin of 60 percent to 40 percent. At present, Oregon is the only state to permit assisted suicide. Forty-four states and the District of Columbia specifically prohibit or condemn assisted suicide, although studies have indicated that the practice is much more prevalent than realized (Quill, Lo, and Brock 1997). Five states have not criminalized assisted suicide per se; in those states, however, one who assisted in a suicide might well face homicide charges.

The federal courts did not get involved in assisted suicide until 1994, when Compassion in Dying, an organization that offers open support to terminally ill patients who desire the option of assisted dying, filed lawsuits in federal district court challenging the constitutionality of laws criminalizing assisted suicide in Washington state and New York. In *Compassion in Dying v. Washington* (850 F.Supp. 1454; [W.D. Wash. 1994]), the district court equated the right to die with the right to have an abortion and concluded that the Due Process Clause guaranteed adults who were mentally competent, terminally ill, and acting under no influence of other people the right to hasten their deaths by taking a lethal dose of physician-prescribed drugs. The court further held that there was no constitutional distinction between the right to refuse or terminate unwanted, life-prolonging medical treatment and the right to physician-assisted suicide by an uncoerced, mentally competent, terminally ill adult. As such, the Equal Protection Clause was violated by the statute because the statute distinguished between two similarly situated groups of mentally competent, terminally adults. Terminally ill patients whose conditions involved the use of life support could lawfully obtain medical assistance for terminating such support, which would hasten death, whereas terminally ill patients whose conditions did not involve life-sustaining equipment were denied the opportunity to hasten death with medical assistance.

While the federal district court in Washington was considering the challenge to the Washington law, a federal district court in New York was debating a New York law that made it a felony to assist in a suicide. In contrast, the district court in *Quill v. Koppell* (870 F.Supp. 78 [S.D.N.Y. 1994]) held that the New York law did not violate either the Due Process or Equal Protection Clause. Because our nation had historically disapproved of suicide and assisted suicide, the court reasoned, physician-assisted suicide was not a fundamental liberty interest protected by the Due Process Clause. The Equal Protection Clause was not violated because it was "hardly unreasonable or irrational" for the state to recognize a difference between allowing death to occur naturally and prescribing lethal doses of medicine or intentionally using an artificial death-producing device.

Both cases were appealed; both appellate courts—the U.S. Courts of Appeals for the Ninth and Second Circuits—held that the Constitution guaranteed some citizens the right to physician-assisted suicide. The Ninth Circuit, which heard en banc the appeal coming from Washington, asserted that the Constitution encompassed a due process liberty interest in controlling "the time and manner of one's own death"—in short, a constitutionally protected right to die (*Compassion in Dying v. Washington,* 79 F.3d 790; 793 [9th Cir. 1996]). (An *en banc* hearing is a session of an appellate court in which a large group of judges assigned to the court participate. En banc hearings are usually reserved for cases of extraordinary importance.) Writing for eight members of an eleven-member panel, Judge Stephen Reinhardt asserted that the right to die belonged under the rubric of constitutional privacy: "A common thread running through these [privacy] cases is that they involved decisions that are highly personal and intimate, as well as of great importance to the individual. Certainly, few decisions are more personal, intimate or important than the decision to end one's life, especially when the reason for doing so is to avoid excessive and protracted pain" (79 F.3d at 813). Judge Reinhardt failed to explain, though, why decisions about death deserved the same constitutional protection as decisions relating to marriage, procreation, and family life—the traditional categories of constitutional privacy. After all, Michael Hardwick, only a decade earlier, had failed to persuade the justices that his choice to participate in homosexual sodomy was protected by the Constitution because it was personal, intimate, and important.

Perhaps conceding the inadequacy of the constitutional privacy argument, Judge Reinhardt analogized the right to die to the right to refuse medical treatment, suggesting that when U.S. Supreme Court recognized a constitutional right to refuse medical treatment in *Cruzan,* it "necessarily recognize[d] a liberty interest in hastening one's one death" (79 F.3d at 816). (In making this claim, however, Judge Reinhardt ignored the portion of *Cruzan* that clearly distinguished refusing medical treatment from committing suicide, as well as *Cruzan*'s explicit endorsement of laws imposing criminal penalties on those who assisted in a suicide.) Accordingly, because physician-assisted suicide was a liberty interest, and because the liberty interest in *Cruzan* was subjected to "ordinary balancing" against state interests, Judge Reinhardt concluded that the state had to satisfy a balancing test less restrictive than strict scrutiny but more stringent than rational basis to justify the impairment of this right (see Table 3.1, "Standards of Review"). As opposed to the unnecessarily rigid strict scrutiny and rational basis tests, both of which depended upon the classification of the asserted right or interest as either fundamental or nonfundamental, this ordinary balancing test operated on a continuum, requiring that the more important the individual's interest, the more persuasive the state's justifications for infringement had to be.

Applying such a test, the Ninth Circuit determined that none of the state's interests—preserving life, preventing suicide, and safeguarding the interests of third-party dependents of people contemplating suicide—were sufficient to justify the curtailment of this liberty interest. Because the court was convinced that substantive due process protected physician-assisted suicide, the Ninth Circuit did not consider the Equal Protection challenge.

The Second Circuit, hearing the appeal from New York, rejected the due process–fundamental rights argument but accepted the equal protection argument (*Quill v. Vacco,* 80 F.3d 716 [3d Cir. 1996]). The opinion, written by Judge Roger Miner, was mindful of Justice Byron White's admonition in *Hardwick* (478 U.S. at 194) that "the Court is most vulnerable and comes nearest illegitimacy when it deals with judge-made constitutional law having little or no cognizable roots in the language and design of the Constitution." Certain that the right to assisted suicide had no cognizable basis in the U.S. Constitution's language or design, the three-judge panel unanimously declined the invitation to identify a new constitutional right to die in the absence of a clear direction from a higher judicial authority. Yet because the law failed to "treat equally all competent persons who are in the final stages of fatal illness and wish to hasten their deaths," it encroached upon the Equal Protection Clause (80 F.3d at 727). By allowing terminally ill patients on life support to hasten their deaths, but prohibiting terminally ill patients who are not on life support from doing so, the law treated similarly circumstanced persons differently. Accordingly, the court held that a willing physician could prescribe drugs to be self-administered by a mentally competent, terminally ill patient seeking to end his or her life during the final stages of a terminal illness. (In reaching this result, Judge Miner, much like his counterpart on the West Coast, failed to acknowledge the legal distinction between refusing medical treatment—historically treated as an omission to cure—and causing death—historically treated as an action to kill.)

In sum, the Court of Appeals for the Ninth Circuit struck down Washington's law forbidding physician-assisted suicide on the grounds that it violated constitutional privacy and the liberty protected by the Due Process Clause of the Fourteenth Amendment. The Court of Appeals for the Second Circuit invalidated New York's law on the basis of the Fourteenth Amendment's Equal Protection Clause upon rejecting the state's distinction between the terminally ill's right to terminate life-support systems and claim to a right to physician-assisted suicide. The following year, in separate unanimous decisions issued on the same day, the U.S. Supreme Court reversed both the Ninth and Second Circuits, declining to find a liberty interest in physician-assisted suicide and dismissing the equal protection argument. Writing for a five-justice majority, Chief Justice William Rehnquist authored the opinion in both cases.

In *Washington v. Glucksberg* (521 U.S. 702; 1997), the case from the Ninth Circuit, the Supreme Court began by acknowledging its reluctance to expand the concept of substantive due process, for when the justices extended constitutional protection to an asserted right, it placed that matter outside of the arena of public debate and legislative action and risked transforming the Due Process Clause into the policy preferences of the justices. Chief Justice Rehnquist then identified the two primary features of the Supreme Court's substantive due process analysis. First, the

Due Process Clause protected only those fundamental rights firmly established in this nation's history and tradition. Second, the asserted fundamental liberty interest had to be carefully described. The right to assisted suicide met neither of these stipulations.

The second requirement was not met because the asserted fundamental liberty interest had been described by the appellate court variously and inaccurately as a right "to determine the time and manner of one's death," the "right to die," a "liberty to choose how to die," a right to "control one's final days," the right "to choose a humane, dignified death," and the "liberty to shape death." Yet the specific question before the justices was whether the liberty protected by the Due Process Clause included a right to commit suicide, which itself included a right to obtain assistance in doing so.

The first requirement was not satisfied, either. After examining the nation's history and legal traditions, the majority found a "consistent, almost universal, and continuing rejection" of this asserted right, even for terminally ill, mentally competent adults (521 U.S. at 723). To hold otherwise would be to reverse centuries of legal doctrine and practice and to strike down laws in almost every state. Unlike the appellate court, the Supreme Court refused to extend constitutional privacy to protect all personal, intimate, and important choices or to extend the holding in *Cruzan* to confer a general right to die. Instead, constitutional privacy provided heightened protection to those personal, intimate, and important choices relating to marriage, procreation, and family life only; and *Cruzan* simply conferred a right to refuse lifesaving medical treatment—a right grounded in the nation's history and tradition, long recognized by the common law, and significantly different than the right to assisted suicide. Thus, the asserted right to assistance in committing suicide was neither a fundamental liberty interest protected by the Due Process Clause nor consistent with the Supreme Court's substantive due process line of cases.

Because assisted suicide was not a fundamental liberty interest, the Supreme Court applied the rational basis test, unlike the ordinary balancing test employed by the Ninth Circuit, to determine the constitutionality of the Washington law (see Table 3.1, "Standards of Review"). The majority unquestionably accepted Washington's unqualified interest in prohibiting intentional killing and preserving human life; in maintaining the ethics and integrity of the medical profession; in protecting vulnerable persons from undue pressure to end their lives; and in avoiding the "slippery slope" toward euthanasia, both voluntary and involuntary. In an interesting footnote, however, the majority left open the possibility that a law prohibiting physician-assisted suicide might be declared unconstitutional "in a more particularized challenge." Without providing specifics, the majority opinion stated that such a claim would have to be "quite different" from the ones advanced in this case (521 U.S. at 735, n. 24).

In *Vacco v. Quill* (521 U.S. 793; 1997), the companion case from New York, the Supreme Court dismissed the equal protection challenge. The New York law, the chief justice reasoned, treated everyone equally: all persons had the right to refuse medical treatment; and all persons were prohibited from assisting another in committing suicide. Furthermore, the Court rejected the Second Circuit's contention that the right to refuse medical treatment was directly comparable to assisted suicide, concluding that there was an important distinction between causation and intent. When a patient disconnected life support, the patient "died from an underlying fatal disease or pathology"; but when a patient swallowed lethal medication prescribed by a physician, the patient was "killed by that medication" (521 U.S. at 802).

In *Glucksberg* and *Quill,* the Supreme Court declined to find a right to assisted suicide. By so doing, however, the Court did not purport to resolve the question once and for all but rather permitted the debate over physician-assisted suicide to continue. Shedding "the robes of the philosopher king" and donning "the more humble garments of judges in a democratic society," the justices expressly recognized that other institutions in our society were often better situated to resolve important issues of principle (McConnell 1997, A14). Although the justices were unanimous in declining to find a right to assisted suicide, the majority (in a footnote) and five justices (in separate concurring opinions) indicated that they might be willing to recognize a constitutional right to physician-assisted suicide under circumstances different than those presented in these cases. Although the majority did not elaborate on those circumstances, four of the five concurring justices expressed concern about a patient's ability to avoid severe physical pain when facing an imminent death; and the fifth articulated some apprehension over the effectiveness of proposed assisted suicide guidelines in preventing involuntary euthanasia.

Justice John Paul Stevens was "convinced" that there were situations— when palliative care could not alleviate intolerable suffering, for example—in which a patient had a legitimate and constitutionally protected interest in hastening death. Because dying patients in Washington and New York could obtain palliative care, even if that care hastened death, Justice Sandra Day O'Connor found it unnecessary to address the question of "whether suffering patients have a constitutionally cognizable interest in obtaining relief from the suffering they may experience in the last days of their lives" (521 U.S. at 737). Her silence on that question, therefore, left open the possibility that there was a constitutional prohibition against laws that barred access to potentially lethal medication to alleviate grave pain. Although she did not write a separate opinion, Justice Ruth Ginsburg agreed "substantially" with the opinion of Justice O'Connor. Justice Stephen Breyer expressed a greater willingness than his colleagues to assert a constitutional right to die, although he formulated the liberty interest as a "right to die with dignity." At the core of that right was "personal control over the manner of death, professional medical assistance, and the avoidance of unnecessary and severe physical suffering—combined" (521 U.S. at 790). He even suggested (by referencing *Griswold v. Connecticut*) that the right to die with dignity was as much a protected liberty as the decision to use birth control. But because the state statutes did not force a dying person to endure serious pain, or prohibit physicians from providing patients with drugs sufficient to control pain despite the risk that the drugs themselves would kill, Justice Breyer deemed it imprudent to decide *in this case* whether the right to die with dignity was constitutionally protected.

In addition to the four justices who articulated concern about a patient's ability to avoid severe physical pain when facing an imminent death, Justice David Souter hinted that he, too, might be willing to revisit the issue under different circumstances. His primary fear relating to the asserted liberty interest was the potential for physicians and others to abuse a limited freedom to assist suicides by pressuring vulnerable persons into suicide decisions. Clearly, the states had the power to protect terminally ill patients from involuntary euthanasia. Even the possibility that similar assisted suicide guidelines in the Netherlands had failed to protect terminally ill patients from involuntary euthanasia was sufficient justification to exercise caution *for the time being.* He noted, "I do not decide for all time that the respondents' claim should not be recognized" (521 U.S. at 789). Justice Souter's concurrence, therefore, left open the possibility that, should procedural safeguards that prevent involuntary euthanasia be adopted, he might be willing to recognize a right to physician-assisted suicide.

Although in each case five justices rejected portions of the majority's analysis and indicated that they might be willing to recognize a right to physician-assisted suicide in different circumstances—which the majority opinion did not entirely rule out, either—two considerations render that possibility remote. First, the number of cases in which a patient's pain cannot be mitigated through palliative care is relatively small. In fact, the American Medical Association asserted in its amicus brief that pain management, if properly administered, can alleviate almost all physical suffering. (A brief *amicus curiae,* literally "friend of the court," is a legal brief submitted by a person or organization not party to the litigation but vitally interested in the outcome of the case.) Other amicus briefs, of course, rejected that assertion and avowed that palliative care cannot mitigate all physical suffering of terminally ill patients. Second, some opponents of physician-assisted suicide question whether courts are competent to determine accurately and objectively if a patient suffers severe pain. Thomas Marzen (1994, 820) and Yale Kamisar (1995, 744–745), for example, argue that judges will either have to accept the rather subjective evaluations of patients or physicians or draw artificial lines between virtually indistinguishable cases. Yet to suggest that a physician is unable to assist a patient "whom he or she confidently diagnoses merely because another case might not provide the requisite degree of confidence" defies the realities of modern medicine (Note 1997, 248).

A close reading of *Glucksberg* and *Quill* reveals that the Supreme Court did not definitely resolve whether some patients have a constitutional right to physician-assisted suicide. For the time being, the justices agreed to let the matter play out in state legislatures, many of which were engaged in a serious and thoughtful debate on the policy and impolicy, the wisdom and inexpediency, of physician-assisted suicide. Moreover, nothing in the Court's decisions prevented a state from allowing physician-assisted suicide, such as Oregon did in November 1997, when the Death with Dignity Act went into effect.

In the same year *Glucksberg* and *Quill* were decided, Congress passed the Assisted Suicide Funding Restriction Act, which barred the use of federal funds to pay for assisted suicide, euthanasia, and mercy killing. The act did not prohibit assisted suicide, euthanasia, or mercy killing, however. Shortly after Oregon's Death with Dignity Act went into effect, Drug Enforcement Agency (DEA) chief Thomas Constantine suggested that Oregon physicians who participated in assisted suicide would be in violation of the federal Controlled Substances Act (1970). In 1998, however, U.S. Attorney General Janet Reno announced that the Department of Justice would not prosecute physicians who were in full compliance with the Oregon law when assisting suicide. Her decision was based on her findings that the Controlled Substances Act was primarily concerned with illegal drug trafficking and was not intended to supplant the individual states as the regulators of medical practice.

Opponents of physician-assisted suicide, led by Representative Henry Hyde (R-IL) and Senator Don Nickles (R-OK), responded to this executive decision by introducing the Lethal Drug Abuse Prevention Act in Congress. This act, deliberately aimed at overthrowing the Oregon law, would have prohibited doctors and pharmacists from dispensing any federally regulated drug for the purpose of suicide. In their haste to introduce the bill after the adverse decision by the attorney general, however, legislators failed to garner the support of the most powerful lobby on health care: the American Medical Association. Without the support of the AMA, the bill never passed. It was withdrawn from floor debate on the day of the scheduled vote in the House of Representatives and was stalled in the Senate.

Undeterred, opposition forces introduced the Pain Relief Promotion Act the following year. Although similar to the Lethal Drug Abuse Prevention Act, this act, according to its sponsors, sought not to discourage assisted suicide but to encourage pain relief. Either way, the Pain Relief Promotion Act, disguised as compassionate legislation for the dying, was an effort to overturn Oregon's physician-assisted suicide law. The bill did not affect physicians who prescribed drugs for pain relief, even if those drugs caused death, but did punish physicians who prescribed drugs intentionally to cause death. Under the act, the DEA was responsible for determining the physician's intentions; and if a physician were found to have prescribed drugs explicitly to hasten death, the physician could be sentenced to twenty years in prison. The AMA endorsed the bill because it recognized that aggressive pain relief was "a legitimate medical purpose," even if it increased the risk of death, and it adequately protected doctors from being punished unless their intent was shown to be assisted suicide, not pain relief. Other powerful lobbies—the American Bar Association and the American Cancer Society, for example—opposed the legislation. The Pain Relief Promotion Act passed the House of Representatives in October 1999 by a vote of 271-156 but failed to reach the Senate floor for a full vote prior to that chamber's adjournment in December 2000.

Less than a year later, the new U.S. attorney general, John Ashcroft, decreed that the federal Controlled Substances Act could be used to prosecute physicians in Oregon who helped terminally ill patients commit suicide by prescribing lethal drugs. Arguing that physician-assisted suicide was not a "legitimate medical purpose," Ashcroft warned Oregon physicians who assisted in suicide that their prescription-writing privileges could be revoked and they could be subject to criminal prosecution. Mindful of what the justices said in *Glucksberg* and *Quill*—that other institutions in our society were often better situated to resolve important issues of principle—Oregon filed a lawsuit to block this federal intervention. In April 2002, a federal judge rejected the Department of Justice's effort to block the state's assisted suicide law, noting that the Controlled Substances Act did not authorize either the attorney general or federal prosecutors to determine what constituted "the legitimate practice of medicine." "The citizens of Oregon, through their democratic initiative process," Judge Robert Jones wrote, "have chosen to resolve the moral, legal, and ethical debate on physician-assisted suicide for themselves by voting—not once, but twice—in favor of the Oregon act" (*Oregon v. Ashcroft*, 192 F.Supp. 2d 1077, 1079 [2002]). The judge left open the question of whether Congress could define what constituted the legitimate practice of medicine.

The Department of Justice resumed its bid to prevent physician-assisted suicide in September 2002 by filing an appeal with the U.S. Court of Appeals for the Ninth Circuit. In that appeal, the attorney general reiterated his position that federal law prohibits physicians from prescribing controlled substances except for legitimate medical purposes, of which suicide was not one. Should this case reach the Supreme Court, however, the justices would be confronted with an entirely different question than those posed in *Glucksberg* and *Quill.* Instead of asking whether the Constitution provided some citizens with a right to a physician's assistance in committing suicide—a question of civil liberties, constitutional privacy, and the liberty interest—the justices would have to ask whether Congress could by federal law prohibit a state from allowing its citizens to exercise a right not protected by the U.S. Constitution—a question of federalism. Generally speaking, the states have the authority to grant more substantial and far-reaching rights than those protected by the U.S. Constitution. In addition, the fact that the justices specifically deferred to the states in *Glucksberg* and *Quill,* knowing full well that Oregon had approved the Death with Dignity Act, may prove to be a major impediment to the federal government's case.

The right to die has been a matter of intense public debate for millennia, yet it has been the subject of judicial debate in this country for only a few decades. Arguments in favor of the right to die—be that the right to refuse medical treatment or the right to obtain assistance for the purposes of ending life—generally derive from some combination of the interrelated rights of liberty, autonomy, privacy, and property (Lewis 2001, 52–63). The essential liberty argument is that freedom is a basic good, and the individual, in the absence of harm to others, must be let alone to do as he or she wishes. A commitment to autonomy holds that the choice of electing to forgo continued life is pivotal to controlling one's own life; failure to respect that right impoverishes other, perhaps less momentous, choices. And the instrumental privacy argument maintains that because constitutional privacy protects personal choices, and because the decision whether to continue living is among the most personal of choices, the right to die merits constitutional protection. Moreover, if the right to privacy protects the right to die naturally (see *Cruzan*), it should also protect the right of the mentally competent, terminally ill patient to opt for a quick and painless death. "It is inconsistent to recognize a terminal patient's legally protected right to self-euthanasia but deny that patient the means of implementing that decision" (Wolhandler 1984, 383). Accordingly, constitutional privacy should protect those patients who choose active euthanasia of their own volition, and it should shield from legal sanctions second parties whose assistance is needed to effectuate such a request.

Arguments against the right to die stem from the rights to life, equal protection, and autonomy. Because the right to life is of a special character—an "inalienable," Creator-given right, according to the Declaration of Independence—any decision to end one's life is an "attempt to alienate the inalienable, to give away what cannot properly be given away" (Feinberg 1978, 93). This particular argument takes on a property bent when religious opponents to the right to die assert that God has a property interest in our bodies and our lives. The equal protection argument is concerned with the impact of the routinization of active euthanasia on already marginalized or discriminated against groups. Opponents fear that the poor, the elderly, the demented, the mentally ill, those without good medical insurance, the physically disabled, perhaps even those who are leading purposeless lives, will endure tremendous pressure to end their lives due to financial constraints or family or societal indifference. And when marginalized members of a society are inundated with the message that suicide is acceptable, responsible, and even expected, their right to autonomy is not enhanced; rather, it is threatened. "The social legitimacy and easy availability of effective assistance to commit suicide that would necessarily follow recognition of suicide as a 'right' would . . . contribute to a climate in which both subtle and obvious forms of duress would cause many who would not otherwise do so to choose suicide" (Marzen 1985, 8). In short, the law must protect against people being bullied into ending their lives prematurely.

The Supreme Court rulings on refusing medical treatment and physician-assisted suicide have not laid to rest the question of whether the Constitution protects the right to die. In *Cruzan*, eight justices construed the Fourteenth Amendment's Due Process Clause to guarantee a liberty interest that protected the right of a *competent* patient to refuse unwanted medical treatment. Those same eight justices further agreed that an *incompetent* patient owned a liberty interest in refusing medical treatment in certain circumstances. *Cruzan* thus asserted that the right to die deserved some constitutional protection. In similar fashion, the Court in *Glucksberg* and *Quill* hinted that the right to physician-assisted suicide, under different circumstances, deserved some constitutional protection also.

In none of these cases, however, did the Supreme Court dismiss the primary countervailing state interest—the preservation of life. Clearly, the outer limits of the right to die have yet to be marked by the Supreme Court. Increases in life expectancy, sizable population growth among the elderly, advances in medical technology, dramatic increases in the cost of quality medical care, and the willingness of at least one state to permit active euthanasia are certain to keep this issue near the forefront of public and judicial debate.

FAMILY AUTONOMY

The twentieth-century judicial discourse on marriage and family life recognized that fundamental rights of marital choice, marital intimacy, and family creation were implied in the penumbras of the Bill of Rights and in the Fourteenth Amendment's guarantee of liberty. To reach into those "intimacies of the marriage relationship" was to invade the privacy that was implicit in a free society. Nevertheless, the right to regulate most aspects of marriage remains the prerogative of the individual states. Each state has the authority to determine the rules regarding a marriage's inception, duration, status, conditions, and termination. As such, without the consent of the state, no marriage can exist. Currently, all states ban polygamy, and forty-nine states refuse to recognize same-sex marriages. Immigrants to the United States, many arriving from nations where polygamy is commonplace and traditional, have expressed concerns about the legal nonrecognition of plural marriages. And support for same-sex marriage appears to be gaining political and legal momentum.

Much like with marriage, each state governs adoptions, the process whereby a legal parent-child relationship is created between individuals who are not biologically related. Recently, a state statute that banned adoption by homosexual adults was challenged as impermissibly infringing upon the fundamental rights of family privacy, intimate association, and family integrity.

Polygamy

Polygamy, the condition of having more than one spouse at a time, has been a widespread practice for centuries (Stack 1998). The Christian Bible does not condemn the practice. In fact, the Old Testament records that the Hebrew patriarchs Abraham, David, and Solomon had multiple wives, with Solomon possessing 700 wives and 300 concubines (women who live with men without being married). Biblical practices aside, the Catholic Church frowned upon the practice, leading to its decline among Western European Christians. Early Jewish law permitted the practice among male believers. In the tenth century A.D., however, a Jewish rabbi named Gershom outlawed polygamy for 1,000 years. (That prohibition expired in 1987.) And the Koran, the sacred book of Islam, permits a husband to take up to four wives, as long as he can treat them with equal fairness.

By the time of the founding of the United States, most of the cultures around the world "held no brief for strict monogamy" (Cott 2000, 9). The peoples of Asia, Africa, and Australia, the Muslims around the Mediterranean, and the natives of North and South America all countenanced polygamy. But Christians in Britain, Europe, and North America strictly opposed the practice. Polygamy did not become prevalent anywhere in the United States until the middle of the nineteenth century, when the Mormon Church, which had been established in Utah, canonized the doctrine of polygamy and encouraged its practice among believers. Encouraged no doubt by the widespread belief among Christians that monogamy was the superior form of marriage—and motivated in part by a strong dislike and equally strong fear of the Mormon Church—Congress passed the Morrill Act in 1862, which made polygamy in the territories of the United States punishable by a fine of up to $500 and imprisonment for as much as five years. When the law was challenged on grounds of free exercise of religion, the U.S. Supreme Court, in *Reynolds v. United States* (98 U.S. 145, 164; 1879), upheld the statute, noting that Congress was free to regulate those actions—even those actions motivated by religious obligation—that were "in violation of social duties or subversive of good order." Stated otherwise, because polygamy impaired the public interest, the First Amendment did not protect it. Accordingly, it was within the authority of any civil government to ban polygamy.

Eleven years later, in *Davis v. Beason* (133 U.S. 333; 1890), a challenge to an Idaho law that denied voting privileges to those who advocated or practiced plural marriages, the Supreme Court reaffirmed the distinction between religious belief and conduct. Religion was a matter of belief and therefore constitutionally protected; but conduct, which included polygamy, was not completely protected by the First Amendment. In a single paragraph, the Court characterized polygamy as uncivilized, un-Christian, destructive of marriage, disturbing to the peace of families, degrading to women, debasing to men, pernicious to the best interests of society, and wholly deserving of punishment. "To call its advocacy a tenet of religion," concluded Justice Stephen Field, "is to offend the common sense of mankind" (133 U.S. at 145). That same year, the Mormon Church, exhausted by its numerous court contests with the federal government, officially disavowed polygamy or, as they liked to call it, "celestial marriage." Subsequently, when Utah petitioned to enter the United States, Congress ordered that the state constitution include a provision that specifically banned polygamy. Utah complied and was admitted in 1896.

Today, although there are nearly 40,000 polygamists in the United States, few U.S. citizens consider plural marriage to be a controversial topic. Most find the practice beyond the accepted norms of American society; many find it abhorrent. Nevertheless, it is practiced in the United States, often illegally and covertly, among Native American tribes, several experimental Christian groups, and Mormons. Not all polygamous marriages are illegal. Because Native American tribes are subject to the laws only of Congress, and because Congress has not prohibited plural marriages among tribal Native Americans, if a tribe has a recognized custom of polygamy, its members may enter into polygamous marriages, including those with nonmembers, even if it conflicts with state law. Religious groups have never been similarly exempted from state law.

The emergence of constitutional privacy in the twentieth century provided a new line of attack for polygamists in their attempts to earn constitutional protection for their conduct. In the late 1960s and early 1970s, the U.S. Supreme Court issued a series of rulings that declared unconstitutional state and federal laws that interfered with the fundamental privacy rights of U.S. citizens. To recall, in *Loving v. Virginia* (388 U.S. 1, 12; 1967), the Court decided that the right to marry was "one of the vital personal rights essential to the orderly pursuit of happiness by free men [and] . . . fundamental to our very existence and survival." Although the justices never fully explained the constitutional basis for this declaration, presumably it was the constitutional right to privacy. Two years earlier, the Court in *Griswold* had held that a married couple had a fundamental right to privacy. That right to privacy, the Court noted, was "older than the Bill of Rights—older than our political parties, older than our school system." And to permit the police to invade a married couple's bedroom to search for signs of the use of proscribed contraceptives was "repulsive to the notions of privacy surrounding the marriage relationship" (381 U.S. 479, 485–486). Read together, *Loving* and *Griswold* can be interpreted to mean that the freedom to marry is fundamental and all married couples have the right to privacy within that marriage.

Todd Gillett (2000, 532) has argued that *Griswold,* if "stretched to its furthest extent," permits polygamous relations within licensed marriages.

> If a polygamous arrangement involves one lawful marriage, the husband and his "legal" wife are entitled to privacy as to their marital relations. In *Griswold,* the Court determined that the government did not have the right to invade a married couple's bedroom to search for proscribed contraceptives. The prosecution of polygamy would demand greater intrusions into a couple's private world than the limited search supposed in *Griswold.* Before a charge could be filed, the police would have to examine the very structure of a couple's marital relationship. This search would encompass everything from the couple's sexual habits, to finances, to family structure, in order to determine if the husband was living with and maintaining more than one "wife." If the charges were true, the fact that the legal wife approved of the arrangement would be of no consequence to the government. If the charges were unsubstantiated, the government would have invaded the couple's privacy in an unconstitutional manner, invading the zone of marital privacy, in its search for improprieties. If the act of searching

> the bedroom for a condom can be considered intrusive, the surveillance necessary to prove a charge of polygamy would be worse.

Accordingly, antipolygamy statutes destroy the polygamist's right to marital privacy.

Unfortunately for polygamists, no state or federal court has ever accepted Gillett's argument. The Supreme Court has not ruled directly on an antipolygamy statute in more than a century, although it stated in a footnote in *Paris Adult Theatre I v. Slaton* (413 U.S. 49, 68, n. 15; 1973) that few individuals "seriously claim that making bigamy a crime violates the First Amendment or any other constitutional provision." (*Bigamy* is the condition of having two wives or two husbands at the same time.) The U.S. Court of Appeals for the Tenth Circuit considered the question of whether constitutional privacy prohibited the state of Utah from sanctioning polygamous marriage in *Potter v. Murray City* (760 F.2d 1065, 1070–1071; [10th Cir. 1985]), ultimately deciding that nothing in any of the Supreme Court's privacy cases—nothing in *Griswold,* nothing in *Loving,* nothing in *Eisenstadt v. Baird,* nothing in *Roe v. Wade*—supported extending the right to protect polygamous marriage. The following year, the U.S. Supreme Court denied certiorari (474 U.S. 849; 1985).

Although the law in the United States has consistently frowned upon plural marriages, in much of the global community, polygamy is common, normal, and accepted (Stack 1998, A1). Polygamy is regularly practiced in Africa, the Middle East, and Asia. Plural marriages are most prevalent in Muslim countries, most of which have no laws against the practice, including Algeria, Egypt, Iran, Iraq, Jordan, Morocco, Sudan, Syria, and Yemen. Estimates suggest that approximately one-third of the world's population belongs to a community that practices polygamy.

The acceptance of polygamy in many parts of the globe has raised anew the question of how a society should deal with immigrant customs that are uncommon, abnormal, and illegal in the new land. In short, how should the law respond when immigrants bring customs that violate societal taboos? Should immigrants be expected to abandon their customs and enter only into monogamous marriages, if any, or should the law recognize those customs and protect them from governmental encroachment? Beginning at least in the 1990s, African and Muslim immigrants to the United States have argued against the cultural and religious bias they perceive to be inherent in state and federal antipolygamy statutes. (State law prohibits polygamy; federal law bars polygamous immigrants.)

Immigrants and members of certain faiths continue to assert that the right to polygamy should be protected under the U.S. Constitution, either as a free exercise of religion, as a freedom of expression, or as a right to privacy for personal relationships among consenting adults. Such assertions have, for now, fallen upon unreceptive legislative and judicial ears.

Same-Sex Marriage

The general rule among the fifty states is that persons of the same sex may not marry each other. Since the mid-1970s, advocates of same-sex marriage, often lacking the political clout to obtain change through the legislative process, have increasingly sought judicial legalization of same-sex marriage and judicial recognition of same-sex marriages for the purposes of qualifying for various marital benefits. Most courts that have considered the question of whether a state must recognize same-sex marriages have concluded that statutes prohibiting such unions are constitutional. Efforts to secure same-sex marriage rights through litigation were wholly unsuccessful until 1993. Since then, courts in Hawaii, Alaska, and Vermont have rendered decisions favorable to same-sex marriage, although the decisions from Hawaii and Alaska were abrogated by state constitutional amendments.

In the early 1990s, Hawaii, like every other state, refused to recognize unions between members of the same sex as a valid marriage. After being denied marriage licenses, three same-sex couples brought suit in state court, claiming violations of their *enumerated* rights to privacy and equal protection under the Hawaii constitution. The state trial court dismissed the case, whereupon the couples appealed. In *Baehr v. Lewin* (852 P.2d 44; [Haw. 1993]), the Hawaii Supreme Court rejected the argument that same-sex couples possessed a fundamental right to marry under the state constitutional right to privacy. After acknowledging that it could give broader privacy protection under the Hawaii constitution than that given by the U.S. Constitution, the court declined to do so, instead holding that the state constitutional right to privacy was similar to the federal constitutional right to privacy. Accordingly, because same-sex marriage was not "so rooted in the traditions and collective conscience of our people," there was no fundamental, constitutional right to same-sex marriage. Nevertheless, the court concluded that the state's refusal to issue marriage licenses to same-sex couples constituted gender-based discrimination. The plurality began by emphasizing that the state's guarantees of equal protection were "more elaborate" than those found in the U.S. Constitution. Although the Fourteenth Amendment prohibited a state from denying "to any person within its jurisdiction the equal protection of the laws," Hawaii's counterpart in law specifically prohibited state-sanctioned discrimination against any person in the exercise of his or her civil rights on the basis of sex. As such, the plurality held that "sex" was a suspect category, and any state action that discriminated against a person because of his or her sex was subject to strict scrutiny. The *Baehr* court thus remanded the case to the trial court to determine whether the discrimination was necessary to serve a compelling state interest and narrowly tailored to achieve that interest.

On remand, a trial court found the state's interest in supporting the upbringing of children in particular types of households unpersuasive and ordered the state to issue marriage licenses irrespective of gender. The trial judge stayed the decision, however, pending the state's appeal to the Hawaii Supreme Court. Before that appeal could be heard, the Hawaii legislature approved a constitutional amendment that gave state lawmakers the power to restrict marriage to heterosexual couples. In late 1998, Hawaii voters overwhelmingly approved (69 percent to 29 percent) the amendment. Shortly thereafter, the Hawaii legislature clarified that marriage was between "a man and a woman," thereby nullifying the trial court's order that the state issue marriage licenses to same-sex couples.

Before the Hawaii constitution was amended, however, opponents of same-sex marriage introduced bills called "Defense of Marriage Acts" (DOMAs) to foreclose that possibility in numerous state legislatures. Today, thirty-six states statutorily ban same-sex marriage. Congressional opponents to same-sex marriage, motivated by fear that a same-sex marriage recognized in one state would have to be honored in other states under the Full Faith and Credit Clause, introduced the Defense of Marriage Act in 1996. (The Full Faith and Credit Clause, located in Article IV, section 1 of the U.S. Constitution, generally requires states to accept the public acts and records and judicial proceedings of other states as valid. Congress, however, has the power to prescribe the manner in which states are to comply with the clause.) The Defense of Marriage Act relieved the states of any obligation under the Full Faith and Credit Clause to recognize same-sex marriages from other states and defined marriage, for the purpose of all federal laws, as "the union of one man and one woman." Supporters of the bill argued that traditional heterosexual marriage was the "fundamental building block of [American] society," that the Judeo-Christian moral tradition considered homosexuality to be immoral and perverse, and that licensing same-sex marriages would eventually lead to licensing polygamy, incest, even marriage to animals. Those who opposed the Defense of Marriage Act reasoned that marriage was a fundamental right, regarding which the states should not discriminate on the basis of gender. They drew analogies between earlier bans on miscegenation and the continuing prohibition of same-sex marriage (Cott 2000, 219–220). The bill easily passed the House of Representatives (H.R. 3396) on July 12, 1996, and the Senate (S. 1740) on September 10, 1996. President William Clinton signed the Defense of Marriage Act into law on September 21, 1996.

In 1998, in *Brause v. Bureau of Vital Statistics* (No. 3AN-95-6562 CI [Alaska Sup. Ct. 1998]), an Alaska trial court held that a male couple was entitled to a marriage license. Relying heavily upon state constitutional privacy protection, the court recognized a fundamental right to choose one's life partner—an intimate personal decision, immune from governmental intrusion. Although it was true that same-sex marriage was not "rooted in our traditions," reasoned Judge Peter Michalski, it was equally obvious that the freedom to choose one's life partner was. Much like in Hawaii, however, this result was subsequently nullified by a state constitutional amendment.

Vermont proved to be the breakthrough for supporters of same-sex marriage. In December 1999, the Vermont Supreme Court, in *Baker v. State* (744 A.2d 864 [Vt. 1999]), ruled that state marriage laws denying equal benefits to committed same-sex partners violated the state constitution's guarantee that the laws be "instituted for the common benefit, protection, and security of the people, nation, or community, and not for the particular emolument or advantage of any single person, family, or set of persons, who are a part only of that community." In short, this Common Benefits Clause, a rough analogue to the Equal Protection Clause of the federal Fourteenth Amendment, prohibited discrimination—including discrimination against someone who wished to marry someone of the same sex—unless "premised on an appropriate and overriding public interest." After considering and dismissing each of the state's asserted interests—fostering the link between procreation and child rearing; promoting child rearing in a setting that provided both male and female role models;

discouraging marriages of convenience for tax, housing, or other benefits; maintaining uniformity with marriage laws in other states; and generally protecting marriage from destabilizing changes—the court held that same-sex couples were entitled to the same benefits and protections afforded by Vermont law to married opposite-sex couples. The court then ordered the state legislature to adopt legislation meeting its constitutional mandate. Four months later, Vermont enacted the nation's first law authorizing *civil unions* between same-sex partners that entitled those entering into such unions all the identical rights—including state benefits—and protections that stem from the marital relationship.

Though asked to do so, the Vermont Supreme Court did not establish same-sex marriage as a fundamental privacy right. Instead, the majority characterized same-sex marriage as involving a right to certain benefits that could not be denied consistent with the equal protection of the laws. As such, no state court of last resort has ever articulated an independent constitutional interest in same-sex marriage. The constitutional interest argument for same-sex marriage asserts

> that there is a fundamental constitutional right to marry or a broader right to privacy or of intimate association; that the essence of this right is the private, intimate association of consenting adults who want to share their lives and commitment with each other; that same-sex couples have just as much intimacy and need for marital privacy as heterosexual couples; and that laws allowing heterosexual, but not same-sex, couples to marry infringe upon and discriminate against this, or any related, fundamental right. (Wardle 1996, 26–27)

Relying largely on the family privacy cases, and emphasizing *Loving,* advocates of this position (Hohengarten 1994; Eskridge 1996) maintain that courts should compel states to permit same-sex marriages in the same manner that the U.S. Supreme Court compelled Virginia and other states to permit interracial marriages—by recognizing the claimed right either as a fundamental right to marry, or of privacy, or of intimate association.

Although it is true that the Supreme Court in *Loving* focused much on the invidious racial discrimination inherent in the antimiscegenation statute, it emphasized that the statute's impingement on the freedom to marry was independently unconstitutional. The Court elaborated on this analysis in *Zablocki v. Redhail* (discussed in Chapter 3). Supporters of same-sex marriage rights assert that *Loving* and *Zablocki* establish a doctrinal structure applicable to same-sex marriage: a state law that places a direct legal obstacle in the path of a person desiring to get married infringes a fundamental right and must be supported by sufficiently important state interests closely tailored to effectuate only those interests. Yet the justifications advanced by the state for prohibiting same-sex marriage—upholding tradition, creating the ideal setting for procreation, and maximizing the possibility that children will be raised in the best possible setting—are neither compelling nor narrowly tailored. Tradition cannot justify discrimination; after all, not long ago, society disapproved of interracial marriages. Excluding same-sex couples from marriage does not foster procreation because there is no evidence that gays and lesbians who cannot marry their same-sex partners will seek opposite-sex partners with whom they can marry and conceive children. And no evidence supports the assertion that children raised by heterosexual married couples fare better than those raised in two-parent gay and lesbian households. According to William Eskridge (1996, 142–143), these various arguments are simply makeweights for the real motivation behind the states' opposition to same-sex marriage—deterring homosexuality and the fear that recognizing same-sex marriage will send the message that the state approves of homosexuality.

Opponents of the constitutional interest argument for same-sex marriage (Wardle 1996; Schowengerdt 2001) acknowledge that marriage is a specially preferred, fundamental constitutional right. Yet they refuse to accept the claim that same-sex marriage is part of that fundamental right because neither of the established criteria for identifying special constitutional rights—that the right be "deeply rooted in our nation's history and tradition" or "implicit in the concept of ordered liberty"—is satisfied by same-sex marriage claims. As recently as 1986, the U.S. Supreme Court, in *Bowers v. Hardwick* (discussed in Chapter 3), considered and rejected the claim that constitutional privacy or any of the Court's prior jurisprudence provided any special protection for homosexual behavior. The justices concluded that constitutional privacy encompassed matters relating to procreation, marriage, and family life and that homosexual sodomy was wholly unrelated to each. Accordingly, commentators suggest that if a state may prohibit homosexual behavior, it logically follows that a state may prohibit homosexual marriage. Although it is true that marriage has received special solicitude and protection from the U.S. Supreme Court, that solicitude and protection have never been extended to same-sex marriage. The privacy protected in *Griswold* was conventional, heterosexual marriage. The privacy protected in *Loving* was heterosexual, though not so conventional, marriage. And the privacy protected in *Zablocki* was conventional, heterosexual marriage. Although the justices expanded the zone of constitutional privacy to include some activities unrelated to marriage, they never included within its protection homosexual behavior. Opponents recognize that a claim to constitutional protection for same-sex marriage would be strengthened if there were a sustained societal consensus for recognition of such marriages. Of course, no such support exists. Our nation's history and traditions have long condemned homosexumal behavior and never permitted same-sex marriages. The past aside, almost three-fourths of the states still ban same-sex marriage.

Opponents of the right to same-sex marriage also reject the *Loving* analogy and the equal protection argument. The *Loving* analogy—laws against same-sex marriage are constitutionally indistinguishable from the outdated prohibitions against interracial marriage—fails because, though the U.S. Supreme Court has found race to be unrelated to any legitimate purpose for distinguishing between couples in marriage regulations, it has never found homosexual behavior to be so unrelated. Moreover, the language and history of the Fourteenth Amendment make clear that its purpose was to forbid racial, and not sexual-orientation, discrimination by state government. Race is the quintessential suspect classification, and any law that discriminates on the basis of race is subject to strict scrutiny. By contrast, sexual orientation is a nonsuspect classification, and any law that discriminates on the basis of such is analyzed under the rational basis test (see Table 3.1). The equal protection argument—laws that permit a man to marry a woman but not another man discriminate on the basis of gender in violation of the Equal Protection Clause of the Fourteenth Amendment or some analogous state constitutional provision—was the basis for the decision of the Vermont Supreme Court. Opponents maintain that this argument is similarly unsupportable because, on its face, the heterosexual marriage requirement equally requires both men and women to marry only persons of the other gender. This line of reasoning was rejected when employed in the context of race in *Loving,* where Virginia argued that the antimiscegenation law treated both races equally by requiring both whites and blacks to marry only persons of the same race. Of course, *Loving* was about racial discrimination, not gender discrimination. As Chief Justice Earl Warren wrote, "Under our Constitution, the freedom to marry . . . a person of another *race* resides with the individual and cannot be infringed by the State" (388 U.S. at 12; emphasis added). And since that time, the Court has consistently refused to equate racial and gender discrimination.

At present, thirty-six states ban same-sex marriages. Only one state, Vermont, officially recognizes same-sex unions. Five states—California, Hawaii, Massachusetts, New York, and Vermont—and more than fifty municipal governments—including Atlanta, the District of Columbia, Los Angeles, New York City, Philadelphia, St. Louis, San Francisco, and Seattle—offer either domestic partnership registries or extend domestic partnership benefits to their employees, a significant increase in recent years.

In 2002, congressional opponents of same-sex marriage, aware of the successful efforts to secure same-sex marriage rights through litigation in Vermont and worried that courts in other states might extend the privilege, introduced in the House of Representatives a constitutional amendment. The proposed Federal Marriage Amendment states, "Marriage in the United States shall consist only of the union of a man and a woman. Neither this constitution nor the constitution of any state, nor state and federal law, shall be construed to require that marital status or the legal incidents thereof be conferred upon married couples or groups." If approved by both houses of Congress and ratified by the states, this constitutional amendment would not only deprive judges of the authority to demand legal recognition of same-sex marriages but also withdraw from state legislatures the power to permit same-sex marriages, even if every voter and every legislator in the state wanted to allow them. The amendment would not prohibit a state legislature from adopting a civil union or domestic partnership scheme, though it would prohibit a state or federal court from requiring a state legislature to do so. Benefits offered by private businesses would be unaffected by such an amendment. Because thirty-six states already have preemptive bans on same-sex marriage, it appears that if the proposal were to be adopted by the House of Representatives and the Senate (it has not yet been introduced in the Senate), supporters would need to locate only two more state legislatures willing to ban same-sex marriage. (To amend the Constitution requires ratification from three-fourths, or thirty-eight, of the states; thirty-six currently ban same-sex marriages.)

Marriage is no doubt a favored institution afforded preferential treatment under the laws of the nation. Many legal rights and responsibilities inhere in the marital relationship. Although the U.S. Supreme Court has repeatedly held that marriage is a fundamental right under the U.S. Constitution, it has not ruled directly on the issue of same-sex marriage. A constitutional challenge to a heterosexual marriage requirement could invoke either the Due Process Clause or the Equal Protection Clause, possibly both. A successful due process claim, however, appears unlikely. As recently as 1986, the Court refused to extend constitutional protection to homosexual behavior when rejecting a due process challenge to a state antisodomy statute. Presumably, if a state may proscribe homosexual behavior, it may similarly proscribe homosexual marriage. Moreover, the justices have always defined the fundamental right to marry exclusively as the freedom that one man and one woman have to enter into a special relationship largely immune from governmental interference. So far, only one court—a state trial court—has defined the fundamental right to marry broadly to include the freedom of all persons to choose their life partners, irrespective of gender. And that decision was promptly nullified by a state constitutional amendment. A successful equal protection claim is similarly doubtful. In *Romer v. Evans* (517 U.S. 620; 1996), the Supreme Court invalidated a state constitutional amendment forbidding legal protections for homosexuals, but it held that homosexuals did not constitute a suspect class for the purpose of equal protection analysis. Thus, though homosexuals are protected by the Equal Protection Clause, government action classifying individuals on the basis of homosexuality or homosexual behavior is subject to the rational basis test, and any such classification will be sustained as long as it is rationally related to a legitimate state interest (see Table 3.1, "Standards of Review"). Although the Court has already noted that public disapprobation alone is insufficient to justify singling out a group of citizens for unfavorable treatment, the justices may be more willing to accept a state's interest in upholding tradition, creating the ideal setting for procreation, and maximizing the possibility that children will be raised in the best possible setting.

Homosexual Adoption

In 1977, Florida became the first state to deny homosexuals the right to adopt children. Accordingly, when Steven Lofton, a homosexual foster parent of three children, filed an application with the Florida Department of Children and Families to adopt one of his three foster children, his application was denied. Lofton then challenged the state law in federal district court as violative of the fundamental rights of family privacy, intimate association, and family integrity protected by the Due Process Clause, as well as of the Equal Protection Clause. In August 2001, in *Lofton v. Kearney* (157 F.Supp. 2d 1372 [S.D. Fla. 2001]), a federal judge rejected both claims. Although acknowledging that biological ties alone did not constitute a family, Judge Lawrence King nevertheless concluded that the Due Process Clause protected "only those social units that share an expectation of continuity justified by the presence of certain basic elements traditionally recognized as characteristic of the family" (157 F.Supp. 2d at 1379). Relying heavily upon the U.S. Supreme Court's decision in *Smith v. Organization for Foster Families for Equality and Reform* (discussed in Chapter 3), the judge concluded that when family bonds originate under state law and contractual arrangements—as is the case with foster families and adoptions—rather than from biological ties, the members of that family have a diminished expectation of family privacy, intimate association, and family integrity. In short, adoption was a privilege created by statute, not a fundamental right.

As to the equal protection argument, the court held that the appropriate standard of review, because adoption was not a fundamental right and because homosexuals did not constitute a suspect class, was the rational basis test (see Table 3.1, "Standards of Review"). The state of Florida argued that the homosexual adoption provision served two legitimate purposes: to express moral disapproval of homosexuality and to promote the best interests of Florida's children. The court rejected the first interest: "Enacting a classification to express society's disapproval of a group burdened by the law is precisely what the Equal Protection Clause does not allow" (157 F.Supp. 2d at 1382.) The second argument, however, proved convincing, and the court concluded that it was rational for the state to conclude that a heterosexual married couple provided a more stable home life for children as compared to homosexual parents.

Currently, Florida is the only state that prohibits homosexuals from adopting. Although the U.S. Supreme Court has yet to rule on the constitutionality of such a prohibition, the holding in *Smith*—that family privacy inheres more in the natural family than in the foster family—may well be dispositive in the area of homosexual adoption.

Sexual Autonomy

Numerous twentieth-century Supreme Court decisions—most notably *Griswold* and *Eisenstadt*—opened the door to claims of sexual autonomy. Nevertheless, it is still not entirely clear how much sexual autonomy is included under the rubric of constitutional privacy. Prisoners, for example, have often asserted that because married and unmarried persons have a fundamental right to privacy in their sexual relations, they should be permitted physical intimacy with their spouses or lovers. Recently, a prisoner argued that his fundamental right to procreate—even if accomplished via overnight mail—survived incarceration. In addition, two state courts have held that constitutional privacy includes the right to obtain and use sexually stimulating devices.

Conjugal Rights, the Right to Procreation, and Prisoners

Prisoners do not shed all of their constitutional rights at the prison gate. The Supreme Court has repeatedly insisted that prison inmates be accorded those rights not fundamentally inconsistent with imprisonment itself or incompatible with the objectives of incarceration. For example, *Skinner v. Oklahoma* (discussed in Chapter 3) held that a forced sterilization program violated a prisoner's constitutional right to maintain his procreative abilities. More recently, *Turner v. Safley* (see Chapter 3) established that inmates have a fundamental right to marry while incarcerated. Even though these and other constitutional guarantees survive incarceration, they may be restricted by legitimate penological objectives, to include security, order, deterrence, incapacitation, reformation, and rehabilitation.

Marital privacy rights—to include cohabitation, conjugal rights, and procreation—may be substantially abridged, even denied, in the prison setting. (*Conjugal rights* are the rights of a husband and wife to each other's company and affection.) Although the right to marry is constitutionally protected, courts have held that the exigencies and operational considerations of the penal system preclude a prisoner from retaining and exercising a fundamental right to cohabitate or to engage in sexual relations with his or her spouse. In other words, constitutional privacy does not create any protected guarantee to cohabitation or conjugal visitation privileges with a spouse while incarcerated. Constitutionally permissible restrictions on conjugal visits had, it was thought until recently, rendered the procreation question moot. As such, the Supreme Court has never directly addressed whether the right to procreate is a right prisoners possess during their time in prison. No court at any level had done so prior to 2000, when William Gerber, a life-term prisoner in California, requested to have a child with his wife via artificial insemination.

Given Gerber's sentence, a state regulation that prohibited conjugal visits for inmates serving lifetime terms, and his wife's age, Gerber alleged that artificial insemination was the only method by which he and his wife could conceive a child together. He thus requested that prison authorities permit him to provide a semen specimen to a laboratory so that his wife could be artificially inseminated with it. Prison authorities denied the request, whereupon Gerber filed suit alleging that the prison's refusal violated his constitutional right to procreate under the Due Process Clause of the Fourteenth Amendment. Although the trial court recognized the right to procreate as fundamental, it held that a prisoner forfeited his or her right to access to a means of procreation while incarcerated (*Gerber v. Hickman,* 103 F.Supp. 2d 1214 [E.D. Cal. 2000]). The U.S. Court of Appeals for the Ninth Circuit initially reversed the decision. Citing *Skinner* and *Turner,* the three-judge panel held that the right to procreation survived incarceration (*Gerber v. Hickman,* 264 F.3d 882 [9th Cir. 2001]). The panel then remanded the case back to the trial court, requesting that prison authorities articulate legitimate penological objectives to justify restricting the exercise of this right.

Before those further proceedings took place, however, the Ninth Circuit, dividing 6-5, reversed the decision en banc (*Gerber v. Hickman,* 291 F.3d 617 [9th Cir. 2002]). Requiring prison authorities to accommodate Gerber's request as a matter of constitutional right, noted the majority opinion, would be "a radical and unprecedented interpretation" of the Constitution. Some familial rights enjoyed by free persons—such as privacy, intimate association, and procreation—were fundamentally inconsistent with incarceration. The dissenters criticized the majority for failing to explain how Gerber's request implicated rights necessarily restricted by incarceration. The prisoner wanted to ejaculate into a plastic cup, which was then to be mailed or given to his lawyer for delivery to a laboratory that would use its content to artificially inseminate his wife. No step of that process was fundamentally inconsistent with incarceration: "Production of the semen and delivery to a laboratory neither compromises security, nor places a strain on prison resources beyond that required to mail any other package" (291 F.3d at 629–630). Prison guards do not patrol cell blocks looking for inmates masturbating; the prison has no penological interest in what prisoners do "with their seed once it's spilt"; there is nothing remotely inconsistent with incarceration in handing a non–security threatening package from an inmate to an inmate's lawyer; and what the lawyer does with the package once it is outside prison walls is irrelevant to prison authorities.

In August 2002, Gerber petitioned the U.S. Supreme Court for a writ of certiorari. On November 18, 2002, the justices, without comment, denied the writ. Accordingly, the Court has never addressed squarely the question of whether the fundamental right to procreate survives incarceration.

Sexually Stimulating Devices

Since the mid-1970s, eight states—Alabama, Colorado, Georgia, Kansas, Louisiana, Mississippi, Texas, and Virginia—have enacted laws criminalizing the sale, distribution, or promotion of sexual devices used primarily for the stimulation of human genital organs. Numerous lower courts have considered constitutional challenges to such laws.

State appellate courts in Georgia and Texas have upheld the constitutionality of their statutes. The Georgia Supreme Court construed the prohibited devices—dildos, vibrators, and artificial vaginas—as obscene; therefore, they were constitutionally unprotected (*Sewell v. State,* 233 S.E.2d 187 [Ga. 1977]). One Texas court avoided the constitutional privacy issue altogether by justifying the statute as an appropriate exercise of state police power, the state's authority to legislate to protect public health, safety, welfare, and morality (*Yorko v. State,* 690 S.W.2d 260 [Tex. Crim. App. 1985]); and a second considered and rejected the constitutional privacy issue, asserting that the U.S. Supreme Court had never expressly recognized a fundamental right to sexual privacy (*Regaldo v. State,* 872 S.W.2d 7 [Tex. App. 1994]).

State supreme courts in Colorado, Kansas, and Louisiana, as well as a federal district court in Alabama, however, have rejected state statutes banning the sale of genital-stimulating devices. The Colorado and Kansas Supreme Courts based their decisions on the constitutional right to privacy but limited their holdings to those individuals seeking to make legitimate medical or therapeutic use of the proscribed devices (*People v. Seven Thirty-Five East Colfax, Inc.,* 697 P.2d 1023 [Colo. 1985]; *State v. Hughes,* 792 P.2d 1023 [Kan. 1990]). Because the legitimate use of these devices was a fundamental right, the courts subjected the statutes to strict scrutiny, ultimately finding that the states' interests were not sufficiently compelling to justify the infringement. By contrast, a federal district court in Alabama and the Louisiana Supreme Court, noting the U.S. Supreme Court's reluctance to expand fundamental rights, refused to expand the fundamental right to privacy to include sexually stimulating devices (*Williams v. Pryor,* 41 F.Supp. 2d 1257 [N.D. Ala. 1999]; *State v. Brenan,* 772 So.2d 64 [La. 2000]). Nevertheless, both courts found that the statutes failed the rational basis test. After accepting the states' interests in promoting public morality, the courts held that absolute bans on such devices, without considering their medical and therapeutic uses, were not rationally related to the state's interest in protecting children and unconsenting adults from viewing obscene material. In January 2001, the U.S. Court of Appeals for the Eleventh Circuit reversed the decision of the federal district court, concluding that Alabama's interest in promoting public morality was a legitimate interest and that the statute prohibiting the sale of sexually stimulating devices was rationally related to that interest. That conclusion aside, however, the Eleventh Circuit remanded the case to the trial court for reconsideration of the fundamental rights/constitutional privacy issues, noting that the statute implicated "important interests in sexual privacy" (*Williams v. Pryor,* 240 F.3d 944, 955 [11th Cir. 2001]).

As is evident from this discussion, lower courts are divided on the question of whether constitutional privacy protects the sale, distribution, and promotion of sexually stimulating devices. This is partly due to the fact that the U.S. Supreme Court has never specifically included sexual autonomy within the protections of constitutional privacy. Some constitutional scholars (Mohr 1986; Kaminer 2001) believe that the Court's prior cases, specifically the contraception and abortion cases, establish a constitutional right to sexual autonomy—that is, that the Constitution protects the second decision (to use contraceptives or to abort an unborn child) necessarily means that the Constitution protects the first decisions (to engage in sexual relations). Read more broadly, constitutional privacy should be extended to all aspects of an individual's private sex life, including the use of sexually stimulating devices. Of course, the justices have never explicitly articulated a fundamental right to sex. And even if previous cases can be so construed, that does not guarantee that there is a fundamental right to sexually stimulating devices. As the Court said in *Glucksberg,* a fundamental right must be "objectively, deeply rooted in this Nation's history and tradition" and "implicit in the concept or ordered liberty, such that 'neither liberty nor justice would exist if [the right] were sacrificed" (521 U.S. at 720–721). The Eleventh Circuit remanded *Williams* precisely because the lower court failed to analyze whether private sexual activity in general (and the right to a vibrator in particular) was deeply rooted in the history and traditions of our nation. Thus, the fate of Alabama's prohibition on sexually stimulating devices, and perhaps the fates of other similar prohibitions, remains undetermined.

INFORMATIONAL PRIVACY

Without question, technological developments over the decades have heightened threats to privacy. Closed-circuit TVs scrutinize activities in supermarkets, shopping malls, workplaces, and along city streets. Traffic monitoring systems record the whereabouts of automobiles. Wireless communications technology can pinpoint the location of cellular phones. Electronic communications systems generate information about an individual's credit-card purchases and Internet browsing habits. Computer technology provides the means for central storage of and easy accessibility to massive amounts of data, making information collection much easier. And the Internet—the ultimate marketplace of ideas unrestricted by geographic distances or national borders—facilitates the unprecedented and rapid dissemination of stored information. This explosive growth in networked acquisition, storage, and dissemination of information, much of which links various facts with identifying characteristics of individuals and is maintained by federal, state, and local authorities, poses a serious threat to informational privacy by increasing the potential for security breaches and subsequent abuse of such information.

Informational privacy is the claim of individuals, groups, and institutions "to determine for themselves when, how, and to what extent information about them is communicated to others" (Westin 1967, 7). Of particular concern here is the acquisition, storage, or dissemination of information by *government.* Individuals have no constitutional protection when private actors acquire and disseminate certain information, although many states provide legal protection through statutes that give individuals the right to sue for damages if their privacy has been invaded in specified ways. Typically, the constitutional right to informational privacy involves an allegation that government has acquired or disclosed highly personal or intimate information about an individual, without that individual's consent and without sufficient justification, resulting in a loss of privacy. To what extent, therefore, do state and federal constitutions protect individuals from unjustifiable encroachments of privacy that occur when government acquires or discloses highly personal or intimate information about them?

The Supreme Court did not explicitly recognize the right to informational privacy under the U.S. Constitution until *Whalen v. Roe* (429 U.S. 589; 1977), a challenge by patients and doctors to a

New York statute that required copies of prescriptions for certain drugs to be recorded and stored in a centralized governmental computer. Although the justices rejected the challenge, finding that the state's interest in controlling the distribution of dangerous drugs was a legitimate exercise of state police power, a majority assumed that, in certain circumstances, the acquisition and disclosure by the government of health care information would violate the constitutional right to informational privacy. Justice John Paul Stevens, writing for the majority, noted that constitutional privacy embraced not only an "interest in independence in making certain kinds of important decisions"—those about marriage, procreation, and family life, for example—but also an "individual interest in avoiding disclosure of personal matters" (429 U.S. at 599–600). As the authority for this other branch of constitutional privacy rights, the Court relied upon Justice Brandeis's dissent in *Olmstead v. United States* (1928; see discussion in Chapter 3), wherein he characterized privacy as the "right to be let alone." By doing so, the Court linked the constitutional right to informational privacy "to the intellectual tradition, rights theory, and concept of privacy" that was reflected in Warren and Brandeis's 1890 *Harvard Law Review* article on privacy (Turkington 1990, 481). (Although it is true that informational privacy was not the focus of that article, its authors discussed the loss of privacy stemming from the publication of personal information.) In affirming the right of the individual to have personal information kept private, the majority concluded:

> A final word about issues we have not decided. We are not unaware of the threat to privacy implicit in the accumulation of vast amounts of personal information in computerized data banks or other massive government files. The collection of taxes, the distribution of welfare and social security benefits, the supervision of public health, the direction of our Armed Forces, and the enforcement of the criminal laws all require the orderly preservation of great quantities of information,

> much of which is personal in character and potentially embarrassing or harmful if disclosed. The right to collect and use such data for public purposes is typically accompanied by a concomitant statutory or regulatory duty to avoid unwarranted disclosures. . . . [I]n some circumstances, that duty arguably has its roots in the Constitution. (429 U.S. at 605)

Whalen thus encouraged lower courts to find violations of the constitutional right to informational privacy when government unjustifiably collected or disseminated certain personal information. Since *Whalen,* seven federal appellate courts have explicitly recognized informational privacy as a constitutionally protected interest, a fundamental right implicit in the concept of liberty under the U.S. Constitution. Because this right is triggered by governmental action that does not constitute a search within the meaning of the Fourth Amendment, it is part of the constitutionally protected liberties that are independent of the Fourth Amendment (Turkington 1990, 481). In addition, numerous state courts have construed their state constitutions to provide similar privacy protection.

In informational privacy cases post-*Whalen,* most of which involve the disclosure of health care information or financial records, lower courts have accepted Justice Brandeis's argument that every intrusion by the government upon the privacy of the individual must be justified. Accordingly, as is true in most other areas of the law, when individuals challenge government's disclosure of certain information about them, courts engage in the delicate task of balancing competing interests. On the one hand, individuals clearly have an interest in controlling the circulation of information about themselves. (For example, individuals treated in state mental health hospitals have a legitimate interest in keeping their mental health records private.) On the other hand, the government's disclosure of certain information is often necessary to accomplish legitimate governmental functions. (For example, the government's obligation to protect citizens may necessitate the release of mental health information in certain situations, such as when an individual with a mental health history seeks a license to carry a firearm or employment as an elementary school teacher.)

Quite obviously, not all disclosures of information by government violate the constitutional right to informational privacy. To determine whether the constitutional right to informational privacy has been violated, courts first must determine the extent to which the individual's privacy has been invaded by government and, second, evaluate the government's need for the information to determine whether the invasion of privacy is justified (Turkington 1990, 504–509). Lower courts have consistently held the constitutional right to informational privacy protects against disclosure only of *some* information and is not a general right to nondisclosure of all private information. More precisely, informational privacy protects against the disclosure only of information implicating privacy—information describing or representing intimate or highly personal facts about a person. Therefore, the threshold requirement question is whether the information acquired or disseminated by government is of an intimate or highly personal nature. Intimate information is information "about a person that is inextricably tied to personhood; it is information that reflects an extension or expression of the person and deals with the very essence of that person." Such information includes information about an individual's physical features, medical conditions, mental states, family relationships, and sexual activities. "Non-consensual acquisition or publication of such information demonstrates a lack of respect to the person and constitutes an affront to the subject's human dignity" (Turkington 1990, 506). Similarly, financial records, although not intimate, are highly personal, and disclosure of such information can lead to unwarranted solicitations, lawsuits, extortion, kidnapping, identity theft, and other potentially harmful consequences.

The threshold requirement is thus met, and the constitutional right to informational privacy implicated, when government discloses highly personal or intimate information without consent. When government does so, and such action is later challenged, courts must then determine whether the privacy intrusion is justified. In *United States v. Westinghouse* (638 F.2d 570 [3d Cir. 1980]), the U.S. Court of Appeals for the Third Circuit, after recognizing that at times the societal interest in disclosing personal information outweighed the privacy interest, promulgated a now well-accepted standard for determining whether the invasion of privacy is constitutionally justified. The factors to be considered in weighing the societal interest in public health and safety against the privacy interests include: (1) the type of information requested; (2) the potential for harm in any nonconsensual disclosure of that information; (3) the injury from disclosure to the relationship in which the record was generated; (4) the adequacy of safeguards to prevent unauthorized disclosure; (5) the degree of the need for access; and (6) whether there is an express statutory mandate, articulated public policy, or other recognizable interest militating toward access. At a minimum, the government must be able to demonstrate that the release of certain information furthers an important governmental interest and that sufficient effort has been taken to prevent unnecessary and excessive public access to such information.

The state statutes known as Megan's Laws offer a good example of the conflict between the government's need to disseminate information and the individual's right to keep certain information private. In 1994, Megan Kanka, a seven-year-old, was brutally raped and murdered near her home. The Kanka's neighbor, a man twice convicted of sexual offenses involving young girls, eventually confessed to the assault. Megan, her parents, local police, and members of the community had no knowledge of the accused murderer's history. New Jersey subsequently enacted the so-called Megan's Law, which required all sex offenders at large to register with local authorities. It also provided for the disclosure of certain information about those required to register. Following congressional encouragement, all states enacted similar laws, which vary greatly from state to state. California, for example, disseminates information about convicted sex offenders on a CD-ROM accessible to the public. Louisiana insists that convicted sex offenders inform their neighbors via postcards. Some states require law enforcement officers to notify the community that a sex offender has moved into the neighborhood; others compel authorities to publish the address of the offender; and still others mandate that the offender submit blood, hair, or saliva samples to a DNA database to be used as evidence if future charges were brought against that person. Opponents of registration and community notification laws like these allege, among other constitutional claims, an invasion of informational privacy. By informing local communities of such intimate and highly personal information, offenders no doubt suffer great harm in the form of shame, harassment, and discrimination. Nevertheless, most courts that have considered the constitutionality of these laws have upheld them. In 1997, for example, in *E. B. v. Verniero* (119 F.3d 1077; [3d Cir. 1997]), a challenge to the New Jersey law, the U.S. Court of Appeals for the Third Circuit did not dismiss the informational privacy argument but instead recognized the legitimate governmental interest in protecting public safety. "[R]egistration and . . . notification can enable law enforcement and those likely to encounter a sex offender to be aware of a potential danger and to stay vigilant against possible re-abuse," the decision said. "This is not an unreasonable premise" (119 F.3d at 1098). Later that year, the U.S. Supreme Court refused to stay the New Jersey community notification statute, thereby allowing the decision of the Third Circuit to stand.

According to Laurence Tribe (1988, 1393), government

> should be recognized to have a duty to provide reasonable assurance (1) that it is not needlessly, or in breach of the terms on which information was gathered, (a) maintaining or (b) releasing (or encouraging maintenance or release of) information about people, however accurate; and (2) that such information as government either maintains or releases (or encourages others to maintain or release) is indeed as accurate as it can reasonably be made.

Although there is no comprehensive law guaranteeing informational privacy in the United States, Congress has enacted scores of statutes that affect informational privacy. Some of those laws apply to government; some apply to private entities; and some apply to both. For example, the Privacy Act of 1974 prohibits the disclosure of a federal agency record containing personal information without the written consent of the subject except in limited circumstances, which include disclosure for routine use (i.e., use consistent with the purpose for which the information was collected), law enforcement purposes, and protecting the health or safety of an individual. The Fair Credit Reporting Act of 1974 requires consumer reporting agencies to adopt procedures to assure that credit information is confidential, accurate, relevant, and used for its proper purposes. The Electronic Communications Privacy Act of 1986 protects against the unauthorized access, interception, or disclosure of private electronic communications by the government (as well as by third parties to the communication). Authorized access, interception, or disclosure by government requires a court-ordered warrant. The Computer Fraud and Abuse Act of 1994 prohibits unauthorized access of private and government computers. The Health Insurance Portability and Accountability Act of 1996 protects the privacy of medical records. Even the Freedom of Information Act and the Right to Know Act—based largely on the notion that citizens in a democratic society have a legal right to examine and investigate the conduct of government—contain provisions that prevent the general dissemination of much intimate and highly personal information in the possession of government. Other federal policies protecting informational privacy include the Family Educational Rights and Privacy Act of 1974, which protects student records; the Driver's Privacy Protection Act of 1994, which regulates the release of motor vehicle records; the Right to Financial Privacy Act of 1994, which forbids most governmental access of the financial records of individuals; the Video Privacy Act of 1994, which safeguards videotape rental records; and various provisions of the Internal Revenue Code, which require the privacy of taxpayer records. In addition, most states have adopted statutes that prevent the general dissemination of intimate and highly personal information by state governmental actors and agencies.

Two other recent issues invoke claims of informational privacy: first, the federal government's request for access to encrypted messages (Etzioni 1999, 75–102); and second, the federal government's warrantless and widespread monitoring of individuals' Internet activities.

To protect against espionage and to ensure customer confidentiality in on-line transactions, private businesses, including banks, regularly use *encrypted*, or specifically coded, messages. As a result of this expanding use of complicated encryption technologies, law enforcement officers, no longer able to decipher encrypted communications, have requested that those who use coding or scrambling devices provide the federal government with the "keys" to obtain access to the encrypted information. Proponents of such an initiative see a necessity based on national security and public safety, even more apparent since the terrorist attacks of September 11, 2001. After all, terrorists and other criminals have regularly used encryption to keep their plans and activities secret. When police arrested Ramszi Yousef, the mastermind behind the truck-bombing of the World Trade Center in New York City in 1993 that killed six people, they discovered encrypted plans to blow up eleven commercial aircraft. Aun Shinrikyo, the cult responsible for the nerve gas attack on a Tokyo subway in 1995, in which nineteen people died, had encrypted files about plans to attack the United States. And Aldrich Ames, a Central Intelligence Agency official who spied for the Soviet Union, used encrypted files.

In July 2000, the Federal Bureau of Investigation (FBI) admitted to its use of Carnivore, a device that intercepts, reads, stores, and classifies Internet transmissions, including e-mail communications, to and from persons or organizations that the FBI thinks may be involved in criminal activity. By cataloging an individual's e-mail and web-browsing habits, Carnivore is capable of providing law enforcement authorities with a detailed picture of that individual's associations, habits, contacts, interests, and activities—all of which occurs without the individual's knowledge and without a typical court-ordered warrant. Proponents of the device point to the fact that Carnivore makes it much more difficult for terrorists, organized crime groups, and drug-trafficking organizations to communicate via the Internet, thereby reducing their ability to defeat effective law enforcement. Moreover, proponents assure critics that the FBI will limit the use of Carnivore to those situations in which a court has authorized the interception of computer communications. Congress initially expressed serious reservations about the use of Carnivore. Nevertheless, in the wake of the events of September 11, 2001, Congress, in passing the USA Patriot Act, broadened the FBI's power to use Carnivore.

Those who oppose the government's request for access to encrypted communications and the government's monitoring of Internet transmissions naturally fear the diminution of privacy, the possibility for the improper capture of data, and the potential abuse of the gathered information. The ability to conduct one's personal affairs away from the prying eyes of government, they assert, is of paramount importance in a free society. Although the government has assured the public that necessary safeguards to protect against unauthorized abuse or misuse of information have been taken, critics continue to disbelieve. Instead, they maintain that modern technology has fulfilled Justice Brandeis's prophesy expressed in dissent in *Olmstead*—that "ways may some day be developed by which the Government, without removing papers from secret drawers, can reproduce them in court, and by which it will be enabled to expose to a jury the most intimate occurrences of the home" (277 U.S. at 473–474).

In 1977, the U.S. Supreme Court held that informational privacy was a constitutionally protected interest. Remarkable advances in technology, leading to the unprecedented acquisition, storage, and sharing of massive amounts of data, have made constitutional protection for informational privacy a much more complex issue than in generations past. Nevertheless, lower courts continue to apply the balancing-of-interests test—weighing the competing interests of the state and the individual, balancing the advantages of disclosure with its accompanying threats to privacy. Courts have thus consistently held that the constitutionally protected interest in informational privacy is mitigated when the dissemination of certain information furthers a legitimate governmental objective. Clearly, some governmental disclosure of intimate or highly personal information is justifiable; allowing government unfettered discretion to disclose all that it knows about an individual is not. Thus, when a court decides that the government's interest legitimately supports the dissemination of intimate or highly personal information, it typically circumscribes the permissible instances to prevent potential abuses.

CONCLUSION

Although neither the Constitution nor the Bill of Rights mentions any right to privacy, the Supreme Court has long recognized that a right to personal privacy exists under the Constitution. No doubt, constitutional privacy exists because our form of democratic government recognizes, and the Constitution imposes, some limits of the authority of government to control the day-to-day activities of its citizens. Justice Louis Brandeis aptly captured the intentions of the Framers in his memorable dissent in *Olmstead:*

> The makers of our Constitution undertook to secure conditions favorable to the pursuit of happiness. They recognized the significance of man's spiritual nature, of his feelings and of his intellect. They knew that only a part of the pain, pleasure and satisfactions of life are to be found in material things. They sought to protect Americans in their beliefs, their thoughts, their emotions and their sensations. They conferred, as against the government, the right to be let alone—the most comprehensive of rights and the right most valued by civilized men. To protect that right, every unjustifiable intrusion by the government upon the privacy of the individual, whatever the means employed, must be deemed a [constitutional] violation. (277 U.S. 438, 478)

In varying contexts, the Supreme Court or individual justices have found that constitutional privacy derives from numerous rights specifically protected in the Bill of Rights, the Ninth Amendment, or the Fourteenth Amendment. Constitutional privacy comes from the "penumbras" and "emanations" of the First, Third, Fourth, and Fifth Amendments, all of which were intended to protect individuals in their privacy; read together, these amendments create "zones of privacy." It stems from the Ninth Amendment, which makes clear that certain rights, though not specifically listed in the Bill of Rights, are still protected against governmental encroachment. And it is found in the "liberty" protected by the Due Process Clause of the Fourteenth Amendment.

Wherever derived, constitutional privacy should not be confused with the expectations of privacy guaranteed by the Fourth Amendment; neither should it be mistaken with the right to privacy protected by tort law. The Fourth Amendment concept of privacy specifically protects against unjustified governmental intrusions into one's person, homes, papers, and effects and is necessary for the full enjoyment of the rights of personal security, personal liberty, and private property. The Fourth Amendment, to be sure, secures privacy, but it is a separate aspect of privacy, one not covered here. The tort law concept of privacy protects against encroachments stemming from the actions of private individuals, and it permits the individual whose privacy has been invaded to request from a court of law an action for damages against the person or persons who have committed the wrong. By contrast, constitutional privacy is the right of the individual: (1) to be free from unwanted and unwarranted governmental intrusion in all matters affecting fundamental rights; and (2) not to have certain private information gathered, preserved, or disseminated by government. Thus, constitutional privacy involves at least two separate kinds of interests: one in independence in making certain kinds of important decisions, and the other in avoiding disclosure by government of personal matters.

The first type of constitutional privacy interest "attaches to the rightholder's own actions." It is about the freedom of the individual to make certain decisions and to act upon those decisions. Constitutional privacy thus immunizes certain conduct from state proscription or penalty (Rubenfeld 1989, 740). For most of the twentieth century and now in the twenty-first, the Supreme Court has debated just "which decisions" should be protected from state proscription or penalty. The Court has said that constitutional privacy encompasses only those personal rights that can be deemed "fundamental" or "implicit in the concept of ordered liberty," and it has extended constitutional privacy to activities relating to procreation, marriage, and family life. We know, for example, that constitutional privacy includes reproductive choices that, if denied, would affect a couple as to whether to conceive a child or force a pregnant woman to bear a child—marital choices that, if denied, would deprive men and women of "one of the vital personal rights essential to the orderly pursuit of happiness for free men." Constitutional privacy also includes family choices that, if denied, would permit government to make children the mere instruments of the state and to limit family living arrangements. More specifically, we know that constitutional privacy protects the right of married and unmarried persons to use contraceptives and of pregnant woman to obtain an abortion; the right to choose one's marital partner irrespective of race and to dissolve a marital relationship irrespective of financial resources; and the right of parents to direct the upbringing of their children and to live with extended family members. Because procreation, marriage, and family life

> are undertakings that go on for years, define roles, direct activities, operate on or even create intense emotional relations, enlist the body, inform values, and in sum substantially shape the totality of a person's daily life and consciousness, . . . [l]aws that force such undertakings on individuals may properly be called 'totalitarian,' and the right to privacy exists to protect against them. (Rubenfeld 1989, 801–802)

We also know that constitutional privacy does *not* include the right to enter into plural marriages; the right to engage in homosexual sodomy; and the right of prisoners to engage in sexual relations with their loved ones or spouses. In these and other matters, the Supreme Court has held that such alleged rights are neither "fundamental" nor "implicit in the concept of ordered liberty."

The second type of constitutional privacy interest attaches to government's actions vis-à-vis the individual's right to control the face he or she presents to the world. As Isaiah Berlin (1969, 155) asked, "Am I not what I am, to some degree in virtue of what others think and feel me to be?" Although this type of constitutional privacy has received much less attention from legal scholars and courts than the other, courts have regularly held that government has an obligation to avoid unwarranted disclosures of certain personal information and that when government opts to disclose such information it be done in furtherance of a legitimate governmental objective. The relatively sparse attention afforded informational privacy, however, should not be interpreted as a lack of importance. Moreover, this type of privacy will become more urgent in the age of the computer and the Internet, with their vast capacities to obtain, retain, and disseminate massive amounts of information.

Several privacy issues remain unresolved. The Supreme Court's rulings on refusing medical treatment and physician-assisted suicide have not fully answered the question of whether constitutional privacy protects the right to die. The justices have yet to address directly the issues of same-sex marriages, homosexual adoptions, a prisoner's right to conceive a child with his wife via artificial insemination, and sexually stimulating devices. And technological developments continue to raise new questions about the limits of governmental power and the boundaries of constitutional privacy. Constitutional privacy thus remains a developing concept.

The right to privacy is firmly established in American constitutional law. Citizens value it; state and federal courts have recognized it; and numerous state constitutions contain explicit protections for it. As such, the constitutional right to privacy is not in jeopardy of being relegated to the fringes of our constitutional jurisprudence.

It remains to be seen, however, where the courts will draw the line between the power of the government and the right of the people to be let alone. The challenge today is the same as it was a century ago: to strike the appropriate balance between our need for order and our desire for liberty. And that is no easy task. A government with too much power breeds despotism. A citizenry with too much freedom invites anarchy. The right to privacy illustrates well this give and take of our constitutional system of governance.

References and Further Reading

"Aided Suicide Law Invalidated Again." *New York Times,* January 28, 1994, at A17.

Aquinas, St. Thomas. [1274] 1988. *Summa Theologica.* Translated and edited by Paul E. Sigmund. New York: W. W. Norton.

Battin, Margaret P., Rosamond Rhodes, and Anita Silvers. 1998. *Physician Assisted Suicide: Expanding the Debate.* New York: Routledge.

Berlin, Isaiah. 1969. *Four Essays on Liberty.* London: Oxford University Press.

Black's Law Dictionary. 1968–1990. 4th–6th eds. St. Paul, MN: West Publishing.

Blackstone, Sir William. 1765–1769. *Commentaries on the Laws of England.* 4 vols. Oxford, UK: Clarendon Press.

de Bracton, Henry. [1268] 1968. *On the Laws and Customs of England.* Translated by Samuel E. Thorne and edited by George S. Woodbine. 4 vols. Buffalo, NY: W. S. Hein.

Cott, Nancy F. 2000. *Public Vows: A History of Marriage and the Nation.* Cambridge, MA: Harvard University Press.

Cruz, David B. 2000. "'The Sexual Freedom Cases'? Contraception, Abortion, Abstinence, and the Constitution." *Harvard Civil Rights and Civil Liberties Law Review* 35: 299–383.

Eskridge, William N. 1996. *The Case for Same-Sex Marriage: From Sexual Liberty to Civilized Commitment.* New York: Free Press.

Etzioni, Amitai. 1999. *The Limits of Privacy.* New York: Basic Books.

Feinberg, Joel. 1978. "Voluntary Euthanasia and the Right to Life." *Philosophy and Public Affairs* 7: 93–123.

Gillett, Todd M. 2000. "The Absolution of *Reynolds:* The Constitutionality of Religious Polygamy." *William and Mary Bill of Rights Journal* 8: 497–534.

Helms, Shawn C. 2001. "Translating Privacy Values with Technology." *Boston University Journal of Science and Technology Law* 7: 288–326.

Hoefler, James M. 1994. "Diffusion and Diversity: Federalism and the Right to Die in the Fifty States." *Publius: The Journal of Federalism* 24: 153–170.

Hoefler, James M., and Brian M. Kamoie. 1994. *Deathright: Culture, Medicine, Politics, and the Right to Die.* Boulder, CO: Westview Press.

Hohengarten, William M. 1994. "Note, Same-Sex Marriage, and the Right of Privacy." *Yale Law Journal* 103: 1495–1531.

Kamen, Al. 1989. "When Exactly Does Life End?" *Washington Post National Weekly Edition,* September 18–24, at 31.

Kaminer, Maggie Ilene. 2001. "How Broad Is the Fundamental Right to Privacy and Personal Autonomy?—On What Grounds Should the Ban on the Sale of Sexually Stimulating Devices Be Considered Unconstitutional?" *American University Journal of Gender, Social Policy, and the Law* 9: 395–422.

Kamisar. Yale. 1993. "Are Laws against Assisted Suicide Unconstitutional?" *Hastings Center Report* 23: 32–41.

———. 1995. "Against Assisted Suicide—Even a Very Limited Form." *University of Detroit Mercy Law Review* 72: 735–769.

Lewis, Penney. 2001. "Rights Discourse and Assisted Suicide." *American Journal of Law and Medicine* 27: 45–99.

Marzen, Thomas J. 1985. "Suicide: A Constitutional Right?" *Duquesne Law Review* 24: 1–100.

———. 1994. "'Out, Out Brief Candle': Constitutionally Prescribed Suicide for the Terminally Ill." *Hastings Constitutional Law Quarterly* 21: 799–826.

McConnell, Michael W. 1997. "Supreme Humility." *Wall Street Journal,* July 2, at A14.

Mohr, Richard D. 1986. "Mr. Justice Douglas at Sodom: Gays and Privacy." *Columbia Human Rights Law Review* 18: 43–110.

Montaigne, Michel. [1580] 1904. *The Essays of Michael Lord of Montaigne.* 3 vols. Translated by John Florio. London: Frowde.

"Physician-Assisted Suicide." Note. 1997. *Harvard Law Review* 111: 237–248.

Quill, Timothy E., Bernard Lo, and Dan W. Brock. 1997. "Palliative Options of Last Resort: A Comparison of Voluntary Stopping Eating and Drinking, Terminal Sedation, Physician-Assisted Suicide, and Voluntary Active Euthanasia." *Journal of the American Medical Association* 278: 2099–2104.

Report of the Ad Hoc Committee of the Harvard Medical School to Examine the Definition of Brain Death. 1968. "A Definition of Irreversible Coma." *Journal of the American Medical Association* 205: 337–340.

Rubenfeld, Jed. 1989. "The Right of Privacy." *Harvard Law Review* 102: 737–807.

Schowengerdt, Dale M. 2001. "Defending Marriage: A Litigation Strategy to Oppose Same-Sex 'Marriage.'" *Regent University Law Review* 14: 487–511.

Stack, Peggy Fletcher. 1998. "Globally, Polygamy Is Commonplace." *Salt Lake Tribune,* Setpember 20, A1.

"Suicide Law Struck Down." *New York Times,* December 14, 1993, at A18.

Sykes, Charles J. 1999. *The End of Privacy.* New York: St. Martin's Press.

Trosino, James. 1993. "Note, American Wedding: Same-Sex Marriage and the Miscegenation Analogy." *Boston University Law Review* 73: 93–120.

Turkington, Richard C. 1990. "Legacy of the Warren and Brandeis Article: The Emerging Unencumbered Constitutional Right to Informational Privacy." *Northern Illinois University Law Review* 10: 479–520.

Urofsky, Melvin I. 1994. *Letting Go: Death, Dying, and the Law.* Norman: University of Oklahoma Press.

———. 2000. *Lethal Judgments: Assisted Suicide and American Law.* Lawrence: University Press of Kansas.

Urofsky, Melvin I., and Philip E. Urofsky. 1996. *The Right to Die: A Two-Volume Anthology of Scholarly Works.* New York: Garland Publications.

Wardle, Lynn D. 1996. "A Critical Analysis of Constitutional Claims for Same-Sex Marriage." *Brigham Young Law Review* 1996: 1–101.

Weir, Robert F., ed. 1997. *Physician-Assisted Suicide.* Bloomington: Indiana University Press.

Westin, Alan F. 1967. *Privacy and Freedom.* New York: Atheneum.

Wolhandler, Steven J. 1984. "Voluntary Active Euthanasia for the Terminally Ill and the Constitutional Right to Privacy." *Cornell Law Review* 69: 363–383.

Woodman, Sue. 1998. *Last Rights: The Struggle Over the Right to Die.* New York: Plenum Trade.

5

Key People, Cases, and Events

Abortion

The intentional termination of a pregnancy. In *Roe v. Wade* (1973), the U.S. Supreme Court held that constitutional privacy was "broad enough to encompass a woman's decision whether or not to terminate her pregnancy."

Active Involuntary Euthanasia

Causing the death of a person who has not requested assistance in dying. Although sometimes known as mercy killing, active involuntary euthanasia is legally akin to homicide.

Active Voluntary Euthanasia

The willing participation of a person in direct action that will cause his or her death. When the person seeking death requires assistance, it is frequently termed *assisted suicide;* when that assistance comes from a medical doctor, it is often termed *physician-assisted suicide.* Perhaps the most common form of this type of euthanasia is an individual voluntarily and knowingly taking a lethal dose of medicine. Active voluntary euthanasia is so closely akin to suicide as to be practically indistinguishable.

Advanced Directive

A legal document expressing a patient's wishes about the kind of health care desired should that person become unable to make his or her own health care decisions. There are two types of advanced directives: the living will, and the durable power of attorney for health care. The Patient Self-Determination Act (1991) requires all hospitals, skilled nursing facilities, home health agencies, hospice programs, and health maintenance organizations to guarantee that every adult receiving medical care be provided written information concerning advanced directives.

Akron v. Akron Center for Reproductive Health (1983)

Decision of the U.S. Supreme Court declaring unconstitutional several restrictions imposed upon abortions, including requirements that all abortions after the first trimester of pregnancy be performed in full-service hospitals (as opposed to clinics); that minors obtain parental or judicial consent for an abortion; that the attending physician provide the woman with specific information relevant to informed consent; that a woman wait twenty-four hours between consenting to and receiving an abortion; and that physicians performing abortions dispose of fetal remains in a "humane and sanitary manner." This decision was overturned in part in *Planned Parenthood of Southeastern Pennsylvania v. Casey* (1992), in which the U.S. Supreme Court upheld requirements relating to parental or judicial consent for a minor; informed consent; and a twenty-four-hour waiting period.

American Civil Liberties Union

The nation's preeminent civil liberties organization, the American Civil Liberties Union has long sought to defend and preserve the individual rights and liberties, including privacy, guaranteed by the U.S. Constitution.

American Medical Association

The nation's most influential and powerful lobby on health care, the American Medical Association has been deeply involved in matters relating to the right to die.

Antifederalists

Those opposed to ratification of the Constitution of 1787. Antifederalists feared that the new government would destroy the sovereignty and autonomy of the states. In addition, during the ratification debate, Antifederalists successfully pushed for a federal Bill of Rights, a list of restrictions on the powers of the national government. Almost two centuries later, the Bill of Rights provided the textual justification for the constitutional right to privacy.

Article III of the U.S. Constitution

The article of the federal constitution dealing with the structure and powers of the judicial branch of the federal government. It is the shortest and least detailed of the institutional articles.

Artificial Hydration and Nutrition

Medical intervention to supply hydration and nutrition by tube, catheter, or needle to patients who cannot or will not drink or eat.

Commonly known as tube-feeding, artificial hydration and nutrition often prolong the lives of patients who would otherwise expire. For example, after swallowing large quantities of alcohol and tranquilizers, Karen Quinlan lapsed into an irreversible coma yet lived for nine more years receiving artificial hydration and nutrition.

Artificial Insemination

The placing of sperm into the cervical canal of a woman for the purposes of procreation. In 2000, William Gerber, a life-term prisoner in California, requested to have a child with his wife via artificial insemination. When prison authorities denied the request, Gerber alleged that the prison's refusal violated his constitutional right to procreate. The Ninth Circuit Court of Appeals eventually rejected his request.

Ashcroft, John

The U.S. attorney general under President George W. Bush. Even though the Oregon Death with Dignity Act permitted physicians in Oregon to help terminally ill patients commit suicide by prescribing lethal drugs, Ashcroft sought to prosecute those assisting physicians under the federal Controlled Substances Act.

Assisted Suicide

Helping an individual commit suicide. When that assistance comes from a medical doctor, it is often termed *physician-assisted suicide.* In an assisted suicide, the assistant either directly brings about death (e.g., by injecting a terminally ill patient, upon his or her request, with controlled substances) or supplies the means of death (e.g., by providing a prescription for a lethal dose of morphine, a supply of carbon monoxide and a facemask, or a machine that will deliver death-inducing medications when prompted) so that the patient can bring about his or her own death.

Assisted Suicide Funding Restriction Act (1997)

Federal law that bars the use of federal funds to pay for assisted suicide, euthanasia, and mercy killing.

Baehr v. Lewin (1993)

Decision of the Hawaii Supreme Court holding that, although there was no state constitutional right to same-sex marriage, the state's refusal to issue marriage licenses to same-sex couples constituted gender-based discrimination in violation of the state constitution. Following this case, opponents of same-sex marriage introduced bills to foreclose that possibility in numerous state legislatures. Congressional opponents, motivated by fear that a same-sex marriage recognized in Hawaii would have to be honored in other states under the Full Faith and Credit Clause, introduced the Defense of Marriage Act in 1996. In 1998, *Baehr* was abrogated by a state constitutional amendment that authorized state lawmakers to restrict marriage to heterosexual couples.

Baker v. State (1999)

Decision of the Vermont Supreme Court holding that state marriage laws that denied equal benefits to committed same-sex partners violated the state constitution's Common Benefits Clause, a rough analogue to the Equal Protection Clause of the federal Fourteenth Amendment. Shortly thereafter, Vermont enacted the nation's first law authorizing *civil unions* between same-sex partners that entitled those entering into such unions all the identical rights—including state benefits—and protections that stem from the marital relationship.

Barron v. Baltimore (1833)

Decision of the U.S. Supreme Court holding that the Bill of Rights was a limitation of power on the federal government, not on state governments. The Bill of Rights did not limit the powers of state governments until well into the twentieth century, following the Supreme Court's selective incorporation of the Bill of Rights.

Bellotti v. Baird (1979)

Decision of the U.S. Supreme Court holding that, though a state may require a minor seeking an abortion to obtain parental consent, the state must allow minors the opportunity to approach a judge for an abortion order *without first consulting* their parents and that those proceedings had to be confidential.

Bigelow v. Virginia (1975)

Decision of the U.S. Supreme Court declaring unconstitutional a Virginia statute that prohibited advertisements for abortions or abortion-related services.

Bill of Rights

The first ten amendments to the U.S. Constitution, collectively ratified in December 1791. This list of restrictions on the powers of the national government was adopted largely because of the Antifederalist fears that the Constitution would destroy the sovereignty and autonomy of the states. Almost two centuries later, the Bill of Rights provided the textual justification for the constitutional right to privacy.

Black, Hugo

Associate justice of the U.S. Supreme Court from 1937 to 1971. Beginning in *Griswold v. Connecticut* (1965), Justice Black argued that no general right to privacy could be found in the Constitution or the Bill of Rights.

Blackmun, Harry

Associate justice of the U.S. Supreme Court from 1970 to 1974. Justice Blackmun authored the majority opinion in *Roe v. Wade* (1973).

Blackstone, William

Perhaps the most influential English jurist of the eighteenth century. His *Commentaries of the Laws of England* (1765–1769) became the primary legal authority for eighteenth- and nineteenth-century lawyers in the United States.

Boddie v. Connecticut (1971)

Decision of the U.S. Supreme Court striking down a state statute that required payment of court costs prior to obtaining a divorce. The majority opinion declared that, because divorce was a "precondition to the adjustment of a fundamental human relationship," it deserved constitutional protection (in much the same manner as the right to marry). Here, the justices held that divorce was protected under the constitutional right to privacy.

Bouvia v. Superior Court of Los Angeles County (1986)

Decision of a California appellate court in which the majority flatly denied that a physician who facilitated death assisted suicide. Concurring justice Lynn D. Compton wrote even more forcefully, noting that the right to die should "include the ability to enlist assistance from others, including the medical profession, in making death as painless as possible." *Bouvia* was one of the first state court cases to address the issue of assisted suicide.

Bowers, Michael

The Georgia attorney general who defended the state's anti-sodomy statute in *Bowers v. Hardwick* (1986).

Bowers v. Hardwick (1986)

Decision of the U.S. Supreme Court holding that homosexual sodomy was not a fundamental right and therefore not protected under the constitutional right to privacy.

Boyd v. United States (1886)

First decision of the U.S. Supreme Court specifically to recognize protection for privacy interests under the Fourth and Fifth Amendments. The justices held that the amendments applied "to all invasions on the part of government and its employees of the sanctity of a man's home and the privacies of his life."

Brain Death

Irreversible loss of function of the brain. The dilemma presented by the possibility of an individual living while in an irreversible coma prompted an ad hoc committee of the Harvard University Medical School in 1968 to recommend that a person who had suffered irreversible loss of function of the brain be considered legally dead. All states have since adopted brain death statutes, with many enacting, sometimes with variations, the Uniform Determination of Death Act definition.

Brandeis, Louis

Coauthor of the famous 1890 *Harvard Law Review* article on privacy; associate justice of the U.S. Supreme Court from 1916 to 1939. In "The Right to Privacy," Brandeis and coauthor Samuel Warren called upon the courts to recognize a specific constitutional right to privacy, a right independent of property and liberty and unrelated to tort law. Almost four decades later, Justice Brandeis, in dissent in *Olmstead v. United States* (1928), defined privacy as "the right to be let alone—the most comprehensive of rights and the right most valued by civilized men." The phrase *right to be let alone* has been repeated often in privacy cases throughout the twentieth century.

Brause v. Bureau of Vital Statistics (1998)

Decision of an Alaska trial court holding that a male couple was entitled to a marriage license. The court recognized a fundamental right to choose one's life partner. This decision was subsequently nullified by a state constitutional amendment.

Buck v. Bell (1927)

Decision of the U.S. Supreme Court upholding a Virginia law that required the sterilization of persons indefinitely confined to state mental health institutions. The justices rejected the contention that compulsory surgical sterilization deprived persons of their constitutional right to bodily integrity and was therefore repugnant to the Due Process Clause of the Fourteenth Amendment.

Calder v. Bull (1798)

The earliest judicial discussion on unenumerated rights. This decision of the U.S. Supreme Court revealed how divided the justices were over the exercise of judicial review. Justice Samuel Chase contended that the judiciary had the power to overturn laws that violated fundamental principles, even if those laws did not run afoul of specific constitutional provisions. By contrast, Justice James Iredell maintained that, even if a law ran counter to principles of "natural justice," the courts still lacked the power to declare it unconstitutional. Judicial review was established five years later in *Marbury v. Madison* (1803). And privacy, though unenumerated, was declared to be a fundamental right in *Griswold v. Connecticut* (1965).

Carey v. Population Services International (1977)

Decision of the U.S. Supreme Court striking down a New York statute that criminalized the distribution of contraceptive devices to anyone under the age of sixteen; the distribution of contraceptive devices by anyone other than a licensed pharmacist; and the advertisement or display of contraceptives. The majority opinion made clear that the decision whether or not to beget or bear a child was "at the very heart of . . . constitutionally protected choices."

Carnivore

A Federal Bureau of Investigation (FBI) device that intercepts, reads, stores, and classifies Internet transmissions to and from persons or organizations that the FBI thinks may be involved in criminal activity. Carnivore is capable of providing law enforcement authorities with a detailed picture of an individual's associations, habits, contacts, interests, and activities, all of which occurs without the individual's knowledge and without a court-ordered warrant.

Certiorari

The primary method by which the U.S. Supreme Court accepts a case for its review.

Checks and Balances

One of the four defining principles of the Constitution. The legislative, executive, and judicial branches of the national government share certain powers so that no branch has exclusive domain over any activity. This way, each branch may "resist encroachment" by the others. For example, the legislature may check the executive by overriding a presidential veto, impeaching and removing the president, and rejecting presidential nominees, including federal judges. The legislature may check the judiciary by determining the jurisdiction of federal courts and by rejecting, impeaching, and removing federal judges. The executive may check the legislature by rejecting bills passed by Congress, and it may check the judiciary by appointing all federal judges and by pardoning those accused or convicted of federal crimes. And the judiciary may check the legislative and executive branches through the exercise of judicial review.

Chicago, Burlington, and Quincy Railroad Company v. Chicago (1897)

Decision of the U.S. Supreme Court holding that the Due Process Clause of the Fourteenth Amendment required that the states honor the provision of the Fifth Amendment that prohibits the taking of private property for public use without just compensation. This case was the first manifestation of the doctrine that held that the Fourteenth Amendment's Due Process Clause made the Bill of Rights, or at least one provision of the Bill of Rights, applicable to the states. Not until well into the twentieth century, however, would the justices accept the argument that the Fourteenth Amendment's Due Process Clause *incorporated* most of the provisions of the Bill of Rights, thereby making most of the provisions of the Bill of Rights binding upon state governments.

"Clear and convincing, inherently reliable evidence"

A standard used to evaluate a patient's wishes if that person is unable to do so. Missouri law permitted a surrogate to act for an incompetent patient in electing to have artificial hydration and nutrition withdrawn in such a way as to cause death, but it established a procedural safeguard to make certain that the decisions of the surrogate conformed as best it may to the wishes expressed by the patient when competent. Specifically, the law required "clear and convincing, inherently reliable evidence" of the patient's wishes not to continue life-sustaining medical treatment. The law was sustained by the U.S. Supreme Court in *Cruzan v. Missouri Department of Health* (1990). The standard of clear and convincing, inherently reliable evidence was permissible because it guarded against potential abuses of the so-called substituted judgment doctrine and prevented irreversible error.

Cleveland Board of Education v. LaFleur (1974)

Decision of the U.S. Supreme Court striking down a school board's policy that mandated unpaid maternity leave five months prior to the expected date of childbirth. The justices noted that, in this situation, concern for the unborn child could not trump the pregnant woman's autonomy.

Common Law

A body of general legal principles derived from judicial decisions. These principles guide contemporary court rulings through the *doctrine of stare decisis,* which implies that a rule established by a court is to be followed in all similar cases.

Commonwealth v. Bonadio (1980)

Decision of the Pennsylvania Supreme Court holding that to regulate the private sexual conduct of consenting adults was beyond the power of the state.

Commonwealth of Kentucky v. Wasson (1992)

Decision of the Kentucky Supreme Court striking down a state law against homosexual sodomy; the court held that the state constitution offered greater protection of the right to privacy than the U.S. Constitution.

Compassion in Dying

An organization that offers open support to terminally ill patients who desire the option of assisted dying. In 1994, Compassion in Dying filed two lawsuits in federal district court challenging the constitutionality of laws criminalizing assisted suicide in Washington state and New York. Those two challenges became *Washington v. Glucksberg* (1997) and *Vacco v. Quill* (1997), two decisions of the U.S. Supreme Court.

Compelling State Interest

To justify laws that curtail fundamental rights or discriminate against suspect classifications, government has the heavy burden of persuading a court that there is a *compelling state interest* in the legislative classification and that there is no other, less restrictive way to accomplish that interest. See Strict Scrutiny.

Computer Fraud and Abuse Act (1994)

Federal law prohibiting unauthorized access of private and government computers.

Comstock Act (1873)

Federal law that made it a crime to sell, lend, distribute, publish, or possess devices or literature pertaining to birth control or abortion. Many states soon followed suit, with twenty-four states criminalizing birth control and abortion.

Concurring Opinion

An opinion written by a judge or justice who agrees with a particular result reached by the court but disagrees with some or all of the reasons for that result. A concurring opinion often outlines different or additional reasons for the same result.

Conjugal Rights

The rights of a husband and wife to each other's company and affection. Courts have consistently held that certain marital privacy rights, to include conjugal rights, may be substantially abridged, even denied, in the prison setting.

Constitution of 1787

Written in 1787 and put into effect in 1789, the document was designed to provide a structure, basic institutions, and a set of powers, principles, and prohibitions for the operations of government in the United States. The four defining principles of the Constitution are federalism, separation of powers, checks and balances, and individual rights.

Constitutional Privacy

The right of the individual to be free from unwanted and unwarranted governmental intrusion in matters affecting fundamental rights; also, the right of the individual not to have certain private information gathered, preserved, or disseminated by government. Constitutional privacy involves at least two separate kinds of interests: one in independence in making certain kinds of important decisions, and the other in avoiding disclosure by government of personal matters.

Constitutional Revolution of 1937

During President Franklin Delano Roosevelt's first term (1933–1937), the U.S. Supreme Court invalidated much of the president's New Deal economic legislation. Following his reelection in 1936, President Roosevelt boldly proposed an increase in the size of the Court. The plan was rendered unnecessary in the spring of 1937, however, when the justices surprisingly sustained both state and federal economic regulations. Since this "switch in time that saved nine" (i.e., justices), the Court has consistently refused to invoke the Due Process Clause to limit the power of government to regulate the economy.

Contraception

The intentional prevention of impregnation through the use of various devices, agents, or drugs. In *Griswold v. Connecticut* (1965), the U.S. Supreme Court struck down a state law on marital privacy grounds that made it a crime for any person to use any drug, article, or instrument to prevent conception. Seven years later, the justices extended the holding in *Griswold* to unmarried persons.

Controlled Substances Act (1970)

Federal law regulating the manufacture and distribution of various narcotics used in the illicit production of controlled substances.

Under the act, U.S. Attorney General John Ashcroft sought to prosecute physicians in Oregon who helped terminally ill patients commit suicide by prescribing lethal drugs, even though the Oregon Death with Dignity Act permitted such assistance.

Cooley, Thomas M.

Nineteenth-century treatise writer and justice of the Michigan Supreme Court from 1864 to 1884. In *A Treatise on the Law of Torts* (1880), Cooley defined privacy as "a right of complete immunity: to be let alone." Ten years later, Samuel Warren and Louis Brandeis used that definition in their landmark article on privacy in the *Harvard Law Review.* Almost four decades later, Justice Brandeis, in dissent in *Olmstead v. United States* (1928), once again borrowed from Cooley when he defined privacy as "the right to be let alone—the most comprehensive of rights and the right most valued by civilized men." The phrase *right to be let alone* has been repeated often in privacy cases throughout the twentieth century.

Cruzan, Nancy

Young woman who suffered permanent brain damage as a result of an automobile accident and the subsequent deprivation of oxygen to her brain. Cruzan lived in a persistent vegetative state with no cognitive functions for nearly five years, at which time her parents requested that the artificial hydration and nutrition, with which their daughter could live indefinitely, be terminated. This request gave rise to the U.S. Supreme Court decision *Cruzan v. Missouri Department of Health* (1990).

Cruzan v. Missouri Department of Health (1990)

Decision of the U.S. Supreme Court holding that a state may require "clear and convincing, inherently reliable evidence" of an incompetent patient's wishes not to continue life-sustaining medical treatment prior to terminating life-sustaining medical treatment. The justices also acknowledged a common law right and constitutionally protected liberty interest, but not a fundamental right to privacy, in a *competent* person's decision to refuse medical treatment, including lifesaving hydration and nutrition.

Davis v. Beason (1890)

Decision of the U.S. Supreme Court sustaining an Idaho law that denied voting privileges to those who advocated or practiced plural marriages. The majority opinion characterized polygamy as uncivilized, un-Christian, destructive of marriage, disturbing to the peace of families, degrading to women, debasing to men, pernicious to the best interests of society, and wholly deserving of punishment.

Declaration of Independence (1776)

Written in 1776 by Thomas Jefferson, this document explained why it was necessary for the colonies to sever all political ties with Great Britain. The Declaration of Independence was a summation of three fundamental principles: (1) individuals possessed rights outside of those granted or recognized by government; (2) government may exercise power only with the consent of the governed; and (3) if the government acted improperly, its contract with the people was broken, and the people could abolish the existing government and institute a new one.

"Deeply rooted in this Nation's history and tradition"

A standard used to evaluate whether rights should be considered fundamental and thus protected by the U.S. Constitution. In determining which individual rights are fundamental, the U.S.

Supreme Court has consistently asked whether the alleged right is "deeply rooted in this Nation's history and tradition." With respect to privacy, the justices have consistently held that only matters relating to procreation, marriage, and family life are so "deeply rooted."

Defense of Marriage Act (1996)

Federal law relieving the states of any obligation under the Full Faith and Credit Clause to recognize same-sex marriages from other states and defining marriage, for the purpose of all federal laws, as "the union of one man and one woman."

Dissenting Opinion

An opinion written by a judge or justice who disagrees with a particular result reached by a court.

Doe v. Bolton (1973)

Decision of the U.S. Supreme Court invalidating several restrictions imposed upon women seeking abortions, including that all abortions be performed in licensed hospitals; that hospital staff committees approve abortions in advance; and that two physicians concur in the abortion decision. The justices struck down the requirements as not reasonably related to the safety or necessity of the abortion.

Douglas, Justice William

Associate justice of the U.S. Supreme Court from 1939 to 1975. Justice Douglas authored the majority opinion in *Griswold v. Connecticut* (1965), the case in which the Court first recognized a constitutional right to privacy.

Driver's Privacy Protection Act (1994)

Federal law regulating the release of motor vehicle records.

Durable Power of Attorney for Health Care

This type of advanced directive allows a patient to specify in advance who should make health care decisions for the patient if the patient is unable to make his or her own health care decisions. In most states, this authority extends to the termination of life-sustaining medical treatment and the discontinuance of artificial hydration and nutrition.

E. B. v. Verniero (1997)

Decision of the U.S. Court of Appeals for the Third Circuit upholding New Jersey's Megan's Law. Opponents of the law alleged, among other constitutional claims, an invasion of informational privacy. By informing local communities of such intimate and highly personal information, paroled sex offenders no doubt suffered great harm in the form of shame, harassment, and discrimination. Nevertheless, the court recognized that registration and notification enabled law enforcement and those likely to encounter a sex offender to be aware of a potential danger and to stay vigilant against possible re-abuse.

Eisenstadt v. Baird (1972)

Decision of the U.S. Supreme Court striking down a Massachusetts law that forbade the use of contraceptives by unmarried persons. In the majority opinion, Justice William Brennan noted: "If the right to privacy means anything, it is the right of the individual, married or single, to be free from unwarranted governmental intrusion into matters so fundamental affecting a person as whether to bear or begat a child."

Electronic Communications Privacy Act (1986)

Federal law protecting against the unauthorized access, interception, or disclosure of private electronic communications by the government (as well as by third parties to the communication). Authorized access, interception, or disclosure by government requires a court-ordered warrant.

Euthanasia

Literally, "a good or happy death"; the means of bringing about a gentle and easy death of a person suffering from an incurable and extremely painful disease. Since the 1970s, euthanasia has come to mean the implementation of any one of four specific practices: passive voluntary euthanasia, passive involuntary euthanasia, active voluntary euthanasia, and active involuntary euthanasia.

Fair Credit Reporting Act (1974)

Federal law requiring consumer reporting agencies to adopt procedures to assure that credit information is confidential, accurate, relevant, and used for its proper purposes.

Family Educational Rights and Privacy Act (1974)

Federal law protecting student records.

Federal Marriage Amendment (2002)

Proposed constitutional amendment introduced in the House of Representatives in mid-2002, the operative sentences of which read, "Marriage in the United States shall consist only of the union of a man and a woman. Neither this constitution nor the constitution of any state, nor state and federal law, shall be construed to require that marital status or the legal incidents thereof be conferred upon married couples or groups."

Federalism

One of the four defining principles of the U.S. Constitution. Federalism is a system of government in which a constitution divides power between a national government and subnational governments. Neither the national government nor any state government receives its powers from the other. Instead, both types of government derive their powers from the Constitution. The Framers of the Constitution viewed the division of governmental authority as a means of checking power with power and providing double security to the people. The national government would keep the state governments in check, and the state governments would prevent excesses by the national government. In a federal system, both governments may act directly upon the people.

Federalist No. 78 (1788)

Written by Alexander Hamilton in 1788, this article asserted a justification for judicial review. Because the Constitution of 1787 granted only limited powers to government, it necessarily followed that other powers were outside the pale of governmental authority. This implied prohibition against certain powers could be preserved in practice "no other way than the medium of courts of justice, whose duty it must be to declare all acts contrary to the manifest tenor of the Constitution void." This article has been consistently cited by judges and courts when declaring legislative acts unconstitutional.

The Federalist Papers (1787–1788)

A series of scholarly articles written by Alexander Hamilton, James Madison, and John Jay in 1787 and 1788 promoting ratification of the Constitution of 1787. Many of these articles were devoted to explanations of the various provisions of the Constitution and to reassurances that the new government would not destroy the states or become an instrument of tyranny. To this day, *The Federalist* remains one of the great treatises on the American constitutional system. *The Federalist* was persuasive in securing ratification in a number of states, most notably Virginia and New York.

Federalists

Those who supported ratification of the Constitution of 1787.

Fetus

An unborn human more than eight weeks after conception.

Fifth Amendment Self-Incrimination Clause

Provision of the Fifth Amendment that prohibits a state from forcing an individual to testify against himself. This clause thus protects the privacy of one's thoughts. In *Griswold v. Connecticut* (1965), the U.S. Supreme Court held that the right to privacy derived from rights explicitly protected in the Bill of Rights, including the Self-Incrimination Clause, which enabled the citizen to create a zone of privacy that government could not force him to surrender to his detriment.

First Amendment

Provision in the Bill of Rights that guarantees freedom of conscience in both religious and political matters and freedom of association. This amendment thus protects the autonomy of the individual. In *Griswold v. Connecticut* (1965), the U.S. Supreme Court held that the right to privacy derived from rights explicitly protected in the Bill of Rights, including the rights guaranteed in the First Amendment, which were intended to secure the rights of private sentiment and private judgment.

Fourteenth Amendment Due Process Clause

Provision of the Fourteenth Amendment that prohibits a state from depriving any person of "life, liberty, or property, without due process of law." Not until well into the twentieth century did the U.S. Supreme Court accept the argument that this clause incorporated most of the provisions of the Bill of Rights, thus making most of its provisions binding upon state governments as well. In the most generic sense, *due process of law* refers to the methods by which governmental authority is exercised; this is commonly known as *procedural due process.* Due process of law has also been interpreted as imposing certain substantive limitations on governmental policies; this concept is often referred to as *substantive due process.*

Fourteenth Amendment Equal Protection Clause

Provision of the Fourteenth Amendment that prohibits a state from denying "to any person within its jurisdiction the equal protection of the Laws." This clause was dispositive in the U.S. Supreme Court's invalidation of Oklahoma's Habitual Criminal Sterilization Act in *Skinner v. Oklahoma* (1942) and Virginia's antimiscegenation statute in *Loving v. Virginia* (1967). The Court rejected an equal protection challenge to a New York state law that criminalized assisted suicide in *Vacco v. Quill* (1997). Supporters of same-sex marriage claim that laws allowing heterosexual, but not same-sex, couples to marry infringe upon this clause.

Fourth Amendment

Provision in the Bill of Rights that affirms the "right of the people to be secure in their persons, houses, papers, and effects, against unreasonable searches and seizures." In *Griswold v. Connecticut* (1965), the U.S. Supreme Court held that the right to privacy derived from rights explicitly protected in the Bill of Rights, including the rights protected in the Fourth Amendment, which prohibited official intrusions into a person's dwelling in the interests of privacy. Thomas Cooley noted that the justification for this amendment was the common law principle that "a man's house is his castle." And in that castle, the citizen was free from "the prying eyes of the government."

Freedom of Access to Clinic Entrances Act (1994)

Federal law that makes the use of force or the threat of force, or physical obstruction for the purpose of injuring, intimidating, or interfering with a person seeking to obtain or provide reproductive health services, a federal offense, with penalties up to ten years' imprisonment. Congress passed this law following a wave of violence directed against abortion clinics and other reproductive health care providers.

Full Faith and Credit Clause

Provision in Article IV of the U.S. Constitution that requires states to accept the public acts and records and judicial proceedings of other states as valid. Congress, however, has the power to prescribe the manner in which states are to comply with the Full Faith and Credit Clause. Congressional opponents to same-sex marriage, motivated by fear that a same-sex marriage recognized in one state would have to be honored in other states, introduced the Defense of Marriage Act in 1996, which relieved the states of any obligation under the Full Faith and Credit Clause to recognize same-sex marriages from other states.

Fundamental Rights

Individual rights deeply rooted in this nation's history and tradition or implicit in the concept of ordered liberty, even if such rights are not mentioned in the U.S. Constitution or recognized by enacted law. In determining what rights are fundamental, judges and justices are not to rely solely or even primarily upon their personal and private notions. Instead, they are to look "to the traditions and [collective] conscience of our people" to determine whether a principle is "so rooted [there] . . . as to be ranked fundamental" (*Snyder v. Massachusetts* 1934). Judges and justices are not to rely solely upon the express language of the Bill of Rights to make that determination either. As such, a judge may restrict the act of a duly elected legislature even if that act does not violate a specific constitutional provision. This approach does not recognize the finite Constitution as the sole authority on individual rights; it is Lockean in nature, holding that individual rights come first and government follows to secure those rights. The U.S. Supreme Court has acknowledged that there are additional fundamental rights, protected against governmental infringement, that exist in addition to those rights specifically articulated in the first eight amendments. Since *Griswold v. Connecticut* (1965), the right to privacy has been one of those additional, fundamental rights, although the right has been limited to matters relating to procreation, marriage, and family life. Contrast this approach with *legal positivism.*

"Great laboratories of democracy"

Phrase used by Justice Louis Brandeis pointing out that state governments provide laboratories for public policy experimentation.

This is one of the many advantages of federalism. If a state adopts a policy that fails, its negative effects are limited. If a state adopts a policy that succeeds, similar policies can be adopted by other states. Missouri, for example, permits a surrogate to act for an incompetent patient in electing to have artificial hydration and nutrition withdrawn in such a way as to cause death, but it requires clear and convincing, inherently reliable evidence of the patient's wishes not to continue life-sustaining medical treatment. Many others states do not insist upon such heightened evidentiary requirements. Oregon is the only state that permits its terminally ill residents to end their lives through the voluntary self-administration of lethal medications, expressly prescribed by a physician for that purpose. Because the U.S. Constitution allows such experimentation, national politicians do not have to resolve every controversial issue. Uniformity is not required.

Griswold, Estelle

The executive director of the Planned Parenthood League of Connecticut who challenged the constitutionality of Connecticut's prohibition on the use of contraceptives by married persons. This challenge gave rise to the landmark U.S. Supreme Court decision *Griswold v. Connecticut* (1965).

Griswold v. Connecticut (1965)

Decision of the U.S. Supreme Court invalidating on constitutional privacy grounds a state prohibition on the use of contraceptives by married persons. *Griswold* was the first case in which the justices specifically recognized an independent and fundamental right to privacy under the U.S. Constitution. This constitutional right to privacy was located in the "penumbras" of various guarantees of the Bill of Rights and was broad enough to include the freedom of married couples to use contraceptives in the privacy of their bedrooms.

Guardian ad litem

An advocate appointed by a court to represent the best interests of a child or incompetent individual. Often, a court will appoint a guardian ad litem to represent the interests of a permanently comatose patient where the wishes of that patient are not known or are unclear.

Hales v. Petit (1562)

Decision of the Court at Common Bench in Great Britain that pronounced the interest of the state in prohibiting suicide. Here, the court referred to suicide as an "Offence against Nature, against God, and against the King."

Hamilton, Alexander

Forceful advocate for a strong national government at the Constitutional Convention; coauthor of *The Federalist Papers.* Hamilton was opposed to a Bill of Rights for two reasons. First, the national government was already limited to specific enumerated rights. Second, he feared that to enumerate certain liberties might in the future lead to the conclusion that the *mentioned* liberties were the *only* liberties. This fear was in large part responsible for the Ninth Amendment.

Hardwick, Michael

A homosexual man arrested for performing consensual oral sex with another adult male in the privacy of his bedroom, in violation of Georgia's antisodomy statute. Hardwick brought a civil suit challenging the constitutionality of Georgia's law punishing heterosexual and homosexual sodomy. This challenge gave rise to the U.S. Supreme Court decision *Bowers v. Hardwick* (1986).

Harlan, John Marshall

Associate justice of the U.S. Supreme Court from 1955 to 1971. In *Poe v. Ullman* (1961), Justice Harlan argued in dissent that a state statute prohibiting the use of contraceptives by married persons violated the right to marital privacy as guaranteed by the Bill of Rights and the Fourteenth Amendment. This dissent had a significant impact on the development of privacy jurisprudence, as evidenced by the Court's opinion to this effect only four years later in *Griswold v. Connecticut* (1965).

Harris v. McRae (1980)

Decision of the U.S. Supreme Court upholding the Hyde Amendment, which limited federal funding for nontherapeutic abortions. The majority opinion noted that a woman's constitutional right to an abortion did not require Congress to appropriate funds to enable an indigent woman to obtain the procedure.

Health Insurance Portability and Accountability Act (1996)

Federal law protecting the privacy of medical records.

Hobbes, Thomas

Seventeenth-century English political philosopher and author of *The Leviathan* (1651). Thomas Hobbes, among others, advanced what would become the animating principle of the American Revolution and its subsequent government: the social contract theory. This theory posits that all men are born free and equal by God-given right and, therefore, must give their consent to be governed.

Hodgson v. Minnesota (1990)

Decision of the U.S. Supreme Court sustaining a Minnesota statute that required a forty-eight-hour waiting period for minors seeking an abortion.

Human Life Amendment (1973)

Proposed constitutional amendment to overturn *Roe v. Wade* (1973). This proposed amendment, which fell far short of the votes required for passage in both houses of the Congress, read:

> Section 1: With respect to the right to life, the word "person" as used in this article and in the Fifth and Fourteenth Amendments to the Constitution of the United States applies to all human beings irrespective of age, health, function, or condition of dependency, including the unborn offspring at every stage of their biological development.
>
> Section 2: No unborn person shall be deprived of life by any person; provided, however, that nothing in this article shall prohibit a law permitting only those medical procedures required to prevent the death of the mother.
>
> Section 3: The Congress and the several States shall have the power to enforce this article by appropriate legislation.

Hyde Amendment (1976)

Federal law excluding abortion from the comprehensive health care services provided to indigent persons by the federal government through Medicaid, though an exception is granted if the abortion is necessary to save the life of the mother. In 1994,

Congress broadened the Hyde Amendment to permit federal funding in cases of rape or incest and when the mother's life was endangered by physical disorder, illness, or injury.

"Implicit in the concept of ordered liberty"

In determining which individual rights are fundamental, and thus protected by the U.S. Constitution, the U.S. Supreme Court has consistently asked whether the alleged right is "implicit in the concept of ordered liberty." With respect to privacy, the justices have consistently held that only matters relating to procreation, marriage, and family life are so implicit.

Incorporation of the Bill of Rights

Process by which most of the provisions of the Bill of Rights have been brought within the scope of the Fourteenth Amendment Due Process Clause, thus making most of the provisions of the Bill of Rights binding upon the states. In *Palko v. Connecticut* (1937), the U.S. Supreme Court rationalized the selective application of the guarantees of the Bill of Rights. According to this theory, often known as *selective incorporation,* only fundamental rights are applied to the states. For a right to be fundamental, it either had to be "implicit in the concept of ordered liberty" or "deeply rooted in the nation's history and tradition." Even now, several provisions of the Bill of Rights—the Second Amendment, the Third Amendment, the Grand Jury Clause of the Fifth Amendment, the Seventh Amendment, and the Excessive Bail and Fines Clauses of the Eighth Amendment—are not applicable to the states.

Individual Rights

One of the four defining principles of the Constitution. Individual rights, often referred to as *civil liberties,* are the freedoms of all persons from governmental interference. The Bill of Rights lists specific freedoms, such as freedom of speech, press, and religion, as well as freedom from unreasonable searches and seizures, and may be properly viewed as a general expression of the Framers' prevalent fear of fundamental rights being deprived by the government. Several of the individual rights protected in the Bill of Rights were adopted to protect individuals in their privacy. The First, Third, Fourth, and Fifth Amendments all contain some privacy component. The driving force behind these grants of freedom was the memory of tyranny under the king of England.

Informational Privacy

The claim of individuals, groups, and institutions "to determine for themselves when, how, and to what extent information about them is communicated to others." Of particular concern is the acquisition, storage, or dissemination of information by *government.* The U.S. Supreme Court did not explicitly recognize the right to informational privacy under the U.S. Constitution until *Whalen v. Roe* (1977).

Informed Consent

This doctrine requires that a patient be fully informed of the risks and benefits of any medical intervention *and* agree to particular medical treatment. The logical corollary of the doctrine of informed consent is the right not to consent. State and federal courts have consistently agreed that a competent patient has the right to refuse or terminate medical treatment, even if doing so will result in certain death.

In re Quinlan (1976)

Decision of the New Jersey Supreme Court recognizing that constitutional privacy protects a competent patient's decision to refuse or withdraw life-prolonging medical treatment *under cer-*

tain circumstances. In addition, the court held that constitutional privacy protects a guardian or family's decision to authorize termination of such treatment for incompetent patients *under certain circumstances.* Because *In re Quinlan* was a decision of the New Jersey Supreme Court, it established no national precedent.

Irreversible Coma

Medical condition in which a patient has no possibility of regaining consciousness yet is capable of existing indefinitely in a persistent vegetative state. This dilemma prompted an ad hoc committee of the Harvard University Medical School in 1968 to recommend that a person who had suffered irreversible loss of function of the brain be considered legally dead. Most states have since adopted brain-death statutes.

Johnson, Darlene

A young unmarried mother of four children (pregnant with the fifth child) who pleaded guilty to child abuse. California state judge Howard Broadman ordered that Johnson spend one year in jail, followed by three years of probation, during which time she would have six matchstick-sized birth control rods implanted into her upper arm. By releasing very small amounts of a hormone that keeps the ovaries from releasing eggs, these rods prevented conception. If Johnson rejected the "temporary" sterilization, the judge would sentence her to more time in jail. In short, Johnson had to choose between contraception and jail. She initially agreed to the conditions but, shortly thereafter, decided against them and requested that the judge reconsider in light of her constitutional right to reproduce.

Judicial Bypass

A process by which minors who are required by law either to obtain consent from or notify a parent of their intent to obtain an abortion can petition a judge for an abortion order *without first consulting* their parents. The U.S. Supreme Court has upheld laws that require parental consent and parental notification, so long as those laws provide for a judicial bypass.

Judicial Review

The power of the federal judiciary to review and, if warranted, declare unconstitutional the acts and proceedings of other branches and levels of government. In effect, judicial review is the power of the federal courts to determine the constitutionality of governmental action; if that action is deemed inconsistent with the U.S. Constitution, then the judiciary has the power to nullify the will of the elected representatives of the people. For example, the U.S. Supreme Court exercised judicial review when it declared several laws (Oklahoma's Habitual Criminal Sterilization Act, Connecticut's prohibition of the use of contraceptives by married persons, Virginia's restriction on miscegenation, and Texas's ban on abortions) violative of the constitutional right to privacy.

Kelley v. Johnson (1976)

Decision of the U.S. Supreme Court concluding that constitutional privacy did not encompass an individual liberty interest in personal appearance. The justices thus sustained a police department regulation directed at personal grooming.

Kevorkian, Dr. Jack

Michigan physician who almost single-handedly elevated assisted suicide to the national agenda. He did so by publicizing widely his assistance in the death of Janet Atkins in 1990 and dozens, perhaps hundreds, of others thereafter. Dubbed "Dr. Death" by the media, Kevorkian was convicted of second-degree murder in 1999. Shortly thereafter, he was sentenced to ten to twenty-five years in prison.

Since his public crusade began in the early 1990s, four states have considered citizen initiatives on physician-assisted suicide.

Legal Positivism

Doctrine in constitutional thought positing that the only rights possessed by the people are those explicitly stated in the Constitution or granted via the legislature. In a phrase, "first comes government, then come individual rights." Legal positivism further holds that judges are authorized to recognize only those rights found in constitutional provisions or legislative statutes. Contrast this approach with *fundamental rights.*

Lehr v. Robertson (1983)

Decision of the U.S. Supreme Court upholding a New York provision that denied notice and opportunity to be heard in a custodial dispute to a father who had never had any significant custodial, personal, or financial relationship with his child. When considered with *Stanley v. Illinois* (1972), this case appears to establish that biological fatherhood *and* an established parental relationship create a constitutionally protected privacy interest in a relationship with a child. Compare *Michael H. v. Gerald D.* (1989).

Lethal Drug Abuse Prevention Act (1998)

Act introduced in Congress by opponents of physician-assisted suicide. Deliberately aimed at overthrowing the Oregon Death with Dignity Act, this act would have prohibited doctors and pharmacists from dispensing any federally regulated drug for the purpose of suicide. Without the support of the American Medical Association, the most powerful lobby on health care, the bill never passed. It was withdrawn from floor debate on the day of the scheduled vote in the House of Representatives, and it stalled in the Senate.

Limited Government

This principle recognizes legal, written restraints on governmental authority and the moral primacy of the private over the public sphere of society. Limited government was a central assumption of American political thought at the time of the Constitutional Convention.

Living Will

This type of an advanced directive is a formal document governing the withholding or withdrawal of life-sustaining medical treatment from a patient in the event that the patient becomes permanently unconscious or terminally ill and is unable to make decisions regarding his or her medical treatment. All fifty states now legitimize the use of living wills for end-of-life decisionmaking.

Lochner v. New York (1905)

Decision of the U.S. Supreme Court striking down New York's labor law that limited the number of hours bakers could work. This case marked the heyday of economic substantive due process. For most of the next four decades, the justices embarked upon a full-scale substantive due process review, invalidating close to 200 state and federal economic (including labor) regulations. The *Lochner* era came to a close with the constitutional revolution of 1937. It was during this era of economic substantive due process, however, that the Court initially acknowledged protection under the Due Process Clause of the Fourteenth Amendment for personal privacy in the areas of education and child rearing.

Locke, John

Seventeenth-century English political philosopher, social-contract theorist, and author of *Two Treatises of Government* (1690). Locke argued that individuals entered into a contract with government to preserve their natural rights. Because these rights preceded government, government was not their source. Instead, government existed to protect preexisting rights. When the government failed to do so, the people possessed the authority to ask the government to cease and desist; and if the government refused to comply, the people could remove the government by revolution and then establish a new government. Locke's *Two Treatises of Government* embodied the principles of natural rights, limited government, and the right of revolution, each widely referenced by the colonists in the years preceding the American Revolution. Locke's works impacted greatly the Declaration of Independence and the Constitution of 1787.

Lofton v. Kearney (2001)

Decision of a federal district court upholding a Florida law that denied homosexuals the right to adopt children. Steven Lofton, a homosexual foster parent of three children, challenged the state law as violative of the fundamental rights of family privacy, intimate association, and family integrity protected by the Due Process Clause, as well as of the Equal Protection Clause. The judge rejected both claims.

Loving v. Virginia (1967)

Decision of the U.S. Supreme declaring unconstitutional a Virginia law that criminalized miscegenation in which a white person was a party. Although the justices invalidated the law on equal protection grounds, the opinion characterized the personal interest in choosing whom to marry as a fundamental right of privacy.

"The freedom to marry has long been recognized as one of the vital personal rights essential to the orderly pursuit of happiness by free men," the majority opinion stated. Advocates of same-sex marriage have used the *Loving* analogy, arguing that courts should compel states to permit same-sex marriages in the same manner that the U.S. Supreme Court compelled Virginia and other states to permit interracial marriages—by recognizing the claimed right either as a fundamental right to marry, or of privacy, or of intimate association. Only one state court, in Alaska, has done so, although that decision was subsequently nullified by a state constitutional amendment.

Madison, James

Forceful advocate for a strong national government at the Constitutional Convention and coauthor of *The Federalist.* At the convention, Madison was present at nearly all of the deliberations and kept detailed notes of them, earning him the title "father of the Constitution." Because he feared "the abuse of the powers of the General Government," Madison authored and introduced into the House of Representatives a bill of rights, several of the provisions of which were intended to protect individuals in their privacy. Much like Alexander Hamilton, Madison was concerned that future generations might conclude that the *mentioned* liberties in the Bill of Rights were the *only* liberties retained by the people. This concern led Madison to suggest the Ninth Amendment, which made it clear that the listing of certain rights did not mean that others did not exist. Almost two centuries later, the U.S. Supreme Court cited various provisions of the first eight amendments and the Ninth Amendment as justification for the constitutional right to privacy.

Maher v. Roe (1977)

Decision of the U.S. Supreme Court upholding a Connecticut law that authorized the reimbursement of Medicaid recipients for medical expenses incident to childbirth but not to abortion. The right to abortion, the majority opinion noted, implied "no limitation on the authority of a State to make a value judgment favoring childbirth over abortion, and to implement that judgment by the allocation of public funds."

Majority Opinion

An opinion that is supported by a majority of the judges or justices who participated in the decision. A majority opinion is often referred to as the opinion of the court.

Marbury v. Madison (1803)

Landmark decision of the U.S. Supreme Court in which the justices, for the first time, declared an act of Congress unconstitutional. The majority opinion justified its exercise of judicial review in terms of the fundamental principles of constitutional government. Recognizing the U.S. Constitution as the "fundamental and paramount law of the nation," the Court held that an act of the legislature repugnant to the Constitution was void. Moreover, it was the duty of the judiciary to make such a declaration. It was in this case that Chief Justice John Marshall made his now famous declaration: "It is emphatically the province and duty of the judicial department to say what the law is. Those who apply the rule to particular cases, must of necessity expound and interpret that rule. If two laws conflict with each other, the courts must decide the operation of each." Each time a judicial body declares an act of elected representatives unconstitutional—as the U.S. Supreme Court did in *Skinner v. Oklahoma* (1942), *Griswold v. Connecticut* (1965), *Loving v. Virginia* (1967), and *Roe v. Wade* (1973), for example—it invokes the legacy of *Marbury v. Madison.*

Megan's Laws

State laws that require all sex offenders at large to register with local authorities and provide for the disclosure of certain information about those required to register. Although opponents of such registration and community notification laws allege an invasion of informational privacy, appellate courts have recognized the legitimate governmental interest in protecting public safety.

Meyer v. Nebraska (1923)

Decision of the U.S. Supreme Court striking down a Nebraska law that prohibited the teaching of any modern foreign language to schoolchildren who had not reached the ninth grade. This was one of the earliest cases to test the limits of public interference with private decisionmaking. The majority opinion noted that individuals possessed certain fundamental rights that had to be respected by government. The source of those fundamental rights was the Due Process Clause of the Fourteenth Amendment, which included rights of autonomous, private decisionmaking. This case is perceived by many to be a companion case to *Pierce v. Society of Sisters* (1925). These two cases are the first cases to hold that the Due Process Clause of the Fourteenth Amendment protected certain noneconomic aspects of individual autonomy. These cases are thus appropriately viewed as denoting the emergence of a new branch of substantive due process, one that surfaced fully four decades later as an important precedent for constitutional privacy. Read together, *Meyer* and *Pierce* are the true progenitors of the privacy decisions. They demarcate limitations on governmental power to intrude upon matters affecting fundamental rights.

Michael H. v. Gerald D. (1989)

Decision of the U.S. Supreme Court holding that a father with a significant relationship to his child lacked paternal rights, including visitation, because the child's mother was married to another man at the time of conception and birth. There was no merit to the father's claim that he had a constitutionally protected liberty interest in the parental relationship he had established with his child because paternal rights between the biological father and his child *in these circumstances* had not traditionally been accorded special protection. To the contrary, the plurality concluded, "our traditions have protected the marital family."

Mill, John Stuart

Nineteenth-century English philosopher, political writer, and author of *On Liberty* (1859), which explored the struggle between individual autonomy and governmental authority. Mill posited that the only justification for interfering with anyone's liberty, against that individual's will, was self-preservation—to prevent harm to others. Governmental power could not be exercised over the individual because it would make him happier or, in the opinions of others, to do so would be wise or even right.

Miscegenation

From the Latin *miscere* (to mix) and *genus* (race), miscegenation is marriage between persons of different races. In *Loving v. Virginia* (1967), the U.S. Supreme Court declared Virginia's antimiscegenation statute violative of the Equal Protection Clause of the Fourteenth Amendment.

Monogamy

The condition of having one spouse at a time.

Moore v. City of East Cleveland (1977)

Decision of the U.S. Supreme Court invalidating a city housing ordinance that essentially limited the occupancy of any dwelling to members of the same nuclear family. The opinion recognized as fundamental the freedom of personal choice in matters of family living arrangements.

Mormon Church

Based largely in Utah during the nineteenth century, the Church of Jesus Christ of Latter Day Saints (the formal name of the Mormon Church) canonized the doctrine of polygamy and encouraged its practice among believers. In 1890, the Mormon Church, exhausted by its numerous court contests with the federal government, officially disavowed the practice of plural marriage.

Morrill Act (1862)

Federal law that made polygamy in U.S. territories punishable by a fine up to $500 and imprisonment for as much as five years. The law was passed in response to the teachings and practices of the Mormon Church.

Ninth Amendment

Provision of the Bill of Rights that makes clear that the inclusion of certain liberties in the Bill of Rights does not mean that others do not exist. James Madison, concerned that future generations might conclude that the *mentioned* liberties were the *only* liberties, suggested the Ninth Amendment: "The enumeration in the Constitution of certain rights, shall not be construed to deny or disparage others retained by the people." Scholars are divided over whether this amendment confers additional rights to the people or whether it simply recognizes that there remains reserved to the people an area of unsurrendered rights. Some conclude that the Ninth Amendment was not meant to add anything to the meaning of the Constitution but was adopted in order to eliminate the grant of powers by implication. Others conclude that the amendment was definitely intended as a general declaration of "individual inherent rights," unenumerated *and* independent of constitutional grant. Such debates aside, the U.S. Supreme Court cited the Ninth Amendment as partial justification for the constitutional right to privacy in *Griswold v. Connecticut* (1965).

Olmstead v. United States (1928)

Decision of the U.S. Supreme Court holding that the use of evidence obtained through a warrantless wiretap in a federal criminal trial did not violate the Fourth Amendment's guarantee against unreasonable searches and seizures. Because the interception of the telephone conversations occurred without *trespass* on private property, there was no *search* of a constitutionally protected area; moreover, conversations were not tangible items that could be *seized.* More important for purposes of constitutional privacy, Justice Louis Brandeis argued in dissent that the U.S. Constitution bestowed upon each individual a general right of privacy, one not confined to traditional categories of searches involving actual trespass on private property or seizures of tangible items. He then concluded that "the makers of our Constitution . . . conferred, as against the government, the right to be let alone—the most comprehensive of rights and the right most valued by civilized men." This statement has been repeated often in privacy cases throughout the twentieth century.

Oregon Death with Dignity Act (1994)

Oregon law that decriminalizes assisted suicide. More specifically, it permits terminally ill Oregon residents to end their lives through the voluntary self-administration of lethal medications, expressly prescribed by a physician for that purpose. Although the act legalizes physician-assisted suicide, it prohibits a physician or other person from directly administering a medication to end another's life. After three years of court challenges, including a petition that was denied by the U.S. Supreme Court, the law went into effect in 1997. At present, Oregon is the only state to permit assisted suicide. Congressional opponents of physician-assisted suicide have introduced a number of bills deliberately aimed at overthrowing the Oregon law, including the Lethal Drug Abuse Prevention Act (1998) and the Pain Relief Promotion Act (1999).

Pain Relief Promotion Act (1999)

A bill introduced in Congress intended to overturn Oregon's Death with Dignity Act. The bill did not affect physicians who prescribed drugs for pain relief, even if those drugs caused death, but punished physicians who prescribed drugs intentionally to cause death. The bill was approved in the House of Representatives but not in the Senate.

Palko v. Connecticut (1937)

Decision of the U.S. Supreme Court rationalizing the selective incorporation of Bill of Rights into the Fourteenth Amendment's Due Process Clause. According to this theory, often known as *selective incorporation,* only fundamental rights are applied to the states. For a right to be fundamental, it either had to be implicit in the concept of ordered liberty or deeply rooted in the nation's history and tradition. Today, most of the provisions of the Bill of Rights are binding upon the states.

Parental Consent/Notification

Common provision found in many state abortion regulations requiring minors seeking to terminate their pregnancy either to get consent from or to notify a parent of their intent to obtain an abortion. Laws requiring parental consent and parental notification have been upheld by the U.S. Supreme Court, as long as those laws provide for a *judicial bypass,* whereby minors can petition a judge for an abortion order without first consulting their parents.

Partial-Birth Abortion

A procedure "in which the person performing the abortion partially delivers vaginally a living unborn child before killing the unborn child and completing the delivery." In *Stenberg v. Carhart* (2000), the U.S. Supreme Court struck down a Nebraska law that prohibited partial-birth abortion.

Passive Involuntary Euthanasia

Hastening the death of a person without that person's consent. Perhaps the most common form of this type of euthanasia is a family member electing to discontinue artificial means of support for a loved one in a persistent vegetative state. Most states permit, within certain limitations, the withdrawal of life-sustaining medical treatment and the termination of artificial hydration and nutrition for patients in a persistent vegetative state through the use of advanced directives, although the U.S. Supreme Court has said the states may require "clear and convincing, inherently reliable evidence" of the patient's wishes not to continue life-sustaining medical treatment.

Passive Voluntary Euthanasia

Hastening the death of a person with that person's consent by discontinuing artificial means of support. Perhaps the most common form of this type of euthanasia is an elderly person requesting to have a respirator or feeding tube removed so as to bring about death. The U.S. Supreme Court, in *Cruzan v. Missouri Depart-*

ment of Health (1990), interpreted the Fourteenth Amendment's Due Process Clause to guarantee a liberty interest that protects the right of a *competent* patient to refuse unwanted medical treatment, even if doing so will most certainly result in death.

Patient Self-Determination Act (1991)

Act of Congress that requires all hospitals, skilled nursing facilities, home health agencies, hospice programs, and health maintenance organizations to guarantee that every adult receiving medical care be provided written information concerning advanced directives.

Pavesich v. New England Life Insurance Company (1905)

Decision of the Georgia Supreme Court expressly recognizing the existence of a general and independent right to privacy under the state constitution. *Pavesich* constituted the first time any court of last resort in the United States acknowledged an independent constitutional right to privacy.

Penumbras of the Bill of Rights

In *Griswold v. Connecticut* (1965), the U.S. Supreme Court held that the right to privacy was located in the penumbras of the First, Third, Fourth, Fifth, and Ninth Amendments. A *penumbra* is a partial shadow surrounding a fuller and darker shadow, as in an eclipse. "[S]pecific guarantees in the Bill of Rights have penumbras, formed by emanations from those guarantees that help give them life and substance," said the majority opinion. In short, the justices acknowledged that certain specifically enumerated rights protected in the U.S. Constitution, when considered along with their "emanations" and "penumbras," implied other rights, including an independent, general right to privacy.

People v. Onofre (1980)

Decision of the New York Court of Appeals, the highest court in the state, invalidating a state law that criminalized sodomy on state constitutional privacy grounds. The opinion held that adults could seek sexual gratification from what "at least once was commonly regarded as 'deviant' conduct," as long as the decision to participate was voluntary and the activity occurred in a private setting.

Persistent Vegetative State

Medical condition in which a patient has no possibility of regaining consciousness yet is capable of existing indefinitely. This dilemma prompted an ad hoc committee of the Harvard University Medical School in 1968 to recommend that a person who had suffered irreversible loss of function of the brain be considered legally dead. Most states have since adopted brain-death statutes.

Pierce v. Society of Sisters (1925)

Decision of the U.S. Supreme Court invalidating an Oregon statute that prohibited private elementary schooling, thus requiring all children between the ages of eight and sixteen to attend public schools. The majority opinion held that the law interfered with the rights of parents and guardians to direct the upbringing and education of their children. This case is perceived by many to be a companion case to *Meyer v. Nebraska* (1923). These two cases are the first cases to hold that the Due Process Clause of the Fourteenth Amendment protected certain noneconomic aspects of individual autonomy. These cases are thus appropriately viewed as denoting the emergence of a new branch of substantive due process, one that surfaced fully four decades later as an important precedent for constitutional privacy. Read together,

Meyer and *Pierce* are the true progenitors of the privacy decisions. They demarcate limitations on governmental power to intrude upon matters affecting fundamental rights.

Planned Parenthood

The nation's largest reproductive health care organization, Planned Parenthood has long sought to assure that individuals have the right to decide freely when and whether to have a child. To that end, this organization supports access to means of contraception and a woman's right to choose to terminate her pregnancy. Planned Parenthood has also provided monetary and legal assistance to individuals wishing to challenge state and federal laws curtailing reproductive freedom. Estelle Griswold, for example, was the executive director of the Planned Parenthood League of Connecticut; her case led to the landmark *Griswold* decision by the Supreme Court.

Planned Parenthood of Central Missouri v. Danforth (1976)

Decision of the U.S. Supreme Court invalidating a Missouri abortion law that required a woman, before submitting to an abortion during the first twelve weeks of pregnancy, to obtain written consent of a spouse and to secure the written consent of a parent or person in loco parentis if unmarried and under the age of eighteen. The justices upheld a requirement that a woman seeking an abortion consent in writing to the procedure and certify that her consent was informed, freely given, and not the result of coercion. Three years later, in *Bellotti v. Baird* (1979), the U.S. Supreme Court upheld a state law that required a minor to obtain parental consent, as long as that law provided for a *judicial bypass,* whereby minors can petition a judge for an abortion order without first consulting their parents. Spousal consent and notification requirements have consistently been struck down by the Court.

Planned Parenthood of Southeastern Pennsylvania v. Casey (1992)

Decision of the U.S. Supreme Court sustaining a Pennsylvania abortion law that required a woman to wait twenty-four hours between consenting to and receiving an abortion; that the woman be given state-mandated information about abortion and offered state-authored materials on fetal development; and that minors obtain consent of one parent or guardian, or a judicial waiver, prior to receiving an abortion. The justices struck down a requirement that a married woman inform her husband of her intent to have an abortion. *Casey* reaffirmed the essential holding of *Roe v. Wade* (1973)—that viability marked the earliest point at which the state's interest in fetal life was constitutionally adequate to justify a legislative ban on nontherapeutic abortions. Nevertheless, the majority rejected the trimester framework of *Roe,* replacing it with the undue burden analysis, which asks whether restrictive laws had the purpose or effect of placing a "substantial obstacle in the path of a woman seeking an abortion of a nonviable fetus." This case was the last major broadside attack on the constitutional right to abortion.

Plurality Opinion

An opinion that states the holding of a court but is supported by less than a majority of the judges or justices participating in the decision.

Poe v. Ullman (1961)

Decision of the U.S. Supreme Court dismissing on technical grounds a constitutional challenge to an 1879 Connecticut statute that criminalized the use of contraceptives by married couples. In dissent, however, Justice John Marshall Harlan argued that the statute violated the right to marital privacy as guaranteed by the

Bill of Rights and the Fourteenth Amendment. This dissent had a profound impact on the development of privacy jurisprudence, as evidenced by the Court's opinion to this effect only four years later in *Griswold v. Connecticut* (1965).

Poelker v. Doe (1977)

Decision of the U.S. Supreme Court upholding a St. Louis ordinance that provided publicly financed hospital services for childbirth without providing analogous services for nontherapeutic abortions. The justices noted that even though abortion was a constitutionally protected right, public hospitals had no obligation to provide for them, even for indigent women.

Police Power

A state's authority to legislate to protect public health, safety, welfare, and morality. For much of the twentieth century the U.S. Supreme Court has attempted to determine the extent to which state police power was limited by specific provisions of the U.S. Constitution.

Polygamy

The condition of having more than one spouse at a time. The emergence of constitutional privacy in the twentieth century provided a new line of attack for polygamists in their attempts to earn constitutional protection for their conduct. Supporters of polygamy have argued that statutes prohibiting plural marriages encroach upon the fundamental right to marital privacy. No state or federal court has ever accepted this argument. In 1973, the U.S. Supreme Court opined that few individuals "seriously claim that making bigamy a crime violates the First Amendment or any other constitutional provision." And in 1985, the U.S. Court of

Appeals for the Tenth Circuit decided that nothing in any of the U.S. Supreme Court's privacy cases supported extending the right to protect polygamous marriage.

Post v. State (1986)

Decision of the Oklahoma Supreme Court of Criminal Appeals striking down a statute that prohibited sodomy between consenting adult heterosexuals. The U.S. Supreme Court denied a request for certiorari in this case.

Potter v. Murray City (1985)

Decision of the U.S. Court of Appeals for the Tenth Circuit holding that nothing in any of the U.S. Supreme Court's privacy cases supported extending the constitutional right to privacy to protect polygamous marriage.

Powell v. State (1998)

Decision of the Georgia Supreme Court invalidating a criminal sodomy statute on state law privacy grounds. The court concluded that the right to be let alone guaranteed by the Georgia constitution was far more extensive than the right of privacy protected by the U.S. Constitution.

Prince v. Massachusetts (1944)

Decision of the U.S. Supreme Court reaffirming constitutional protection for family privacy. The majority opinion spoke of a "private realm of family life which the state cannot enter."

Privacy, Significance of

Privacy is valued condition of human life because it satisfies primary human needs, including personal autonomy, emotional release, self-evaluation, and protected communication; promotes human personhood; and fosters healthy human relationships.

Privacy Act (1974)

Federal law prohibiting the disclosure of a federal agency record containing personal information without the written consent of the subject except in limited circumstances, which include disclosure for routine use (i.e., use consistent with the purpose for which the information was collected), law enforcement purposes, and protecting the health or safety of an individual.

Procedural Due Process of Law

This concept maintains that the Due Process Clause of the Fourteenth Amendment obliges government to provide an individual with fair notice and a fair hearing prior to depriving that individual of "life, liberty, or property." In short, procedural due process places limits on *how* government may exercise its power.

Prochoice Movement

General term describing the efforts of individuals and organizations committed to preserving the constitutional right to abortion.

Prolife Movement

General term describing the efforts of individuals and organizations opposed to the constitutional right to abortion.

"Procreation, marriage, and family life"

Broadly speaking, the U.S. Supreme Court has limited constitutional privacy to activities relating to "procreation, marriage, and family life."

Quickening

The stage of pregnancy at which the unborn child shows signs of life. The first abortion statutes in the United States, enacted between 1820 and 1840, prohibited only those abortions that occurred postquickening.

Quinlan, Karen

Young woman who became permanently comatose after swallowing large quantities of alcohol and tranquilizers. When it became evident that she would not regain consciousness, her parents requested that she be removed from the respirator. This request gave rise to the New Jersey Supreme Court decision *In re Quinlan* (1976).

Rational Basis Test

Standard of review under the Equal Protection and Due Process Clauses used by courts to evaluate laws that discriminate against nonsuspect classifications or curtail nonfundamental rights. When the rational basis test is applied, the burden is on those attacking the law, and the courts are likely to sustain the law as long as it is reasonably related to a legitimate state interest. For example, because terminally ill patients are not a suspect classification and because assisted suicide is not a fundamental right, this particular test was used by the U.S. Supreme Court in *Washington v. Glucksberg* (1997). Compare this with the *strict scrutiny* test.

Ravin v. State (1975)

Decision of the Alaska Supreme Court holding that the right to privacy under both the federal and state constitutions protected the possession of small quantities of marijuana for personal, private use by adults in their homes.

Reynolds v. United States (1879)

Decision of the U.S. Supreme Court sustaining a federal statute that banned polygamy. The majority opinion held that Congress was free to regulate those actions—even those actions motivated by religious obligation—that were "in violation of social duties or subversive of good order."

"Right to be let alone"

Attributed to Thomas Cooley, this phrase is often used as the most basic definition of constitutional privacy. Justice Louis Brandeis, dissenting in *Olmstead v. United States* (1928), employed the phrase when he defined privacy as "the right to be let alone—the most comprehensive of rights and the right most valued by civilized men." The phrase has been repeated often in privacy jurisprudence.

The Right to Die

Controlling the timing and manner of one's own death. More specifically, it is the right to refuse unwanted medical treatment or to have ongoing medical care withdrawn even though the refusal or withdrawal will most likely result in death; also, the right to terminate one's own life or obtain assistance for the purpose of doing so. The U.S. Supreme Court has not answered definitively the question of whether the Constitution protects the right to die. The justices have interpreted the Fourteenth Amendment's Due Process Clause to guarantee a liberty interest that protects the right of a *competent* patient to refuse unwanted medical treatment. The Court has also acknowledged that an *incompetent* patient owns a liberty interest in refusing medical treatment under certain circumstances. Thus, the right to die deserves some constitutional protection. In similar fashion, at least five justices have hinted that, under certain circumstances, the right to physician-assisted suicide may merit some constitutional protection also.

Right to Financial Privacy Act (1994)

Federal law forbidding most governmental access to the financial records of individuals.

"The Right to Privacy," *Harvard Law Review* (1890)

Landmark article calling upon the courts to recognize a specific constitutional right to privacy, a right independent of property and liberty and unrelated to tort law. This article traced the genealogy of privacy back to the common law of England, concluding that each individual possessed a general right "to enjoy life, . . . to be let alone." "The Right to Privacy" has assumed a hallowed place in legal circles; it has been dubbed by more than a few scholars as the most influential law review article in history.

Roberson v. Rochester Fielding Box Company (1902)

Decision of the New York Court of Appeals, the highest court in the state, specifically refusing to recognize privacy as an independent right under the state constitution.

Roe, Jane

Pseudonym for Norma McCorvey, who unsuccessfully sought an abortion in Texas, which, like most other states in the early 1970s, prohibited abortions unless necessary to save a woman's life. McCorvey challenged the constitutionality of the Texas abortion law and became "Jane Roe" in a test case. McCorvey claimed that she had a right to choose to terminate her pregnancy, a right found in the concept of personal liberty found in the Due Process Clause of the Fourteenth Amendment; in personal, marital, familial, and sexual privacy protected by the Bill of Rights and its penumbras; and among those rights reserved to the people by the Ninth Amendment. Her challenge gave rise to the U.S. Supreme Court decision *Roe v. Wade* (1973).

Roe v. Wade (1973)

Decision of the U.S. Supreme Court declaring that constitutional privacy was "broad enough to encompass a woman's decision whether or not to terminate her pregnancy." This case elevated abortion to the national political agenda and has become the most debated privacy case ever. It is praised by many for its recognition that control over a woman's body and her reproductive destiny belonged to the woman; and it is criticized by an equal number for its lack of concern for potential life and perceived support of infanticide.

Romer v. Evans (1996)

Decision of the U.S. Supreme Court invalidating a state constitutional amendment forbidding legal protections for homosexuals but holding that homosexuals are not a suspect class for the purposes of equal protection analysis. Thus, though homosexuals are protected by the Equal Protection Clause, government action classifying individuals on the basis of homosexuality or homosexual behavior is subject to the rational basis test, and any such classification will be sustained as long as it is rationally related to a legitimate state interest. This holding may prove dispositive in equal protection challenges to bans on same-sex marriages; it was cited by a federal district judge in *Lofton v. Kearney* (2001) in upholding a Florida law that denied homosexuals the right to adopt children.

Schloendorff v. Society of New York Hospital (1914)

Decision of the New York Court of Appeals, the highest court in the state, in which Justice Benjamin Cardozo opined that "[e]very human being of adult years and sound mind has a right to determine what shall be done with his own body." This statement is often cited as the genesis of the common law's recognition of the patient's right to control the decisionmaking of the physician; today, the doctrine is commonly referred to as *informed consent.*

Separation of Powers

One of the four defining principles of the Constitution. Separation of powers is a way of parceling out power among the three branches of the national government. The Constitution assigns the legislative, executive, and judicial powers of the national government to three separate, independent branches of government. This separation, James Madison maintained, provided an "essential precaution in favor of liberty."

Sexually Stimulating Devices

Devices used primarily for the stimulation of human genital organs, banned in a number of states. At least two state supreme courts have held that the use of such devices is a fundamental right and thus protected by the constitutional right to privacy.

Skinner v. Oklahoma (1942)

Decision of the U.S. Supreme Court striking down Oklahoma's Habitual Criminal Sterilization Act. Although the justices relied upon the Equal Protection Clause in invalidating the act, the majority opinion noted that procreation was "one of the basic civil rights of man . . . fundamental to the very existence and survival of the race." *Skinner* was thus the first major ruling extending constitutional protection to procreation.

Smith v. Organization for Foster Families for Equality and Reform (1977)

Decision of the U.S. Supreme Court holding that the privacy interest between foster parent and child was less protected than the privacy interest between biological parent and child. Because the natural family had its origins entirely apart from the power of the state, its privacy was based upon intrinsic human rights. The foster family, by contrast, had its origins in state law and contractual arrangements. This precedent was cited by a lower federal court in *Lofton v. Kearney* (2001) in upholding a Florida law that denied homosexuals the right to adopt children.

Social Contract Theory

Made prominent in the seventeenth century by philosophers Thomas Hobbes and John Locke, this theory posits that all men are born free and equal by God-given right and, therefore, must give their consent to be governed. This theory became the animating principle of the American Revolution and the subsequent government of the United States.

Sodomy

Oral or anal copulation; prohibited in most states. The U.S. Supreme Court held in *Bowers v. Hardwick* (1986) that private homosexual sodomy between consenting adults was not a constitutionally protected privacy interest.

Sousna v. Iowa (1975)

Decision of the U.S. Supreme Court sustaining an Iowa law requiring a one-year residency as a precondition to obtaining a divorce. Even though divorce is a constitutionally protected privacy interest, the justices held that states could regulate divorce in reasonable ways.

Spousal Consent/Notification

Common provision found in many state abortion regulations requiring married women either to get consent from or notify their spouse of their intent to obtain an abortion. Laws requiring spousal consent and notification have been struck down by the U.S. Supreme Court as imposing an "undue burden" upon women seeking an abortion.

Stanley v. Georgia (1969)

Decision of the U.S. Supreme Court holding that a state could not punish the mere private possession of obscene material in the home. The justices based their holding on three constitutional rights: freedom of speech, freedom from unreasonable searches and seizures, *and* the right to privacy.

Stanley v. Illinois (1972)

Decision of the U.S. Supreme Court acknowledging that a father, though unwed, had a constitutional privacy interest in the children he had sired and raised.

State v. Bateman (1976)

Decision of the Arizona Supreme Court concluding that the state constitutional right to privacy did not give unmarried heterosexual adults the right to perform "unnatural copulation." The majority opinion clarified, however, that similar activity conducted by married persons could not be criminalized.

State v. Pilcher (1976)

Decision of the Iowa Supreme Court invalidating an antisodomy statute as an invasion of fundamental rights, including the personal right of privacy, as applied to private heterosexual sodomy between consenting adults.

State v. Saunders (1977)

Decision of the New Jersey Supreme Court striking down an antifornication statute, as applied to private consensual, noncommercial, heterosexual activity between adults.

Sterilization

The act of depriving an individual of his or her ability to produce offspring. In *Skinner v. Oklahoma* (1942), the U.S. Supreme Court, in striking down a statute that required sterilization for thrice-convicted felons, declared procreation to be a fundamental right protected by the U.S. Constitution.

Strict Scrutiny

Standard of review under the Equal Protection and Due Process Clauses used by courts to evaluate laws that discriminate against suspect classifications or curtail fundamental rights. A *suspect classification* is a class of people deliberately subjected to such unequal treatment in the past, or relegated by society to a position of such political powerlessness, as to require extraordinary judicial protection. A *fundamental right* is a right either implicit in the concept of ordered liberty or deeply rooted in the nation's history and tradition. A law that discriminates against a suspect classification or curtails a fundamental right is inherently suspect. Operationally, this means that the law is presumptively unconstitutional. To justify such a restriction, the government has the heavy burden of persuading a court that there is a compelling state interest in the law and that there is no other, less restrictive way to accomplish that interest. For example, because race is a suspect classification, this particular test was used by the U.S. Supreme Court in *Loving v. Virginia* (1967). Because procreation is a fundamental right, this particular test was employed by the justices in *Skinner v. Oklahoma* (1942). Compare this with the rational basis test.

Substantive Due Process of Law

This concept maintains that the Due Process Clause of the Fourteenth Amendment imposes certain *substantive* limitations on governmental policies. Substantive due process holds that the government is barred from adopting and enforcing policies that are irrational, unreasonable, unfair, or unjust, even though those policies may not infringe upon specific constitutional prohibitions. In short, this doctrine places limits on *what* government may do. Many scholars trace the genesis of substantive due process to *Wynehamer v. People of the State of New York* (1856), a decision of the New York Court of Appeals, the highest court in the state.

Substituted Judgment/ Substitute Decisionmakers

In a case of substituted judgment, the person previously authorized by the patient, when competent, to give consent on behalf of the incompetent patient attempts to determine what the patient would have wanted done had the patient understood the circumstances. The substitute decisionmaker's best guess as to the wishes of the incompetent patient is then substituted for the expressed wishes of the incompetent patient, which cannot be obtained. The purpose of substituted judgment is to respect the autonomy of the incompetent patient by enforcing his or her likely wishes regarding medical care.

Suicide

The deliberate termination of one's own life.

Suicide Machine

Apparatus designed by Dr. Jack Kevorkian to assist individuals in committing suicide. The Kevorkian suicide machine has three canisters attached to a metal frame. The first canister contains ordinary saline; the second barbiturates; and the third potassium chloride. Each canister has a syringe connected to an intravenous line in the person's arm. After the saline begins to flow, the person who wishes to die prompts the machine to deliver the sleep-inducing barbiturates. Once the person is asleep, a mechanical device triggered by the person's falling arm releases the lethal mixture of potassium chloride into the bloodstream. Death usually occurs within minutes.

Third Amendment

Provision in the Bill of Rights that protects the privacy of the home in peacetime from soldiers seeking quarters without the owner's consent. In *Griswold v. Connecticut* (1965), the U.S. Supreme Court held that the right to privacy derived from rights explicitly protected in the Bill of Rights, including the right secured by the Third Amendment, the obvious purpose of which was "to secure the perfect enjoyment of that great right, of the [English] common law, that a man's house shall be his own castle, privileged against all civil and military intrusion."

Thornburgh v. American College of Obstetricians and Gynecologists (1986)

Decision of the U.S. Supreme Court invalidating numerous provisions of a Pennsylvania abortion statute and reaffirming the general principles laid down in *Roe v. Wade* (1973). Generally speaking, *Thornburgh* held that states could not, under the guise of protecting maternal health or potential life, intimidate women into continuing their pregnancies. Restrictions similar to those invalidated here were upheld in *Planned Parenthood of Southeastern Pennsylvania v. Casey* (1992).

Tort Privacy

Certain privacy encroachments stem from the actions of private individuals. A *tort* is a private or civil injury to a person, property, or reputation. The individual who has been injured may bring a lawsuit against the wrongdoer, requesting that a court provide a remedy in the form of an action for damages. Tort privacy permits those who are of the opinion that their privacy has been invaded or denied to request from a court of law an action for damages against the person or persons who have committed the wrong.

Trimester Framework

Framework contrived by Justice Harry Blackmun in *Roe v. Wade* (1973) to balance the interests of a woman seeking an abortion with those of the states seeking to regulate or proscribe abortion. This approach divides the nine-month pregnancy into three successive three-month periods. Prior to the end of the first trimester of pregnancy, the state cannot interfere with a woman's decision to terminate her pregnancy. After the first trimester, and until the point in time when the fetus becomes viable, the state can regulate the abortion procedure but only in ways that are reasonably related to the preservation and protection of maternal health. From the point of viability, the state may regulate, and even prohibit altogether, abortions, except those necessary to preserve the life or health of the mother. The trimester framework was rejected in *Planned Parenthood of Southeastern Pennsylvania v. Casey* (1992), the justices replacing it with the undue burden analysis.

Troxel v. Granville (2000)

Decision of the U.S. Supreme Court striking down a Washington law that allowed a judge to order child visitation rights to grandparents against the wishes of the child's parents and reaffirming the right of parents to direct the upbringing of their children. "The liberty interest at issue in this case—the interests of parents in the care, custody, and control of their children—is perhaps the oldest of the fundamental liberty interests recognized by this Court," noted the plurality opinion.

Turner v. Safley (1987)

Decision of the U.S. Supreme Court striking down a Missouri statute that prohibited most marriages involving prison inmates as impermissibly burdening a fundamental liberty. The justices reaffirmed their earlier characterization of marriage as a constitutional right.

Undue Burden Analysis

Standard adopted by the U.S. Supreme Court in *Planned Parenthood of Southeastern Pennsylvania v. Casey* (1992) to determine the constitutionality of abortion regulations. Under this analysis, the justices ask whether the challenged regulation has the purpose or effect of placing a "substantial obstacle in the path of a woman seeking an abortion of a nonviable fetus."

Unenumerated Rights

Rights not mentioned in the U.S. Constitution or the Bill of Rights. The Ninth Amendment makes clear that the inclusion of certain liberties in the Bill of Rights does not mean that others do not exist. To be certain, the right to privacy is nowhere specifically mentioned in the U.S. Constitution or the Bill of Rights. Nevertheless, constitutional privacy flows from the general concept that there are certain unlisted yet fundamental freedoms beyond the power of government to restrict.

Uniform Determination of Death Act

All states have adopted brain-death statutes, with many enacting, sometimes with variations, the Uniform Determination of Death Act definition: "An individual who has sustained either (1) irreversible cessation of circulatory and respiratory function, or (2) irreversible cessation of all functions of the entire brain, including the brain stem, is dead."

Union Pacific Railroad v. Botsford (1891)

Decision of the U.S. Supreme Court in which the majority opinion mentioned, for the first time, the "right to be let alone."

United States v. Westinghouse (1980)

Decision of the U.S. Court of Appeals for the Third Circuit promulgating a now well-accepted standard for determining whether an invasion of informational privacy is constitutionally justified. At a minimum, the government must be able to demonstrate that the release of certain information furthers an important governmental interest and that sufficient effort has been taken to prevent unnecessary and excessive public access to such information.

USA Patriot Act (2001)

Federal law passed following the terrorist attacks of September 11, 2001, that broadened the power of the Federal Bureau of Investigation to use Carnivore (a device that intercepts, reads, stores, and classifies Internet transmissions; see the specific entry for Carnivore).

Vacco v. Quill (1997)

Decision of the U.S. Supreme Court dismissing an equal protection challenge to a New York law that prohibited assisted suicide.

Viability

The point in a pregnancy when the unborn child becomes capable of maintaining a separate existence outside of the mother's womb.

Video Privacy Act (1994)

Federal law safeguarding videotape rental records.

Wade, Henry

The criminal district attorney for Dallas County, Texas, who argued in support of the Texas law that prohibited abortions in *Roe v. Wade* (1973).

Waiting Period

Common provision found in many state abortion regulations requiring women seeking an abortion to wait a certain period of time, usually twenty-four or forty-eight hours, between consenting to and receiving an abortion. Such laws have been upheld by the U.S. Supreme Court.

Warren, Samuel

Coauthor of the famous 1890 *Harvard Law Review* article on privacy. In "The Right to Privacy," Warren and coauthor Louis Brandeis called upon the courts to recognize a specific constitutional right to privacy, a right independent of property and liberty and unrelated to tort law.

Washington v. Glucksberg (1997)

Decision of the U.S. Supreme Court holding that assisted suicide was not a fundamental right and therefore not protected under the constitutional right to privacy.

Webster v. Reproductive Health Services (1989)

Decision of the U.S. Supreme Court upholding a Missouri abortion statute that forbade the use of public facilities for abortions not necessary to save a woman's life and required physicians to perform viability testing prior to performing an abortion. This case marked a turning point in abortion adjudication. Prior to this time, most state restrictions on abortion had been struck down. After *Webster*, states possessed far greater power to regulate when, where, and how a woman could terminate her pregnancy.

Whalen v. Roe (1977)

Decision of the U.S. Supreme Court explicitly recognizing the constitutional right to informational privacy. The majority opinion noted held that constitutional privacy embraced not only an "interest in independence in making certain kinds of important decisions" but also an "individual interest in avoiding disclosure of personal matters."

Wynehamer v. People of the State of New York (1856)

Decision of the New York Court of Appeals overturning a state law that prohibited the sale of liquor. Many scholars trace the genesis of substantive due process to this case. For the first time, a court of last resort discovered that the concept of due process encompassed more than procedures. It mattered not that the New York legislature followed proper procedures in enacting the criminal statute, for the statute deprived individuals of certain *substantive* rights protected under the New York Constitution.

Zablocki v. Redhail (1978)

Decision of the U.S. Supreme Court striking down a Wisconsin statute that denied parents who failed to meet child-support obligations the right to remarry without a court's permission; also reaffirmed the fundamental character of the right to marry.

Zones of Privacy

In a series of decisions going back as far as the late nineteenth century, the U.S. Supreme Court recognized that a guarantee of certain areas or zones of privacy existed under the Constitution and that the right had application to activities relating to procreation, marriage, and family life. In *Griswold v. Connecticut* (1965), the Court was more specific, formally acknowledging that the First, Third, Fourth, Fifth, and Ninth Amendments created "zones of privacy" free from governmental encroachment.

6

DOCUMENTS

This chapter presents thirteen primary documents. Because the constitutional right to privacy evolves principally through judicial decisions, twelve of these documents are excerpts from cases, of which ten are decisions of the U.S. Supreme Court. Preceding the cases is a reprint of "The Right to Privacy," the 1890 *Harvard Law Review* article written by Samuel Warren and Louis Brandeis, calling upon the courts to recognize an independent constitutional right to privacy.

Pavesich v. New England Life Insurance Company (1905), the first state Supreme Court case specifically to recognize the existence of a general and independent right to privacy under a state constitution, is included. And Justice Louis Brandeis's dissent in *Olmstead v. United States* (1928), which foreshadowed the modern constitutional right to privacy, is excerpted also.

In the twentieth century, constitutional privacy has gravitated around three principle areas: procreation, marriage, and family life. In addition, it has been argued that constitutional privacy should include private sexual activity between consenting adults and the right to control the timing and manner of one's death. Four of the cases excerpted deal with reproductive autonomy—one with procreation, *Skinner v. Oklahoma* (1942); one with contraception, *Griswold v. Connecticut* (1965); and two with abortion, *Roe v. Wade* (1973) and *Planned Parenthood of Southeastern Pennsylvania v. Casey* (1992). One case involves the marital relationship—*Loving v. Virginia* (1967); one pertains to family life—*Meyer v. Nebraska* (1923); and one relates to sexual autonomy—*Bowers v. Hardwick* (1986). The final two cases—*Cruzan v. Missouri Department of Health* (1990) and *Washington v. Glucksberg* (1997)—raise important questions about the right to die.

Finally, *Commonwealth of Kentucky v. Wasson* (1992), a decision of the Kentucky Supreme Court invalidating a criminal sodomy statute on state law privacy grounds, is included. This case demonstrates well how one state constitution offers greater protection of the right to privacy than the U.S. Constitution.

The cases appear chronologically. This will allow the reader to trace the evolution and perhaps devolution of the constitutional right to privacy in the twentieth century. Each case is preceded by a headnote, a brief statement of the circumstances that brought about the case, identifying the parties and the holding of the lower courts, stating concisely the holding of the U.S. Supreme Court, and explaining the significance of the case. To appreciate better the various sides of the argument, selected separate opinions, both concurring and dissenting, are excerpted.

"THE RIGHT TO PRIVACY," BY SAMUEL D. WARREN AND LOUIS D. BRANDEIS (1890)

"It could be done only on principles of private justice, moral fitness, and public convenience, which, when applied to a new subject, make common law without a precedent; much more when received and approved by usage."

—*Willes, J., in* Millar v. Taylor,
4 Burr. 2303, 2312 (1769)

THAT the individual shall have full protection in person and in property is a principle as old as the common law; but it has been found necessary from time to time to define anew the exact nature and extent of such protection. Political, social, and economic changes entail the recognition of new rights, and the common law, in its eternal youth, grows to meet the new demands of society. Thus, in very early times, the law gave a remedy only for physical interference with life and property, for trespasses *vi et armis.* Then the "right to life" served only to protect the subject from battery in its various forms; liberty meant freedom from actual restraint; and the right to property secured to the individual his lands and his cattle. Later, there came a recognition of man's spiritual nature, of his feelings and his intellect. Gradually the scope of these legal rights broadened; and now the right to life has come to mean the right to enjoy life,—the right to be let alone; the right to liberty secures the exercise of extensive civil privileges; and the term "property" has grown to comprise every form of possession—intangible, as well as tangible.

Thus, with the recognition of the legal value of sensations, the protection against actual bodily injury was extended to prohibit mere attempts to do such injury; that is, the putting another in fear of such injury. From the action of battery grew that of assault. Much later there came a qualified protection of the individual against offensive noises and odors, against dust and smoke, and excessive vibration. The law of nuisance was developed. So regard for human emotions soon extended the scope of personal immunity beyond the body of the individual. His reputation, the standing among his fellow-men, was considered, and the law of slander and libel arose. Man's family relations became a part of the legal conception of his life, and the alienation of a wife's affections was held remediable. Occasionally the law halted, as in its refusal to recognize the intrusion by seduction upon the honor of the family. But even here the demands of society were met. A mean fiction, the action *per quod servitium amisit,* was resorted to, and by allowing damages for injury to the parents' feelings, an adequate remedy was ordinarily afforded. Similar to the expansion of the right to life was the growth of the legal conception of property. From corporeal property arose the incorporeal rights issuing out of it; and then there opened the wide realm of intangible property, in the products and processes of the mind, as works of literature and art, goodwill, trade secrets, and trademarks.

This development of the law was inevitable. The intense intellectual and emotional life, and the heightening of sensations which came with the advance of civilization, made it clear to men that only a part of the pain, pleasure, and profit of life lay in physical things. Thoughts, emotions, and sensations demanded legal recognition, and the beautiful capacity for growth which characterizes the common law enabled the judges to afford the requisite protection, without the interposition of the legislature.

Recent inventions and business methods call attention to the next step which must be taken for the protection of the person, and for securing to the individual what Judge Cooley calls the right "to be let alone." Instantaneous photographs and newspaper enterprise have invaded the sacred precincts of private and domestic life; and numerous mechanical devices threaten to make good the prediction that "what is whispered in the closet shall be proclaimed from the house-tops." For years there has been a feeling that the law must afford some remedy for the unauthorized circulation of portraits of private persons; and the evil of invasion of privacy by the newspapers, long keenly felt, has been but recently discussed by an able writer. The alleged facts of a somewhat notorious case brought before an inferior tribunal in New York a few months ago, directly involved the consideration of the right of circulating portraits; and the question whether our law will recognize and protect the right to privacy in this and in other respects must soon come before out courts for consideration.

Of the desirability—indeed of the necessity—of some such protection, there can, it is believed, be no doubt. The press is overstepping in every direction the obvious bounds of propriety and of decency. Gossip is no longer the resource of the idle and of the vicious, but has become a trade, which is pursued with industry as well as effrontery. To satisfy a prurient taste the details of sexual relations are spread broadcast in the columns of the daily papers. To occupy the indolent, column upon column is filled with idle gossip, which can only be procured by intrusion upon the domestic circle. The intensity and complexity of life, attendant upon advancing civilization, have rendered necessary some retreat from the world, and man, under the refining influence of culture, has become more sensitive to publicity, so that solitude and privacy have become more essential to the individual; but modern enterprise and invention have, through invasions upon his privacy, subjected him to mental pain and distress, far greater than could be inflicted by mere bodily injury. Nor is the harm wrought by such invasions confined to the suffering of those who may be the subjects of journalistic or other enterprise. In this, as in other branches of commerce, the supply creates the demand. Each crop of unseemly gossip, thus harvested, becomes the seed of more, and, in direct proportion to its circulation, results in the lowering of social standards and of morality. Even gossip apparently harmless, when widely and persistently circulated, is potent for evil. It both belittles and perverts. It belittles by inverting the relative importance of things, thus dwarfing the thoughts and aspirations of a people. When personal gossip attains the dignity of print, and crowds the space available for matters of real interest to the community, what wonder that the ignorant and thoughtless mistake its relative importance. Easy of comprehension, appealing to that weak side of human nature which is never wholly cast down by the misfortunes and frailties of our neighbors, no one can be surprised that it usurps the place of interest in brains capable of other things. Triviality destroys at once robustness of thought and delicacy of feeling. No enthusiasm can flourish, no generous impulse can survive under its blighting influence.

It is our purpose to consider whether the existing law affords a principle which can properly be invoked to protect the privacy of the individual; and, if it does, what the nature and extent of such protection is.

Owing to the nature of the instruments by which privacy is invaded, the injury inflicted bears a superficial resemblance to the wrongs dealt with by the law of slander and of libel, while a legal remedy for such injury seems to involve the treatment of mere wounded feelings, as a substantive cause of action. The principle on which the law of defamation rests, covers, however, a radically different class of effects from those for which attention is now asked. It deals only with damage to reputation, with the injury done to the individual in his external relations to the community, by lowering him in the estimation of his fellows. The matter published of him, however widely circulated, and however unsuited to publicity, must, in order to be actionable, have a direct tendency to injure him in his intercourse with others, and even if in writing or in print, must subject him to the hatred, ridicule, or contempt of his fellowmen,—the effect of the publication upon his estimate of himself and upon his own feelings nor forming an essential element in the cause of action. In short, the wrongs and correlative rights recognized by the law of slander and libel are in their nature material rather than spiritual. That branch of the law simply extends the protection surrounding physical property to certain of the conditions necessary or helpful to worldly prosperity. On the other hand, our law recognizes no principle upon which compensation can be granted for mere injury to the feelings. However painful the mental effects upon another of an act, though purely wanton or even malicious, yet if the act itself is otherwise lawful, the suffering inflicted is *dannum absque injuria.* Injury of feelings may indeed be taken account of in ascertaining the amount of damages when attending what is recognized as a legal injury; but our system, unlike the Roman law, does not afford a remedy even for mental suffering which results from mere contumely and insult, but from an intentional and unwarranted violation of the "honor" of another.

It is not however necessary, in order to sustain the view that the common law recognizes and upholds a principle applicable to cases of invasion of privacy, to invoke the analogy, which is but superficial, to injuries sustained, either by an attack upon reputation or by what the civilians called a violation of honor; for the legal doctrines relating to infractions of what is ordinarily termed the common-law right to intellectual and artistic property are, it is believed, but instances and applications of a general right to privacy, which properly understood afford a remedy for the evils under consideration.

The common law secures to each individual the right of determining, ordinarily, to what extent his thoughts, sentiments, and emotions shall be communicated to others. Under our system of government, he can never be compelled to express them (except when upon the witness stand); and even if he has chosen to give them expression, he generally retains the power to fix the limits of the publicity which shall be given them. The existence of this right does not depend upon the particular method of expression adopted. It is immaterial whether it be by word or by signs, in painting, by sculpture, or in music. Neither does the existence of the right depend upon the nature or value of the thought or emotions, nor upon the excellence of the means of expression. The same protection is accorded to a casual letter or an entry in a diary and to the most valuable poem or essay, to a botch or daub and to a masterpiece. In every such case the individual is entitled to decide whether that which is his shall be given to the public. No other has the right to publish his productions in any form, without his consent. This right is wholly independent of the material on which, the thought, sentiment, or emotions is expressed. It may exist independently of any corporeal being, as in words spoken, a song sung, a drama acted. Or if expressed on any material, as in a poem in writing, the author may have parted with the paper, without forfeiting any proprietary right in the composition itself. The right is lost only when the author himself communicates his production to the public,—in other words, publishes it. It is entirely independent of the copyright laws, and their extension into the domain of art. The aim of those statutes is to secure to the author, composer, or artist the entire profits arising from publication; but the common-law protection enables him to control absolutely the act of publication, and in the exercise of his own discretion, to decide whether there shall be any publication at all. The statutory right is of no value, *unless* there is a publication; the common-law right is lost *as soon as* there is a publication.

What is the nature, the basis, of this right to prevent the publication of manuscripts or works of art? It is stated to be the enforcement of a right of property; and no difficulty arises in accepting this view, so long as we have only to deal with the reproduction of literary and artistic compositions. They certainly possess many of the attributes of ordinary property; they are transferable; they have a value; and publication or reproduction is a use by which that value is realized. But where the value of the production is found not in the right to take the profits arising from publication, but in the peace of mind or the relief afforded by the ability to prevent any publication at all, it is difficult to regard the right as one of property, in the common acceptation of that term. A man records in a letter to his son, or in his diary, that he did not dine with his wife on a certain day. No one into whose hands those papers fall could publish them to the world, even if possession of the documents had been obtained rightfully; and the prohibition would not be confined to the publication of a copy of the letter itself, or of the diary entry; the restraint extends also to a publication of the contents. What is the thing which is protected? Surely, not the intellectual act of recording the fact that the husband did not dine with his wife, but that fact itself. It is not the intellectual product, but the domestic occurrence. A man writes a dozen letters to different people. No person would be permitted to publish a list of the letters written. If the letters or the contents of the diary were protected as literary compositions, the scope of the protection afforded should be the same secured to a published writing under the copyright law. But the copyright law would not prevent an enumeration of the letters, or the publication of some of the facts contained therein. The copyright of a series of paintings or etchings would prevent a reproduction of the paintings as pictures; but it would not prevent a publication of list or even a description of them. Yet in the famous case of *Prince Albert v. Strange,* the court held that the common-law rule prohibited not merely the reproduction of the etchings which the plaintiff and Queen Victoria had made for their own pleasure, but also "the publishing (at least by printing or writing), though not by copy or resemblance, a description of them, whether more or less limited or summary, whether in the form of a catalogue or otherwise." Likewise, an unpublished collection of news possessing no element of a literary nature is protected from privacy.

That this protection cannot rest upon the right to literary or artistic property in any exact sense, appears the more clearly when the subject-matter for which protection is invoked is not even in the form of intellectual property, but has the attributes of ordinary tangible property. Suppose a man has a collection of gems or curiosities which he keeps private: it would hardly be contended that any person could publish a catalogue of them, and yet the articles enumerated are certainly not intellectual property in the legal sense, any more than a collection of stoves or of chairs.

The belief that the idea of property in its narrow sense was the basis of the protection of unpublished manuscripts led an able court to refuse, in several cases, injunctions against the publication of private letters, on the ground that "letters not possessing the attributes of literary compositions are not property entitled to protection;" and that it was "evident the plaintiff could not have considered the letters as of any value whatever as literary productions, for a letter cannot be considered of value to the author which he never would consent to have published." But those decisions have not been followed, and it may not be considered settled that the protection afforded by the common law to the author of any writing is entirely independent of its pecuniary value, its intrinsic merits, or of any intention to publish the same and, of course, also, wholly independent of the material, if any, upon which, or the mode in which, the thought or sentiment was expressed.

Although the courts have asserted that they rested their decisions on the narrow grounds of protection to property, yet there are recognitions of a more liberal doctrine. Thus in the case of *Prince Albert v. Strange,* already referred to, the opinions of both the Vice-Chancellor and of the Lord Chancellor, on appeal, show a more or less clearly defined perception of a principle broader than those which were mainly discussed, and on which they both place their chief reliance. Vice-Chancellor Knight Bruce referred to publishing of a man that he had "written to particular persons or on particular subjects" as an instance of possibly injurious disclosures as to private matters, that the courts would in a proper case prevent; yet it is difficult to perceive how, in such a case, any right of privacy, in the narrow sense, would be drawn in question, or why, if such a publication would be restrained when it threatened to expose the victim not merely to sarcasm, but to ruin, it should not equally be enjoined, if it threatened to embitter his life. To deprive a man of the potential profits to be realized by publishing a catalogue of his gems cannot *per se* be a wrong to him. The possibility of future profits is not a right of property which the law ordinarily recognizes; it must, therefore, be an infraction of other rights which constitutes the wrongful act, and that infraction is equally wrongful, whether its results are to forestall the profits that the individual himself might secure by giving the matter a publicity obnoxious to him, or to gain an advantage at the expense of his mental pain and suffering. If the fiction of property in a narrow sense must be preserved, it is still true that the end accomplished by the gossip-monger is attained by the use of that which is another's, the facts relating to his private life, which he has seen fit to keep private. Lord Cottenham stated that a man "is that which is exclusively his," and cited with approval the opinion of Lord Eldon, as reported in a manuscript note of the case of *Wyatt v. Wilson,* in 1820, respecting an engraving of George the Third during his illness, to the effect that "if one of the late king's physicians had kept a diary of what he heard and saw, the court would not, in the king's lifetime, have permitted him to print and publish it;" and Lord Cottenham declared, in respect to the acts of the defendants in the case before him, that "privacy is the right invaded." But if privacy is once recognized as a right entitled to legal protection, the interposition of the courts cannot depend on the particular nature of the injuries resulting.

These considerations lead to the conclusion that the protection afforded to thoughts, sentiments, and emotions, expressed through the medium of writing or of the arts, so far as it consists in preventing publication, is merely an instance of the enforcement of the more general right of the individual to be let alone. It is like the right not be assaulted or beaten, the right not be imprisoned, the right not to be maliciously prosecuted, the right not to be defamed. In each of these rights, as indeed in all other rights recognized by the law, there inheres the quality of being owned or possessed—and (as that is the distinguishing attribute of property) there may some propriety in speaking of those rights as property. But, obviously, they bear little resemblance to what is ordinarily comprehended under that term. The principle which protects personal writings and all other personal productions, not against theft and physical appropriation, but against publication in any form, is in reality not the principle of private property, but that of an inviolate personality.

If we are correct in this conclusion, the existing law affords a principle from which may be invoked to protect the privacy of the individual from invasion either by the too enterprising press, the photographer, or the possessor of any other modern device for rewording or reproducing scenes or sounds. For the protection afforded is not confined by the authorities to those cases where any particular medium or form of expression has been adopted, not to products of the intellect. The same protection is afforded to emotions and sensations expressed in a musical composition or other work of art as to a literary composition; and words spoken, a pantomime acted, a sonata performed, is no less entitled to protection than if each had been reduced to writing. The circumstance that a thought or emotion has been recorded in a permanent form renders its identification easier, and hence may be important from the point of view of evidence, but it has no significance as a matter of substantive right. If, then, the decisions indicate a general right to privacy for thoughts, emotions, and sensations, these should receive the same protection, whether expressed in writing, or in conduct, in conversation, in attitudes, or in facial expression.

It may be urged that a distinction should be taken between the deliberate expression of thoughts and emotions in literary or artistic compositions and the casual and often involuntary expression given to them in the ordinary conduct of life. In other words, it may be contended that the protection afforded is granted to the conscious products of labor, perhaps as an encouragement to effort. This contention, however plausible, has, in fact, little to recommend it. If the amount of labor involved be adopted as the test, we might well find that the effort to conduct one's self properly in business and in domestic relations had been far greater than that involved in painting a picture or writing a book; one would find that it was far easier to express lofty sentiments in a diary than in the conduct of a noble life. If the test of deliberateness of the act be adopted, much casual correspondence which is now accorded full protection would be excluded from the beneficent operation of existing rules. After the decisions denying the distinction attempted to be made between those literary productions which it was intended to publish and those which it was not, all considerations of the amount of labor involved, the degree of deliberation, the value of the product, and the intention of publishing must be abandoned, and no basis is discerned upon which the right to restrain publication and reproduction of such so-called literary and artistic works can be rested, except the right to privacy, as a part of the more general right to the immunity of the person,—the right to one's personality.

It should be stated that, in some instances where protection has been afforded against wrongful publication, the jurisdiction has been asserted, not on the ground of property, or at least not wholly on that ground, but upon the ground of an alleged breach of an implied contract or of a trust or confidence.

Thus, in *Abernethy v. Hutchinson,* 3 L. J. Ch. 209 (1825), where the plaintiff, a distinguished surgeon, sought to restrain the publication in the "Lancet" of unpublished lectures which he had delivered as St. Bartholomew's Hospital in London, Lord Eldon doubted whether there could be property in lectures which had not been reduced to writing, but granted the injunction on the ground of breach of confidence, holding "that when persons were admitted as pupils or otherwise, to hear these lectures, although they were orally delivered, and although the parties might go to the extent, if they were able to do so, of putting down the whole by means of short-hand, yet they could do that only for the purposes of their own information, and could not publish, for profit, that which they had not obtained the right of selling."

In *Prince Albert v. Strange,* I McN. & G. 25 (1849), Lord Cottenham, on appeal, while recognizing a right of property in the etchings which of itself would justify the issuance of the injunction, stated, after discussing the evidence, that he was bound to assume that the possession of the etching by the defendant had "its foundation in a breach of trust, confidence, or contract," and that upon such ground also the plaintiff's title to the injunction was fully sustained.

In *Tuck v. Priester,* 19 Q.B.D. 639 (1887), the plaintiffs were owners of a picture, and employed the defendant to make a certain number of copies. He did so, and made also a number of other copies for himself, and offered them for sale in England at a lower price. Subsequently, the plaintiffs registered their copyright in the picture, and then brought suit for an injunction and damages. The Lords Justices differed as to the application of the copyright acts to the case, but held unanimously that independently of those acts, the plaintiffs were entitled to an injunction and damages for breach of contract.

In *Pollard v. Photographic Co.,* 40 Ch. Div. 345 (1888), a photographer who had taken a lady's photograph under the ordinary circumstances was restrained from exhibiting it, and also from selling copies of it, on the ground that it was a breach of an implied term in the contract, and also that it was a breach of confidence. Mr. Justice North interjected in the argument of the plaintiff's counsel the inquiry: "Do you dispute that if the negative likeness were taken on the sly, the person who took it might exhibit copies?" and counsel for the plaintiff answered: "In that case there would be no trust or consideration to support a contract." Later, the defendant's counsel argued that "a person has no property in his own features; short of doing what is libellous or otherwise illegal, there is no restriction on the photographer's using his negative." But the court, while expressly finding a breach of contract and of trust sufficient to justify its interposition, still seems to have felt the necessity of resting the decision also upon a right of property, in order to bring it within the line of those cases which were relied upon as precedents.

This process of implying a term in a contract, or of implying a trust (particularly where a contract is written, and where these is no established usage or custom), is nothing more nor less than a judicial declaration that public morality, private justice, and general convenience demand the recognition of such a rule, and that the publication under similar circumstances would be considered an intolerable abuse. So long as these circumstances happen to present a contract upon which such a term can be engrafted by the judicial mind, or to supply relations upon which a trust or confidence can be erected, there may be no objection to working out the desired protection though the doctrines of contract or of trust. But the court can hardly stop there. The narrower doctrine may have satisfied the demands of society at a time when the abuse to be guarded against could rarely have arisen without violating a contract or a special confidence; but now that modern devices afford abundant opportunities for the perpetration of such wrongs without any participation by the injured party, the protection granted by the law must be placed upon a broader foundation. While, for instance, the state of the photographic art was such that one's picture could seldom be taken without his consciously "sitting" for the purpose, the law of contract or of trust might afford the prudent man sufficient safeguards against the improper circulation of his portrait; but since the latest advances in photographic art have rendered it possible to take pictures surreptitiously, the doctrines of contract and of trust are inadequate to support the required protection, and the law of tort must be resorted to. The right of property in its widest sense, including all possession, including all rights and privileges, and hence embracing the right to an inviolate personality, affords alone that broad basis upon which the protection which the individual demands can be rested.

Thus, the courts, in searching for some principle upon which the publication of private letters could be enjoined, naturally came upon the ideas of a breach of confidence, and of an implied contract; but it required little consideration to discern that this doctrine could not afford all the protection required, since it would not support the court in granting a remedy against a stranger; and so the theory of property in the contents of letters was adopted. Indeed, it is difficult to conceive on what theory of the law the casual recipient of a letter, who proceeds to publish it, is guilty of a breach of contract, express or implied, or of any breach of trust, in the ordinary acceptation of that term. Suppose a letter has been addressed to him without his solicitation. He opens it, and reads. Surely, he has not made any contract; he has not accepted any trust. He cannot, by opening and reading the letter, have come under any obligation save what the law declares; and, however expressed, that obligation is simply to observe the legal right of the sender, whatever it may be, and whether it be called his right or property in the contents of the letter, or his right to privacy.

A similar groping for the principle upon which a wrongful publication can be enjoined is found in the law of trade secrets. There, injunctions have generally been granted on the theory of a breach of contract, or of an abuse of confidence. It would, of course, rarely happen that any one would be in possession of a secret unless confidence had been reposed in him. But can it be supposed that the court would hesitate to grant relief against one who had obtained his knowledge by an ordinary trespass,—for instance, by wrongfully looking into a book in which the secret was recorded, or by eavesdropping? Indeed, in *Yovatt v. Winyard,* I J.&W. 394 (1820), where an injunction was granted against making any use or of communicating certain recipes for veterinary medicine, it appeared that the defendant while in the plaintiff's employ, had surreptitiously got access to his book of recipes, and copied them. Lord Eldon "granted the injunction, upon the ground of there having been a breach of trust and confidence;" but it would seem difficult to draw any sound legal distinction between such a case and one where a mere stranger wrongfully obtained access to the book.

We must therefore conclude that the rights, so protected, whatever their exact nature, are not rights arising from contract or from special trust, but are rights as against the world; and, as above stated, the principle which has been applied to protect these rights is in reality not the principle of private property, unless that word be used in an extended and unusual sense. The principle which protects personal writings and any other productions of the intellect of or the emotions, is the right to privacy, and the law has no new principle to formulate when it extends this protection to the personal appearance, sayings, acts, and to personal relation, domestic or otherwise.

If the invasion of privacy constitutes a legal *injuria,* the elements for demanding redress exist, since already the value of mental suffering, caused by an act wrongful in itself, is recognized as a basis for compensation.

The right of one who has remained a private individual, to prevent his public portraiture, presents the simplest case for such extension; the right to protect one's self from pen portraiture, from a discussion by the press of one's private affairs, would be a more important and far-reaching one. If casual and unimportant statements in a letter, if handiwork, however inartistic and valueless, if possessions of all sorts are protected not only against reproduction, but also against description and enumeration, how much more should the acts and sayings of a man in his social and domestic relations be guarded from ruthless publicity. If you may not reproduce a woman's face photographically without her consent, how much less should be tolerated the reproduction of her face, her form, and her actions, by graphic descriptions colored to suit a gross and depraved imagination.

The right to privacy, limited as such right must necessarily be, has already found expression in the law of France.

It remains to consider what are the limitations of this right to privacy, and what remedies may be granted for the enforcement of the right. To determine in advance of experience the exact line at which the dignity and convenience of the individual must yield to the demands of the public welfare or of private justice would be a difficult task; but the more general rules are furnished by the legal analogies already developed in the law of slander and libel, and in the law of literary and artistic property.

I. The right to privacy does not prohibit any publication of matter which is of public or general interest.

In determining the scope of this rule, aid would be afforded by the analogy, in the law of libel and slander, of cases which deal with the qualified privilege of comment and criticism on matters of public and general interest. There are of course difficulties in applying such a rule; but they are inherent in the subject-matter, and are certainly no greater than those which exist in many other branches of the law,—for instance, in that large class of cases in which the reasonableness or unreasonableness of an act is made the test of liability. The design of the law must be to protect those persons with whose affairs the community has no legitimate concern, from being dragged into an undesirable and undesired publicity and to protect all persons, whatsoever; their position or station, from having matters which they may properly prefer to keep private, made public against their will. It is the unwarranted invasion of individual privacy which is reprehended, and to be, so far as possible, prevented. The distinction, however, noted in the above statement is obvious and fundamental. There are persons who may reasonably claim as a right, protection from the notoriety entailed by being made the victims of journalistic enterprise. There are others who, in varying degrees, have renounced the right to live their lives screened from public observation. Matters which men of the first class may justly contend, concern themselves alone, may in those of the second be the subject of legitimate interest to their fellow-citizens. Peculiarities of manner and person, which in the ordinary individual should be free from comment, may acquire a public importance, if found in a candidate for public office. Some further discrimination is necessary, therefore, than to class facts or deeds as public or private according to a standard to be applied to the fact or deed *per se.* To publish of a modest and retiring individual that he suffers from an impediment in his speech or that he cannot spell correctly, is an unwarranted, if not an unexampled, infringement of his rights, while to state and comment on the same characteristics found in a would-be congressman could not be regarded as beyond the pale of propriety. The general object in view is to protect the privacy of private life, and to whatever degree and in whatever connection a man's life has ceased to be private, before the publication under consideration has been made, to that extent the protection is likely to be withdrawn. Since, then, the propriety of publishing the very same facts may depend wholly upon the person concerning whom they are published, no fixed formula can be used to prohibit obnoxious publications. Any rule of liability adopted must have in it an elasticity which shall take account of the varying circumstances of each case,—a necessity which unfortunately renders such a doctrine not only more difficult of application, but also to a certain extent uncertain in its operation and easily rendered abortive. Besides, it is only the more flagrant breaches of decency and propriety that could in practice be reached, and it is not perhaps desirable even to attempt to repress everything which the nicest taste and keenest sense of the respect due to private life would condemn.

In general, then, the matters of which the publication should be repressed may be described as those which concern the private life, habits, acts, and relations of an individual, and have no legitimate connection with his fitness for a public office which he seeks or for which he is suggested, or for any public or quasi public position which he seeks or for which he is suggested, and have no legitimate relation to or bearing upon any act done by him in a public or quasi public capacity. The foregoing is not designed as a wholly accurate or exhaustive definition, since that which must ultimately in a vast number of cases become a question of individual judgment and opinion is incapable of such definition; but it is an attempt to indicate broadly the class of matters referred to. Some things all men alike are entitled to keep from popular curiosity, whether in public life or not, while others are only private because the persons concerned have not assumed a position which makes their doings legitimate matters of public investigation.

2. The right to privacy does not prohibit the communication of any matter, though in its nature private, when the publication is made under circumstances which would render it a privileged communication according to the law of slander and libel. Under this rule, the right to privacy is not invaded by any publication made in a court of justice, in legislative bodies, or the committees of those bodies; in municipal assemblies, or the committees of such assemblies, or practically by any communication in any other public body, municipal or parochial, or in any body quasi public, like the large voluntary associations formed for almost every purpose of benevolence, business, or other general interest; and (at least in many jurisdictions) reports of any such proceedings would in some measure be accorded a like privilege. Nor would the rule prohibit any publication made by one in the discharge of some public or private duty, whether legal or moral, or in conduct of one's own affairs, in matters where his own interest is concerned.

3. The law would probably not grant any redress for the invasion of privacy by oral publication in the absence of special damage. The same reasons exist for distinguishing between oral and written publications of private matters, as is afforded in the law of defamation by the restricted liability for slander as compared with the liability for libel. The injury resulting from such oral communications would ordinarily be so trifling that the law might well, in the interest of free speech, disregard it altogether.

4. The right to privacy ceases upon the publication of the facts by the individual, or with his consent.

This is but another application of the rule which has become familiar in the law of literary and artistic property. The cases there decided establish also what should be deemed a publication,—the important principle in this connection being that a private communication of circulation for a restricted purpose is not a publication within the meaning of the law.

5. The truth of the matter published does not afford a defence. Obviously this branch of the law should have no concern with the truth or falsehood of the matters published. It is not for injury to the individual's character that redress or prevention is sought, but for injury to the right of privacy. For the former, the law of slander and libel provides perhaps a sufficient safeguard. The latter implies the right not merely to prevent

inaccurate portrayal of private life, but to prevent its being depicted at all.

6. The absence of "malice" in the publisher does not afford a defence.

Personal ill-will is not an ingredient of the offence, any more than in an ordinary case of trespass to person or to property. Such malice is never necessary to be shown in an action for libel or slander at common law, except in rebuttal of some defence, *e.g.*, that the occasion rendered the communication privileged, or, under the statutes in this State and elsewhere, that the statement complained of was true. The invasion of the privacy that is to be protected is equally complete and equally injurious, whether the motives by which the speaker or writer was actuated are taken by themselves, culpable or not; just as the damage to character, and to some extent the tendency to provoke a breach of the peace, is equally the result of defamation without regard to motives leading to its publication. Viewed as a wrong to the individual, this rule is the same pervading the whole law of torts, by which one is held responsible for his intentional acts, even thought they care committed with no sinister intent; and viewed as a wrong to society, it is the same principle adopted in a large category of statutory offences.

The remedies for an invasion of the right of privacy are also suggested by those administered in the law of defamation, and in the law of literary and artistic property, namely:—

I. An action of tort for damages in all cases. Even in the absence of special damages, substantial compensation could be allowed for injury to feelings as in the action of slander and libel.

2. An injunction, in perhaps a very limited class of cases.

It would doubtless be desirable that the privacy of the individual should receive the added protection of the criminal law, but for this, legislation would be required. Perhaps it would be deemed proper to bring the criminal liability for such publication within narrower limits; but that the community has an interest in preventing such invasions of privacy, sufficiently strong to justify the introduction of such a remedy, cannot be doubted. Still, the protection of society must come mainly through a recognition of the rights of the individual. Each man is responsible for his own acts and omissions only. If he condones what he reprobates, with a weapon at hand equal to his defence, he is responsible for the results. If he resists, public opinion will rally to his support. Has he then such a weapon? It is believed that the common law provides him with one, forged in the slow fire of the centuries, and to-day fitly tempered to his hand. The common law has always recognized a man's house as his castle, impregnable, often, even to his own officers engaged in the execution of its command. Shall the courts thus close the front entrance to constituted authority, and open wide the back door to idle or prurient curiosity?

Samuel D. Warren, Louis D. Brandeis.
BOSTON, December 1890.

Pavesich v. New England Life Insurance Company (1905)

Without consent, the New England Life Insurance Company made use of Pavesich's name and picture, along with a testimonial, in an advertisement. Pavesich sued, claiming one count of libel and one count of invasion of privacy and seeking $25,000. The City Court of Atlanta, Georgia, dismissed the case, whereupon Pavesich appealed to the Georgia Supreme Court. Pavesich became the first case in which any court in the United States specifically recognized a general and independent right to privacy.

Argued February 3, 1905; Decided March 3, 1905.

JUDGES: Cobb, J. All the Justices concur.

. . . The individual surrenders to society many rights and privileges which he would be free to exercise in a state of nature, in exchange for the benefits which he receives as a member of society. But he is not presumed to surrender all those rights, and the public has no more right, without his consent, to invade the domain of those rights which it is necessarily to be presumed he has reserved than he has to violate the valid regulations of the organized government under which he lives. The right of privacy has its foundation in the instincts of nature. It is recognized intuitively, consciousness being the witness that can be called to establish its existence. Any person whose intellect is in a normal condition recognizes at once that as to each individual member of society there are matters private and there are matters public so far as the individual is concerned. Each individual as instinctively resents any encroachment by the public upon his rights which are of a private nature as he does the withdrawal of those of his rights which are of a public nature. A right of privacy in matters purely private is therefore derived from natural law. . . .

The right to withdraw from the public gaze at such times as a person may see fit, when his presence in public is not demanded by any rule of law is also embraced within the right of personal liberty. Publicity in one instance and privacy in the other is each guaranteed. If personal liberty embraces the right of publicity, it no less embraces the correlative right of privacy; and this is no new idea in Georgia law. . . .

[A] violation of the right of privacy is a direct invasion of a legal right of the individual. It is a tort, and it is not necessary that special damages should have accrued from its violation in order to entitle the aggrieved party to recover. . . . In an action for an invasion of such right the damages to be recovered are those for which the law authorizes a recovery in torts of that character; and if the law authorizes a recovery of damages for wounded feelings in other torts of a similar nature, such damages would be recoverable in an action for a violation of this right. . . . [C]ases may arise where it is difficult to determine on which side of the line of demarkation which separates the right of privacy from the well-established rights of others they are to be found; but we have little difficulty in arriving at the conclusion that the present case is one in which it has been established that the right of privacy has been invaded, and invaded by one who can not claim exemption under the constitutional guaranties of freedom of speech and of the press. The form and features of the plaintiff are his own. The defendant insurance company and its agent had no more authority to display them in public for the purpose of advertising the business in which they were engaged than they would have had to compel the plaintiff to place himself upon exhibition for this purpose. The latter procedure would have been unauthorized and unjustifiable, as every one will admit; and the former was equally an invasion of the rights of his person. . . .

So thoroughly satisfied are we that the law recognizes within proper limits, as a legal right, the right of privacy, and that the publication of one's picture without his consent by another as an advertisement . . . is an invasion of this right. . . .

MEYER V. NEBRASKA (1923)

In the early 1920s, Nebraska prohibited the teaching of any modern foreign language to schoolchildren who had not reached the ninth grade.

Robert Meyer, a parochial school instructor, was convicted of teaching German to a child of ten. The Nebraska Supreme Court upheld his conviction. It was argued before the U.S. Supreme Court that the purpose of the statute was to promote "civic development." By "inhibiting . . . education of the immature in foreign tongues and ideals," students could learn English and acquire the preferable American ideals. The justices rejected that argument and declared the statute outside of the competency of the state, noting that the individual had certain fundamental rights that had to be respected. The source of those fundamental rights was the Due Process Clause of the Fourteenth Amendment. Meyer is the true progenitor of the constitutional privacy decisions. It is the first U.S. Supreme Court case to demarcate limitations on governmental power to intrude upon matters affecting fundamental rights.

Argued February 23, 1923; Decided June 4, 1923.

MR. JUSTICE McREYNOLDS delivered the opinion of the Court.

. . . The problem for our determination is whether the statute as construed and applied unreasonably infringes the liberty guaranteed to the plaintiff in error by the Fourteenth Amendment. "No State shall . . . deprive any person of life, liberty, or property, without due process of law."

While this Court has not attempted to define with exactness the liberty thus guaranteed, the term has received much consideration and some of the included things have been definitely stated. Without doubt, it denotes not merely freedom from bodily restraint but also the right of the individual to contract, to engage in any of the common occupations of life, to acquire useful knowledge, to marry, establish a home and bring up children, to worship God according to the dictates of his own conscience, and generally to enjoy those privileges long recognized at common law as essential to the orderly pursuit of happiness by free men. . . . The established doctrine is that this liberty may not be interfered with, under the guise of protecting the public interest, by legislative action which is arbitrary or without reasonable relation to some purpose within the competency of the State to effect. Determination by the legislature of what constitutes proper exercise of police power is not final or conclusive but is subject to supervision by the courts. . . . The American people have always regarded education and acquisition of knowledge as matters of supreme importance which should be diligently promoted. . . . Corresponding to the right of control, it is the natural duty of the parent to give his children education suitable to their station in life; and nearly all the States, including Nebraska, enforce this obligation by compulsory laws. Practically, education of the young is only possible in schools conducted by especially qualified persons who devote themselves thereto. The calling always has been regarded as useful and honorable, essential, indeed, to the public welfare. Mere knowledge of the German language cannot reasonably be regarded as harmful. Heretofore it has been commonly looked upon as helpful and desirable. Plaintiff in error taught this language in school as part of his occupation. His right thus to teach and the right of parents to engage him so to instruct their children, we think, are within the liberty of the Amendment. The challenged statute forbids the teaching in school of any subject except in English; also the teaching of any other language until the pupil has attained and successfully passed the eighth grade, which is not usually accomplished before the age of twelve. . . . Evidently the legislature has attempted materially to interfere with the calling of . . . language teachers, with the opportunities of pupils to acquire knowledge, and with the power of parents to control the education of their own. . . .

That the State may do much, go very far, indeed, in order to improve the quality of its citizens, physically, mentally and morally, is clear; but the individual has certain fundamental rights which must be respected. The protection of the Constitution extends to all, to those who speak other languages as well as to those born with English on the tongue. Perhaps it would be highly advantageous if all had ready understanding of our ordinary speech, but this cannot be coerced by methods which conflict with the Constitution—a desirable end cannot be promoted by prohibited means. . . .

The desire of the legislature to foster a homogeneous people with American ideals prepared readily to understand current discussions of civic matters is easy to appreciate. Unfortunate experiences during the late war and aversion toward every characteristic of truculent adversaries were certainly enough to quicken that aspiration. But the means adopted, we think, exceed the limitations upon the power of the State and conflict with rights assured to plaintiff in error. The interference is plain enough and no adequate reason therefore in time of peace and domestic tranquility has been shown.

Olmstead v. United States (1928) (Brandeis, J., dissenting)

Roy Olmstead was convicted in federal district court of transporting and selling liquor in violation of the National Prohibition Act. The evidence used to convict Olmstead was secured by a warrantless wiretap placed by federal agents on telephone lines between Olmstead's home and office. Olmstead challenged the admission of this evidence on the grounds that it was obtained in violation of the Fourth Amendment's guarantee against unreasonable searches and seizures. The Supreme Court held that because the interception of telephone conversations occurred without "trespass" on private property there was no "search" of a constitutionally protected area. Moreover, conversations were not tangible items that could be "seized." In dissent, Justice Louis Brandeis contended that the Constitution conferred upon each individual a general right of privacy, thus foreshadowing the modern constitutional right to privacy.

Argued February 20–21, 1928; Decided June 4, 1928.

MR. JUSTICE BRANDEIS, dissenting.

... The Government makes no attempt to defend the methods employed by its officers. Indeed, it concedes that if wire-tapping can be deemed a search and seizure within the Fourth Amendment, such wire-tapping as was practiced in the case at bar was an unreasonable search and seizure, and that the evidence thus obtained was inadmissible. But it relies on the language of the Amendment; and it claims that the protection given thereby cannot properly be held to include a telephone conversation. When the Fourth and Fifth Amendments were adopted, "the form that evil had theretofore taken," had been necessarily simple. Force and violence were then the only means known to man by which a Government could directly effect self-incrimination. It could compel the individual to testify—a compulsion effected, if need be, by torture. It could secure possession of his papers and other articles incident to his private life—a seizure effected, if need be, by breaking and entry. Protection against such invasion of "the sanctities of a man's home and the privacies of life" was provided in the Fourth and Fifth Amendments by specific language.... Subtler and more far-reaching means of invading privacy have become available to the Government. Discovery and invention have made it possible for the Government, by means far more effective than stretching upon the rack, to obtain disclosure in court of what is whispered in the closet. . . . The progress of science in furnishing the Government with means of espionage is not likely to stop with wire-tapping. Ways may some day be developed by which the Government, without removing papers from secret drawers, can reproduce them in court, and by which it will be enabled to expose to a jury the most intimate occurrences of the home. . . . Can it be that the Constitution affords no protection against such invasions of individual security? . . .

The protection guaranteed by the Amendments is much broader in scope. The makers of our Constitution undertook to secure conditions favorable to the pursuit of happiness. They recognized the significance of man's spiritual nature, of his feelings and of his intellect. They knew that only a part of the pain, pleasure and satisfactions of life are to be found in material things. They sought to protect Americans in their beliefs, their thoughts, their emotions and their sensations. They conferred, as against the Government, the right to be let alone—the most comprehensive of rights and the right most valued by civilized men. To protect that right, every unjustifiable intrusion by the Government upon the privacy of the individual, whatever the means employed, must be deemed a violation of the Fourth Amendment. . . .

It is . . . immaterial where the physical connection with the telephone wires leading into the defendant's premises was made. And it is also immaterial that the intrusion was in aid of law enforcement. Experience should teach us to be most on our guard to protect liberty when the Government's purposes are beneficent. Men born to freedom are naturally alert to repel invasion of their liberty by evil-minded rulers. The greatest dangers to liberty lurk in insidious encroachment by men of zeal, well-meaning but without understanding. . . .

Decency, security and liberty alike demand that government officials shall be subjected to the same rules of conduct that are commands to the citizen. In a government of laws, existence of the government will be imperilled if it fails to observe the law scrupulously. Our Government is the potent, the omnipresent teacher. For good or for ill, it teaches the whole people by its example. Crime is contagious. If the Government becomes a lawbreaker, it breeds contempt for law; it invites every man to become a law unto himself; it invites anarchy. To declare that in the administration of the criminal law the end justifies the means—to declare that the Government may commit crimes in order to secure the conviction of a private criminal—would bring terrible retribution. Against that pernicious doctrine this Court should resolutely set its face.

Skinner v. Oklahoma (1942)

The Oklahoma Habitual Criminal Sterilization Act provided for the sterilization of "habitual criminals," defined therein as any person who had been convicted three or more times for "felonies involving moral turpitude." Interestingly, though, the act exempted persons convicted of prohibitory laws, revenue acts, embezzlement, and political offenses. Jack Skinner was a thrice-convicted felon—once for stealing chickens and twice for robbery with firearms. Two years after his third conviction, the state attorney general instituted proceedings against him under the act. Skinner challenged the constitutionality of the law, alleging that it violated both the Equal Protection and Due Process Clauses of the Fourteenth Amendment. His challenge was unsuccessful in the lower courts. The U.S. Supreme Court held that the statute violated the Equal Protection Clause. Because compulsory sterilization laws deprived individuals of a fundamental liberty—the right to produce offspring—the justices concluded that such laws should be evaluated under a higher standard: strict scrutiny. Skinner *was thus the first major ruling extending constitutional protection to procreation.*

Argued May 6, 1942; Decided June 30, 1946.

MR. JUSTICE DOUGLAS delivered the opinion of the Court.

This case touches a sensitive and important area of human rights. Oklahoma deprives certain individuals of a right which is basic to the perpetuation of a race—the right to have offspring. . . .

. . . [T]here is a feature of the Act which clearly condemns it. That is, its failure to meet the requirements of the equal protection clause of the Fourteenth Amendment. We do not stop to point out all of the inequalities in this Act. A few examples will suffice. A clerk who appropriates over $20 from his employer's till and a stranger who steals the same amount are thus both guilty of felonies. If the latter repeats his act and is convicted three times, he may be sterilized. But the clerk is not subject to the pains and penalties of the Act no matter how large his embezzlements nor how frequent his convictions. A person who enters a chicken coop and steals chickens commits a felony; and he may be sterilized if he is thrice convicted. If, however, he is a bailee of the property and fraudulently appropriates it, he is an embezzler. Hence, no matter how habitual his proclivities for embezzlement are and no matter how often his conviction, he may not be sterilized.

... We are dealing here with legislation which involves one of the basic civil rights of man. Marriage and procreation are fundamental to the very existence and survival of the race. The power to sterilize, if exercised, may have subtle, far-reaching and devastating effects. In evil or reckless hands it can cause races or types which are inimical to the dominant group to wither and disappear. There is no redemption for the individual whom the law touches. Any experiment which the State conducts is to his irreparable injury. He is forever deprived of a basic liberty. ... The guaranty of "equal protection of the laws is a pledge of the protection of equal laws." When the law lays an unequal hand on those who have committed intrinsically the same quality of offense and sterilizes one and not the other, it has made as invidious a discrimination as if it had selected a particular race or nationality for oppressive treatment. Sterilization of those who have thrice committed grand larceny, with immunity for those who are embezzlers, is a clear, pointed, unmistakable discrimination. Oklahoma makes no attempt to say that he who commits larceny by trespass or trick or fraud has biologically inheritable traits which he who commits embezzlement lacks. Oklahoma's line between larceny by fraud and embezzlement is determined, as we have noted, "with reference to the time when the fraudulent intent to convert the property to the taker's own use" arises. We have not the slightest basis for inferring that that line has any significance in eugenics, nor that the inheritability of criminal traits follows the neat legal distinctions which the law has marked between those two offenses. ... The equal protection clause would indeed be a formula of empty words if such conspicuously artificial lines could be drawn.

GRISWOLD V. CONNECTICUT (1965)

A Connecticut statute made the use of contraceptives a criminal offense. Estelle Griswold, executive director of the Planned Parenthood League of Connecticut, and Dr. C. Lee Buxton, a licensed physician and medical director for the league, were convicted on a charge of having violated the statute as accessories by giving information, instruction, and advice to married persons as to the means of preventing conception. An intermedi-

ate appellate court and the state's highest court affirmed the judgment. The U.S. Supreme Court reversed, invalidating the statute on constitutional privacy grounds. Griswold *was the first case in which the justices specifically recognized an independent and fundamental right to privacy under the U.S. Constitution. This constitutional right to privacy was located in the "penumbras" of various guarantees of the Bill of Rights and was broad enough to include the freedom of married couples to use contraceptives in the privacy of their bedrooms.*

Argued March 29–30, 1965; Decided June 7, 1965.

MR. JUSTICE DOUGLAS delivered the opinion of the Court.

... Coming to the merits, we are met with a wide range of questions that implicate the Due Process Clause of the Fourteenth Amendment. Overtones of some arguments suggest that *Lochner v. New York* ... should be our guide. But we decline that invitation.... We do not sit as a super-legislature to determine the wisdom, need, and propriety of laws that touch economic problems, business affairs, or social conditions. This law, however, operates directly on an intimate relation of husband and wife and their physician's role in one aspect of that relation.

The association of people is not mentioned in the Constitution nor in the Bill of Rights. The right to educate a child in a school of the parents' choice—whether public or private or parochial—is also not mentioned. Nor is the right to study any particular subject or any foreign language. Yet the [Constitution] has been construed to include certain of those rights. By *Pierce v. Society of Sisters,* the right to educate one's children as one chooses is made applicable to the States by the force of the First and Fourteenth Amendments. By *Meyer v. Nebraska,* the same dignity is given the right to study the German language in a private school.... Without those peripheral rights the specific rights would be less secure. And so we reaffirm the principle of the *Pierce* and the *Meyer* cases. In *NAACP v. Alabama,* ... we protected the "freedom to associate and privacy in one's associations," noting that freedom of association was a peripheral First Amendment right.... In other words, the First Amendment has a penumbra where privacy is protected from governmental intrusion. In like context, we have protected forms of "association" that are not political in the customary sense but pertain to the social, legal, and economic benefit of the members.

[Previous] cases suggest that specific guarantees in the Bill of Rights have penumbras, formed by emanations from those guarantees that help give them life and substance. . . . Various guarantees create zones of privacy. The right of association contained in the penumbra of the First Amendment is one. . . . The Third Amendment in its prohibition against the quartering of soldiers "in any house" in time of peace without the consent of the owner is another facet of that privacy. The Fourth Amendment explicitly affirms the "right of the people to be secure in their persons, houses, papers, and effects, against unreasonable searches and seizures." The Fifth Amendment in its Self-Incrimination Clause enables the citizen to create a zone of privacy which government may not force him to surrender to his detriment. The Ninth Amendment provides: "The enumeration in the Constitution, of certain rights, shall not be construed to deny or disparage others retained by the people." We have had many controversies over these penumbral rights of "privacy and repose." . . . These cases bear witness that the right of privacy which presses for recognition here is a legitimate one.

The present case, then, concerns a relationship lying within the zone of privacy created by several fundamental constitutional guarantees. And it concerns a law which, in forbidding the *use* of contraceptives rather than regulating their manufacture or sale, seeks to achieve its goals by means having a maximum destructive impact upon that relationship. Such a law cannot stand in light of the familiar principle, so often applied by this Court, that a "governmental purpose to control or prevent activities constitutionally subject to state regulation may not be achieved by means which sweep unnecessarily broadly and thereby invade the area of protected freedoms." . . . Would we allow the police to search the sacred precincts of marital bedrooms for telltale signs of the use of contraceptives? The very idea is repulsive to the notions of privacy surrounding the marriage relationship. We deal with a right of privacy older than the Bill of Rights—older than our political parties, older than our school system. Marriage is a coming together for better or for worse, hopefully enduring, and intimate to the degree of being sacred. It is an association that promotes a way of life, not causes; a harmony in living, not political faiths; a bilateral loyalty, not commercial or social projects. Yet it is an association for as noble a purpose as any involved in our prior decisions.

MR. JUSTICE GOLDBERG, with whom the CHIEF JUSTICE and MR. JUSTICE BRENNAN join, concurring.

I agree with the Court that Connecticut's birth-control law unconstitutionally intrudes upon the right of marital privacy, and I join in its opinion and judgment. . . . I add these words to emphasize the relevance of [the Ninth] Amendment to the Court's holding. . . . The language and history of the Ninth Amendment reveal that the Framers of the Constitution believed that there are additional fundamental rights, protected from governmental infringement, which exist alongside those fundamental rights specifically mentioned in the first eight constitutional amendments. [The Ninth Amendment] . . . was proffered to quiet expressed fears that a bill of specifically enumerated rights could not be sufficiently broad to cover all essential rights and that the specific mention of certain rights would be interpreted as a denial that others were protected. . . .

While this Court has had little occasion to interpret the Ninth Amendment, "it cannot be presumed that any clause in the constitution is intended to be without effect." . . .

I agree fully with the Court that, applying these tests, the right of privacy is a fundamental personal right. . . .

Although the Constitution does not speak in so many words of the right of privacy in marriage, I cannot believe that it offers these fundamental rights no protection. The fact that no particular provision of the Constitution explicitly forbids the State from disrupting the traditional relation of the family—a relation as old and as fundamental as our entire civilization—surely does not show that the Government was meant to have the power to do so. Rather, as the Ninth Amendment expressly recognizes, there are fundamental personal rights such as this one, which are protected from abridgment by the Government though not specifically mentioned in the Constitution. . . . In sum, I believe that the right of privacy in the marital relation is fundamental and basic—a personal right "retained by the people" within the meaning of the Ninth Amendment. Connecticut cannot constitutionally abridge this fundamental right, which is protected by the Fourteenth Amendment from infringement by the States. I agree with the Court that petitioners' convictions must therefore be reversed.

MR. JUSTICE HARLAN, concurring in the judgment.

In my view, the proper constitutional inquiry in this case is whether this Connecticut statute infringes the Due Process Clause of the Fourteenth Amendment because the enactment violates basic values "implicit in the concept of ordered liberty." . . . I believe that it does. While the relevant inquiry may be aided by resort to one or more of the provisions of the Bill of Rights, it is not dependent on them or any of their radiations. The Due Process Clause of the Fourteenth Amendment stands . . . on its own bottom.

MR. JUSTICE BLACK, with whom MR. JUSTICE STEWART joins, dissenting.

The Court talks about a constitutional "right of privacy" as though there is some constitutional provision or provisions forbidding any law ever to be passed which might abridge the "privacy" of individuals. But there is not. . . .

One of the most effective ways of diluting or expanding a constitutionally guaranteed right is to substitute for the crucial word or words of a constitutional guarantee another word or words, more or less flexible and more or less restricted in meaning. This fact is well illustrated by the use of the term "right of privacy" as a comprehensive substitute for the Fourth Amendment's guarantee against "unreasonable searches and seizures." "Privacy" is a broad, abstract and ambiguous concept which can easily be shrunken in meaning but which can also, on the other hand, easily be interpreted as a constitutional ban against many things other than searches and seizures. . . .

I get nowhere in this case by talk about a constitutional "right of privacy" as an emanation from one or more constitutional provisions. I like my privacy as well as the next one, but I am nevertheless compelled to admit that government has a right to invade it unless prohibited by some specific constitutional provision. For these reasons I cannot agree with the Court's judgment and the reasons it gives for holding this Connecticut law unconstitutional.

. . . Surely it has to be admitted that no provision of the Constitution specifically gives such blanket power to courts to exercise such a supervisory veto over the wisdom and value of legislative policies and to hold unconstitutional those laws which they believe unwise or dangerous. . . . While I completely subscribe to the holding of *Marbury v. Madison* . . . that our Court has constitutional power to strike down statutes, state or federal, that violate commands of the Federal Constitution, I do not believe that we are granted power by the Due Process Clause or any other constitutional provision or provisions to measure constitutionality by our belief that legislation is arbitrary, capricious or unreasonable, or accomplishes no justifiable purpose, or is offensive to our own notions of "civilized standards of conduct." Such an appraisal of the wisdom of legislation is an attribute of the power to make laws, not of the power to interpret them.

I realize that many good and able men have eloquently spoken and written, sometimes in rhapsodical strains, about the duty of this Court to keep the Constitution in tune with the times. The idea is that the Constitution must be changed from time to time and that this Court is charged with a duty to make those changes. For myself, I must with all deference reject that philosophy. The Constitution makers knew the need for change and provided for it. Amendments suggested by the people's elected representatives can be submitted to the people or their selected agents for ratification. That method of change was good for our Fathers, and being somewhat old-fashioned I must add it is good enough for me. And so, I cannot rely on the Due Process Clause or the Ninth Amendment or any mysterious and uncertain natural law concept as a reason for striking down this state law. . . .

So far as I am concerned, Connecticut's law as applied here is not forbidden by any provision of the Federal Constitution as that Constitution was written, and I would therefore affirm.

MR. JUSTICE STEWART, with whom MR. JUSTICE BLACK joins, dissenting.

. . . [T]his is an uncommonly silly law. As a practical matter, the law is obviously unenforceable, except in the oblique context of the present case. As a philosophical matter, I believe the use of contraceptives in the relationship of marriage should be left to personal and private choice. . . . As a matter of social policy, I think professional counsel about methods of birth control should be available to all, so that each individual's choice can be meaningfully made. But we are not asked in this case to say whether we think this law is unwise, or even asinine. We are asked to hold that it violates the United States Constitution. And that I cannot do. . . .

. . . It is the essence of judicial duty to subordinate our own personal views, our own ideas of what legislation is wise and what is not. If, as I should surely hope, the law before us does not reflect the standards of the people of Connecticut, the people of Connecticut can freely exercise their true Ninth and Tenth Amendment rights to persuade their elected representatives to repeal it. That is the constitutional way to take this law off the books.

LOVING V. VIRGINIA (1967)

In 1958, two residents of Virginia, Mildred Jeter, a black woman, and Richard Loving, a white man, were married in the District of Columbia. Shortly thereafter, the Lovings established residency in Virginia. The following year, the Lovings were charged with violating Virginia's antimiscegenation law, which prohibited miscegenation in which a white person was a party. The Lovings pleaded guilty and were sentenced to one year in jail. The trial judge, however, suspended the sentence for twenty-five years, upon the condition that the Lovings leave the state and not return during that period. A unanimous Supreme Court invalidated the law as an invidious racial classification patently lacking a legitimate overriding purpose and therefore inconsistent with the Equal Protection Clause. Eight of the nine justices, however, were also willing to declare the statute violative of the Due Process Clause as well. In Loving, the Supreme Court affirmed that marital choice was among those personal and private decisions that the individual had the freedom to make without unwanted and unwarranted governmental interference.

Argued April 10, 1967; Decided June 12, 1967.

MR. CHIEF JUSTICE WARREN delivered the opinion of the Court.

... There can be no question but that Virginia's miscegenation statutes rest solely upon distinctions drawn according to race. The statutes proscribe generally accepted conduct if engaged in by members of different races. Over the years, this Court has consistently repudiated "distinctions between citizens solely because of their ancestry" as being "odious to a free people whose institutions are founded upon the doctrine of equality." ... At the very least, the Equal Protection Clause demands that racial classifications, especially suspect in criminal statutes, be subjected to the "most rigid scrutiny" ... and, if they are ever to be upheld, they must be shown to be necessary to the accomplishment of some permissible state objective, independent of the racial discrimination which it was the object of the Fourteenth Amendment to eliminate....

There is patently no legitimate overriding purpose independent of invidious racial discrimination which justifies this classification. The fact that Virginia prohibits only interracial marriages involving white persons demonstrates that the racial classifications must stand on their own justification, as measures designed to maintain White Supremacy. We have consistently denied the constitutionality of measures which restrict the rights of citizens on account of race. There can be no doubt that restricting the freedom to marry solely because of racial classifications violates the central meaning of the Equal Protection Clause. These statutes also deprive the Lovings of liberty without due process of law in violation of the Due Process Clause of the Fourteenth Amendment. The freedom to marry has long been recognized as one of the vital personal rights essential to the orderly pursuit of happiness by free men. Marriage is one of the "basic civil rights of man," fundamental to our very existence and survival. . . . To deny this fundamental freedom on so unsupportable a basis as the racial classifications embodied in these statutes, classifications so directly subversive of the principle of equality at the heart of the Fourteenth Amendment, is surely to deprive all the State's citizens of liberty without due process of law. The Fourteenth Amendment requires that the freedom of choice to marry not be restricted by invidious racial discriminations. Under our Constitution, the freedom to marry, or not marry, a person of another race resides with the individual and cannot be infringed by the State.

Roe v. Wade (1973)

In 1969, Norma McCorvey unsuccessfully sought an abortion in Texas. Texas, like most other states at the time, prohibited abortions unless necessary to save a woman's life and provided for a prison term of up to ten years. McCorvey challenged the constitutionality of the law and became "Jane Roe" in a test case against Henry Wade, the criminal district attorney for Dallas County, Texas. The district court held that the statute violated rights protected by the Ninth Amendment, but it refused to enjoin further enforcement of the statute. Both parties appealed to the U.S. Court of Appeals for the Fifth Circuit, which ordered the appeals be held in abeyance pending decision on the appeal taken by both parties to the U.S. Supreme Court. In Roe, *the U.S. Supreme Court declared that constitutional privacy was "broad enough to encompass a woman's decision whether or not to terminate her pregnancy." This case elevated abortion to the national political agenda and became the most debated privacy case ever.*

Argued December 13, 1972, reargued October 11, 1972; Decided January 22, 1973.

MR. JUSTICE BLACKMUN delivered the opinion of the Court.

The principal thrust of appellant's attack on the Texas statutes is that they improperly invade a right, said to be possessed by the pregnant woman, to choose to terminate her pregnancy. Appellant would discover this right in the concept of personal "liberty" embodied in the Fourteenth Amendment's Due Process Clause; or in personal, marital, familial, and sexual privacy said to be protected by the Bill of Rights or its penumbras; . . . or among those rights reserved to the people by the Ninth Amendment. . . . Before addressing this claim, we feel it desirable briefly to survey, in several aspects, the history of abortion, for such insight as that history may afford us, and then to examine the state purposes and interests behind the criminal abortion laws. It perhaps is not generally appreciated that the restrictive criminal abortion laws in effect in a majority of States today are of relatively recent vintage. Those laws, generally proscribing abortion or its attempt at any time during pregnancy except when necessary to preserve the pregnant woman's life, are not of ancient or even of common-law origin. Instead, they derive from statutory changes effected, for the most part, in the latter half of the 19th century. . . .

It is thus apparent that at common law, at the time of the adoption of our Constitution, and throughout the major portion of the 19th century, abortion was viewed with less disfavor than under most American statutes currently in effect. Phrasing it another way, a woman enjoyed a substantially broader right to terminate a pregnancy than she does in most States today. . . .

Three reasons have been advanced to explain historically the enactment of criminal abortion laws in the 19th century and to justify their continued existence. It has been argued occasionally that these laws were the product of a Victorian social concern to discourage illicit sexual conduct. Texas, however, does not advance this justification in the present case. . . .

A second reason is concerned with abortion as a medical procedure. When most criminal abortion laws were first enacted, the procedure was a hazardous one for the woman. . . .

Modern medical techniques have altered this situation. . . . Mortality rates for women undergoing early abortions, where the procedure is legal, appear to be as low as or lower than the rates for normal childbirth. Consequently, any interest of the State in protecting the woman from an inherently hazardous procedure, except when it would be equally dangerous for her to forgo it, has largely disappeared. Of course, important state interests in the areas of health and medical standards do remain. The State has a legitimate interest in seeing to it that abortion, like any other medical procedure, is performed under circumstances that insure maximum safety for the patient. . . . Moreover, the risk to the woman increases as her pregnancy continues. Thus, the State retains a definite interest in protecting the woman's own health and safety when an abortion is proposed at a late stage of pregnancy.

The third reason is the State's interest—some phrase it in terms of duty—in protecting prenatal life. Some of the argument for this justification rests on the theory that a new human life is present from the moment of conception. The State's interest and general obligation to protect life then extends, it is argued, to prenatal life. Only when the life of the pregnant mother herself is at stake, balanced against the life she carries within her, should the interest of the embryo or fetus not prevail. Logically, of course, a legitimate state interest in this area need not stand or fall on acceptance of the belief that life begins at conception or at some other point prior to live birth. In assessing the State's interest, recognition may be given to the less rigid claim that as long as at least *potential* life is involved, the State may assert interests beyond the protection of the pregnant woman alone. . . .

It is with these interests, and the weight to be attached to them, that this case is concerned. . . .

The Constitution does not explicitly mention any right of privacy. In a [long] line of decisions, however, . . .the Court has recognized that a right of personal privacy, or a guarantee of certain areas or zones of privacy, does exist under the Constitution. . . . These decisions make it clear that only personal rights that can be deemed "fundamental" or "implicit in the concept of ordered liberty," . . . are included in this guarantee of personal privacy. They also make it clear that the right has some extension to activities relating to marriage, . . . procreation, . . . contraception, . . . family relationships, . . . and child rearing and education. . . .

This right of privacy . . . is broad enough to encompass a woman's decision whether or not to terminate her pregnancy. The detriment that the

State would impose upon the pregnant woman by denying this choice altogether is apparent. Specific and direct harm medically diagnosable even in early pregnancy may be involved. Maternity, or additional offspring, may force upon the woman a distressful life and future. Psychological harm may be imminent. Mental and physical health may be taxed by child care. There is also the distress, for all concerned, associated with the unwanted child, and there is the problem of bringing a child into a family already unable, psychologically and otherwise, to care for it. In other cases, as in this one, the additional difficulties and continuing stigma of unwed motherhood may be involved. All these are factors the woman and her responsible physician necessarily will consider in consultation. . . .

As noted above, a State may properly assert important interests in safeguarding health, in maintaining medical standards, and in protecting potential life. At some point in pregnancy, these respective interests become sufficiently compelling to sustain regulation of the factors that govern the abortion decision. The privacy right involved, therefore, cannot be said to be absolute. . . .

We, therefore, conclude that the right of personal privacy includes the abortion decision, but that this right is not unqualified and must be considered against important state interests in regulation. Where certain "fundamental rights" are involved, the Court has held that regulation limiting these rights may be justified only by a "compelling state interest," . . . and that legislative enactments must be narrowly drawn to express only the legitimate state interests at stake. . . .

The appellee and certain *amici* argue that the fetus is a "person" within the language and meaning of the Fourteenth Amendment. . . . On the other hand, the appellee conceded on reargument that no case could be cited that holds that a fetus is a person within the meaning of the Fourteenth Amendment. The Constitution does not define "person" in so many words. Section 1 of the Fourteenth Amendment contains three references to "person." . . . "Person" is used in other places in the Constitution. . . . But in nearly all these instances, the use of the word is such that it has application only postnatally. None indicates, with any assurance, that it has any possible pre-natal application.

All this . . . persuades us that the word "person," as used in the Fourteenth Amendment, does not include the unborn.

This conclusion, however, does not of itself fully answer the contentions raised by Texas, and we pass on to other considerations.

The pregnant woman cannot be isolated in her privacy. She carries an embryo and, later, a fetus, if one accepts the medical definitions of the developing young in the human uterus.... The situation therefore is inherently different from marital intimacy, or bedroom possession of obscene material, or marriage, or procreation, or education.... As we have intimated above, it is reasonable and appropriate for a State to decide that at some point in time another interest, that of health of the mother or that of potential human life, becomes significantly involved. The woman's privacy is no longer sole and any right of privacy she possesses must be measured accordingly.

Texas urges that, apart from the Fourteenth Amendment, life begins at conception and is present throughout pregnancy, and that, therefore, the State has a compelling interest in protecting that life from and after conception. We need not resolve the difficult question of when life begins. When those trained in the respective disciplines of medicine, philosophy, and theology are unable to arrive at any consensus, the judiciary, at this point in the development of man's knowledge, is not in a position to speculate as to the answer.... [W]e do not agree that, by adopting one theory of life, Texas may override the rights of the pregnant woman that are at stake. We repeat, however, that the State does have an important and legitimate interest in preserving and protecting the health of the pregnant woman, whether she be a resident of the State or a nonresident who seeks medical consultation and treatment there, and that it has still *another* important and legitimate interest in protecting the potentiality of human life. These interests are separate and distinct. Each grows in substantiality as the woman approaches term and, at a point during pregnancy, each becomes "compelling." With respect to the State's important and legitimate interest in the health of the mother, the "compelling" point, in the light of present medical knowledge, is at approximately the end of the first trimester. This is so because of the now-established medical fact... that until the end of the first trimester mortality in abortion may be less than mortality in normal childbirth. It follows that, from and after this point, a State may regulate the abortion procedure to the extent that the regulation reasonably relates to the preservation and protection of maternal health. Examples of permissible state regulation in this area are requirements as to the qualifications of the person who is to perform the abortion; as to the licensure of that person; as to the facility in which the procedure is to be performed, that is, whether it must be a hospital or may be a clinic or some other place of less-than-hospital status; as to the licensing of the facility; and the like.

This means, on the other hand, that, for the period of pregnancy prior to this "compelling" point, the attending physician, in consultation with his patient, is free to determine, without regulation by the State, that, in his medical judgment, the patient's pregnancy should be terminated. If that decision is reached, the judgment may be effectuated by an abortion free of interference by the State.

With respect to the State's important and legitimate interest in potential life, the "compelling" point is at viability. This is so because the fetus then presumably has the capability of meaningful life outside the mother's womb. State regulation protective of fetal life after viability thus has both logical and biological justifications. If the State is interested in protecting fetal life after viability, it may go so far as to proscribe abortion during that period, except when it is necessary to preserve the life or health of the mother. Measured against these standards, . . . the Texas Penal Code . . . sweeps too broadly. The statute makes no distinction between abortions performed early in pregnancy and those performed later, and it limits to a single reason, "saving" the mother's life, the legal justification for the procedure. The statute, therefore, cannot survive the constitutional attack made upon it here. . . .

To summarize and to repeat: 1. A state criminal abortion statute of the current Texas type, that excepts from criminality only a *lifesaving* procedure on behalf of the mother, without regard to pregnancy stage and without recognition of the other interests involved, is violative of the Due Process Clause of the Fourteenth Amendment. (a) For the stage prior to approximately the end of the first trimester, the abortion decision and its effectuation must be left to the medical judgment of the pregnant woman's attending physician.

(b) For the stage subsequent to approximately the end of the first trimester, the State, in promoting its interest in the health of the mother, may, if it chooses, regulate the abortion procedure in ways that are reasonably related to maternal health.

(c) For the stage subsequent to viability, the State in promoting its interest in the potentiality of human life may, if it chooses, regulate, and even proscribe, abortion except where it is necessary, in appropriate medical judgment, for the preservation of the life or health of the mother. . . .

MR. JUSTICE REHNQUIST, dissenting.

. . . I have difficulty in concluding, as the Court does, that the right of "privacy" is involved in this case. . . .

If the Court means by the term "privacy" no more than that the claim of a person to be free from unwanted state regulation of consensual transactions may be a form of "liberty" protected by the Fourteenth Amendment, there is no doubt that similar claims have been upheld in our earlier decisions on the basis of that liberty. . . . But that liberty is not guaranteed absolutely against deprivation, only against deprivation without due process of law. The test traditionally applied in the area of social and economic legislation is whether or not a law such as that challenged has a rational relation to a valid state objective. . . . The Due Process Clause of the Fourteenth Amendment undoubtedly does place a limit, albeit a broad one, on legislative power to enact laws such as this. If the Texas statute were to prohibit an abortion even where the mother's life is in jeopardy, I have little doubt that such a statute would lack a rational relation to a valid state objective. . . . But the Court's sweeping invalidation of any restrictions on abortion during the first trimester is impossible to justify under that standard, and the conscious weighing of competing factors that the Court's opinion apparently substitutes for the established test is far more appropriate to a legislative judgment than to a judicial one. The Court eschews the history of the Fourteenth Amendment in its reliance on the "compelling state interest" test. . . . But the Court adds a new wrinkle to this test by transposing it from the legal considerations associated with the Equal Protection Clause of the Fourteenth Amendment to this case arising under the Due Process Clause of the Fourteenth Amendment. Unless I misapprehend the consequences of this transplanting of the "compelling state interest test," the Court's opinion will accomplish the seemingly impossible feat of leaving this area of the law more confused than it found it. . . . [T]he adoption of the compelling state interest standard will inevitably require this Court to examine the legislative policies and pass on the wisdom of these policies in the very process of deciding whether a particular state interest put forward may or may not be "compelling." The decision here to break pregnancy into three distinct terms and to outline the permissible restrictions the State may impose in each one, for example, partakes more of judicial legislation than it does of a determination of the intent of the drafters of the Fourteenth Amendment.

The fact that a majority of the States reflecting, after all, the majority sentiment in those States, have had restrictions on abortions for at least a century is a strong indication . . . that the asserted right to an abortion is not "so rooted in the traditions and conscience of our people as to be ranked as fundamental." . . .

To reach its result, the Court necessarily has had to find within the scope of the Fourteenth Amendment a right that was apparently completely unknown to the drafters of the Amendment. . . . By the time of the adoption of the Fourteenth Amendment in 1868, there were at least 36 laws enacted by state or territorial legislatures limiting abortion. While many States have amended or updated their laws, 21 of the laws on the books in 1868 remain in effect today. . . .

There apparently was no question concerning the validity of this provision or of any of the other state statutes when the Fourteenth Amendment was adopted. The only conclusion possible from this history is that the drafters did not intend to have the Fourteenth Amendment withdraw from the States the power to legislate with respect to this matter. . . .

Bowers v. Hardwick (1986)

After being arrested for violating a Georgia statute that criminalized sodomy by committing that act with another adult male in the bedroom of his home, Michael Hardwick challenged the constitutionality of the statute insofar as it criminalized consensual sodomy. The federal district court dismissed the action for failure to state a claim. The U.S. Court of Appeals for the Eleventh Circuit, however, reversed, holding that the Georgia statute violated the respondent's fundamental rights. More specifically, the Eleventh Circuit held that the constitutional right to privacy protected individuals from punishment for their "consensual sexual behavior." That ruling was appealed by Georgia's attorney general, Michael Bowers, to the U.S. Supreme Court, which reversed the Eleventh Circuit, holding that the Due Process Clause of the Fourteenth Amendment did not confer a fundamental right on homosexuals to engage in consensual sodomy, even in the privacy of the home.

Argued March 31, 1986; Decided June 30, 1986.

JUSTICE WHITE delivered the opinion of the Court.

This case does not require a judgment on whether laws against sodomy between consenting adults in general, or between homosexuals in particular, are wise or desirable. It raises no question about the right or propriety of state legislative decisions to repeal their laws that criminalize homosexual sodomy, or of state-court decisions invalidating those laws on state constitutional grounds. The issue presented is whether the Federal Constitution confers a fundamental right upon homosexuals to engage in sodomy and hence invalidates the laws of the many States that still make such conduct illegal and have done so for a very long time. The case also calls for some judgment about the limits of the Court's role in carrying out its constitutional mandate. We first register our disagreement with the . . . respondent that the Court's prior cases have construed the Constitution to confer a right of privacy that extends to homosexual sodomy and for all intents and purposes have decided this case. . . .

[N]one of the rights announced in [previous] cases bears any resemblance to the claimed constitutional right of homosexuals to engage in acts of sodomy that is asserted in this case. No connection between family, marriage, or procreation on the one hand and homosexual activity on the other has been demonstrated. . . . Moreover, any claim that these cases nevertheless stand for the proposition that any kind of private sexual conduct between consenting adults is constitutionally insulated from state proscription is unsupportable. . . .

Precedent aside, however, respondent would have us announce . . . a fundamental right to engage in homosexual sodomy. This we are quite unwilling to do. It is true that despite the language of the Due Process Clauses of the Fifth and Fourteenth Amendments . . . the cases are legion in which those Clauses have been interpreted to have substantive content, subsuming rights that to a great extent are immune from federal or state regulation or proscription. Among such cases are those recognizing rights that have little or no textual support in the constitutional language. . . . Striving to assure itself and the public that announcing rights not readily identifiable in the Constitution's text involves much more than the imposition of the Justices' own choice of values on the States and the Federal Government, the Court has sought to identify the nature of the rights qualifying for heightened judicial protection. In *Palko v. Connecticut*, . . . it was said that this category includes those fundamental liberties that are "implicit in the concept of ordered liberty." . . . A different description of fundamental liberties appeared in

Moore v. East Cleveland, ... where they are characterized as those liberties that are "deeply rooted in this Nation's history and tradition."

... It is obvious to us that neither of these formulations would extend a fundamental right to homosexuals to engage in acts of consensual sodomy. Proscriptions against that conduct have ancient roots.... Sodomy was a criminal offense at common law and was forbidden by the laws of the original 13 States when they ratified the Bill of Rights. In 1868, when the Fourteenth Amendment was ratified, all but 5 of the 37 States in the Union had criminal sodomy laws. In fact, until 1961, all 50 States outlawed sodomy, and today, 24 States and the District of Columbia continue to provide criminal penalties for sodomy performed in private and between consenting adults.... Against this background, to claim that a right to engage in such conduct is "deeply rooted in this Nation's history and tradition" or "implicit in the concept of ordered liberty" is, at best, facetious.

Nor are we inclined to take a more expansive view of our authority to discover new fundamental rights imbedded in the Due Process Clause. The Court is most vulnerable and comes nearest to illegitimacy when it deals with judge-made constitutional law having little or no cognizable roots in the language or design of the Constitution. There should be, therefore, great resistance to expand the substantive reach of those Clauses, particularly if it requires redefining the category of rights deemed to be fundamental. Otherwise, the Judiciary necessarily takes to itself further authority to govern the country without express constitutional authority. The claimed right pressed on us today falls far short of overcoming this resistance.

Respondent, however, asserts that the result should be different where the homosexual conduct occurs in the privacy of the home. He relies on *Stanley v. Georgia,* ... where the Court held that the First Amendment prevents conviction for possessing and reading obscene material in the privacy of one's home....

Stanley did protect conduct that would not have been protected outside the home, and it partially prevented the enforcement of state obscenity laws; but the decision was firmly grounded in the First Amendment. The right pressed upon us here has no similar support in the text of the Constitution, and it does not qualify for recognition under the prevailing principles for construing the Fourteenth Amendment. Its limits are also difficult to discern. Plainly enough, otherwise illegal conduct is not always immunized whenever it occurs in the home. Victimless crimes, such as the possession and use of illegal drugs, do not escape the law where they are committed at home. *Stanley* itself recognized that its holding offered no protection for the possession in the home of drugs, firearms, or stolen goods. . . . And if respondent's submission is limited to the voluntary sexual conduct between consenting adults, it would be difficult, except by fiat, to limit the claimed right to homosexual conduct while leaving exposed to prosecution adultery, incest, and other sexual crimes even though they are committed in the home. We are unwilling to start down that road.

Even if the conduct at issue here is not a fundamental right, respondent asserts that there must be a rational basis for the law and that there is none in this case other than the presumed belief of a majority of the electorate in Georgia that homosexual sodomy is immoral and unacceptable. This is said to be an inadequate rationale to support the law. The law, however, is constantly based on notions of morality, and if all laws representing essentially moral choices are to be invalidated under the Due Process Clause, the courts will be very busy indeed. Even respondent makes no such claim, but insists that majority sentiments about the morality of homosexuality should be declared inadequate. We do not agree, and are unpersuaded that the sodomy laws of some 25 States should be invalidated on this basis. . . .

CHIEF JUSTICE BURGER, concurring.

. . . [T]he proscriptions against sodomy have very "ancient roots." . . . To hold that the act of homosexual sodomy is somehow protected as a fundamental right would be to cast aside millennia of moral teaching.

JUSTICE POWELL, concurring.

I join the opinion of the Court. I agree with the Court that there is no fundamental right—*i.e.*, no substantive right under the Due Process Clause—such as that claimed by respondent Hardwick, and found to exist by the Court of Appeals. This is not to suggest, however, that respondent may not be protected by the Eighth Amendment of the Constitution. The Georgia statute at issue in this case . . . authorizes a court to imprison a person for up to 20 years for a single private, consensual act of sodomy. In my view, a prison sentence for such conduct—certainly a sentence of long duration—would create a serious Eighth Amendment issue. . . .

In this case, however, respondent has not been tried, much less convicted and sentenced. Moreover, respondent has not raised the Eighth Amendment issue below. For these reasons this constitutional argument is not before us.

JUSTICE BLACKMUN, with whom JUSTICE BRENNAN, JUSTICE MARSHALL, and JUSTICE STEVENS join, dissenting.

This case is no more about "a fundamental right to engage in homosexual sodomy," as the Court purports to declare . . . than *Stanley v. Georgia* . . . was about a fundamental right to watch obscene movies, or *Katz v. United States* . . . was about a fundamental right to place interstate bets from a telephone booth. Rather, this case is about "the most comprehensive of rights and the right most valued by civilized men," namely, "the right to be let alone."

. . . The statute at issue . . . denies individuals the right to decide for themselves whether to engage in particular forms of private, consensual sexual activity. The Court concludes that [it] is valid essentially because "the laws of . . . many States . . . still make such conduct illegal and have done so for a very long time." . . . But the fact that the moral judgments expressed by statutes like [these] may be "natural and familiar . . . ought not to conclude our judgment upon the question whether statutes embodying them conflict with the Constitution of the United States." . . . I believe we must analyze respondent Hardwick's claim in the light of the values that underlie the constitutional right to privacy. If that right means anything, it means that, before Georgia can prosecute its citizens for making choices about the most intimate aspects of their lives, it must do more than assert that the choice they have made is an "abominable crime not fit to be named among Christians." . . . A fair reading of the statute and of the complaint clearly reveals that the majority has distorted the question this case presents. . . . [T]he Court's almost obsessive focus on homosexual activity is particularly hard to justify in light of the broad language Georgia has used. . . . The sex or status of the persons who engage in the act is irrelevant as a matter of state law. . . . Michael Hardwick's standing may rest in significant part on Georgia's apparent willingness to enforce against homosexuals a law it seems not to have any desire to enforce against heterosexuals. . . . But his claim that § 16–6–2 involves an unconstitutional intrusion into his privacy and his right of intimate association does not depend in any way on his sexual orientation. . . . The Court concludes today that none of our prior cases dealing with various decisions that individuals are entitled to make free of governmental interference "bears any resemblance to the claimed constitutional right of homosexuals to engage in acts of sodomy that is asserted in this case." ... While it is true that these cases may be characterized by their connection to protection of the family, ... the Court's conclusion that they extend no further than this boundary ignores the warning ... against "[closing] our eyes to the basic reasons why certain rights associated with the family have been accorded shelter under the Fourteenth Amendment's Due Process Clause." We protect those rights not because they contribute, in some direct and material way, to the general public welfare, but because they form so central a part of an individual's life. "[The] concept of privacy embodies the 'moral fact that a person belongs to himself and not others nor to society as a whole.'"

... The Court claims that its decision today merely refuses to recognize a fundamental right to engage in homosexual sodomy; what the Court really has refused to recognize is the fundamental interest all individuals have in controlling the nature of their intimate associations with others.... Indeed, the right of an individual to conduct intimate relationships in the intimacy of his or her own home seems to me to be the heart of the Constitution's protection of privacy.

CRUZAN V. MISSOURI DEPARTMENT OF HEALTH (1990)

As a result of an automobile accident and the subsequent deprivation of oxygen to the brain, Nancy Cruzan suffered permanent brain damage. Despite rehabilitative efforts, she lived in a persistent vegetative state with no cognitive functions for nearly five years. When convinced that their daughter had no hope of regaining consciousness, Cruzan's parents requested that the artificial hydration and nutrition, with which their daughter could live indefinitely, be terminated. The hospital refused to act without a court order. The parents then successfully petitioned a Missouri state court for authorization of their request. On appeal, however, the Missouri Supreme Court reversed, upholding the state's living will statute, which required "clear and convincing, inherently reliable evidence" of the patient's wishes not to continue life-sustaining medical treatment. Although affirming the judgment of the Missouri Supreme

Court, the U.S. Supreme Court construed the Fourteenth Amendment's Due Process Clause to guarantee a liberty interest that protected the right of a competent patient to refuse unwanted medical treatment; it also agreed that an incompetent patient owned a liberty interest in refusing medical treatment, as long as that patient had clearly expressed a desire to have medical treatment terminated in the event of permanent incapacitation.

Argued December 6, 1989; Decided June 25, 1990.

CHIEF JUSTICE REHNQUIST delivered the opinion of the Court.

At common law, even the touching of one person by another without consent and without legal justification was a battery. . . . This notion of bodily integrity has been embodied in the requirement that informed consent is generally required for medical treatment. Justice Cardozo, while on the Court of Appeals of New York, aptly described this doctrine: "Every human being of adult years and sound mind has a right to determine what shall be done with his own body; and a surgeon who performs an operation without his patient's consent commits an assault, for which he is liable in damages." . . .

The logical corollary of the doctrine of informed consent is that the patient generally possesses the right not to consent, that is, to refuse treatment. . . .

. . . [T]he common-law doctrine of informed consent is viewed as generally encompassing the right of a competent individual to refuse medical treatment. . . . In this Court, the question is simply and starkly whether the United States Constitution prohibits Missouri from choosing the rule of decision which it did. This is the first case in which we have been squarely presented with the issue whether the United States Constitution grants what is in common parlance referred to as a "right to die." . . . [I]n deciding "a question of such magnitude and importance . . . it is the [better] part of wisdom not to attempt, by any general statement, to cover every possible phase of the subject." . . .

The principle that a competent person has a constitutionally protected liberty interest in refusing unwanted medical treatment may be inferred from our prior decisions. . . . But determining that a person has a "liberty interest" under the Due Process Clause does not end the inquiry; "whether respondent's constitutional rights have been violated must be determined by balancing his liberty interests against the relevant state interests." . . .

. . . [F]or purposes of this case, we assume that the United States Constitution would grant a competent person a constitutionally protected right to refuse lifesaving hydration and nutrition. Petitioners go on to assert that an incompetent person should possess the same right in this respect as is possessed by a competent person. . . .

The difficulty with petitioners' claim is that in a sense it begs the question: An incompetent person is not able to make an informed and voluntary choice to exercise a hypothetical right to refuse treatment or any other right. Such a "right" must be exercised for her, if at all, by some sort of surrogate. Here, Missouri has in effect recognized that under certain circumstances a surrogate may act for the patient in electing to have hydration and nutrition withdrawn in such a way as to cause death, but it has established a procedural safeguard to assure that the action of the surrogate conforms as best it may to the wishes expressed by the patient while competent. Missouri requires that evidence of the incompetent's wishes as to the withdrawal of treatment be proved by clear and convincing evidence. The question, then, is whether the United States Constitution forbids the establishment of this procedural requirement by the State. We hold that it does not. Whether or not Missouri's clear and convincing evidence requirement comports with the United States Constitution depends in part on what interests the State may properly seek to protect in this situation. Missouri relies on its interest in the protection and preservation of human life. . . . As a general matter, the States—indeed, all civilized nations—demonstrate their commitment to life by treating homicide as a serious crime. Moreover, the majority of States . . . have laws imposing criminal penalties on one who assists another to commit suicide. We do not think a State is required to remain neutral in the face of an informed and voluntary decision by a physically able adult to starve to death.

But in the context presented here, a State has more particular interests at stake. The choice between life and death is a deeply personal decision of obvious and overwhelming finality. We believe Missouri may legitimately seek to safeguard the personal element of this choice through the imposition of heightened evidentiary requirements. It cannot be disputed that the Due Process Clause protects an interest in life as well as an interest in refusing life-sustaining medical treatment. Not all incompetent patients will have loved ones available to serve as surrogate decisionmakers. And even where family members are present, "there will, of course, be some unfortunate situations in which family members will not act to protect a patient." . . . A State is entitled to guard against potential abuses in such situations. . . .

In our view, Missouri has permissibly sought to advance these interests through the adoption of a "clear and convincing" standard of proof to govern such proceedings. . . .

. . . We believe that Missouri may permissibly place an increased risk of an erroneous decision on those seeking to terminate an incompetent individual's life-sustaining treatment. An erroneous decision not to terminate results in a maintenance of the status quo; the possibility of subsequent developments such as advancements in medical science, the discovery of new evidence regarding the patient's intent, changes in the law, or simply the unexpected death of the patient despite the administration of life-sustaining treatment at least create the potential that a wrong decision will eventually be corrected or its impact mitigated. An erroneous decision to withdraw life-sustaining treatment, however, is not susceptible of correction. . . .

In sum, we conclude that a State may apply a clear and convincing evidence standard in proceedings where a guardian seeks to discontinue nutrition and hydration of a person diagnosed to be in a persistent vegetative state. We note that many courts which have adopted some sort of substituted judgment procedure in situations like this, whether they limit consideration of evidence to the prior expressed wishes of the incompetent individual, or whether they allow more general proof of what the individual's decision would have been, require a clear and convincing standard of proof for such evidence. . . .

JUSTICE O'CONNOR, concurring.

I write separately to emphasize that the Court does not today decide the issue whether a State must also give effect to the decisions of a surrogate decisionmaker. . . . In my view, such a duty may well be constitutionally required to protect the patient's liberty interest in refusing medical treatment.

JUSTICE SCALIA, concurring.

While I agree with the Court's analysis today, and therefore join in its opinion, I would have preferred that we announce, clearly and promptly, that the federal courts have no business in this field; that American law has always accorded the State the power to prevent, by force if necessary, suicide—including suicide by refusing to take appropriate measures necessary to preserve one's life; . . . and, hence, that even when it *is* demonstrated by clear and convincing evidence that a patient no longer wishes certain measures to be taken to preserve his or her life, it is up to the citizens of Missouri to decide, through their elected representatives, whether that wish will be honored.

JUSTICE BRENNAN, with whom JUSTICE MARSHALL and JUSTICE BLACKMUN join, dissenting.

Because I believe that Nancy Cruzan has a fundamental right to be free of unwanted artificial nutrition and hydration, which right is not outweighed by any interests of the State, and because I find that the improperly biased procedural obstacles imposed by the Missouri Supreme Court impermissibly burden that right, I respectfully dissent. Nancy Cruzan is entitled to choose to die with dignity. . . .

[I]f a competent person has a liberty interest to be free of unwanted medical treatment, as both the majority and JUSTICE O'CONNOR concede, it must be fundamental. . . . Whatever other liberties protected by the Due Process Clause are fundamental, "those liberties that are 'deeply rooted in this Nation's history and tradition'" are among them. . . .

The right to be free from medical attention without consent, to determine what shall be done with one's own body, *is* deeply rooted in this Nation's traditions, as the majority acknowledges. . . . This right has long been "firmly entrenched in American tort law" and is securely grounded in the earliest common law. . . . Thus, freedom from unwanted medical attention is unquestionably among those principles "so rooted in the traditions and conscience of our people as to be ranked as fundamental." . . .

Although the right to be free of unwanted medical intervention, like other constitutionally protected interests, may not be absolute, no state interest could outweigh the rights of an individual in Nancy Cruzan's position. Whatever a State's possible interests in mandating life-support treatment under other circumstances, there is no good to be obtained here by Missouri's insistence that Nancy Cruzan remain on life-support systems if it is indeed her wish not to do so. . . .

The only state interest asserted here is a general interest in the preservation of life. But the State has no legitimate general interest in someone's life, completely abstracted from the interest of the person living that life, that could outweigh the person's choice to avoid medical treatment. . . .

. . . Missouri may constitutionally impose only those procedural requirements that serve to enhance the accuracy of a determination of Nancy Cruzan's wishes or are at least consistent with an accurate determination. The Missouri "safeguard" that the Court upholds today does not meet that standard. The determination needed in this context is whether the incompetent person would choose to live in a persistent vegetative state on life support or to avoid this medical treatment. Missouri's rule of decision imposes a markedly asymmetrical evidentiary burden. Only evidence of specific statements of treatment choice made by the patient when competent is admissible to support a finding that the patient, now in a persistent vegetative state, would wish to avoid further medical treatment. Moreover, this evidence must be clear and convincing. No proof is required to support a finding that the incompetent person would wish to continue treatment. . . .

Finally, I cannot agree with the majority that where it is not possible to determine what choice an incompetent patient would make, the State's role as *parens patriae* permits the State automatically to make that choice itself.

PLANNED PARENTHOOD OF SOUTHEASTERN PENNSYLVANIA V. CASEY (1992)

The Pennsylvania Abortion Control Act required "informed consent" counseling, a twenty-four-hour waiting period, parental consent for minors (with a judicial bypass option), and spousal notification. The district court enjoined enforcement of all the restrictions. The U.S. Court of Appeals for the Third Circuit reversed, sustaining all of the requirements except for the spousal-notification requirement. The U.S. Supreme Court affirmed the appellate court. Casey also reaffirmed the essential holding of Roe*—that viability marked the earliest point at which the state's interest in fetal life was constitutionally adequate to justify a legislative ban on nontherapeutic abortions.*

In an extraordinary opinion written jointly by Justices O'Connor, Kennedy, and Souter, and joined in part by Justices Blackmun and Stevens, the majority said that *Roe* established a "rule of law and a component of liberty we cannot renounce." Nevertheless, the majority rejected the trimester framework, replacing it with the undue burden analysis, which asked whether restrictive laws had the purpose or effect of placing a "substantial obstacle in the path of a woman seeking an abortion of a nonviable fetus."

Argued April 22, 1992; Decided June 29, 1992.

JUSTICE O'CONNOR, JUSTICE KENNEDY, AND JUSTICE SOUTER announced the decision of the Court.

Liberty finds no refuge in a jurisprudence of doubt. Yet 19 years after our holding that the Constitution protects a woman's right to terminate her pregnancy in its early stages, . . . that definition of liberty is still questioned. . . .

After considering the fundamental constitutional questions resolved by *Roe*, principles of institutional integrity, and the rule of *stare decisis*, we are led to conclude this: the essential holding of *Roe v. Wade* should be retained and once again reaffirmed. It must be stated at the outset and with clarity that *Roe's* essential holding, the holding we reaffirm, has three parts. First is a recognition of the right of the woman to choose to have an abortion before viability and to obtain it without undue interference from the State. Before viability, the State's interests are not strong enough to support a prohibition of abortion or the imposition of a substantial obstacle to the woman's effective right to elect the procedure. Second is a confirmation of the State's power to restrict abortions after fetal viability, if the law contains exceptions for pregnancies which endanger the woman's life or health. And third is the principle that the State has legitimate interests from the outset of the pregnancy in protecting the health of the woman and the life of the fetus that may become a child. These principles do not contradict one another; and we adhere to each. . . .

Our law affords constitutional protection to personal decisions relating to marriage, procreation, contraception, family relationships, child rearing, and education. . . . These matters, involving the most intimate and personal choices a person may make in a lifetime, choices central to personal dignity and autonomy, are central to the liberty protected by the Fourteenth Amendment. . . . Though abortion is conduct, it does not follow that the State is entitled to proscribe it in all instances. That is because the liberty of the woman is at stake in a sense unique to the human condition and so unique to the law. The mother who carries a child to full term is subject to anxieties, to physical constraints, to pain that only she must bear. That these sacrifices have from the beginning of the human race been endured by woman with a pride that ennobles her in the eyes of others and gives to the infant a bond of love cannot alone be grounds for the State to insist she make the sacrifice. Her suffering is too intimate and personal for the State to insist, without more, upon its own vision of the woman's role, however dominant that vision has been in the course of our history and our culture. The destiny of the woman must be shaped to a large extent on her own conception of her spiritual imperatives and her place in society. . . .

While we appreciate the weight of the arguments made on behalf of the State in the cases before us, arguments which in their ultimate formulation conclude that *Roe* should be overruled, the reservations any of us may have in reaffirming the central holding of *Roe* are outweighed by the explication of individual liberty we have given combined with the force of *stare decisis*. . . .

Although *Roe* has engendered opposition, it has in no sense proven "unworkable." . . .

. . . An entire generation has come of age free to assume *Roe's* concept of liberty in defining the capacity of women to act in society, and to make reproductive decisions; no erosion of principle going to liberty or personal autonomy has left *Roe's* central holding a doctrinal remnant; *Roe* portends no developments at odds with other precedent for the analysis of personal liberty; and no changes of fact have rendered viability more or less appropriate as the point at which the balance of interests tips. Within the bounds of normal *stare decisis* analysis, then, and subject to the considerations on which it customarily turns, the stronger argument is for affirming *Roe's* central holding, with whatever degree of personal reluctance any of us may have, not for overruling it. . . .

. . . A decision to overrule *Roe's* essential holding under the existing circumstances would address error, if error there was, at the cost of both profound and unnecessary damage to the Court's legitimacy, and to the Nation's commitment to the rule of law. It is therefore imperative to adhere to the essence of *Roe's* original decision, and we do so today. . . . [I]t is a constitutional liberty of the woman to have some freedom to terminate her pregnancy. We conclude that the basic decision in *Roe* was based on a constitutional analysis which we cannot now repudiate. The woman's liberty is not so unlimited, however, that from the outset the State cannot show its concern for the life of the unborn, and at a later point in fetal development the State's interest in life has sufficient force so that the right of the woman to terminate the pregnancy can be restricted. . . .

We conclude the line should be drawn at viability, so that before that time the woman has a right to choose to terminate her pregnancy. . . .

We give this summary: (a) To protect the central right recognized by *Roe v. Wade* while at the same time accommodating the State's profound interest in potential life, we will employ the undue burden analysis. . . . An undue burden exists, and therefore a provision of law is invalid, if its purpose or effect is to place a substantial obstacle in the path of a woman seeking an abortion before the fetus attains viability. (b) We reject the rigid trimester framework of *Roe v. Wade.* To promote the State's profound interest in potential life, throughout pregnancy the State may take measures to ensure that the woman's choice is informed, and measures designed to advance this interest will not be invalidated as long as their purpose is to persuade the woman to choose childbirth over abortion. These measures must not be an undue burden on the right. (c) As with any medical procedure, the State may enact regulations to further the health or safety of a woman seeking an abortion. Unnecessary health regulations that have the purpose or effect of presenting a substantial obstacle to a woman seeking an abortion impose an undue burden on the right.

(d) Our adoption of the undue burden analysis does not disturb the central holding of *Roe v. Wade,* and we reaffirm that holding. Regardless of whether exceptions are made for particular circumstances, a State may not prohibit any woman from making the ultimate decision to terminate her pregnancy before viability.

(e) We also reaffirm *Roe's* holding that "subsequent to viability, the State in promoting its interest in the potentiality of human life may, if it chooses, regulate, and even proscribe, abortion except where it is necessary, in appropriate medical judgment, for the preservation of the life or health of the mother."

JUSTICE BLACKMUN, concurring in part and dissenting in part.

I do not underestimate the significance of today's joint opinion. Yet I remain steadfast in my belief that the right to reproductive choice is entitled to the full protection afforded by this Court. . . . And I fear for the darkness as four Justices anxiously await the single vote necessary to extinguish the light. . . .

But, we are reassured, there is always the protection of the democratic process. While there is much to be praised about our democracy, our country since its founding has recognized that there are certain fundamental liberties that are not to be left to the whims of an election. A woman's right to reproductive choice is one of those fundamental liberties. Accordingly, that liberty need not seek refuge at the ballot box.

JUSTICE SCALIA, with whom the CHIEF JUSTICE, JUSTICE WHITE, and JUSTICE THOMAS join, concurring in the judgment and dissenting in part.

The States may, if they wish, permit abortion on demand, but the Constitution does not *require* them to do so. The permissibility of abortion, and the limitations upon it, are to be resolved like most important questions in our democracy: by citizens trying to persuade one another and then voting.... A State's choice between two positions on which reasonable people can disagree is constitutional even when (as is often the case) it intrudes upon a "liberty" in the absolute sense. Laws against bigamy, for example—with which entire societies of reasonable people disagree—intrude upon men and women's liberty to marry and live with one another. But bigamy happens not to be a liberty specially "protected" by the Constitution. That is, quite simply, the issue in these cases: not whether the power of a woman to abort her unborn child is a "liberty" in the absolute sense; or even whether it is a liberty of great importance to many women. Of course it is both. The issue is whether it is a liberty protected by the Constitution of the United States. I am sure it is not. I reach that conclusion . . . for the same reason I reach the conclusion that bigamy is not constitutionally protected—because of two simple facts: (1) the Constitution says absolutely nothing about it, and (2) the longstanding traditions of American society have permitted it to be legally proscribed....

The Court's description of the place of *Roe* in the social history of the United States is unrecognizable. Not only did *Roe* not, as the Court suggests, *resolve* the deeply divisive issue of abortion; it did more than anything else to nourish it, by elevating it to the national level where it is infinitely more difficult to resolve. National politics were not plagued by abortion protests, national abortion lobbying, or abortion marches on Congress before *Roe v. Wade* was decided. Profound disagreement existed among our citizens over the issue—as it does over other issues, such as the death penalty—but that disagreement was being worked out at the state level. As with many other issues, the division of sentiment within each State was not as closely balanced as it was among the population of the Nation as a whole, meaning not only that more people would be satisfied with the results of state-by-state resolution, but also that those results would be more stable. Pre-*Roe,* moreover, political compromise was possible. *Roe's* mandate for abortion on demand destroyed the compromises of the past, rendered compromise impossible for the future, and required the entire issue to be resolved uniformly, at the national level. At the same time, *Roe* created a vast new class of abortion consumers and abortion proponents by eliminating the moral opprobrium that had attached to the act. ("If the Constitution *guarantees* abortion, how can it be bad?"—not an accurate line of thought, but a natural one.) Many favor all of those developments, and it is not for me to say that they are wrong. But to portray *Roe* as the statesmanlike "settlement" of a divisive issue . . . is nothing less than Orwellian. *Roe* fanned into life an issue that has inflamed our national politics in general, and has obscured with its smoke the selection of Justices to this Court in particular, ever since. And by keeping us in the abortion-umpiring business, it is the perpetuation of that disruption, rather than of any *Pax Roeana,* that the Court's new majority decrees. . . .

We should get out of this area, where we have no right to be, and where we do neither ourselves nor the country any good by remaining.

Commonwealth of Kentucky v. Wasson (1992)

Jeffrey Wasson was charged with violating a Kentucky law that criminalized "deviate sexual intercourse with another person of the same sex." The trial judge dismissed the charge, declaring that the statute violated the state constitution's right to privacy and guarantee of equal protection. A state appellate court affirmed, as did the Kentucky Supreme Court. This case demonstrates well how one state constitution offers greater protection of the right to privacy than the U.S. Constitution. Excerpts here are limited to the right to privacy argument.

Rendered September 24, 1992.

Opinion of the Court by Justice LEIBSON.

The Commonwealth maintains that the United States Supreme Court's decision in *Bowers v. Hardwick* . . . is dispositive of the right to privacy issue; that the "Kentucky Constitution did not intend to confer any greater right to privacy than was afforded by the U.S. Constitution." . . .

Bowers v. Hardwick . . . [does not] speak to rights of privacy under the state constitution. . . .

[W]e hold the guarantees of individual liberty provided in our 1891 Kentucky Constitution offer greater protection of the right of privacy than provided by the Federal constitution as interpreted by the United States Supreme Court, and that the statute in question is a violation of such rights. . . . No language specifying "rights of privacy," as such, appears in either the Federal or State Constitution. The Commonwealth recognizes such rights exist, but takes the position that, since they are implicit rather than explicit, our Court should march in lock step with the United States Supreme Court in declaring when such rights exist. Such is not the formulation of federalism. On the contrary, under our system of dual sovereignty, it is our responsibility to interpret and apply our state constitution independently. We are not bound by decisions of the United States Supreme Court when deciding whether a state statute impermissibly infringes upon individual rights guaranteed in the State Constitution so long as state constitutional protection does not fall below the federal floor, meaning the minimum guarantee of individual rights under the United States Constitution as interpreted by the United States Supreme Court. . . . Kentucky cases recognized a legally protected right of privacy based on our own constitution and common law tradition long before the United States Supreme Court first took notice of whether there were any rights of privacy inherent in the Federal Bill of Rights. . . .

[In addition,] . . . the United States Supreme Court is extremely reticent in extending the reach of the Due Process Clauses in substantive matters. . . . *Bowers v. Hardwick* . . . expresses this reticence. The United States Supreme Court, defining the reach of the zone of privacy in terms of federal due process analysis, limits rights of privacy to "liberties that are 'deeply rooted in this Nation's history and tradition.'" . . . Sodomy is not one of them. *Bowers v. Hardwick* decides that rights protected by the Due Process Clauses in the Fifth and Fourteenth Amendments to the United States Constitution do not "extend a fundamental right to homosexuals to engage in acts of consensual sodomy."

Bowers decides nothing beyond this. But state constitutional jurisprudence in this area is not limited by the constraints inherent in federal due process analysis. Deviate sexual intercourse conducted in private by consenting adults is not beyond the protections of the guarantees of individual liberty in our Kentucky Constitution. . . .

The clear implication [from the Kentucky Constitution and subsequent state cases] is that immorality in private which does "not operate to the detriment of others," is placed beyond the reach of state action by the guarantees of liberty in the Kentucky Constitution.

WASHINGTON V. GLUCKSBERG (1997)

In 1994, a group known as Compassion in Dying challenged the constitutionality of a Washington law that criminalized assisted suicide. The district court struck down the statute, holding that it restricted the exercise of a constitutionally protected liberty interest and violated the Equal Protection Clause. The U.S. Court of Appeals for the Ninth Circuit heard the appeal en banc, concluding that the Constitution encompassed a due process liberty interest in controlling "the time and manner of one's own death." The appellate court did not consider the equal protection argument. The U.S. Supreme Court then reversed, holding that Washington's prohibition did not offend a fundamental liberty interest protected by the Due Process Clause. In a case decided on the same day, Vacco v. Quill *(521 U.S. 793; 1997), the justices declared that a similar statute from New York did not offend the Equal Protection Clause.*

Argued January 8, 1997; Decided June 26, 1997.

CHIEF JUSTICE REHNQUIST delivered the opinion of the Court.

In almost every State—indeed, in almost every western democracy—it is a crime to assist a suicide. The States' assisted-suicide bans are not innovations. Rather, they are longstanding expressions of the States' commitment to the protection and preservation of all human life. . . . Indeed, opposition to and condemnation of suicide—and, therefore, of assisting suicide—are consistent and enduring themes of our philosophical, legal, and cultural heritages. . . .

More specifically, for over 700 years, the Anglo-American common-law tradition has punished or otherwise disapproved of both suicide and assisting suicide. . . .

. . . [C]olonial and early state legislatures and courts did not retreat from prohibiting assisting suicide. . . . And the prohibitions against assisting suicide never contained exceptions for those who were near death. . . .

The earliest American statute explicitly to outlaw assisting suicide was enacted in New York in 1828 . . . and many of the new States and Territories followed New York's example. . . . In this century, the Model Penal Code also prohibited "aiding" suicide, prompting many States to enact or revise their assisted-suicide bans. The Code's drafters observed that "the interests in the sanctity of life that are represented by the criminal homicide laws are threatened by one who expresses a willingness to participate in taking the life of another, even though the act may be accomplished with the consent, or at the request, of the suicide victim." . . .

Attitudes toward suicide itself have changed . . . but our laws have consistently condemned, and continue to prohibit, assisting suicide. Despite changes in medical technology and notwithstanding an increased emphasis on the importance of end-of-life decisionmaking, we have not retreated from this prohibition. Against this backdrop of history, tradition, and practice, we now turn to respondents' constitutional claim.

The Due Process Clause guarantees more than fair process, and the "liberty" it protects includes more than the absence of physical restraint. . . . The Clause also provides heightened protection against government interference with certain fundamental rights and liberty interests. . . . In a long line of cases, we have held that, in addition to the specific freedoms protected by the Bill of Rights, the "liberty" specially protected by the Due Process Clause includes the rights to marry, . . . to have children, . . . to direct the education and upbringing of one's children, . . . to marital privacy, . . . to use contraception, . . . to bodily integrity, . . . and to abortion. . . . We have also assumed, and strongly suggested, that the Due Process Clause protects the traditional right to refuse unwanted lifesaving medical treatment. . . .

But we "have always been reluctant to expand the concept of substantive due process because guideposts for responsible decisionmaking in this unchartered area are scarce and open-ended." . . . By extending constitutional protection to an asserted right or liberty interest, we, to a great extent, place the matter outside the arena of public debate and legislative action. We must therefore "exercise the utmost care whenever we are asked to break new ground in this field," . . . lest the liberty protected by the Due Process Clause be subtly transformed into the policy preferences of the members of this Court. . . .

Our established method of substantive-due-process analysis has two primary features: First, we have regularly observed that the Due Process Clause specially protects those fundamental rights and liberties which are, objectively, "deeply rooted in this Nation's history and tradition" [or] "implicit in the concept of ordered liberty." . . . Second, we have required in substantive-due-process cases a "careful description" of the asserted fundamental liberty interest. . . .

We now inquire whether this asserted right has any place in our Nation's traditions. Here, . . . we are confronted with a consistent and almost universal tradition that has long rejected the asserted right, and continues explicitly to reject it today, even for terminally ill, mentally competent adults. To hold for respondents, we would have to reverse centuries of legal doctrine and practice, and strike down the considered policy choice of almost every State. . . .

Respondents contend, however, that the liberty interest they assert *is* consistent with this Court's substantive-due-process line of cases, if not with this Nation's history and practice. Pointing to *Casey* and *Cruzan*, respondents read our jurisprudence in this area as reflecting a general tradition of "self-sovereignty," . . . and as teaching that the "liberty" protected by the Due Process Clause includes "basic and intimate exercises of personal autonomy." . . . According to respondents, our liberty jurisprudence, and the broad, individualistic principles it reflects, protects the "liberty of competent, terminally ill adults to make end-of-life decisions free of undue government interference." . . . The question presented in this case, however, is whether the protections of the Due Process Clause include a right to commit suicide with another's assistance. . . .

The history of the law's treatment of assisted suicide in this country has been and continues to be one of the rejection of nearly all efforts to permit it. That being the case, our decisions lead us to conclude that the asserted "right" to assistance in committing suicide is not a fundamental liberty interest protected by the Due Process Clause. The Constitution also requires, however, that Washington's assisted-suicide ban be rationally related to legitimate government interests. . . . This requirement is unquestionably met here. . . . Washington's assisted-suicide ban implicates a number of state interests. . . .

First, Washington has an "unqualified interest in the preservation of human life." . . . The State's prohibition on assisted suicide, like all homicide laws, both reflects and advances its commitment to this interest. . . .

Those who attempt suicide—terminally ill or not—often suffer from depression or other mental disorders. . . .

Research indicates, however, that many people who request physician-assisted suicide withdraw that request if their depression and pain are treated. . . . [B]ecause depression is difficult to diagnose, physicians and medical professionals often fail to respond adequately to seriously ill patients' needs. . . . Thus, legal physician-assisted suicide could make it more difficult for the State to protect depressed or mentally ill persons, or those who are suffering from untreated pain, from suicidal impulses. The State also has an interest in protecting the integrity and ethics of the medical profession. . . . [T]he American Medical Association, like many other medical and physicians' groups, has concluded that "physician-assisted suicide is fundamentally incompatible with the physician's role as healer." . . .

Next, the State has an interest in protecting vulnerable groups—including the poor, the elderly, and disabled persons—from abuse, neglect, and mistakes. . . . If physician-assisted suicide were permitted, many might resort to it to spare their families the substantial financial burden of end-of-life health-care costs. The State's interest here goes beyond protecting the vulnerable from coercion; it extends to protecting disabled and terminally ill people from prejudice, negative and inaccurate stereotypes, and "societal indifference." . . . The State's assisted-suicide ban reflects and reinforces its policy that the lives of terminally ill, disabled, and elderly people must be no less valued than the lives of the young and healthy, and that a seriously disabled person's suicidal impulses should be interpreted and treated the same way as anyone else's.

Finally, the State may fear that permitting assisted suicide will start it down the path to voluntary and perhaps even involuntary euthanasia. . . . [W]hat is couched as a limited right to "physician-assisted suicide" is likely, in effect, a much broader license, which could prove extremely difficult for police to contain. Washington's ban on assisting suicide prevents such erosion. This concern is further supported by evidence about the practice of euthanasia in the Netherlands. The Dutch government's own study . . . suggests that, despite the existence of various reporting procedures, euthanasia in the Netherlands has not been limited to competent, terminally ill adults who are enduring physical suffering, and that regulation of the practice may not have prevented abuses in cases involving vulnerable persons, including severely disabled neonates and elderly persons suffering from dementia. . . .

We need not weigh exactingly the relative strengths of these various interests. They are unquestionably important and legitimate, and Washington's ban on assisted suicide is at least reasonably related to their promotion and protection. We therefore hold that [the challenged statute] does not violate the Fourteenth Amendment, either on its face or "as applied to competent, terminally ill adults who wish to hasten their deaths by obtaining medication prescribed by their doctors." Throughout the Nation, Americans are engaged in an earnest and profound debate about the morality, legality, and practicality of physician-assisted suicide. Our holding permits this debate to continue, as it should in a democratic society.

Chronology

1610	English jurist Sir Edward Coke declares in *Dr. Bonham's Case* that "when an act of Parliament is against common right and reason, . . . the common law will controul it and adjudge such act to be void."
1690	English political philosopher John Locke publishes *Two Treatises of Government,* in which he argues that the purpose of government is to preserve natural rights—"lives, liberties, and estates."
1776	Virginia adopts a Bill of Rights, which declares that all men are "by nature equally free and independent, and have certain inherent rights." Other states soon follow.
1776	The Continental Congress approves the Declaration of Independence, which announces and justifies the colonies' separation from Great Britain.
1787	The modern Constitution is written and sent to the states for ratification.
1789	The U.S. Constitution is formally adopted.
1789	Congress proposes twelve amendments to the U.S. Constitution, calling them the Bill of Rights. They are sent to the states for ratification.
1791	The states ratify ten of the proposed twelve amendments, thus adding the Bill of Rights to the U.S. Constitution. Several of the amendments contain some privacy component.

1803 The U.S. Supreme Court, led by Chief Justice John Marshall, holds in *Marbury v. Madison* that an act repugnant to the U.S. Constitution is void and that the judiciary has the duty to make such a declaration.

1859 British political philosopher John Stuart Mill publishes *On Liberty,* in which he argues that the only reason for government to interfere with anyone's liberty, against that individual's will, is self-preservation—to prevent harm to others.

1868 The Fourteenth Amendment is added to the U.S. Constitution. The Due Process Clause of this amendment becomes the medium through which parts of the Bill of Rights are applied to the states.

1880 Thomas Cooley publishes *A Treatise of the Law of Torts,* in which he refers to privacy as "a right of complete immunity: to be let alone."

1886 The U.S. Supreme Court recognizes protection for privacy under the Fourth and Fifth Amendments in *Boyd v. United States.*

1890 Samuel Warren and Louis Brandeis publish "The Right to Privacy" in the *Harvard Law Review.* The article calls upon the court to recognize a specific and independent constitutional right to privacy.

1891 The U.S. Supreme Court specifically mentions "the right to be let alone" in *Union Pacific Railroad v. Botsford.*

1897 The U.S. Supreme Court begins the process of applying parts of the Bill of Rights to the states in *Chicago, Burlington, and Quincy Railroad Company v. Chicago.*

1902 The Court of Appeals of New York, the highest court in the state, refuses to recognize an independent right to privacy under the state constitution in *Roberson v. Rochester Folding Box Company.*

1905 The Georgia Supreme Court becomes the first court to recognize privacy as a distinct and independent right under a state constitution in *Pavesich v. New England Life Insurance Company.*

1923 In *Meyer v. Nebraska,* the U.S. Supreme Court acknowledges protection under the Due Process Clause of the Fourteenth Amendment for personal privacy.

1925 The U.S. Supreme Court grants constitutional protection to personal privacy in the areas of education and family in *Pierce v. Society of Sisters.*

1928 In dissent in *Olmstead v. United States,* Justice Louis Brandeis argues that the U.S. Constitution confers upon each individual a general right to privacy.

1942 Referring to procreation as one of the "basic civil rights of man," the U.S. Supreme Court extends constitutional protection to procreation in *Skinner v. Oklahoma.*

1965 The U.S. Supreme Court specifically recognizes an independent and fundamental right to privacy under the U.S. Constitution in *Griswold v. Connecticut,* striking down a state statute that prohibits the use of contraceptives as applied to married couples. The Court also applies this right to privacy to the states through the Due Process Clause of the Fourteenth Amendment.

1967 In *Loving v. Virginia,* the U.S. Supreme Court characterizes the personal interest in choosing whom to marry as a fundamental privacy right.

1971 Referring to divorce as a "precondition to the adjustment of a fundamental human relationship," the U.S. Supreme Court extends constitutional protection to divorce in *Boddie v. Connecticut.*

1972 In *Eisenstadt v. Baird,* the U.S. Supreme Court declares unconstitutional a state statute that prohibits the use of contraceptives as applied to unmarried persons, holding that constitutional privacy guarantees an individual the freedom from unwarranted governmental intrusion in matters so fundamental affecting a person as whether to bear or begat a child.

1973 The U.S. Supreme Court holds that constitutional privacy encompasses a woman's decision whether or not to terminate her pregnancy in *Roe v. Wade.* Congressional opponents of the constitutional right to abortion propose the Human Life Amendment, which declares that life begins at conception. The proposed amendment, the first of many of this type, fails to gain the necessary votes to be reported out of Congress.

1976 The New Jersey Supreme Court holds that the constitutional privacy protects a patient's decision to refuse or withdraw life-sustaining medical treatment and a guardian or family's decision to authorize the termination of such treatment under certain circumstances in *In re Quinlan.*

1977 The U.S. Supreme Court treats as fundamental the freedom of personal choice in matters of family living arrangements in *Moore v. City of East Cleveland.*

1985 The Colorado Supreme Court declares that constitutional privacy encompasses the right of individuals to make legitimate medical or therapeutic use of sexually stimulating devices in *People v. Seven Thirty-Five East Colfax, Inc.* The Kansas Supreme Court hands down a similar ruling in 1990.

1986 In *Bowers v. Hardwick,* the U.S. Supreme Court holds that homosexual sodomy is not a fundamental right and thus not protected under the constitutional right to privacy.

1990s Jack Kevorkian publicizes his assistance in the death of Janet Atkins in 1990 and dozens, perhaps hundreds, of others thereafter, thereby elevating assisted suicide to the national agenda.

1990 The U.S. Supreme Court declares that the right to die is not a fundamental privacy right, but it acknowledges a constitutionally protected liberty interest in a competent person's decision to refuse life-sustaining medical treatment in *Cruzan v. Missouri Department of Health.*

1992 In *Planned Parenthood of Southeastern Pennsylvania v. Casey,* the U.S. Supreme Court reaffirms the central holding in *Roe*—that viability marks the earliest point at which the state's interest in fetal life was constitutionally adequate to justify a legislative ban on nontherapeutic abortions.

1992 In *Commonwealth of Kentucky v. Wasson,* the Kentucky Supreme Court declares that its constitution offers greater protection of the right to privacy than the U.S. Constitution, at least with respect to consensual sexual acts between adults.

1993 The Hawaii Supreme Court concludes that the state's refusal to issue marriage licenses to same-sex couples constitutes gender-based discrimination in violation of the Hawaii Constitution in *Baehr v. Lewin.* The decision is later nullified by a state constitutional amendment.

1994 Oregon voters approve the Death with Dignity Act, which statutorily decriminalizes physician-assisted suicide.

1996 Congress passes the Defense of Marriage Act, which relieves the states of any obligation under the Full Faith and Credit Clause to recognize same-sex marriages from other states.

1997 The U.S. Supreme Court declines to find a constitutionally protected privacy right to assisted suicide in *Washington v. Glucksberg.*

1998 An Alaska trial court recognizes a fundamental privacy right to choose one's life partner, irrespective of gender, in *Brause v. Bureau of Vital Statistics.* The decision is later overturned by a state constitutional amendment.

1999 The Vermont Supreme Court rules that state marriage laws denying equal benefits to committed same-sex partners violates the state constitution's guarantee of equal protection. Vermont becomes the first state to authorize civil unions between same-sex partners that entitle those entering into such unions all the identical rights and protections that stem from the marital relationship.

2001 In *Lofton v. Kearney,* a federal judge rules that constitutional privacy does not confer upon a homosexual adult a fundamental right to adopt a child.

2001 The U.S. Court of Appeals for the Eleventh Circuit remands a case back to a federal district court, instructing the judge to reconsider a state ban on sexually stimulating devices in light of the "important interest in sexual privacy."

Table of Cases

Akron v. Akron Center for Reproductive Health, 462 U.S. 416 (1983)
Allgeyer v. Louisiana, 165 U.S. 578 (1897)
Baehr v. Lewin, 852 P.2d 44 (Haw. 1993)
Baker v. State, 744 A.2d 864 (Vt. 1999)
Barron v. Baltimore, 32 U.S. 243 (1833)
Bellotti v. Baird, 443 U.S. 622 (1979)
Bigelow v. Virginia, 421 U.S. 809 (1975)
Boddie v. Connecticut, 401 U.S. 371 (1971)
Bolling v. Sharpe, 347 U.S. 497 (1954)
Bouvia v. Superior Court of Los Angeles County, 179 Cal. App. 3d 127 (Cal. 1986)
Bowers v. Hardwick, 478 U.S. 186 (1986)
Boyd v. United States, 116 U.S. 616 (1886)
Brause v. Bureau of Vital Statistics, No. 3AN-95-6562 CI (Alaska Sup. Ct. 1998)
Brown v. Board of Education, 347 U.S. 483 (1954)
Buck v. Bell, 274 U.S. 200 (1927)
Butchers' Benevolent Association v. Crescent City Livestock Landing & Slaughterhouse Company, 83 U.S. 36 (1873)
Calder v. Bull, 3 U.S. 386 (1798)
Carey v. Population Services International, 431 U.S. 678 (1977)
Chicago, Burlington, and Quincy Railway Company v. Chicago, 166 U.S. 226 (1897)

Cleveland Board of Education v. LaFleur, 414 U.S. 632 (1974)
Coffin v. United States, 156 U.S. 432 (1895)
Commonwealth of Kentucky v. Wasson, 842 S.W.2d 487 (Ky. 1992)
Commonwealth v. Bonadio, 415 A.2d 47 (Pa. 1980)
Commonwealth v. Lovett, 6 Pa. L.J.R. 226 (Pa. 1831)
Compassion in Dying v. Washington, 850 F.Supp. 1454 (W.D. Wash. 1994)
Compassion in Dying v. Washington, 79 F.3d 790 (9th Cir. 1996)
Cruzan v. Missouri Department of Health, 497 U.S. 261 (1990)
Davis v. Beason, 133 U.S. 333 (1890)
DeMay v. Roberts, 9 N.W. 146 (Mich. 1881)
Dennis v. Leclerc, 1 Mart. (o.s.) 297 (La. 1811)
Dr. Bonham's Case, 8 Coke Reports 114 (1610)
Doe v. Bolton, 410 U.S. 179 (1973)
Doe v. Commonwealth's Attorney, 425 U.S. 901 (1976)
E. B. v. Verniero, 119 F.3d 1077 (3d Cir. 1997)
Eisenstadt v. Baird, 405 U.S. 438 (1972)
Ex parte Jackson, 96 U.S. 727 (1878)
Gerber v. Hickman, 103 F.Supp. 2d 1214 (E.D. Cal. 2000)
Gerber v. Hickman, 264 F.3d 882 (9th Cir. 2001)
Gerber v. Hickman, 291 F.3d 617 (9th Cir. 2002)
Griffin v. Illinois, 351 U.S. 12 (1956)
Griswold v. Connecticut, 381 U.S. 489 (1965)
Hales v. Petit, 1 Plowd. Com. 253 (1562)
Harris v. McRae, 448 U.S. 297 (1980)
Hodgson v. Minnesota, 497 U.S. 417 (1990)
In re Gault, 387 U.S. 1 (1967)
In re Quinlan, 355 A.2d 647 (N.J. 1976)
Kelley v. Johnson, 425 U.S. 238 (1976)
Kent v. Dulles, 357 U.S. 116 (1958)
Lawrence v. State (41 S.W.3d 349, 2001)
Lawrence v. Texas (2003 U.S. Lexis 5013)
Lehr v. Robertson, 463 U.S. 248 (1983)

Lochner v. New York, 198 U.S. 45 (1905)
Lofton v. Kearney, 157 F.Supp. 2d 1372 (S.D. Fla. 2001)
Loving v. Virginia, 388 U.S. 1 (1967)
Maher v. Roe, 432 U.S. 464 (1977)
Manola v. Stevens (N.Y. Supreme Court 1890)
Mapp v. Ohio, 367 U.S. 643 (1961)
Marbury v. Madison, 5 U.S. 137 (1803)
Meyer v. Nebraska, 262 U.S. 390 (1923)
Michael H. v. Gerald D., 491 U.S. 110 (1989)
Moore v. City of East Cleveland, 431 U.S. 494 (1977)
Munn v. Illinois, 94 U.S. 13 (1877)
NAACP v. Alabama, 357 U.S. 449 (1958)
National Labor Relations Board v. Jones & Laughlin Steel, 301 U.S. 1 (1937)
Olmstead v. United States, 277 U.S. 438 (1928)
Oregon v. Ashcroft, 192 F.Supp. 2d 1077 (2002)
Palko v. Connecticut, 302 U.S. 319 (1937)
Parham v. J.R., 442 U.S. 584 (1979)
Paris Adult Theatre I v. Slaton, 413 U.S. 49 (1973)
Pavesich v. New England Life Insurance Company, 50 S.E. 68 (Ga. 1905)
People v. Onofre, 415 N.E.2d 936 (N.Y. 1980)
People v. Seven Thirty-Five East Colfax, Inc., 697 P.2d 1023 (Colo. 1985)
Pierce v. Society of Sisters, 268 U.S. 510 (1925)
Planned Parenthood of Central Missouri v. Danforth, 428 U.S. 52 (1976)
Planned Parenthood of Southeastern Pennsylvania v. Casey, 505 U.S. 833 (1992)
Poe v. Ullman, 367 U.S. 497 (1961)
Poelker v. Doe, 432 U.S. 519 (1977)
Post v. State, 715 P. 1105 (Okla. 1986)
Potter v. Murray City, 760 F.2d 1065 (10th Cir. 1985)
Powell v. State, 510 S.E.2d 18 (Ga. 1998)

Prince v. Massachusetts, 321 U.S. 158 (1944)
Quill v. Koppell, 870 F.Supp. 78 (S.D.N.Y. 1994)
Quill v. Vacco, 80 F.3d 716 (3d Cir. 1996)
Ravin v. State, 537 P.2d 494 (Alaska 1975)
Regaldo v. State, 872 S.W.2d 7 (Tex. App. 1994)
Reynolds v. Sims, 377 U.S. 533 (1964)
Reynolds v. United States, 98 U.S. 145 (1879)
Roberson v. Rochester Fielding Box Company, 64 N.E. 442 (N.Y. 1902)
Rochin v. California, 342 U.S. 165 (1952)
Roe v. Wade, 410 U.S. 113 (1973)
Romer v. Evans, 517 U.S. 620 (1996)
Runyon v. McCrary, 427 U.S. 160 (1976)
Santa Clara County v. Southern Pacific Railroad Company, 118 U.S. 398 (1886)
Schloendorff v. Society of New York Hospital, 105 N.E. 92 (N.Y. 1914)
Sewell v. State, 233 S.E.2d 187 (Ga. 1977)
Skinner v. Oklahoma, 316 U.S. 535 (1942)
Smith v. Organization for Foster Families for Equality and Reform, 431 U.S. 816 (1977)
Snyder v. Massachusetts, 291 U.S. 97 (1934)
Sousna v. Iowa, 419 U.S. 393 (1975)
Stanley v. Georgia, 394 U.S. 557 (1969)
Stanley v. Illinois, 405 U.S. 645 (1972)
State v. Bateman, 547 P.2d 6 (Ariz. 1976)
State v. Brenan, 772 So.2d 64 (La. 2000)
State v. Hughes, 792 P.2d 1023 (Kan. 1990)
State v. Poe, 252 S.E.2d 843 (N.C. App. 1979)
State v. Pilcher, 242 N.W.2d 348 (Iowa 1976)
State v. Santos, 413 A.2d 58 (R.I. 1980)
State v. Saunders, 381 A.2d 333 (N.J. 1977)
Stenberg v. Carhart, 530 U.S. 914 (2000)

Thornburgh v. American College of Obstetricians and Gynecologists, 476 U.S. 747 (1986)
Troxel v. Granville, 530 U.S. 57 (2000)
Truax v. Raich, 239 U.S. 33 (1915)
Turner v. Safley, 482 U.S. 78 (1987)
Union Pacific Railroad v. Botsford, 141 U.S. 250 (1891)
United States v. Westinghouse, 638 F.2d 570 (3d Cir. 1980)
Vacco v. Quill, 521 U.S. 793 (1997)
Washington v. Glucksberg, 521 U.S. 702 (1997)
Webster v. Reproductive Health Services, 492 U.S. 490 (1989)
Weimer v. Bunbury, 30 Mich. 201 (Mich. 1874)
West Coast Hotel v. Parrish, 300 U.S. 379 (1937)
West Virginia Board of Education v. Barnette, 319 U.S. 624 (1943)
Whalen v. Roe, 429 U.S. 589 (1977)
Willliams v. Pryor, 41 F.Supp. 2d 1257 (N.D. Ala. 1999)
Williams v. Pryor, 240 F.3d 944 (11th Cir. 2001)
Wynehamer v. People of the State of New York, 13 N.Y. 378 (N.Y. 1856)
Yorko v. State, 690 S.W.2d 260 (Tex. Crim. App. 1985)
Zablocki v. Redhail, 434 U.S. 374 (1978)

Annotated Bibliography

Abraham, Henry J. 1998. *Freedom and the Court: Civil Rights and Liberties in the United States.* New York: Oxford University Press. A classic text on civil rights and liberties, including a careful look at the Bill of Rights and its applicability to the states.

Adams, Elbridge. 1905. "The Right to Privacy, and Its Relation to the Law of Libel." *American Law Review* 39: 37–58. An influential turn-of-the-century article asserting that laws protecting privacy were fraught with serious legal difficulties.

Agre, Philip E., and Marc Rotenberg, eds. 1997. *Technology and Privacy: The New Landscape.* Cambridge: Massachusetts Institute of Technology Press. A collection of essays written from a worldwide perspective on how technology is altering our common understanding of privacy.

Alderman, Ellen, and Caroline Kennedy. 1997. *The Right to Privacy.* New York: Vintage Books. A popular book that addresses privacy in a number of contexts by "telling the stories of people who struggled to exercise that right."

Allen, Anita L. 1988. *Uneasy Access: Privacy for Women in a Free Society.* Totowa, NJ: Rowman and Littlefield. An indictment of the law's protection for privacy rights for women.

Baer, Judith A., ed. 2002. *Historical and Multicultural Encyclopedia of Women's Reproductive Rights in the United States.* Westport, CT: Greenwood Press. A reference work on reproductive rights.

Baird, Robert M., and Stuart E. Rosenbaum, eds. 1997. *Same-Sex Marriage: The Moral and Legal Debate.* Amherst, NY: Prometheus Books. A collection of articles, both for and against same-sex marriage.

Ball, Howard. 2002. *The Supreme Court in the Intimate Lives of Americans: Birth, Sex, Marriage, Childbearing, and Death.* New York: New York University Press. A detailed analysis of the legal, political, and ethical issues relating to a number of privacy rights.

Barnett, Randy E. 1987. "Are Enumerated Rights the Only Rights We Have? The Case of Associational Freedom." *Harvard Journal of Law and Public Policy* 10: 101–115. A critique of legal positivism, which holds that the only rights individuals have are those that are explicitly specified in the Constitution or those that are given by the legislature.

———. 1989. *The Rights Retained by the People: The History and Meaning of the Ninth Amendment.* 2 vols. Fairfax, VA: George Mason University Press. The definitive study of the Ninth Amendment and a first-rate collection of essays on general principles of constitutional interpretation, concluding that the lack of mention of some right in the Bill of Rights does not necessarily mean that the right does not exist.

Barnett, Walter. 1973. *Sexual Freedom and the Constitution.* Albuquerque: University of New Mexico Press. An inquiry into the constitutionality of repressive sex laws.

Barron, James H. 1979. "Warren and Brandeis: The Right to Privacy, 4 *Harv. L. Rev.* 193 (1890): Demystifying a Landmark Citation." *Suffolk University Law Review* 13: 875–922. A detailed critique of the Warren and Brandeis article, concluding that, instead of deserving high praise, the piece is a quaint example of misguided legal scholarship and is of limited utility to those seeking solutions to modern-day privacy problems.

Bates, Alan. 1964. "Privacy—A Useful Concept." *Social Forces* 42: 429–434. A discussion of the basic functions privacy performs for individuals.

Battin, Margaret P., Rosamond Rhodes, and Anita Silvers. 1998. *Physician Assisted Suicide: Expanding the Debate.* New York: Routledge. A collection of essays from philosophers, physicians, theologians, social scientists, lawyers, and economists considering the implications of physician-assisted suicide.

Berger, Raoul. 1977. *Government by Judiciary: The Transformation of the Fourteenth Amendment.* Cambridge, MA: Harvard University Press. An influential text arguing that the U.S. Supreme Court's incorporation of the Bill of Rights has dangerously disregarded the intentions of the amendment's Framers and has resulted in a judiciary that has become the nation's paramount policymaker, a superlegislature.

———. 1980. "The Ninth Amendment." *Cornell Law Review* 66: 1–26. A well-documented examination of the legislative discussions relating to the Ninth Amendment, concluding that the Ninth Amendment adds no unspecified rights to the Bill of Rights.

Blackstone, Sir William. 1765–1769. *Commentaries on the Laws of England.* 4 vols. Oxford, UK: Clarendon Press. The most influential law book and primary legal authority for eighteenth- and nineteenth-century lawyers in the United States.

Boonin, David. 2002. *A Defense of Abortion.* New York: Cambridge University Press. A justification for abortion rights.

Bork, Robert H. 1971. "Neutral Principles and Some First Amendment Problems." *Indiana Law Journal* 47: 1–35. An influential law review article criticizing the Supreme Court for "creating" the constitutional right to privacy.

Brant, Irving. 1965. *The Bill of Rights: Its Origin and Meaning.* New York: Mentor Books. A study on the Bill of Rights from its roots in English common law to the decisions of the Supreme Court.

Breckenridge, Adam Carlyle. 1970. *The Right to Privacy.* Lincoln: University of Nebraska Press. A text examining the extent to which the individual is protected by the Bill of Rights from arbitrary and unreasonable intrusions into personal privacy.

Brill, Alida. 1990. *Nobody's Business: The Paradoxes of Privacy.* Reading, MA: Addison-Wesley. A personal essay on the struggle for privacy rights in the 1970s and 1980s.

Brovins, Joan M., and Thomas Oehmke. 1993. *Dr. Death.* Hollywood, FL: Lifetime Books. A biographical piece on Dr. Jack Kevorkian, the most outspoken advocate and practitioner of physician-assisted suicide, and his patients.

Bullough, Vern L. 2001. *Encyclopedia of Birth Control.* Santa Barbara, CA: ABC-CLIO. A standard reference work on birth control.

Burt, Robert A. 1979. "The Constitution and the Family." *Supreme Court Review* 1979: 329–395. A criticism of the use of the privacy doctrine in *Moore v. City of East Cleveland.*

Carr, Robert K. 1942. *The Supreme Court and Judicial Review.* New York: Farrer and Rinehart. A thorough discussion of the establishment, justification, and exercise of judicial review by the Supreme Court.

Chase, Harold W., and Craig R. Ducat. 1974. *Edward S. Corwin's The Constitution and What It Means Today.* Princeton, NJ: Princeton University Press. A basic resource in the study of the Constitution, the Bill of Rights, and other amendments.

Cogan, Neil H., ed. 1997. *The Complete Bill of Rights: The Drafts, Debates, Sources, and Origins.* New York: Oxford University Press. Perhaps the most complete and useful analysis of the Bill of Rights, including all documentary records and relevant debates in the First Congress and in the state ratifying conventions.

Colby, William H. 2002. *Long Goodbye: The Death of Nancy Cruzan.* Carlsbad, CA: Hay House. The story of Nancy Cruzan and her parents' legal battles with the state of Missouri.

Commager, Henry Steele. 1958. *Documents of American History.* 6th ed. New York: Appleton-Century-Crofts. A reference work containing virtually every significant document in American history, beginning in the fifteenth century.

"The Constitutional Status of Sexual Orientation: Homosexuality as a Suspect Classification." 1985. *Harvard Law Review* 98: 1285–1309. A law review article arguing that courts should recognize homosexuality as a suspect classification under the Equal Protection Clause of the Fourteenth Amendment and therefore subject laws that discriminate on such basis to heightened scrutiny.

Cooley, Thomas McIntyre. 1878. *A Treatise on Constitutional Limitations which Rests upon the Legislative Power of the States.* 4th ed. Boston: Little, Brown. An early constitutional law treatise justifying judicial review for legislative acts that infringe upon natural law rights.

———. 1880. *A Treatise on the Law of Torts.* Chicago: Callaghan. An early constitutional law treatise defining privacy as "a right of complete immunity: to be let alone."

Corwin, Edward S. [1929] 1955. *The Higher Law Background of American Constitutional Law.* Reprint. Ithaca, NY: Cornell University Press. A classic text rejecting the doctrine of legislative supremacy and advocating the exercise of judicial review to preserve natural law rights.

Cott, Nancy F. 2000. *Public Vows: A History of Marriage and the Nation.* Cambridge, MA: Harvard University Press. A thorough examination of the evolution and impact of marriage law on the American social structure, including discussions on polygamy and same-sex marriage.

Craig, Barbara Hinkson, and David M. O'Brien. 1993. *Abortion and American Politics.* Chattam, NJ: Chattam House. An unbiased analysis of the abortion controversy and how it has played out in the U.S. political system.

Cruz, David B. 2000. "'The Sexual Freedom Cases'? Contraception, Abortion, Abstinence, and the Constitution." *Harvard Civil Rights and Civil Liberties Law Review* 35: 299–383. An exploration of whether, and to what extent, constitutional privacy protects sexual autonomy.

DeCew, Judith Wagner. 1997. *In Pursuit of Privacy: Law, Ethics, and the Rise of Technology.* Ithaca, NY: Cornell University Press. A defense of a broad conception of privacy, including analysis on abortion, homosexual sodomy, and informational privacy.

Dixon, Robert G., Jr. 1971. *The Right of Privacy.* New York: DaCapo Press. A symposium on the implications of *Griswold v. Connecticut* and the right to privacy.

———. 1976. "The 'New' Substantive Due Process and the Democratic Ethic: A Prolegomenon." *Brigham Young University Law Review* 1976: 43–88. A criticism of the Supreme Court for finding privacy as a derivative or penumbral right.

Dumbauld, Edward. 1957. *The Bill of Rights and What It Means Today.* Norman: University of Oklahoma Press. A standard reference work on the origins and meaning of the Bill of Rights.

Dunbar, Leslie. 1956. "James Madison and the Ninth Amendment." *Virginia Law Review* 42: 627–643. A law review article discussing the "proper place" of the Ninth Amendment in American constitutionalism.

Elliot, Jonathan. [1836] 1974. *The Debates in the Several State Conventions on the Adoption of the Federal Constitution.* 4 vols. Reprint. New York: Burt Franklin. A massive compilation of the documentary records of the state ratifying conventions.

Ely, John Hart. 1973. "The Wages of Crying Wolf: A Comment on *Roe v. Wade.*" *Yale Law Review* 82: 920–949. A critique of *Roe v. Wade.*

———. 1980. *Democracy and Distrust.* Cambridge, MA: Harvard University Press. A well-researched text that includes a lengthy analysis of the legislative debates pertaining to the Ninth Amendment, concluding that the amendment does not grant Congress authority to create additional rights.

Emanuel, Ezekiel. 1997. "Whose Right to Die?" *Atlantic Monthly,* March 1, 1997: 73–79. A word of caution to advocates of physician-assisted suicide.

Eskridge, William N. 1996. *The Case for Same-Sex Marriage: From Sexual Liberty to Civilized Commitment.* New York: Free Press. A justification for legal and constitutional protection of same-sex marriage.

Etzioni, Amitai. 1999. *The Limits of Privacy.* New York: Basic Books. A communitarian's examination of privacy rights, arguing that in certain situations privacy rights should be limited in the interest of the public good.

Fairman, Charles. 1949. "Does the Fourteenth Amendment Incorporate the Bill of Rights?" *Stanford Law Review* 2: 5–139. A lengthy examination of the original understanding of the Fourteenth Amendment, concluding that it was not intended to make the Bill of Rights applicable to the states.

Faux, Marian. 2001. Roe v. Wade: *The Untold Story of the Landmark Supreme Decision the Made Abortion Legal.* Totowa, NJ: Rowman and Littlefield. An in-depth look at *Roe v. Wade.*

Flaherty, David H. 1972. *Privacy in Colonial New England.* Charlottesville: University Press of Virginia. A thorough investigation of personal privacy in colonial New England.

Freund, Paul A. 1971. "Privacy: One Concept or Many." In *Privacy,* edited by J. Roland Pennock and John W. Chapman. New York: Atherton Press. A collection of essays discussing various aspects of privacy.

Fried, Charles. 1968. "Privacy." *Yale Law Journal* 77: 475–493. An oft-cited article examining the foundations of the right to privacy.

Garfinkel, Simson. 2000. *Database Nation: The Death of Privacy in the 21st Century.* Cambridge, MA: O'Reilly and Associates. A look at how modern-day advances in technology endanger privacy.

Garrow, David J. 1994. *Liberty and Sexuality: The Right to Privacy and the Making of* Roe v. Wade. New York: Macmillan Publishing. The most well-researched and readable exposition of abortion and *Roe v. Wade.*

Gerety, Tom. 1977. "Redefining Privacy." *Harvard Civil Rights-Civil Liberties Law Review* 12: 233–296. A law review article discussing the shortcomings of defining privacy broadly as "the right to be let alone" and suggesting that privacy be defined more narrowly as "an autonomy or control over the intimacies of personal identity."

Gerstmann, Evan. 1999. *The Constitutional Underclass: Gays, Lesbians, and the Failure of Class-Based Equal Protection.* Chicago: University of Chicago Press. A critique of current judicial doctrine on the Equal Protection Clause, specifically as it impacts homosexuals.

Gillett, Todd M. 2000. "The Absolution of *Reynolds:* The Constitutionality of Religious Polygamy." *William and Mary Bill of Rights Journal* 8: 497–534. An inquiry in to the constitutionality of antipolygamy laws, concluding that statutes prohibiting polygamy interfere with a polygamist's right to privacy.

Gindin, Susan E. 1997. "Lost and Found in Cyberspace: Informational Privacy in Age of the Internet." *San Diego Law Review* 34: 1153–1223. A critical assessment of legislative efforts to protect informational privacy, encouraging Congress to adopt a comprehensive policy guaranteeing individuals the right to control the collection and distribution of their personal information.

Ginsburg, Ruth Bader. 1985. "Some Thoughts on Autonomy and Equality in Relation to *Roe v. Wade.*" *North Carolina Law Review* 63: 375–386. A critique of the approach used, but not the result reached, in *Roe v. Wade,* suggesting that the majority opinion should have relied upon sex equality considerations.

Glancy, Dorothy J. 1979. "The Invention of the Right to Privacy." *Arizona Law Review* 21: 1–39. An examination of Warren and Brandeis's "invention" of the right to privacy in historical perspective.

Godkin, E. L. 1890. "The Rights of the Citizen—IV: To His Reputation." *Scribner's* 8: 58–68. An influential article arguing that it was in the interest of the state to safeguard in every possible way the good reputation of its citizens and to throw around their personal affairs the hedge of secrecy and privacy.

Goldstein, Leslie Friedman. 1994. *Contemporary Cases in Women's Rights.* Madison: University of Wisconsin Press. A look at Supreme Court cases relating to marital and procreative freedom.

Gordon, Sarah Barringer. 2002. *The Mormon Question: Polygamy and Constitutional Conflict in Nineteenth Century America.* Chapel Hill: University of North Carolina Press. An interdisciplinary study on the Mormon practice of plural marriage and American constitutional thought.

Gormley, Ken. 1992. "One Hundred Years of Privacy." *Wisconsin Law Review* 1992: 1335–1441. A comprehensive analysis of privacy law between 1890 and 1990.

Gorney, Cynthia. 1998. *Article of Faith: A Frontline History of the Abortion Wars.* New York: Simon and Schuster. An intriguing look at the prolife and prochoice movements in Missouri.

Grey, Thomas. 1980. "Eros, Civilization, and the Burger Court." *Law and Contemporary Problems* 43: 83–100. A law review article containing an appendix summarizing all of the law review literature between 1965 and 1979 relating to the relationship between constitutional privacy and legal prohibitions on consensual adult sex.

Grossberg, Michael. 1985. *Governing the Hearth: Law and Family in Nineteenth Century America.* Chapel Hill: University of North Carolina Press. A thorough examination of family law in the nineteenth century.

Hafen, Bruce. 1983. "The Constitutional Status of Marriage, Kinship, and Sexual Privacy—Balancing the Individual and Social Interests." *Michigan Law Review* 81: 463–574. An exhaustively documented consideration of whether courts should recognize privacy claims by unrelated individuals who seek the same constitutional and legal protection as that given to formal relationships based on legal marriage or kinship.

Hamilton, Alexander, James Madison, and John Jay. [1787–1788] 1961. *The Federalist Papers.* New York: Mentor. A collection of eighty-five essays written in defense of the Constitution of 1787.

Hayden, Trudy. 1980. *Your Right to Privacy.* New York: Avon Books. A basic guide to privacy rights, published under the auspices of the American Civil Liberties Union.

Hendricks, Evan. 1990. *Your Right to Privacy.* Carbondale: Southern Illinois University Press. A basic guide to informational privacy rights, published under the auspices of the American Civil Liberties Union.

Heymann, Philip B., and Douglas E. Barzelay. 1973. "The Forest and the Trees: *Roe v. Wade* and Its Critics." *Boston University Law Review* 53: 765–784. A defense of *Roe v. Wade,* arguing that the decision is amply justified both by precedent and long-standing principles.

Hickey, Adam. 2002. "Between Two Spheres: Comparing State and Federal Approaches to the Right to Privacy and Prohibitions against Sodomy." *Yale Law Journal* 111: 93–1030. A comparison between state and federal privacy jurisprudence with respect to antisodomy laws.

Hixson, Richard F. 1987. *Privacy in Public Society: Human Rights in Conflict.* New York: Oxford University Press. A collection of key essays on privacy.

Hoefler, James M. 1994. "Diffusion and Diversity: Federalism and the Right to Die in the Fifty States." *Publius: The Journal of Federalism* 24: 153–170. A look at the policy activity in state legislatures and the judicial decisions in state courts relating to right-to-die issues.

Hoefler, James M., and Brian M. Kamoie. 1994. *Deathright: Culture, Medicine, Politics, and the Right to Die.* Boulder, CO: Westview Press. A discussion of the primary forces that shape right-to-die policy across the fifty states.

Hofstadter, Samuel H. 1954. *The Development of the Right of Privacy in New York.* New York: Grosby Press. A historical examination of the various legislative acts and judicial decisions pertaining to privacy in the state of New York in the late nineteenth and early twentieth centuries.

Hohengarten, William M. 1994. "Same-Sex Marriage and the Right of Privacy." *Yale Law Journal* 103: 1495–1531. A law review note arguing that the constitutional right to privacy requires states to sanction and recognize same-sex marriages.

Holmes, Oliver Wendell, Jr. 1897. "The Path of the Law." *Harvard Law Review* 10: 457–478. A landmark speech discussing the development and advantages of the common law.

Holt, Angela. 2002. "From My Cold Dead Hands: *Williams v. Pryor* and the Constitutionality of Alabama's Anti-Vibrator Law." *Alabama Law Review* 53: 927–947. A law review article arguing that the private use of sexually stimulating devices should be protected under the rubric of constitutional privacy.

Hull, N. E. H. 2001. Roe v. Wade: *The Abortion Rights Controversy in American History.* Lawrence: University Press of Kansas. A historical account of abortion in the United States since 1800.

Humphry, Derek, and Mary Clement. 1998. *Freedom to Die: People, Politics, and the Right-to-Die Movement.* New York: St. Martin's Press. A well-researched examination of the right-to-die movement in the United States.

Hunter, Nan D. 1992. *The Rights of Lesbians and Gay Men.* Carbondale: Southern Illinois University Press. A basic guide to a gay person's rights, published under the auspices of the American Civil Liberties Union.

Inness, Julie C. 1992. *Privacy, Intimacy, and Isolation.* New York: Oxford University Press. A difficult-to-read text focusing on intimacy as the core value of privacy.

Kaminer, Maggie Ilene. 2001. "How Broad Is the Fundamental Right to Privacy and Personal Autonomy?—On What Grounds Should the Ban on the Sale of Sexually Stimulating Devices by Considered Unconstitutional?" *American University Journal of Gender, Social Policy and the Law* 9: 395–422. A law review article suggesting that the courts expand the fundamental right to privacy to include private access and use of genital-stimulating devices.

Kamisar, Yale. 1993. "Are Laws against Assisted Suicide Unconstitutional?" *Hastings Center Report* 23: 32–41. A defense of laws against assisted suicide.

———. 1995. "Against Assisted Suicide—Even a Very Limited Form." *University of Detroit Mercy Law Review* 72: 735–769. A well-researched article opposing assisted suicide.

Kappelhoff, Mark John. 1988. "*Bowers v. Hardwick:* Is There a Right to Privacy?" *American University Law Review* 37: 487–512. A critical examination of *Bowers v. Hardwick* and its impact on the constitutional protection of sexual privacy.

Katz, Pamela S. 1999. "The Case for Legal Recognition of Same-Sex Marriage." *Journal of Law and Policy* 8: 61–106. A law review article arguing that the right to choose one's partner in marriage, irrespective of gender, should not be subjected to governmental interference.

Kauper, Paul C. 1965. "Penumbras, Peripheries, Emanations, Things Fundamental, and Things Forgotten." *Michigan Law Review* 64: 235–258. A defense of the doctrine of unenumerated rights, the right to privacy, and *Griswold v. Connecticut.*

Keynes, Edward. 1996. *Liberty, Property, and Privacy.* University Park: Pennsylvania State University Press. A well-researched text discussing the development of the fundamental rights philosophy and jurisprudence that affords constitutional protection to unenumerated liberty rights, including privacy.

Konvitz, Milton R. 1966. "Privacy and the Law: A Philosophical Prelude." *Law and Contemporary Problems* 31: 272–280. A philosophical look at the intrinsic value of privacy.

Kurland, Philip B. 1976. *Some Reflections on Privacy and the Constitution.* Chicago: University of Chicago Center for Policy Study. A general examination of the constitutional right to privacy ten years after *Griswold v. Connecticut.*

Ladd, Everett Carll. 1997. *Public Opinion about Abortion: Twenty-five Years after* Roe v. Wade. Washington, DC: AEI Press. A look at how public opinion on abortion has changed since *Roe v. Wade.*

Larremore, Wilbur. 1912. "The Law of Privacy." *Columbia Law Review* 12: 693–708. An examination of privacy cases in state courts prior to 1912.

Lewis, Penney. 2001. "Rights Discourse and Assisted Suicide." *American Journal of Law and Medicine* 27: 45–99. A balanced discussion of the common and serious problems that divide those who support and those who oppose assisted suicide.

Locke, John. [1690] 1960. "An Essay Concerning Civil Government." In *Two Treatises of Government.* Reprint. New York: Mentor. An essay concerning the limits of governmental authority, highly influential on the drafters of the Declaration of Independence and the Constitution.

Magnuson, Roger J. 1990. *Are Gay Rights Right?* Portland, OR: Multnomah. An examination of the controversy over homosexual rights.

Marzen, Thomas J. 1985. "Suicide: A Constitutional Right?" *Duquesne Law Review* 24: 1–100. The most comprehensive and heavily documented law review article ever written on suicide.

———. 1994. "'Out, Out Brief Candle': Constitutionally Prescribed Suicide for the Terminally Ill." *Hastings Constitutional Law Quarterly* 21: 799–826. An article arguing against a constitutional right to assisted suicide.

McClellan, Grant S., ed. 1976. *The Right to Privacy.* New York: H. H. Wilson. A look at the constitutional foundations of the right to privacy.

McWhirter, Darien A., and Jon D. Bible. 1992. *Privacy as a Constitutional Right.* New York: Quorum. An easy-to-follow discussion of the development and nature of the constitutional right to privacy.

Mill, John Stuart. [1859] 1956. *On Liberty.* Reprint. Indianapolis, IN: Bobbs-Merrill. A classic text exploring the limits on governmental authority over the individual.

Mohr, Richard D. 1986. "Mr. Justice Douglas at Sodom: Gays and Privacy." *Columbia Human Rights Law Review* 18: 43–110. A law review article arguing in favor of a constitutional right to homosexual sodomy.

Neeley, G. Steven. 1994. *The Constitutional Right to Suicide: A Legal and Philosophical Examination.* New York: P. Lang. A justification for cloaking suicide with constitutional protection.

Nossiff, Rosemary. 2001. *Before* Roe: *Abortion Policy in the States.* Philadelphia: Temple University Press. An analysis of abortion policy in the United States prior to *Roe v. Wade.*

O'Brien, David M. 1979. *Privacy, Law, and Public Policy.* New York: Praeger. A detailed analysis of privacy jurisprudence, including an examination of the different conceptions of privacy and policy recommendations on the subject of informational privacy.

O'Brien, Denis. 1902. "The Right of Privacy." *Columbia Law Review* 2: 437–448. A defense of the New York Court of Appeals' decision not to recognize privacy as a constitutional right in a turn-of-the-century case.

O'Neill, Kevin Francis. 1993. "The Road Not Taken: State Constitutions as an Alternative Source of Protection for Reproductive Rights." *New York Law School Journal of Human Rights* 11: 5–77. An analysis of how state guarantees of liberty, equal protection, and privacy can be used to challenge abortion restrictions.

Palmer, Louis J., Jr. 2002. *Encyclopedia of Abortion in the United States.* Jefferson, NC: McFarland. A reference work on abortion in the United States.

Parker, Richard B. 1974. "A Definition of Privacy." *Rutgers Law Review* 1974: 275–296. An attempt to define more clearly a legal and philosophical definition of privacy.

Parry, Joseph Hyrum. 1890. *Constitutional and Governmental Rights of the Mormons.* Salt Lake City, UT: J. H. Parry. A collection of primary sources on the Mormon Church, including a digest of the decisions of the Supreme Court applicable to polygamy.

Patterson, Bennett. 1955. *The Forgotten Ninth Amendment.* Indianapolis, IN: Bobbs-Merrill. A thorough examination of the legislative history of the Ninth Amendment, concluding that there are "individual inherent rights" that are unenumerated and independent of constitutional grant.

Paul, Ellen Frankel, Jeffrey Paul, and Fred D. Miller Jr., eds. 2000. *The Right of Privacy.* New York: Cambridge University Press. A collection of essays written by philosophers and academic lawyers examining various aspects of the right to privacy as well as the roles that this right plays in moral philosophy, legal theory, and public policy.

Plasencia, Madeline Mercedes. 1999. *Right to Privacy and the Constitution.* New York: Taylor and Francis. A massive compendium examining the major decision of the Supreme Court with respect to privacy rights.

Posner, Richard A. 1979. "The Uncertain Protection of Privacy by the Supreme Court." *Supreme Court Review* 1979: 173–216. An examination of the Supreme Court's decisions dealing with privacy after *Griswold v. Connecticut.*

Pratt, Walter F. 1975. "The Warren and Brandeis Argument for a Right to Privacy." *Public Law* 1975: 161–179. A comparison between the English and American protections for privacy.

Prosser, William L. 1960. "Privacy." *California Law Review* 48: 383–423. A seminal work postulating that the law of privacy comprises four distinct kinds of invasions: intrusion, public disclosure of private facts, false light, and appropriation of character for commercial work.

Quill, Timothy E., Bernard Lo, and Dan W. Brock. 1997. "Palliative Options of Last Resort: A Comparison of Voluntary Stopping Eating and Drinking, Terminal Sedation, Physician-Assisted Suicide, and Voluntary Active Euthanasia." *Journal of the American Medical Association* 278: 2099–2104. An explanation of various end-of-life options for elderly or terminally ill patients.

Reagan, Leslie J. 1997. *When Abortion Was a Crime: Women, Medicine, and Law in the United States, 1867–1973.* Berkeley: University of California Press. A look at abortion in the century preceding *Roe v. Wade.*

Redlich, Norman. 1962. "Are There 'Certain Rights . . . Retained by the People'?" *New York University Law Review* 37: 787–812. An examination of the history of the Ninth Amendment, concluding that it is intended to permit the judicial definition of rights adjacent to, or analogous with, the pattern of rights found in the Constitution.

Reiman, Jeffery. 1976. "Privacy, Intimacy, and Personhood." *Philosophy and Public Affairs* 6: 26–44. A discussion on the value of the right to privacy.

Rhode, Debra. 1989. *Justice and Gender: Sex Discrimination and the Law.* Cambridge, MA: Harvard University Press. A historical examination of gender and the law in the United States from the nineteenth century to the present, including a look at contraception and abortion.

Richard, David A. J. 1986. *Toleration and the Constitution.* New York: Oxford University Press. A highly readable historical review of several constitutional issues, including privacy.

"The Right to Privacy in Nineteenth Century America." 1981. *Harvard Law Review* 94: 1892–1910. A well-documented note examining the extent to which nineteenth-century courts and legislatures recognized privacy as an independent interest.

Rosen, Jeffrey. 2000. *The Unwanted Gaze: The Destruction of Privacy in America.* New York: Random House. An examination of the legal, technical, and cultural changes that have undermined the individual's ability to control how much information about himself or herself is communicated to others.

Rubenfeld, Jed. 1989. "The Right of Privacy." *Harvard Law Review* 102: 737–807. A penetrating analysis of the profound consequences that are brought about laws that prohibit abortion and ban private sexual relations between consenting adults.

Samar, Vincent Joseph. 1991. *The Right to Privacy: Gays, Lesbians, and the Constitution.* Philadelphia: Temple University Press. An examination of privacy jurisprudence relating to homosexual relations.

Schowengerdt, Dale M. 2001. "Defending Marriage: A Litigation Strategy to Oppose Same-Sex 'Marriage.'" *Regent University Law Review* 14: 487–511. An overview of litigation techniques to limit marriage to traditional heterosexual marriage.

Shapiro, Ian. 2001. *Abortion: The Supreme Court Decisions, 1965–2000.* A reference work on every major Supreme Court decision on abortion in the last forty years.

Solinger, Rickie. 1998. *Abortion Wars: A Half Century of Struggle, 1950–2000.* Berkeley: University of California Press. A penetrating account of abortion politics and history in the United States since 1950.

Stewart, Chuck. 2001. *Homosexuality and the Law: A Dictionary.* Santa Barbara, CA: ABC-CLIO. A reference work on homosexuality and the law.

Story, Joseph. 1851. *Commentaries on the Constitution of the United States.* 2d ed. Boston: C. C. Little and J. Brown. An early and oft-cited treatise on the U.S. Constitution.

Strasser, Mark. 2000. "Sex, Law, and the Sacred Precincts of the Marital Bedroom: On State and Federal Right to Privacy Jurisprudence." *Notre*

Dame Journal of Law, Ethics, and Public Policy 14: 753–789. A law review article arguing that any plausible reading of the right to privacy jurisprudence must include the right of same-sex couples to marry.

———. 2002. "Same-Sex Marriages and Civil Unions: On Meaning, Free Exercise, and Constitutional Guarantees." *Loyola University Chicago Law Journal* 33: 597–630. A plea for constitutional protection for same-sex marriages.

Strickman, Leonard P. 1982. "Marriage, Divorce, and the Constitution." *Family Law Quarterly* 15: 259–348. A well-documented consideration of the constitutional issues surrounding marriage and divorce.

Strum, Phillippa. 1998. *Privacy: The Debate in the United States Since 1945.* Fort Worth, TX: Harcourt Brace. A look at the constitutional foundations of privacy and the various ways in which government has interfered with privacy since the end of World War II.

Suhr, Charles. 1991. "*Cruzan v. Director, Missouri Department of Health:* A Clear and Convincing Call for Comprehensive Legislation to Protect Incompetent Patients' Rights." *American University Law Review* 40: 1477–1519. An examination of the approach used by the Supreme Court in addressing the issue of an incompetent patient's right to die.

Sykes, Charles J. 1999. *The End of Privacy.* New York: St. Martin's Press. An analysis of the challenges to informational privacy posed by technological advancements.

Thomsen, Judith Jarvis. 1975. "The Right to Privacy." *Philosophy and Public Affairs* 4: 295–314. A philosopher's look into the status and nature of the right to privacy.

Tribe, Laurence H. 1988. *American Constitutional Law.* 2d ed. New York: Foundation Press. The most comprehensive modern treatise on American constitutional law, including a chapter on rights of privacy and personhood.

Trosino, James. 1993. "Note, American Wedding: Same-Sex Marriage and the Miscegenation Analogy." *Boston University Law Review* 73: 93–120. A law review article suggesting that courts compel states to permit same-sex marriages in the same manner that the U.S. Supreme Court compelled states to permit interracial marriages—by recognizing the claimed right either as a fundamental right to marry, or of privacy, or of intimate association.

Turkington, Richard C. 1990. "Legacy of the Warren and Brandeis Article: The Emerging Unencumbered Constitutional Right to Informational Privacy." *Northern Illinois University Law Review* 10: 479–520. A penetrating discussion of the constitutional right to informational privacy.

Turkington, Richard C., and Anita L. Allen. 1999. *Privacy Law.* St. Paul, MN: West Group. A comprehensive casebook, with comments, on the law of privacy.

Tushnet, Mark. 1991. "Two Notes on the Jurisprudence of Privacy." *Constitutional Commentary* 8: 75–85. A defense of Justice Douglas's opinion in *Griswold v. Connecticut.*

Urofsky, Melvin I. 1994. *Letting Go: Death, Dying, and the Law.* Norman: University of Oklahoma Press. A discussion of the legal, historical, ethical, and medical issues related to the right to die.

———. 2000. *Lethal Judgments: Assisted Suicide and American Law.* Lawrence: University Press of Kansas. A discussion of the legal, historical, ethical, and medical issues related to assisted suicide.

Urofsky, Melvin I., and Philip E. Urofsky. 1996. *The Right to Die: A Two-Volume Anthology of Scholarly Works.* New York: Garland. A collection of articles on the right to die.

Wadlington, Walter. 1966. "The *Loving* Case: Virginia's Anti-Miscegenation Statute in Historical Perspective." *Virginia Law Review* 52: 1189–1223. An examination of Virginia's antimiscegenation laws in historical context, together with the problems created by such laws.

Wardle, Lynn D. 1996. "A Critical Analysis of Constitutional Claims for Same-Sex Marriage." *Brigham Young Law Review* 1996: 1–101. A well-written law review article asserting that same-sex marriage is not a part of the fundamental right to marry and is inconsistent with our nation's history and traditions.

Warren, Samuel D., and Louis D. Brandeis. 1890. "The Right to Privacy." *Harvard Law Review* 9: 193–220. The starting point in any discussion on constitutional privacy, calling upon the courts to recognize a specific constitutional right to privacy, a right independent of property and liberty and unrelated to tort law.

Weddington, Sarah. 1992. *A Question of Choice.* New York: G. P. Putnam's Sons. A behind-the-scenes look at *Roe v. Wade,* written by the lawyer who won the case.

Weir, Robert F., ed. 1997. *Physician-Assisted Suicide.* Bloomington: Indiana University Press. A balanced collection of essays on physician-assisted suicide written by academics, lawyers, and physicians.

Westin, Alan F. 1967. *Privacy and Freedom.* New York: Atheneum. An oft-cited text examining the functions of privacy as well as the advances in the technology of privacy-invasion devices.

Whiting, Raymond. 2002. *A Natural Right to Die: Twenty-three Centuries of Debate.* Westport, CT: Greenwood Press. A look at the right-to-die question beyond the borders of the United States, demonstrating how current U.S. attitudes and practices have been influenced by the legal and cultural development of the ancient Western world.

Wolhandler, Steven J. 1984. "Voluntary Active Euthanasia for the Terminally Ill and the Constitutional Right to Privacy." *Cornell Law Review* 69: 363–383. An early law review article on the right to die, arguing that the constitutional right to privacy protects a competent terminal patient's right to determine the time and manner of his or her death.

Woodhouse, Barbara Bennett. 1992. "Who Owns the Child? *Meyer* and *Pierce* and the Child as Property." *William and Mary Law Review* 33: 995–1122. A revisionist history of two liberal icons, *Meyer v. Nebraska* and *Pierce v. Society of Sisters,* and a discussion of the ways in which the legacy of these two cases continues to shape family law and family policy.

Woodman, Sue. 1998. *Last Rights: The Struggle over the Right to Die.* New York: Plenum Trade. An examination of the right-to-die movement worldwide.

Zucker, Marjorie B. 1999. *The Right to Die Debate: A Documentary History.* Westport, CT: Greenwood Press. A collection of primary documents tracing the history and development of the right to die in the United States.

Index

About the Author

Richard A. Glenn (Ph.D., Tennessee, 1995) is associate professor of government and political affairs at Millersville University. He is the author of more than thirty articles, chapters, essays, and reviews appearing in many journals, books, and other publications, on a variety of U.S. political subjects. He lives with his wife, Lorena, and their sons, Ryan and Andrew, in Lancaster, Pennsylvania.